THE NEW
BABY CARE
BOOK

THE NEW BABY CARE BOOK

Miriam Stoppard MD MRCP

Photography by Anthea Sieveking

A DORLING KINDERSLEY BOOK

*For Oliver, Barnaby, William, Edmund,
Oona, and Slater*

LONDON, NEW YORK, MUNICH,
MELBOURNE, DELHI

A Penguin Company

Second edition first published in Great Britain 1990 by
Dorling Kindersley Limited, 80 Strand, London WC2R 0RL

4 6 8 10 9 7 5

First published 1983
Reprinted 1984, 1985, 1986 (three times),
1987, 1988, 1989, 1991, 1995, 1996, 2001, 2002

First edition

Editor Fiona MacIntyre
Art Editor Anne-Marie Bulat
Managing Editor Amy Carroll

Second edition
revised, edited, and designed by

CARROLL & BROWN LTD.

British Library Cataloguing in Publication Data
Stoppard, Miriam, *1937* -

The new baby care book.
1. Babies. Home care
1. Title
649.122

ISBN 0-7513-3609-2

Printed in Hong Kong by Wing King Tong

Preface

Many years have now passed since Dorling Kindersley and I published the *Baby Care Book*. How much has changed in that time? Research is continuing into the cause or causes of Sudden Infant Death Syndrome (cot death), and there is evidence to suggest that babies who are laid down on their stomachs are more vulnerable. It would seem advisable, therefore, that newborn and very young babies should be placed on their backs to sleep. It is no longer believed that in this position there is an increased risk of the baby bringing up his feed and possibly choking.

There has been much in the news recently abouth the dangers of listeria, salmonella and campylobacter in foodstuffs such as eggs and milk. While these bacteria have always been present, the seriousness of their effects on babies, children, and even the unborn fetus, is now being documented, and advice about appropriate precautions is now available.

Of course there have been advances in baby equipment – not least in the field of disposable nappies with their wetness indicators, leakproof legs, and more carefully positioned padding. Ever-improving, too, is the design of baby transport, with more easily folding and manoeuvrable push-chair-carrycot systems.

Most of all, I think attitudes have changed in at least two important respects. We parents are beginning to recognize that our children have rights; they are not our property, but treasured human beings who must be treated with dignity. It is not on to pull rank anymore: children have a voice which must be heard and their rights must be taken into consideration when making decisions.

We are also realizing that parents have a major role to play as teachers and educators. Children learn some of their most important lessons before they ever start school, and we must take our jobs as teachers very seriously if we want to give them a flying start to life.

Contents

1 On being a parent

There must be parents who feel nothing but continual joy at the news of an expected baby, but they are few and far between. Once the initial joy is over the majority of parents would confess to having mixed feelings about the prospect of having a baby.

Your fears are natural

Probably the most common anxiety is simply fear of parenthood – of whether you will be a good parent and of whether you can cope with bringing up a child, and on top of this will be the worry about your child's happiness if you don't make a good job of it.

There will be economic anxieties. Even if both partners are working, the money that was once enough for two now has to cover the needs of three so it has to spread a little more thinly, and luxuries and comforts, expensive holidays, a new car or decoration of the house will have to go by the board.

Another cause for anxiety will be the undoubted loss of freedom. No longer will you both be able to jump into the car and whizz off anywhere you like, go to a party on the spur of the moment, come back late or stay away on holiday for an extra few days if the fancy takes you.

All of these fears and anxieties are natural, but they are remediable. There is nothing abnormal about fearing that you won't make the grade as a parent. Your feelings may be easier to cope with if you understand that both you and your child will constantly change. Your family unit, the way it develops and the feelings it engenders, are dynamic. They are never stationary. Sometimes things will be very good and harmony will reign, and at other times you will get rather depressed at the amount of disharmony that there seems to be in your home. This is the natural rhythm of human relationships, especially relationships in the home.

All the feelings of love that you have for your child will be mixed at one time or another with resentment, bitterness, anger, hostility and frustration. This is inevitable, in the same way that it's inevitable in any human relationship. The difference is that from your child you will gain rewards that no other person can give you. One of the rules that I have learned about parenting is that whatever you put in you will get back five hundred times over. So not only will your freedom increase as your child gets older, but so will the pleasures that he or she gives you. The sacrifices you make when your baby is very young will be replaced by more and more pleasures. One of the greatest will be to see him or her turn from a dependent, demanding creature into a charming and thoughtful companion, an entertaining friend and a good pal.

How a family evolves

The basic family unit as we know it today has been found in every race or tribe since people first inhabited the earth. The family has always been, and still is, the cornerstone of society and its main function is to create a secure environment in which children can be raised.

There is no-one to whom the family is more important than a baby; it forms his or her entire universe. Within the family

11

your child learns all the basic aspects of human relationships. And within its security, your child learns about the good things in life: the happiness, the love and the laughter, as well as the bad things, the problems, the tensions and the anxieties. As your child grows, the family will provide the steadying, optimistic, strengthening influence that will help him or her cope with new and possibly difficult situations. It should always be the sanctuary to which your child can return when any conflicts seem too confusing to sort out.

The way the family is constructed and the roles played by the members of it, vary from culture to culture and family to family. In modern Western society the man has traditionally taken the role of breadwinner, provider and worker while the woman was the housekeeper and child-rearer and was mainly confined to the home. While today's society has accepted this as the norm it is in fact a very recent development in the evolution of the family.

Prior to the Industrial Revolution the family was a working unit with mother and father and children all working towards the common good. Because of this, many aspects of family life were shared experiences; no distinction was made between worker and nurturer of children as we have it today. Women and children were very often out in the fields as well as the men, and there was no sense at all that a woman's duty was to rear children and do the household chores. It was a much more egalitarian arrangement.

The Industrial Revolution tore apart this happy working family unit. Instead of being together the family was split up. The wage earner, of whichever sex, but usually the man, had to go to the factory in order to do his work instead of being close to his family. At about the same time parents abdicated their role as educators of children to schools, and so the family lost much of its educational function. Thirdly, the mother was often left at home with the children and because the wage earner had to work long hours, she had to shoulder

most of the responsibility for childrearing, for everyday care and for discipline.

Continuing industrialization and urbanization, and the increased scope for travel, meant that families became geographically separate. As a result mothers could no longer rely on their mothers, sisters and grandmothers for help as they had done in the past. They were left alone. The family unit became small, isolated and unsupported; for the mother it became boring, repetitive, tedious and frustrating. She had no time to herself, suffered from a loss of identity and had no other outlet for her skills and capabilities. Only recently, and largely because of the feminist movement, has there been a move back towards the kind of egalitarian marriage that existed before.

The modern mother

Modern mothers can be divided into two main categories. The first consists of those who feel that while their children are very young they want to look after them themselves and they feel that this activity is the most worthwhile job that they can do. However, even a mother who loves her child dearly will be prepared to admit that looking after small children isn't easy. A woman who finds herself a mother shortly after leaving a job is unlikely to be well prepared for the demands, not to mention the isolation of being a mother.

Motherhood has its pleasures and fulfillment but it is very tough. It is a twenty-four hour job and it is rather badly paid. It's repetitive and tedious; it is extremely demanding and wearing. No mother undervalues what she is doing but society does. Consequently when a young mother, particularly if she has been well trained to do a job, is asked what she is doing and all she can say is that she's a mother, she feels that the admission classifies her as inferior to women who are holding down a job. It is up to society to take a more realistic view of motherhood than the present rather idealized one.

The other category is the working mother. For some reason the term "work ing mother" is still a perjorative one in our society. If women aren't prepared to devote themselves entirely to the upbringing of their children it's generally felt that they aren't maternal, that they're selfish and heartless. If we go back to the pre-Industrial Revolution family we find that mothers were always working mothers. They did an equal amount of work to the father and they shared the work of the family with the father.

It is a natural instinct for a mother to want to go on working even although she has had children. Also, many women today work because they have to – either because they have no partner or because there is insufficient income. Women have always made a useful contribution to the support of their families, whether it was growing food, spinning wool, making pots, weaving cotton, grinding flour, curing bacon or tanning leather. Over the centuries the economic importance of women has been equal to their domestic importance. It is only now that we seem to have got things reversed.

Women who work nearly always have a strong drive to be independent outside the home. They want to have their own lives, their own interests, and their own source of income. They cherish their own area of activity where they are respected and their efforts are prized and where they are needed for their skills and expertise. These are perfectly valid and reasonable motives for wanting to work after a child is born. However, the woman who opts to do this is putting herself into the category of people who work hardest and are the most stressed. In Western society today the hardest working person has proven to be the working mother. She has two full-time jobs; that of a mother and that of wage-earner.

The modern father

The modern father is a father who takes responsibility for the general care of his child. Fewer fathers nowadays are prepared to be strangers to their children, missing out on all the good times in the family and, most important, missing out on their children growing up. The modern father is active rather than passive. He will arrange his day to come home early from work to see his children; he will spend time playing with them, showing them new things, helping them with their hobbies, taking them with him when he enjoys his own. He will participate from day one with the care of the baby, with nappy changing, with getting up in the middle of the night, doing the two a.m. feed, helping with bath times, reading stories, playing games and singing songs before bedtime. The modern father is a full-time parent, not a part-time stranger, and everyone in the family benefits from this.

A father who has a high interest in the pregnancy generally stays interested after the baby is born. Interest is positively related to how much he holds the baby in the first six weeks of life and also whether he goes to the baby when he or she cries. Not unexpectedly, his attitude affects his wife's enjoyment of pregnancy and motherhood. The happier he is about the pregnancy and the more he looks forward to fatherhood, the more she enjoys the first few weeks of her baby's life and, of course, the better the start to the baby's life. The better the father is at playing his role, the more important he becomes. As a woman I'm surprised that men aren't more prepared to manipulate the situation in their favour.

A new lifestyle

As a new parent you'll notice quite a few changes in your life. A life of free and easy egocentricity will be nailed down to your new baby's inner alarm clock, to the necessity for feeds, to changing nappies and tending your baby at any time of the day and night. It will almost be a complete reversal of lifestyle, and at first it may not be easy to accept. Some parents don't accept it and never let the baby dominate their lives. They try to carry on with their free and easy way of life with a baby basket tagging along. Other parents do exactly the opposite and give up every-

13

thing to look after their baby. The baby becomes the centre of their lives and they devote all their energy towards his or her care. Neither of these extremes is a good idea; far and away the best is a happy medium in which the needs and emotions of the baby and parents dovetail.

Meeting different needs

Children need certain things from their parents. They need security and love; they need to be introduced to new experiences and they need to be recognized and loved as individuals. If a parent fulfills these needs, particularly love and affection which are the most important things that you can give a child, then that child will develop normally and establish a pattern for forming all future relationships.

After love the next most important thing that you can give your child is stimulation. A small child is like a sponge soaking up practically every new idea and experience he or she comes in contact with. Your new baby has a great potential look on his mind

learn and is just dying to be given the opportunity. So, to be good parents, start introducing your child to the outside world with all its wonders and excitements, first through yourselves and the immediate family, and then through your extended family.

Children also need to know that the adults they love most, their parents, approve of them. The way you should show this approval is by praise. It has often been noted that children respond much better to praise than to blame, and a positive attitude of teaching and education is far more effective than a negative one. A child who is loved has self-respect; a child who is unloved has none. He or she responds to this situation by being difficult to manage, and generally antisocial.

Although children have needs, parents have needs too. Your needs don't disappear just because you've become a parent. The elation of having a baby will be quickly dispelled if you feel that your needs go completely unheeded. All parents

make sacrifices but there is no need for you to be a martyr. If your needs and those of your child are not well balanced, then resentment will build up and the chances of creating a happy, loving, domestic atmosphere will be minimal.

In looking at the needs of the parents the needs of *both* must be taken into consideration. In this day and age parents can be nothing but equal, and parenting and childrearing must be equally shared. It should really be viewed as a contract: you're equally responsible for your child's conception so you should take equal responsibility for rearing him or her. The least that must happen is that you and your partner both agree with each other on the roles that you have to play. It is just not good enough for a woman to be ex-

pected to take on the role of nursemaid, childminder and babysitter, confined to the house with its limited horizons and interests, while the father leaves early in the morning and doesn't return home before the baby is asleep. This situation is insupportable if the woman is an unwilling partner.

In an ideal world the needs of parents and children would complement each other. In other words, the need of parent to love and nurture a small baby would be matched by the infant's dependency and need for care. One of the things that triggers off conflict in a family is when the two sets of needs do not match – especially if the demands of the child are greater than the stage of maturity of the parents can handle.

Your role is important

As a parent you will be called upon to play many roles for your child. You will be your child's first friend and probably his or her best friend for life. At one time we thought that a child was not alert to the world around it until it reacted overtly to what was going on. Indeed Saint Thomas Aquinas saw it on even a longer scale. He said give me a boy until he's seven and then take him, the idea being that a person could be formed completely during the first seven years.

We now know that this formative time is much shorter. A child starts to absorb information about its environment from the second it is born. The fact that it can't focus its eyes on a distant object until the age of about six weeks does not mean that it cannot see. It can. A newborn baby can focus perfectly well at a distance of eight to ten inches and that's where your face and your hands should be if you want your baby to recognize you and watch you.

Babies are responding to sights, sounds, smells, touches, conversations, ambiences as soon as they enter the world. If parents realize this and take this fact seriously it puts them in a highly responsible position. It means that they, and not teachers, are totally responsible for a child's first learning.

You will not only be teacher but playmate, counsellor, educator and disciplinarian. Your influence will be pivotal. A child learns from its parents friendship and hostility, happiness and sadness, content and discontent, the blueprint for a loving relationship, the architecture of a conversation (indeed a baby is conversing in as short a time as two weeks if you learn how to recognize primitive baby conversation). All the early skills, walking, talking, socializing, intellectual development are absolutely in the parents' hands and no-one else is culpable if things go wrong. This means that modern parents have to be active, interested parents who take on their roles as teachers with seriousness and dedication, from the moment the baby is born.

All children require one strong, constant, emotional bond early in their lives. If this bond is missing because the parents are inconsistent in giving their child love, sympathy and reassurance, or because the mother has been replaced by several inadequate mother substitutes, your baby's early need for a secure relationship may be thwarted.

Part of your role will be to teach your child to respect other people's rights and property, and this will be enforced through discipline. For discipline to be effective it should be firm but it should always be sympathetic, understanding and considerate. Very often a child's delinquent act is directed at a neglectful parent with whom he cannot communicate. A parent who does not talk to his or her child has very little chance of influencing him or her, whereas a mother or father who has observed and respected each step in a child's development and accepted his or her idiosyncracies and failures, will nearly always be in a position to talk over problems with that child.

Research has shown that children actually do not like a lack of discipline nor do they thrive when they are undisciplined. In fact they do best when the limits of behaviour are clearly defined for them. It is your role to set standards for behaviour and conduct appropriate for the age of your child, and to create a framework in which your child can get on with his or her life free of unnecessary control. Research into child development has shown that both over-restrictiveness and inconsistency have adverse effects on children. Ideal parents are warm, affectionate, accepting, understanding and encouraging of independence.

One of the most important aspects of parenting is being a model for your developing child. A boy observes his father and quickly realizes what is going to be expected of him as he grows up. He models himself on his father, he copies what his father does, he picks up habits from his father. In the same way a daughter learns

17

from her mother what is expected of her and what it will be like to be a woman. It's the atmosphere and behaviour inside the home from which the children first learn social behaviour and social roles. As they grow older they will determine their own moral values and their standards from those which are displayed by their parents. A child can do quite well with only one parent to learn from, but he or she is obviously better off with two models to check against rather than one. It's my belief that children need the interest, the help, the support, the teaching, the counselling and the love of fathers. Certainly in matters of discipline, both parents are needed because families should make important decisions as a unit, and children should see both their parents taking an interest in and making decisions about the important times in their lives.

The importance of touching

"Spare the rod and spoil the child" was something which my mother and many of her generation quoted to her children, and most people of my age were disciplined not only with words, actions, rewards and punishments, but with some kind of physical punishment. To my mind the

word spoil is a very dangerous one because most people confuse spoiling with loving, and no baby or child can have too much loving.

The first introduction to loving which a newborn baby experiences is the touch of the mother's arms. The second is the sound of her voice. I do believe that babies "bond" to these two things. In other words they recognize the mother's touch, her smell and the sound of her voice as belonging to their carer, the person who feeds and takes an interest in them, soothes away discomfort and generally makes life happier and more pleasant.

One of the most important aspects of this loving relationship is touch and the first touches are soft, gentle, welcoming and cushioning.

We are not the only animal to whom touch is important; it is important throughout the whole animal kingdom, as some beautiful and rather moving animal experiments show. Some of the first of these were done with baby chimpanzees. They were divided into two groups, having both been taken away from their mothers rather early, but old enough to survive on their own. The two groups were given different kinds of "mother": one was given a "wire mother" which was simply the

shape and body of a mother chimp made out of wire and from it protruding a small teat through which the baby chimp could obtain food at will.

The second group was given a "soft mother" which was the wire body covered in material like lambs wool. The special effect of lambs wool is that when the baby chimps moved their bodies against it the lambs wool was so soft that it felt like a mother touching them. The experiment showed that the baby chimps were prepared to go without food in order to snuggle up to the "soft mother", so great was their need for softness, comfort and touching.

Even now in intensive care units where premature babies are nurtured the babies are put on lambs wool sheets because this makes the babies feel as though they are being touched. The astonishing fact is they thrive better and put on weight more quickly than a child who lies on a smooth linen or cotton sheet.

The upshot of all this information is very important for a parent. If you want your baby to be happy, to thrive and to put on weight, one of the most important things you can do for him or her is to cuddle, and cuddle, and give more cuddles. Take opportunities throughout the day to stroke, pat, touch and love through gestures. If you can accompany these touching movements with a soft, loving voice, a big smile and your face eight to ten inches away from your newborn baby, you will be giving it a flying start.

Love is not exclusive

Until quite recently the commonly held view of the mother/child bond was that it was exclusive. It was thought that a strong, healthy bond between mother and child was essential for a child's mental health, but more importantly that a child's care should be monopolized by one mother figure. It was also felt that a child was unable to form attachments to more than one person who was, of course, the mother. This placed an enormous psychological burden on the mother and made her the subject of great leverage by everyone who cared to exert it, be it partner or family.

Research has shown that this is almost certainly not the case. Babies are not confined to a single bond. Once your baby has reached the stage of forming an attachment to anyone then he or she is probably capable of maintaining a number of attachments at the same time. Most babies as they grow up form specific attachments simultaneously – as many as five or more. By the time children are 18 months old almost a third have formed attachments with neighbours and grandparents but, above all, with fathers. Another aspect of the research has shown that being attached to several people at the same time does not mean that the baby has a shallower feeling towards each one. An infant's capacity for attachment is not like a cake that has to be cut. Love in babies has no limits.

Given this basis of a baby's ability to form attachments with several people there is no reason why mothering cannot be shared by several people. Furthermore, the mother need not be the biological mother. There is no evidence at all to suggest that firm attachments won't grow between children and unrelated adults who take over the role of parenting by fostering or adoption, for instance. The belief that the mother, simply by virtue of being the biological mother, is uniquely capable of caring for her child is completely without foundation. There are no medical, physiological or biological reasons for confining childcare to women. The argument in favour of equal sharing of parenting between both parents is irresistible.

An infant can form multiple attachments and research has shown that such attachments depend more on the *quality* of the interaction than on its duration. Controversy about whether the mother has to be the infant's constant companion throughout each day is over. A minimum period of togetherness is desirable, but there is nothing that can be said about how much. It is the personal qualities that the adult brings to the interaction that are the most important. Provided that these can be given full play there is no reason why mother and baby should not spend a portion of the day apart (the mother at work for instance and the child in some kind of day care arrangement which the family is comfortable with).

There is, however, one important proviso: that is the stability and quality of substitute care. If the people responsible for the child's care are constantly changing the child could well become disturbed. A child may not need uniformity of care, but he does need consistency of care. It's your job to make sure this is given if neither of you is going to stay at home.

21

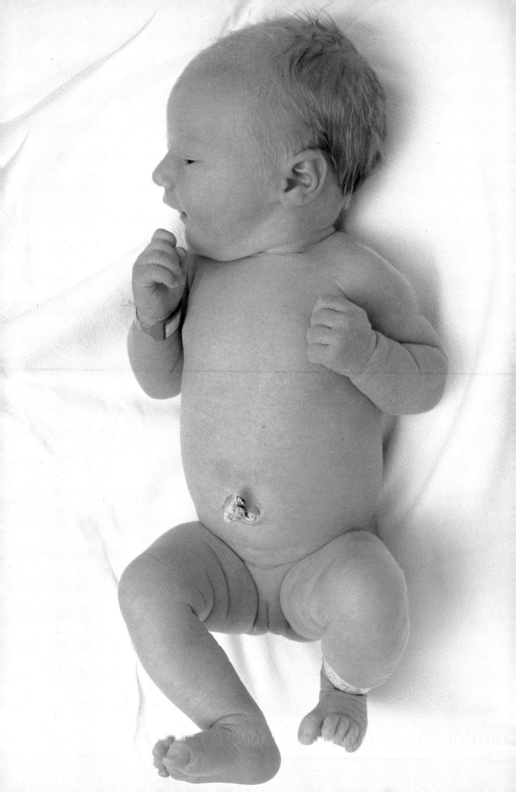

The newborn

Soon after delivery your baby will have an initial examination when his weight, head circumference and possibly his length will be measured in order to form a baseline against which his future development will be measured. Incidentally, don't try to compare your baby with others; doctors and midwives don't. The only comparisons that should be made are with himself at difference stages.

The average birth weight is 2500g to 4500g (5lb 8oz to 9lb 12oz), but if your baby is on the small side don't be concerned about it. The normal range is enormous and varies according to such factors as genetics, race and nutrition, amongst others.

The average length of a baby at term is 48 to 51cm (19 to 20in), but again huge variations are common.

Your baby will almost certainly seem to be oddly proportioned. His abdomen, because of the initial weakness of his abdominal muscles, will seem surprisingly rounded, and his head will be large in comparison with the rest of his body. In contrast to this his arms and legs may appear stick-like, but these proportions are normal.

PHYSICAL IMPRESSIONS

The head

Size
The average newborn baby's head circumference is about 35cm (14in) and is disproportionately larger than the rest of his body. It comprises a quarter of his entire length compared to one eighth in the adult.

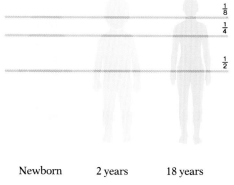

Newborn   2 years   18 years

At birth, the head is a quarter of entire length. At two years it's a fifth and by the eighteenth year it's only an eighth.

Shape
Your baby's head is unlikely to be perfectly rounded after birth, but no matter how bumpy or swollen it looks your baby's brain will not have been damaged. This is because the bones in the head are specially designed to move over each other during birth so that the head, which is the largest part of the baby's body, can pass down the birth canal easily. It will soon regain its rounded shape.

Sometimes the baby has a large, firm swelling on one or both sides of the head which doesn't go down immediately. Called a cephalhaematoma, this is again caused by the natural pressure exerted by the uterine muscle during labour. It's really a large bruise of the scalp and it's outside the skull. The swelling puts no pressure on the baby's brain and subsides, without treatment, within a few weeks.

Bruising is quite common after a forceps delivery, as are shallow indentations on either side of the head. They are both rectified naturally within a couple of days.

23

The fontanelle

The fontanelle is the soft spot in the top of your baby's head and it is the space where the skull bones have not yet joined. They don't fuse until your baby is about two years old. The baby's scalp covers this space and is really quite tough, but you should make sure that the fontanelle is never pressed very hard. The purpose of the fontanelle is to allow the soft skull bones to "mould" (this means to ride over one another) without damage to the baby's brain as it passes through the birth canal. You need take no special care of the skin and hair which cover the fontanelle. However, if you ever notice that the skin over the area is taut, if there's a bulge or if the area's abnormally shrunken you should contact your doctor immediately.

The eyes

Condition
Most babies are born with rather puffy eyes as a result of the natural pressure during birth. The swelling usually goes down within a couple of days.

Never accept a discharge from your baby's eyes as normal. In all probability it's a common, mild infection called "sticky eye", but it should always be treated by a doctor, not by yourself. Never use proprietary drops or ointments.
Colour
All babies are born with blue eyes. This is because melanin, the body's natural pigment is not present in the skin or eyes at birth. If a baby is going to have brown eyes or a dark brown skin, the colour will gradually develop over a period of weeks or months. The eyes and skin may not reach their permanent colour until the baby is six months old.

Eye function
You may find it difficult to get your baby to open his eyes at first but you should never try to force them open. One of the easiest ways I have found to get a baby to open his eyes is to hold him above my head. The tendency then is to open them.

You might notice when your baby does open his eyes that he appears to squint. Don't worry about this. Your baby hasn't yet learnt to use his eyes synchronously, as a pair, to focus on things. The squinting will gradually disappear as he learns to focus when he's one or two months old. You should consult your doctor if your baby is still squinting after three months.
Tears
Babies don't shed tears, as you'll find when your baby cries. It usually takes about four or five months for a baby to produce them.

The mouth

Lip blisters
Such blisters, usually in the centre of the mouth, are caused by the baby's sucking. They cause no harm and will go away of their own accord.
Tongue-tie
Your baby's tongue may appear to be almost fully attached to the bottom of his mouth. This should not be a cause of worry. The baby's tongue grows mainly from the tip throughout the first year.

The skin

The vernix
The skin of your newborn will probably be covered with this white, greasy substance. Some babies have vernix all over their face and body, while others only have it on isolated parts like their face and hands. Hospital practices in relation to the vernix vary. Whereas in some hospitals it is left on because it provides a natural barrier against minor skin infections, in others it is meticulously cleaned off after birth. This is generally considered unnecessary nowadays, not only because of the vernix's protective qualities, but also because it is naturally absorbed into the skin within

two or three days. However, if there are large accumulations of the vernix in the skin folds it may be wiped away in case it causes any irritation.

Texture

Your baby may be born with a dry peeling skin (most noticeable on the palms of the hands and soles of the feet). This is not eczema nor does it mean that your baby will be permanently dry-skinned. In most cases the dryness disappears within a couple of days.

Colour

The top half of your baby's body may be pale while the lower half is red. This is due to the baby's immature circulation which causes the blood to pool in the lower limbs. The difference is rectified by moving the baby.

You may notice that your baby's hands or feet have turned rather blue, especially if he's been lying down. Once again, this is due to the baby's relatively inefficient circulation. The colour will change if you pick up or move the baby. Try to keep the baby's room at an equable temperature, around 16-20°C (65-68°F). Blue marks (also called Mongolian blue spots), which look like bruises, often occur on the lower backs of babies with dark skin tones (nearly all African and Asian babies have them). They are completely harmless and fade away naturally.

Jaundice

It is not uncommon for a baby to suffer jaundice - a yellowish discolouration of the skin and the whites of the eyes. It is scary but nothing to worry about. Many healthy newborn infants develop jaundice on the third day of life and this is known as physiological jaundice, because it is not a disease. It is due to the baby's blood having a high content of primitive red cells, which are broken down after birth. When red cells care broken down, one of their constituent parts, the yellow pigment call bilirubin, increases in the blood and causes the skin and eyes to colour. Physiological jaundice should clear by the end of the first week as long as the baby is feeding well.

Birthmarks

Quite commonly there are small red marks on a baby's skin, particularly on the eyelids, on the forehead and, if you lift up the hair, at the back of the neck just under the hairline. They are due to the enlargement of tiny blood vessels near the surface of the skin and are traditionally called stork beak marks. Both of my sons had them and they disappeared, as they do in most children, by the time they were six months old. In some babies it may take up to eighteen months.

Another common birthmark is the so-called strawberry mark. This appears after a couple of days but gradually fades over the years (it should have disappeared by the time he's three years old). If you're at all worried by your baby's birthmark ask your doctor for advice and reassurance.

Spots

It is not unusual for a baby to have small white spots over the bridge of the nose, called milia. These spots are not abnormal so *never*, ever squeeze them. They are caused by the temporary blockage of the sweat glands and sebaceous glands which secrete sebum to lubricate the skin. They nearly always disappear after a few days.

Weals and rashes

Many babies develop a skin condition which looks rather like nettle rash, called urticaria neonatorum. The baby's skin becomes red and blotchy, with small white spots which appear and disappear quite rapidly. The whole rash only lasts for a couple of days and will disappear without treatment. If you're in doubt consult your doctor.

Body hair

Babies are born with varying amounts of hair, called lanugo hair, on their bodies. Some babies have only a soft down on their heads, others are covered in quite coarse hair over their shoulders and down their spines. Both are quite normal, and the hair usually rubs off quite soon after birth.

The umbilicus

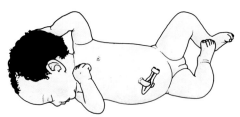

Immediately after birth the umbilical cord is cut about 8 to 10cm from the baby's stomach. Pressure is exerted on it by a clamp and the stump shrivels and drops off within ten days or so. Some babies develop umbilical hernias (small swellings near the navel), but these nearly always clear up within a year of their own accord. If your baby has one and it enlarges or persists consult your doctor.

The breasts

Both male and female babies can have swollen breasts at birth; they may even have a slight discharge of milk. This is caused by the presence of maternal hormones in the baby's body and it resolves itself naturally. *Never* try to squeeze any of the milk out. The swelling will subside within a couple of days.

The genitals

The genitals of both boys and girls are naturally larger at birth than the rest of their bodies. The scrotum or vulva may even look rather red and inflamed. This is a natural occurence and is caused by the mother's hormones crossing the placenta into the baby's bloodstream. Such hormones may also cause a clear or white discharge in female babies, and even a small amount of vaginal bleeding. Once again, this is perfectly normal and will clear up naturally after a couple of days. However, if you're at all worried by this, contact your doctor for reassurance.

Stools

A baby's first stools are usually dark green and sticky and have very little smell. This is because they are mainly meconium which is digested mucus from the mucus glands in the bowel. It is the only kind of motion your baby will pass for the first two or three days. Gradually over the next three or four days you will notice that the stools change colour. The appearance and consistency will depend on whether your baby is having breast or formula milk (see p. 155 and p. 156).

NEWBORN BEHAVIOUR

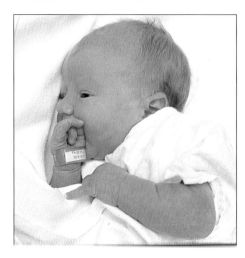

If you concentrate on your baby and observe him carefully over the first two or three days of life you will become familiar with normal infant behaviour and will get accustomed to your baby's idiosyncracies. It is essential that you learn to understand your baby's signals to you, and the only way to do this is to stay with him as much as possible, to watch him, nurse him, play with and look after him.

If you watch him closely you may notice that he does several unexpected things: he may shiver quite suddenly for no reason; he may make such snuffling noises that you wonder if his nose and air passages are blocked; he may even stop breathing all together for several seconds. None of these is abnormal.

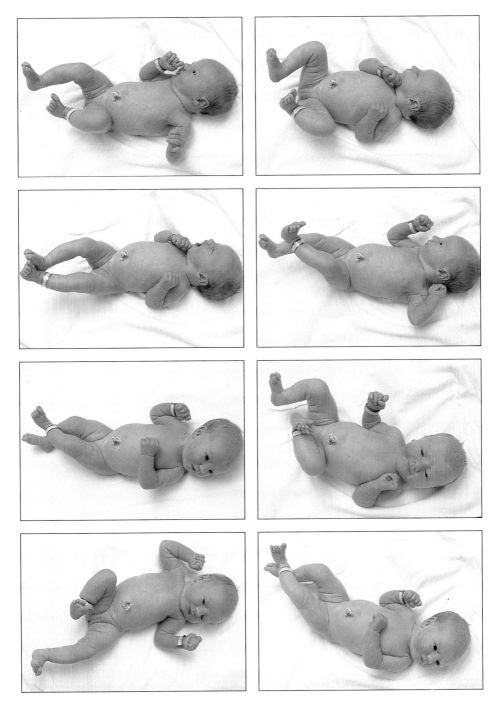

Sounds

Breathing
A neonate's lungs are small and breathing will seem shallow when compared to ours. When you first go to your baby you may be unable to detect that he is breathing. Don't be frightened by this because the breathing will get stronger each day.

All newborn babies make strange sounds when they breathe. Sometimes the breathing is fast and noisy and at other times it may be irregular. Your baby may snuffle with each breath in and out and you may think he has got a cold. This is not necessarily so. In most babies it is because the bridge of the nose is low, and the snuffling noise is caused by the air trying to get through the very small nasal passages. As your baby grows older the bridge of the nose will get higher and the snuffling sound will gradually stop.

On the other hand, if the snuffling interferes with your baby's freedom to suck then you should consult your doctor because he may need treatment with nose drops before feeding (see p. 116). Nose drops should only be used under medical supervision.

You should, however, be concerned about your baby's breathing if it ever becomes laboured, especially if you notice that the chest is being sharply drawn in with each breath and the breathing rate has risen to 60 or more breaths per minute. Any of these signs in your child warrants immediate medical attention (see p. 339).

Sneezing
Babies are very sensitive to bright lights and sometimes sneeze whenever they open their eyes for the first few days. This is because the light stimulates the nerves to the nose as well as to the eyes. (You can try this out for yourself the next time you feel a sneeze coming on: if you look into a bright light you will find that you are able to precipitate the sneeze.) Even if your baby is sneezing quite a lot it doesn't necessarily mean that he has a cold. The lining of a baby's nose is sensitive, and sneezing is essential to clear out the nasal passages and prevent dust from getting down into the lungs.

Hiccups
Newborn babies hiccup quite a lot. This is normal, too, and it shouldn't bother you. Hiccups are caused by sudden, irregular contractions of the diaphragm and are a sign that the muscles involved in respiration, those between the ribs, the diaphragm, and the abdomen, are getting stronger and trying to work in harmony.

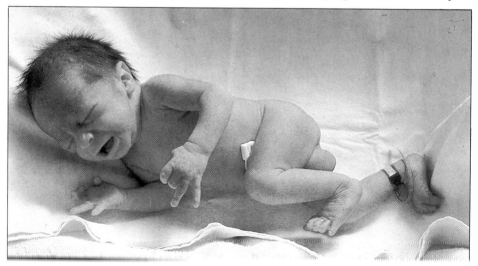

Reflexes and movements

All newborn babies have reflexes which are instinctive movements designed to protect them. They last until voluntary movements on your baby's part take their place, generally around 3 months old. Two of the most easy reflexes to elicit are those to protect the eyes and to maintain breathing: your baby will close his eyes if you touch his eyelids and will make struggling movements with his hands if you gently hold his nose between your thumb and forefinger.

The rooting reflex

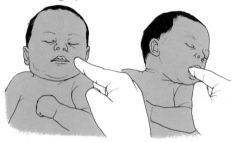

If you gently stroke your baby's cheek you will find that he turns his head in the direction of your finger and opens his mouth. He makes this rooting movement when he is searching for your breast to start feeding (see p. 108).

The sucking reflex

Every baby is born with the reflex to suck and yours will begin to do so if something is put in his mouth or if you press on the upper palate just behind the gums. Sucking movements are extremely strong and they last for quite a long time after the stimulation to suck, like a finger or a nipple, has been removed. If you want to breast-feed it is important that you put the baby to the breast as soon after delivery as possible. Your baby has to get used to the actual technique of breast-feeding, just as you do, so it helps if he has the powerful desire to suck as a stimulus.

The swallowing reflex

All babies can swallow the instant they are born. This means that they can swallow colostrum or milk straight away.

The "walking" reflex

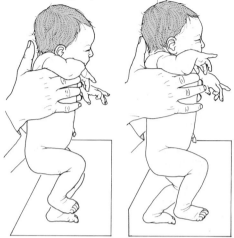

A newborn baby will move his legs in a walking or stepping action if you hold him upright underneath the arms and let his feet touch a firm surface. This is not the reflex that encourages a baby to stand upright and walk (see p. 210). If you hold your baby upright and let the front of his legs gently touch the edge of a solid object he'll automatically bring his foot up in a kind of stepping movement.

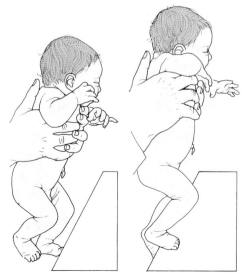

29

The "crawling" reflex

When placed on his stomach your newborn baby will assume what appears to be a crawling position. This is because his legs are still curled up towards his body as they were in the womb. When he kicks his legs he may well be able to shuffle in a vague crawling manner and actually move up his cot slightly. This "reflex" will disappear as soon as his legs uncurl and he lies flat.

The grasp reflex

The startle or Moro reflex

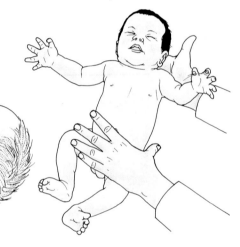

A newborn baby automatically tightens his fingers around anything which is pressed into the palm of his hand. He can grasp very tightly, and immediately after birth this reflex is so strong and powerful that his whole weight can be supported if he grasps on to your fingers. This reflex is generally lost around three months old. If you touch the soles of your baby's feet you will also notice that his toes curl downwards as if to grip something.

If your baby hears a loud noise close to him, or if he's been roughly handled, he will throw up his arms and legs with fingers outstretched in an attempt to catch on to something. He'll let his limbs fall back slowly towards his body and will then bend his knees and clench his fists. This is a large or "gross" response to a stimulus and many newborn responses are like this. For instance, when your young baby sees you he uses the whole of his body to greet you. It's only when he gets to about eight or nine months old that he simply smiles and reaches out his arms to you as a more mature greeting.

30

BONDING

A newborn baby sleeps for most of his first days, so you should spend all of his waking time with him. Research has shown that physical contact with you, the sound of your voice and the smell of your body are very important during the first few days of life. During this time your baby forms a bond with you which, if encouraged, is unique and unbreakable.

This bonding process is nature's way of ensuring that children are nurtured and that the human race, as a whole, survives. However, in the normal course of events, whether you are breast- or bottle-feeding your baby, he will automatically get the close contact he needs while you are feeding, changing and holding him. He will get to know you, your smell, and the sound of your voice.

If, for any reason, your baby is taken away to the nursery for observation, or to the special care unit, you should make every effort to visit him as often as possible. Even if he has to be cared for in an incubator, you can touch and caress him through the portholes, talk to him and, if possible, feed him. It is important to take all the steps you can to reduce the time you are separated from your baby.

Eye contact is essential

All research points to the fact that physical contact between mother and baby should start as soon after birth as possible. Furthermore, eye contact should follow immediately after birth wherever possible. Most child development experts used to say that babies could not see properly until their eyes could focus, but babies *can* interpret shapes and outlines. The shape and outline of your face will be recognized by your baby within 36 hours. Research has shown that it is your eyes that your baby searches for and concentrates on once he has found them. Furthermore, babies can do this within a few hours of birth. Certainly when my second son was born and I lifted him on to my stomach and called his name he opened his eyes instantly on hearing my voice and flicked them around the room until they came to rest on my face.

It has been shown that mothers who make early eye contact with their babies and continue to do so, particularly during feeding times when they face their babies and look deeply into their eyes, are much more likely to be sympathetic, understanding mothers who tend to solve problems calmly and by logical discussion. They rarely resort to physical punishment of their children.

Early physical contact

Following on from the first few days you should try to keep your baby in contact with you as much as possible. By contact I mean on your body, for instance in a sling. It has been known for decades that the children who are carried on their mother's backs, such as those in Indian, Eskimo and some African tribes, rarely cry. The newborn infant finds the close physical presence of the mother very reassuring. She is soft and warm, her smell is familiar. When the baby lays his head against the mother's body he hears the familiar heartbeat that he has been hearing for nine months in the womb. The baby feels secure and at home in his surroundings. It is more natural for your baby to be jogged

about on his mother's body than to lie completely still on a mattress in a cot, especially as it could bring back memories of his cushioned ride in the womb.

The importance of smell

We know that your smell is one of the first associations that your baby makes with you. You give off a smell to which your baby is very sensitive and to which he responds biologically. Whenever you go into your sleeping baby's room he wakes. When other people, even your partner, go in he stays asleep. This is because the baby's very sensitive sense of smell picks up your chemicals called pheromones, and he wakes because he recognizes you as his main source of comfort, pleasure and food.

Sounds and their effects

Newborn babies do not like loud noises. While your baby is becoming used to your voice, speak or sing in a soft, gentle, soothing, cooing voice. Research work at Oxford has shown that babies respond better to the high-pitched female voice rather than to the lower-pitched male voice. To a baby the mother's voice is almost like therapy. You should chat, sing or croon to your baby whenever you are with him. It is surprising how even young babies enjoy nursery rhymes and simple songs, particularly if they have a pronounced rhythm and rhyming sound. Some child development research suggests that children who are sung to early in their lives rapidly develop a feeling for and a facility with words. They tend to speak and read slightly earlier than other children.

Mother love

Most mothers are exhilarated, although exhausted, after the delivery of a baby and feel great love for the child. Some mothers, however, find that they feel nothing towards their babies.

We now know that mother love, put very simply, is a response to hormones. There are certain hormones produced in the brain almost immediately after childbirth, namely oxytocin or prolactin, which trigger off lactation and are also responsible for maternal feelings. Different women have different emotional responses to these hormones and may find that their love for their babies lags behind.

A mother's feelings for her baby can also be affected by other factors, like the actual delivery and her own expectations of the birth and the baby. It's not uncommon for the baby's arrival to be something of an anti-climax. Even if it is short and perfectly normal, labour is a very dramatic event and it is a hard act to follow. Conversely, if the labour has been very hard and long, and if drugs have been used, the mother may be too tired and numbed to feel great love for her child. Also, she may have unrealistic expectations of her response to her newborn baby. She may, for instance, expect to recognize him instantly as her own flesh and blood, and to look physically similar to herself and her partner – this very rarely happens and unless it is realized as a possibility it could cause problems.

Most women, however, find that their love grows gradually over the 48 or 72 hours after their babies' births until on the third day they feel a palpable love for their new babies. But don't be surprised if it takes two weeks – it's not that rare.

Spend time with your baby

A mother's response to her baby can be affected by the amount of time she spends with him during the first few days of life. A group of mothers who were permitted nothing more than routine contact with their babies on a hospital ward was studied. Another group of mothers in the same ward was allowed to have contact with their babies for an extra fifteen hours during their three days in hospital. The two groups were interviewed one month after delivery and a year later and revealed a number of quite surprising differences. The mothers who had been given extended contact were found to be more reluctant to leave their babies, to be more responsive to their crying, to engage in more eye-to-

eye contact during feeding and to be generally more attentive to their babies. The remarkable thing is that these differences are accounted for by just fifteen hours of additional contact during the first three days of life.

While it's undoubtedly true that early physical contact helps bonding, it's not the only factor involved in the development of maternal or paternal feelings. In a study of premature babies, where the most extreme form of early separation arises because the baby has to stay in an incubator for an extended period, mothers were allocated to two groups. In the first, the standard hospital procedure was used and each mother was permitted only to look at her baby during the several weeks he stayed in the incubator. In the second group the mothers were permitted to handle their babies in the incubator from the second day onwards. The mothers were questioned after one week and one month and then after discharge from hospital. It was impossible to find any consistent differences between the two groups. This important piece of research suggests that a mother's attachment to her baby may not be seriously affected by a temporary separation immediately after her baby's birth. That's just as well, otherwise there would be little hope for adoptive parents and their children. Mothering is much more complex than a simple dependency on the hormonal changes that occur at childbirth. The most likely explanation for the way a woman develops mothering and maternal instincts is that it stems from the mother's own childhood. Love develops early on in life on a reciprocal basis. It stems from the experience of being loved by parents who give a child the capacity for loving others. It enables the child to return love when it is given and to transfer it to others later on in life. In other words, when a child is loved it makes him fit for love; if a child is deprived of this experience the ability to love is stunted. This is why it's so important for your child to have your loving attention, care and concern.

Equipment

It's advisable to go shopping in the last couple of months before your baby's born, while you're still unfettered and feel reasonably energetic. You'll be faced with a seemingly endless choice of equipment, all of which will be labelled "essential" by the manufacturers. Don't be swayed by clever advertising. If you can, ask friends or relatives which items of equipment they found useful and, more important, which they bought and never used. Shop around and find out what's available before you make your final decision, and always think of the equipment in relation to your lifestyle. For example, if you feel perfectly relaxed about washing your baby in a sink, don't bother buying a baby bath just because most people do. Similarly, if you really like the idea of a large carriage pram and if you have an adequately large hall, if you have an easy route to any shops or parks without too many steps or other obstructions and if you have the cash, then

you should go ahead and buy it. Some people think it unlucky to buy too much before the birth. Check to see if you can choose what you need but not pick it up.

It isn't essential to buy all-new equipment. Babies grow so quickly that some items, which are essential at one stage, are useless within a couple of months. Many families are quite happy to lend or sell such items, so keep an eye open in newsagents, local papers and clinics as well as at house and garage sales. The only stipulation I'd make when buying secondhand, apart from checking for general wear and tear, is that the surfaces are smooth and rust-free and that, where applicable, they still comply with the latest safety regulations. Car restraints are the only items which should not be bought secondhand.

Delay buying clothes until as late as possible. Relatives love buying for a baby and you'll probably find that many items are duplicated.

ESSENTIAL EQUIPMENT

Sleeping
Carry cot, crib or cot
Mattress
1 waterproof cover
3 fitted towelling sheets
3 cellular blankets
2 swaddling shawls

Transport
Sling
Buggy, push-chair or
   carry-cot pram
Infant car seats

Bathing and changing
Baby bath
Cotton wool
Baby oil
Baby lotion
Large soft towel
Flannel or sponge
Baby brush
Blunt-ended scissors
Changing mat
Nappy liners
4 packs disposable
   nappies
or
24 towelling nappies
Pins
Plastic pants
2 nappy buckets

Clothing
4 stretch suits
4 singlets
2 nightdresses
2 jumpers

Feeding
If breast-feeding:
Breast pads
2 bottles with teats
Sterilizing tablets
1 tin formula
If bottle-feeding:
Bottle-feeding kit
1 month's supply of
   formula
Infant seat
High chair

35

Changing and bathing

If you like the idea of having a special changing area, but don't want to build one or convert a piece of furniture like a chest of drawers, then the changing unit is probably right for you. Make sure that it's stable and has plenty of storage space.

Unless you decide to do without a baby bath, choosing instead to use the sink or a household basin, you'll have to buy a specially-designed one. The specially-moulded, rigid plastic ones generally come with stands. There is also another practical style which fits astride the bath so you don't have to carry the tub from water source to stand.

CHANGING EQUIPMENT

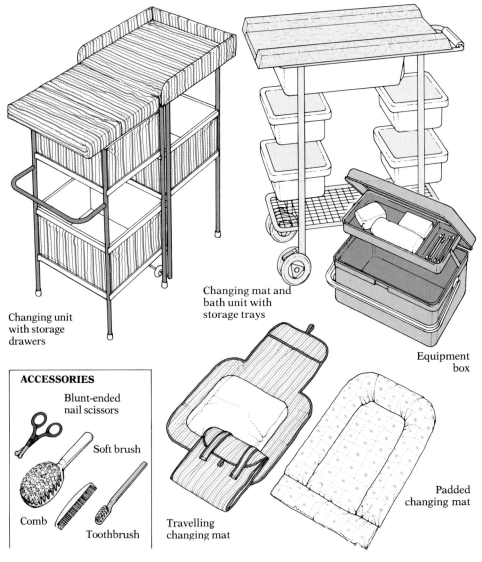

Changing unit with storage drawers

Changing mat and bath unit with storage trays

Equipment box

ACCESSORIES

Blunt-ended nail scissors

Soft brush

Comb

Toothbrush

Travelling changing mat

Padded changing mat

BATHING AND HYGIENE

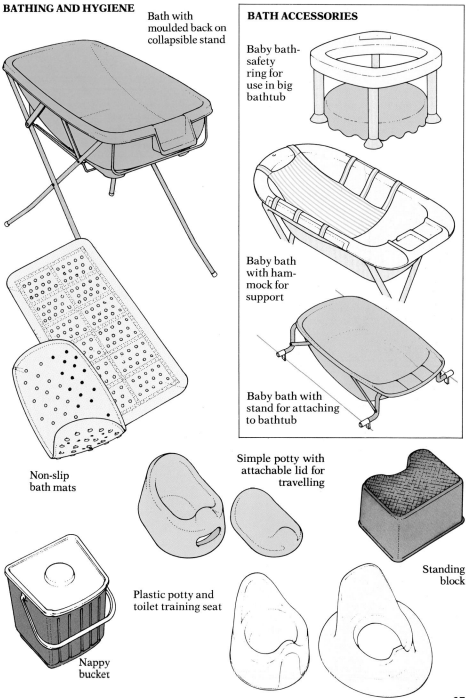

Bath with moulded back on collapsible stand

BATH ACCESSORIES

Baby bath-safety ring for use in big bathtub

Baby bath with hammock for support

Baby bath with stand for attaching to bathtub

Non-slip bath mats

Simple potty with attachable lid for travelling

Standing block

Plastic potty and toilet training seat

Nappy bucket

37

Feeding

If you're breast-feeding you'll need the minimum of equipment – a couple of bottles just in case you want to express some milk, or in case you become ill. Bottle-feeding mothers will have to buy a complete feeding kit (see p. 120).

When your baby starts on solids you'll need equipment which will mash the food into a smooth enough purée. You'll also need an unbreakable dish to serve it in. Special dishes which keep the food hot are available although they're not essential. Bibs, however, are. Probably the most efficient style is the plastic bib with a trough which catches all drips or pieces of food and can be washed off easily.

You'll also need some form of high chair. There is a wide variety to choose from, many of which adapt to other things like swings or tables. Make sure that the chair is stable, that it has washable surfaces, a tray with a rim to catch spilt liquids and safety harness hooks.

BOTTLES AND STERILIZING UNITS

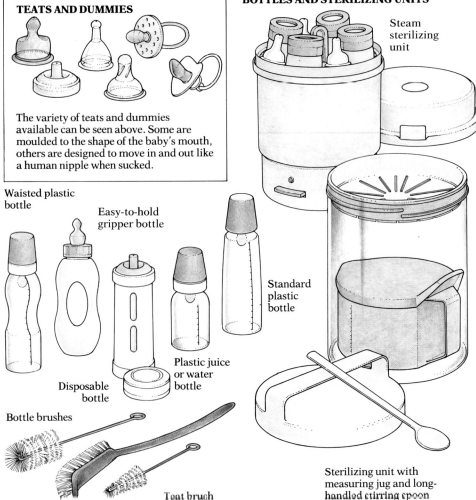

TEATS AND DUMMIES

The variety of teats and dummies available can be seen above. Some are moulded to the shape of the baby's mouth, others are designed to move in and out like a human nipple when sucked.

Steam sterilizing unit

Waisted plastic bottle

Easy-to-hold gripper bottle

Standard plastic bottle

Disposable bottle

Plastic juice or water bottle

Bottle brushes

Teat brush

Sterilizing unit with measuring jug and long-handled stirring spoon

WEANING EQUIPMENT

Grater

Hand blenders

Sieve

Electric
liquidizer

Steamer

Plastic bowl
with handle
and suction
pad

Double-handled,
easy-grip cup

Beaker with
drinking spout

Warmer bowl
with suction pad

Slanted cup with
handles for easy
drinking

Electric baby
food and bottle
heater

Easily-held
weaning spoons
and forks

HIGH CHAIRS

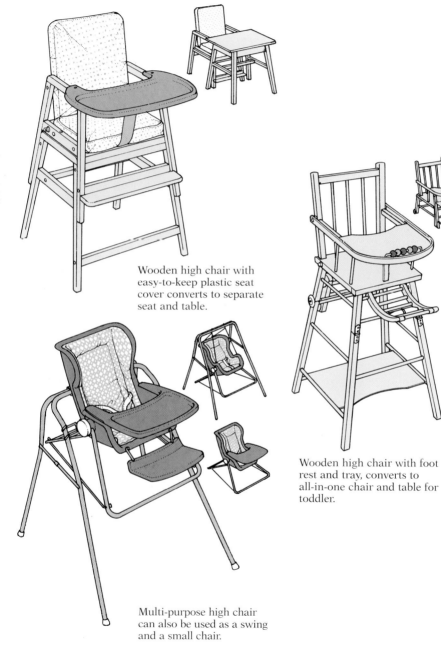

Wooden high chair with easy-to-keep plastic seat cover converts to separate seat and table.

Wooden high chair with foot rest and tray, converts to all-in-one chair and table for toddler.

Multi-purpose high chair can also be used as a swing and a small chair.

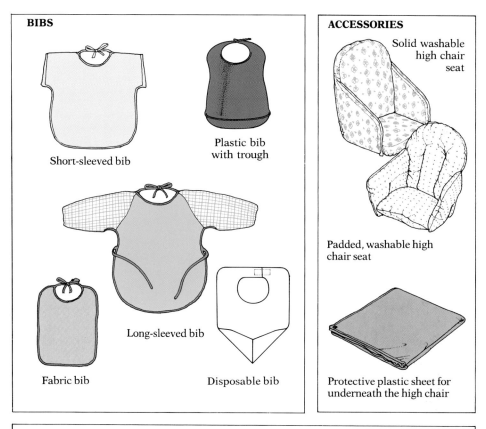

BIBS

Short-sleeved bib

Plastic bib with trough

Long-sleeved bib

Fabric bib

Disposable bib

ACCESSORIES

Solid washable high chair seat

Padded, washable high chair seat

Protective plastic sheet for underneath the high chair

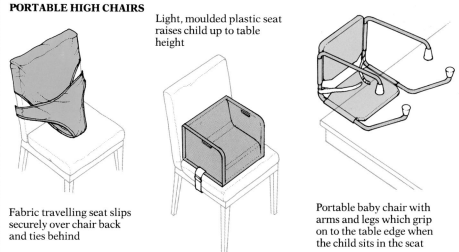

PORTABLE HIGH CHAIRS

Light, moulded plastic seat raises child up to table height

Fabric travelling seat slips securely over chair back and ties behind

Portable baby chair with arms and legs which grip on to the table edge when the child sits in the seat

Sleeping

Wooden rocking cribs are attractive to look at, but if your budget is tight I suggest that you don't buy one; your baby could easily have outgrown it within twelve or thirteen weeks of being born. Instead, use a relatively cheap baby basket or carry-cot pram which can also be used as a push-chair when he's older. When he outgrows whichever of them you've chosen use a cot. The mattress you buy for the cot should fit snugly, allowing no more than one finger to slide between the mattress and the cot side. Do make sure that any side rails are set closely together, so your baby's head can't get stuck, and buy the cot with sides which drop down – it's much easier to get at the baby this way. Fabric-sided travel cots, which collapse and roll up into easily-manageable units, are ideal for both holidays and going out with the baby in the evening. Once the baby can clamber out you'll need to buy a bed – some are actually designed to convert from cots.

CRIBS AND COTS

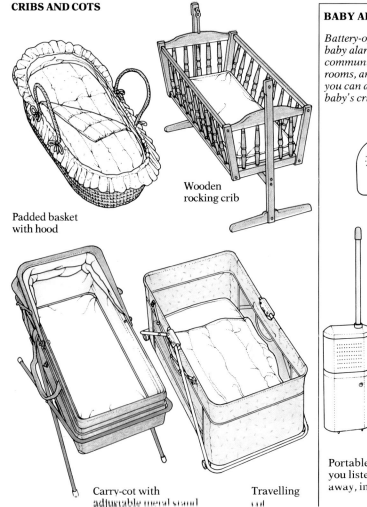

Padded basket
with hood

Wooden
rocking crib

Carry-cot with
adjustable metal stand

Travelling
cot

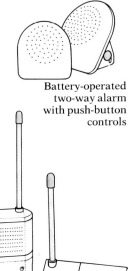

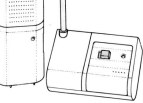

BABY ALARMS

Battery-operated or electronic baby alarms provide good communication between rooms, and even outside, so you can always hear your baby's cries.

Battery-operated
two-way alarm
with push-button
controls

Portable alarm system lets you listen to baby 100 metres away, in house or garden

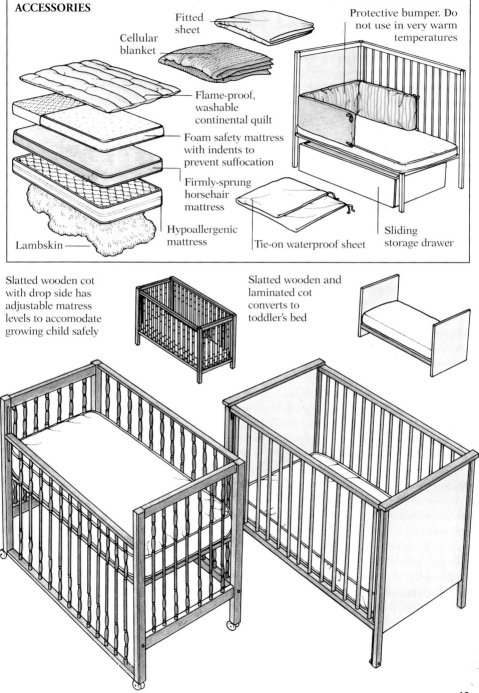

ACCESSORIES

Fitted sheet

Cellular blanket

Protective bumper. Do not use in very warm temperatures

Flame-proof, washable continental quilt

Foam safety mattress with indents to prevent suffocation

Firmly-sprung horsehair mattress

Hypoallergenic mattress

Lambskin

Tie-on waterproof sheet

Sliding storage drawer

Slatted wooden cot with drop side has adjustable matress levels to accomodate growing child safely

Slatted wooden and laminated cot converts to toddler's bed

43

Outings and travel

One of the most straightforward ways of carrying your baby around is in a sling, and you can use these until he grows too heavy; the sling should be used with a neck attachment until he can support his own head. You'll also need some form of push-chair. The one you choose will depend on both your budget and your lifestyle. A large carriage pram is impractical if you live in a small flat, three flights up; a foldable lightweight push-chair or a pram with a removable carry-cot would be much more suitable. Whatever you buy, it should be easy to push, have good brakes, rings for a safety harness and rings to prevent the handle from collapsing.

Whenever you take your child in a car you must comply with safety regulations and restrain him either in a car seat or his carry-cot with straps. If you ride on a bike you'll have to use a specially-designed seat.

BACKPACKS AND SLINGS

Front-carrying fabric sling with neck support for newborns

Adjustable carrier allows newborn to be completely enclosed and older baby to have his legs out

Lightweight and shower-proof carry cape with a warm, fleecy lining

Steel-framed fabric backpack with adjustable neck support and sunshade

Lightweight fabric backpack with adjustable inside seat for both babies and toddlers

PUSH-CHAIRS

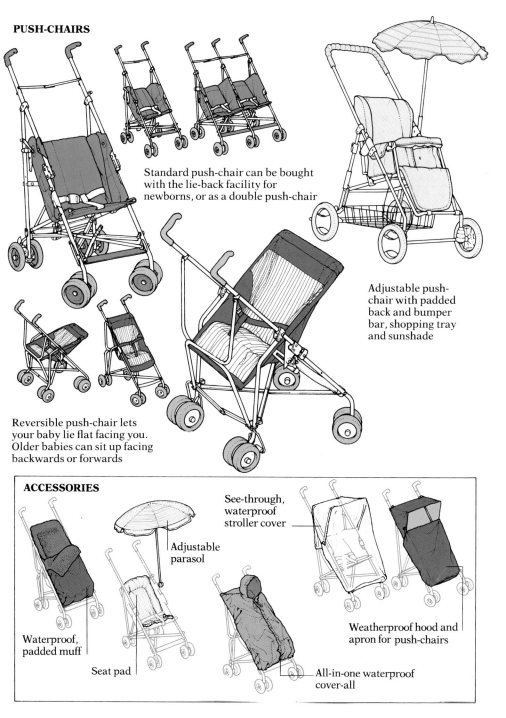

Standard push-chair can be bought with the lie-back facility for newborns, or as a double push-chair

Adjustable push-chair with padded back and bumper bar, shopping tray and sunshade

Reversible push-chair lets your baby lie flat facing you. Older babies can sit up facing backwards or forwards

ACCESSORIES

See-through, waterproof stroller cover

Adjustable parasol

Weatherproof hood and apron for push-chairs

Waterproof, padded muff

Seat pad

All-in-one waterproof cover-all

PRAMS

Carriage pram with solid body
and collapsible fabric hood

Pram with removable
carry-cot

Carry-cot pram converts for
use as push-chair

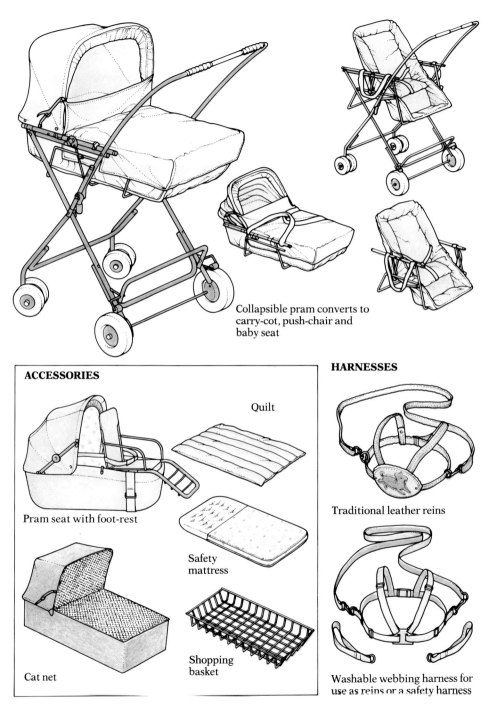

Collapsible pram converts to carry-cot, push-chair and baby seat

ACCESSORIES

Quilt

Pram seat with foot-rest

Safety mattress

Cat net

Shopping basket

HARNESSES

Traditional leather reins

Washable webbing harness for use as reins or a safety harness

47

CAR SAFETY

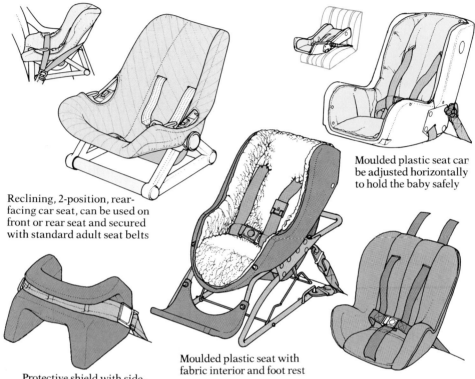

Moulded plastic seat can be adjusted horizontally to hold the baby safely

Reclining, 2-position, rear-facing car seat, can be used on front or rear seat and secured with standard adult seat belts

Moulded plastic seat with fabric interior and foot rest

Protective shield with side-buckling belt

Brushed nylon seat for use as soon as the baby can sit unsupported

---

ACCESSORIES

Standard side-fitting pram carry cot

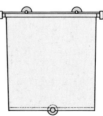

Roller car sunscreen protects babies from direct sunlight. Attached with suction pads

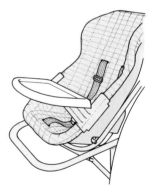

Reclining seat with detachable play and feeding tray

Additional equipment

Even young babies like to see what's going on around them and baby chairs, which are light and portable, are a more solid alternative to pillows. The fabric variety bounces up and down when the baby kicks his legs; the plastic styles are rigid but the angle of the back can be altered. Your baby will need occupying when he's awake so consider hanging a baby bouncer from a door frame. Do, however, try your baby out in a friend's before you buy one – he may not like the sensation it gives him. Although many people find play pens reminiscent of a baby prison, some find them invaluable. If you decide to buy one your choice will be between a wooden or a steel and net one.

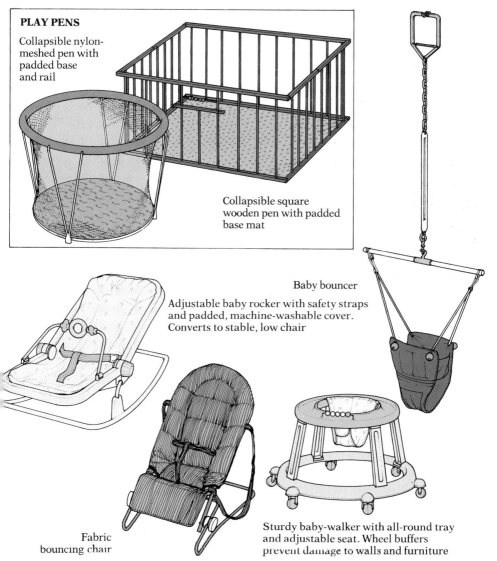

PLAY PENS

Collapsible nylon-meshed pen with padded base and rail

Collapsible square wooden pen with padded base mat

Baby bouncer

Adjustable baby rocker with safety straps and padded, machine-washable cover. Converts to stable, low chair

Fabric bouncing chair

Sturdy baby-walker with all-round tray and adjustable seat. Wheel buffers prevent damage to walls and furniture

49

Arranging a nursery

It is worth planning the lay-out of your nursery well in advance of delivery, after which you'll probably be too busy and too tired to think of anything apart from feeding and changing the baby. Whichever room you choose, make sure that it is as hygenic as possible, with easy-to-wipe surfaces. All furniture should have smooth, rounded edges and should be painted with non-toxic, lead-free paint. There should be plenty of storage space, especially above or to the side of the changing area. If you plan to build your own you'll want a wide, flat surface on which to place the changing mat. Wide-topped chests of drawers make ideal changing tables because they have a large surface area and plenty of storage space. All you have to do is build shelves above wherever you place it. Make sure that the surface is smooth then cover it with a washable covering and put a padded changing mat on top. The floor covering should be warm but hard-wearing; cork tiles and haircord carpets are ideal.

The baby's room has to be kept at a constant temperature of 16-20°C (65-68°F). If you don't want to run the entire house at this level, especially during the day, buy a thermostatically-controlled heater for this purpose.

The lighting should ideally be controlled by a dimmer switch so that you can gently bring up the lights without frightening the baby, and so that you can leave it on low instead of a night light.

Always try to decorate you baby's room in light, cheerful colours. The colours of nature, that is yellow, blue and bright apple or grassy green, have been shown to be good colours for children. Splashes of primary colours also help to brighten and enliven the room.

Make sure that you put interesting pictures on the wall and hang several mobiles above your baby's cot and the changing area. Buy fabrics and wallcoverings with lively designs so that the baby is visually (and therefore mentally) stimulated.

Easily-accessible sink for cleaning baby

Blind with lined curtains

Easy-wipe walls

Cupboard with shelves and hanging space

Portable bath and stand

Washable cotton rug with non-slip backing

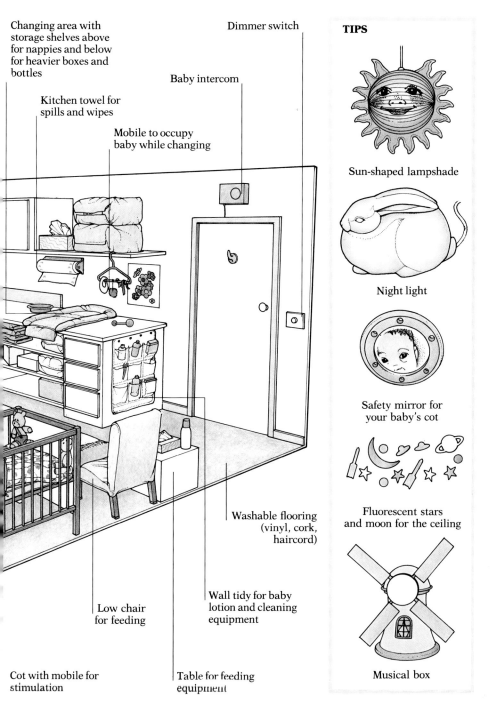

Changing area with storage shelves above for nappies and below for heavier boxes and bottles

Dimmer switch

Baby intercom

Kitchen towel for spills and wipes

Mobile to occupy baby while changing

Washable flooring (vinyl, cork, haircord)

Wall tidy for baby lotion and cleaning equipment

Low chair for feeding

Cot with mobile for stimulation

Table for feeding equipment

TIPS

Sun-shaped lampshade

Night light

Safety mirror for your baby's cot

Fluorescent stars and moon for the ceiling

Musical box

Adapting the nursery for a toddler

Your baby's room is going to have to change to accommodate his needs as he becomes more mobile. The major difference will be the amount of floor space that should be left. He'll be crawling and then walking so there should be as little furniture lying in his way as is possible. And any furniture that's left in his room must be completely stable so that there's no risk of his pulling it down on top of himself. Be extra aware of the safety risks linked with a small, inquisitive toddler and follow all of the recommendations given on p. 324.

As soon as he shows signs of being able to clamber out of his cot you'll have to buy a bed. Beds with drawers underneath are invaluable if storage space is restricted. Position the bed so that you leave as large a space as possible in the centre of the room, whether it's tucked into the corner or flush against the wall. These days many families find that space is at a premium and it makes more sense to put beds on top of each other rather than take up valuable floor space with two single beds. So, if you're planning to have more children, think about buying a bed that forms part of a bunk unit, or buy a double riser in which one bed fits below the other during the day but can be brought out for use at night. You could even consider buying a bed which folds down from the wall.

Your toddler will accumulate more toys, more clothes and more shoes over the next couple of years and you'll correspondingly have to provide plenty of storage. This needn't be straightforward shelves and drawers or ready-made toy boxes; wicker baskets, plastic stacking boxes or laundry baskets all provide good storage for children's things.

Your toddler will enjoy sitting at his own table so if you didn't buy the kind of high chair which converts to a table and chair you'll have to provide one. A blackboard or a special wall area where your toddler knows that he can scribble and chalk on may also be welcome as soon as he's co-ordinated enough to do so.

Safety-step for toddler to reach basin

Pin board for special pictures

Towel ring for toddler's own towel

Blackboard

Safety rail

Changing area converted to bookshelves and toy store

Easy-reach hooks for coats and scarves

Height chart

Cupboards added for extra storage

STORAGE TIPS

Plastic crate for shoe storage

Painted baskets for toys and dressing-up clothes

Plastic toy box on castors for easy pushing

Low table and chair for drawing and playing on

Table moved nearer bed for night light, books and drinks

Suitable single bed with duvet and safety pillow

See-through shoe rack for small toys

4 Clothing

All parents take great pride in their new baby's appearance and there's a great temptation to rush out and buy lots of clothes for her. As long as you realize that your child is going to grow rapidly during these three years, and that the clothes will have a relatively short life, the styles you choose and the amount you spend are up to you. However, no matter what the age of your child, clothing must be comfortable to wear, easy to put on and, above all, washable.

CHOOSING CLOTHES   0–1

Buying the layette
Choosing baby clothes is an occupation most mothers enjoy and while you might like to buy some dress-up clothes for special occasions there's absolutely no need to spend a lot of money.

Your newborn baby won't be very active but that does not mean that she's going to stay scrupulously clean. There will inevitably be accidents and leaks from nappies, despite plastic pants, and she's bound to posset and dribble throughout the day – all of which will mean fairly frequent changes of clothing. Make sure that you have enough clothes to keep up with your baby's needs.

For a summer baby buy:

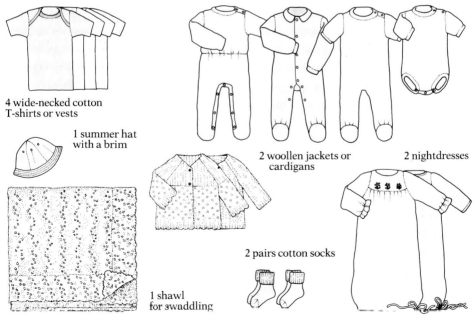

4 summer-weight all-in-one stretch suits

4 wide-necked cotton
T-shirts or vests

1 summer hat
with a brim

2 woollen jackets or
cardigans

2 nightdresses

2 pairs cotton socks

1 shawl
for swaddling

55

For a winter baby buy: 4 all-in-one stretch suits

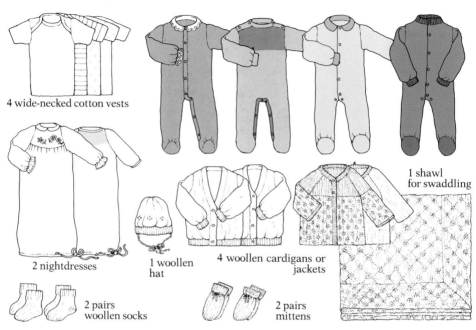

4 wide-necked cotton vests

1 shawl for swaddling

2 nightdresses

1 woollen hat

4 woollen cardigans or jackets

2 pairs woollen socks

2 pairs mittens

CLOTHING TIPS

● Whatever size notation the manufacturer uses, make sure that you buy the size that will last until your baby's at least two months old. She won't be bothered if it's slightly too big and it's more practical than the newborn size which she'll quickly grow out of.

● Buy only machine-washable, colour-proof clothing.

● Make sure that any clothing that you buy allows easy access to the nappy, so there's the minimum of undressing involved. Buy stretch towelling suits with poppers in the crotch or right down the front and leg.

● In the early weeks you may find it easy to use nightdresses which can just be lifted up to get at the nappy.

● Clothes which open down the front or have wide, envelope necks are the best because babies hate having their faces covered.

● Clothes which do up the front also mean that you don't have to turn the baby over when you're dressing her.

● Material should be soft and comfortable with no hard seams or rough stitching; check the neck and waistband before buying. Buy towelling, cotton or pure wool clothes; if you buy clothes made of man-made fibres do check that they feel soft and comfortable.

● Buy non-flammable clothing.

● Avoid lacy shawls or cardigans – your baby's tiny fingers can easily get caught in the holes.

● Avoid white – it gets dirty quickly and needs more care when washing. Babies suit bright colours just as much as the pastels traditionally specified for them.

● If you do buy a hat either buy one with a chin strap, or sew some ribbons on. Many babies hate wearing hats and pull them off unless they're tied on under their chins.

● Clothes with poppers at the neck quite often last longer. Babies often outgrow clothes because their heads can no longer go through the neck opening; with poppers you can just leave them undone to accommodate the head.

Buying additional clothing

The kind of clothes you buy on top of your layette will basically be determined by finance and personal taste. There is no one essential piece of clothing for your baby but there are some items which are more practical than others. In the summer, for example, cotton T-shirts and shorts or cotton dresses are the most suitable because they're cool and leave the baby's limbs free; in the winter mini track suits and dungarees are practical alternatives to all-in-one stretch suits. Once your baby is mobile she'll need clothing like this which gives adequate knee protection. As before, stick to clothes which give you easy access to the baby's nappy because by the time she's crawling she's not going to want to lie still for very long. All clothes that you buy should be machine washable.

Keep an eye on how tight the legs, neck and wrists are on all the clothes and buy the next size up accordingly. You'll probably learn how to gauge your baby's size quite accurately, but if you're at all worried always go by the height and weight charts given, not by age. Unfortunately, different countries and different manufacturers use varying size notations so if you're in any doubt about what sizes mean ask the sales assistant's advice. If you haven't got your child with you check that clothing can be exchanged.

TOP CLOTHES

Neck-buttoned jumper with crotch-opening dungarees

Pull-on track suit

Matching dress and pants set

Wool boots with non-slip soles

Pull-on play suit

NIGHTCLOTHES AND UNDERWEAR

Initially, there is no need to make a distinction between day- and nightwear, and by far the most suitable nightclothes are stretch suits. As your baby gets older sleep suits make a cosy alternative. On very cold nights sleeping bags solve the problem of kicked-off blankets.
If you buy vests make sure you buy wide-necked ones so that they go on easily. Buy brightly patterned sets that can be used as T-shirts.

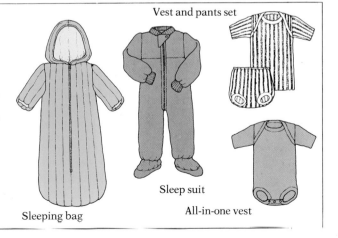

Vest and pants set

Sleeping bag

Sleep suit

All-in-one vest

CHOOSING CLOTHES 1–3

As your baby grows your main concern when buying clothes will be that they're comfortable and, when she's more active, that they allow easy movement. Your baby will no longer spend most of the time asleep and as she starts to run about more she's going to need more clothes. Like an adult's, they'll have to be suitable for various weather conditions (rain, cold, sun), and they'll also have to be tough enough to withstand the wear and tear that your toddler will give them. Once she can crawl she'll need sturdy protection for the knees and once she can walk she'll need shoes to protect her feet.

As before, buy clothing in a material that moves with your child so that however active she is there's no risk of uncomfortableness, or of the material tearing. Towelling, cottons and corduroys are ideal. When she's being "toilet trained" the clothing must be easily pulled down or up, and when she's learning how to dress or undress you should avoid buying clothes with zips or fiddly fastenings, and use elasticated waists as long as possible.

BUYING TIPS

● Always keep your child's measurements jotted down in your diary and, when your child is growing so quickly, make sure that you take new measurements frequently.
● Buy unisex clothes whenever you can. There is no reason why a girl shouldn't wear boys' clothes, and they are usually sturdier anyway.
● Get outdoor clothes on the large side so that extra layers can be worn underneath. As such clothes are often more expensive, the larger size should allow your child to "grow into" it. In items which are worn every day, buy the best quality you can afford; they will last longer and may even be passed on to successive children.
● Brightly-coloured clothes are useful if your toddler wanders off – she'll be easier to spot.
● T-shirts can double-up perfectly well as pyjama tops.
● Buy patterned vests so that they can double up as T-shirts.

● Put extra buttons on dungaree straps so that they can be gradually lengthened as your child gets taller.
● Small boys find short zips difficult to manipulate so buy trousers with elasticated waists for as long as possible.
● Buy tube socks without shaped heels so that they "grow" with the child. Buy all socks in the same brand and the same colour so that you don't have trouble matching them. For articles of clothing like pyjamas try to stick to one brand and one colour, and one design. That way you can match up trousers and tops from various pairs if your child's size and proportions change.
● Buy clothes with elasticated waistbands and trousers or skirts with shoulder straps so that they can be let down.
● Avoid "fitted" clothes – your toddler will grow out of them more quickly than loose-fitting clothes.
● Avoid man-made fabrics – they don't "breathe" like natural fibres and could make your child uncomfortably hot, especially in summer.
● A loose coat, like a duffel coat, will last two winters: one as a coat with the sleeves rolled back, and the second as a jacket with the sleeves at their usual length.

● Some sleepsuits have plastic soles on the feet. So that your child's feet don't sweat, cut a small hole in the middle to let the air circulate.

58

OUTDOOR CLOTHES

Splash suits, which fit over outdoor and indoor clothes, protect your child from puddles and dirt. Two-piece pram suits keep your child warm in cold weather and are essential when she's being carried in a sling with her legs out. The trousers can be pulled down quickly when you need to change the nappy. Thick winter coats should be bought large enough to "grow into".

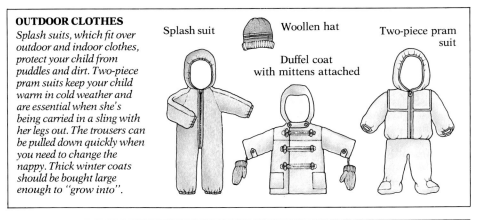

Splash suit

Woollen hat

Two-piece pram suit

Duffel coat with mittens attached

Making clothes last

☐ When sleepsuits get too short for comfort cut off the feet for an extra month's wear

☐ Reinforce the knees on the inside of new jeans with the extra fabric you trim from the bottoms of the legs, or use iron-on patches.

☐ Add another tier to a tiered skirt using identical or contrasting fabric.

☐ Make summer pyjamas from winter pyjamas by cutting down the legs and cutting off the sleeves.

☐ Make summer shorts from long winter trousers that are too short or have got worn at the knees.

☐ When your child outgrows an expensive jacket, cut out the sleeves and let your child wear it as a waistcoat.

☐ Run a dark blue crayon, indelible pencil or a fountain pen filled with blue/black ink over the white line when jeans have been let down.

☐ To allow for growth choose one-piece garments with raglan or dolman sleeves and undefined waistlines.

Choosing shoes

There's absolutely no need to put your baby into shoes until she's walking. The bones in your baby's feet are soft and pliable – so pliable that even the pressure of tightly-fitting socks can misshape the toes if your baby wears them regularly. When it's very cold, or when she starts to crawl, you can put on socks or woollen bootees, but do make sure that there's plenty of room for the foot to move about.

When the time comes to buy your child shoes go to a reputable shoe shop and make sure that you deal with an assistant who's been trained to measure and fit children's shoes. She should always measure the foot for width and length before bringing any shoes for your child to try on. Once the shoes are on she should press the joints of the foot to check that the foot's not restricted in any way and she should check that the buckle or laces hold it firmly in place and don't let it slip about.

You should get your child to stand up and move about in the shoes to check that the toe doesn't crease up and hurt when she's walking and to double-check that there's no slipping.

The type of shoe that you buy will be determined by when and where it is to be worn. For example, it's advisable to buy a sturdy, well-made pair of leather shoes for general outdoor wear, especially once the child is running about and playing. However, when it is raining it's only sensible to put your child in Wellington boots instead of shoes. And in summer, although leather sandals look, and are, solid and sensible, there is nothing wrong with canvas shoes or sneakers as long as care is taken to check that they fit properly. What you should never do is buy second-hand shoes. No matter how expensive children's shoes are, they are an essential means of ensuring that your child has good feet in adult life.

The uppers *should have no hard seams or stitching which might hurt the foot and cause chafing.*

The toe *should be wide enough for the child's toes to fan out without restriction. The box on the toe should be high enough so that no pressure is exerted on the toenails.*

The sole *should be light, flexible and non-slip.*

The heel *should grip snugly. It should be no higher than 3.8 cm (1½ in)*

The fastenings *should be adjustable and the foot held firmly in the shoe. Initially, children find it easier to use buckles than they do laces.*

The arch *should be well-formed to give support.*

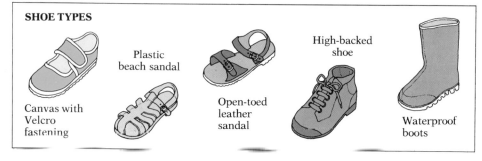

SHOE TYPES

Canvas with Velcro fastening

Plastic beach sandal

Open-toed leather sandal

High-backed shoe

Waterproof boots

Washing

Once your baby starts eating solids she's bound to get messy, even when she's wearing a bib, and once she starts walking the clothing will get dirtier as well. Make sure all the clothing you buy is colour fast so that it can go into the family wash. Obviously, the more changes of clothing you have the less often you'll have to do the washing.

To minimize your wash load put some kind of protective overall on your child whenever she plays messy games; you could even use a cut-down shirt of your own.

DEALING WITH STAINS

Egg
If there is an egg stain on clothing, soak in cold water for an hour before laundering in the usual way.

Grass
Remove grass stains with alcohol if they are resistant to laundering.

Fruit and Chocolate
Douse tough stains such as chocolate or grape juice with soda water, rub until the discolouration has gone and then wash as usual.

Blood
Soak blood stains in cold water for thirty minutes; if they don't come out use an enzyme-containing washing powder. If this fails, try a few drops of ammonia on the stain.

Milk
Remove milk stains by rinsing the clothing thoroughly in cold water and then using an enzyme-containing washing powder.

Chewing gum
Soften the gum with carbon tetrachloride or methylated spirits before gently pulling the gum away from the fabric.

Lipstick
Gently rub vaseline or glycerine into the stain before washing it in warm, soapy water. Once it's dry, sponge it clean with carbon tetrachloride.

Vomit
Use an enzyme-containing washing powder after you've removed the vomit and rinsed the garment with cold water.

DRESSING AND UNDRESSING 0–1

Babies need changing quite frequently in the first months and, initially, you may not be fully confident about supporting your rather floppy baby and dealing with the clothes at the same time. Don't worry: it's perfectly normal to be a bit awkward at first, and any fears that you have are easily overcome with a little bit of practice, patience and gentleness on your part.

With a new baby, always dress and undress her on a flat surface: a changing mat, a bed or the floor are all ideal because they allow you both hands free. Secondly, keep the amount of time that she's undressed to a minimum and don't get flustered when your baby cries as you take off her clothes. Young babies hate being undressed; they're scared of the air on their naked bodies and the removal of the comforting fabric that they were wearing makes them feel very insecure. When your baby feels like this she's going to cry, very loudly. It's not because of you, so don't think that you're a bad parent. Keep calm and get on with the task in hand, but always have something to attract your baby's attention, like a mobile (see p. 169).

DRESSING A NEWBORN

1 *Lay your baby on a flat surface. Make sure that the nappy is clean and change it if necessary. If you're putting on a vest, concertina it up and pull the neck apart with your thumbs.*

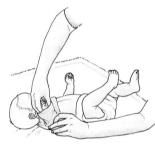

2 *Put it over the baby's head, raising your baby's head slightly as you do so. Widen the right armhole and gently guide your baby's arm through it; repeat with the other side.*

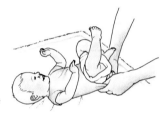

3 *Pull the vest down and then undo the poppers of the all-in-one stretch suit, keeping an eye on your baby as you do so.*

4 *Lay the suit out flat so that it's ready to put on. Pick up your baby and place her on top of it.*

5 *Concertina up the right sleeve and put it over your baby's fist. Guide the arm through, pulling the sleeve up the arm as you do so. Repeat with the other side.*

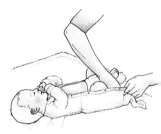

6 *Guide your baby's right leg in to the foot of the suit; repeat with the other leg. Do up the suit.*

Using your lap

When your baby has more muscle control and you feel more confident you can sit the baby on your lap to take off the clothes. If you sit with your legs crossed your baby can sit neatly in the hollow of your legs; your arm should cradle the baby. Alternatively, you could combine sitting the baby on your lap with using a flat surface. For example, it may be easier to put on the top layer in your lap, but to deal with the bottom half on a flat surface. You'll probably need to distract your baby in some way, so have some toys for her to hold.

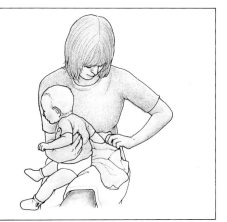

UNDRESSING A NEWBORN

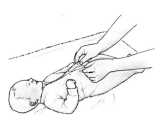

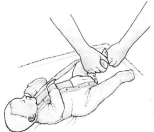

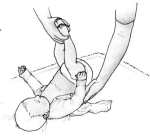

1 *Lay your baby on a flat surface and undo the suit down the front.*

2 *Because you'll probably have to change the nappy, gently pull both legs out first. Change the nappy if necessary.*

3 *Lift the baby's legs up and slide the suit up the baby's back to her shoulders.*

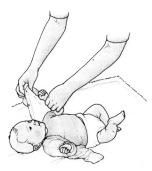

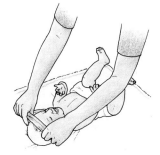

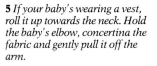

4 *Slide the baby's left hand out gently. Repeat on the other side.*

5 *If your baby's wearing a vest, roll it up towards the neck. Hold the baby's elbow, concertina the fabric and gently pull it off the arm.*

6 *Open out the neck and lift the vest carefully over her head so that it doesn't touch your baby's face.*

Dressing the older baby

Once your baby can crawl she won't want to stay still for long and dressing may proceed "on the move". However, towards the end of the year this will be coupled with the ability to help as you put on the clothes. For example, if you ask your eleven-month-old baby to make a fist, or stretch out an arm, she'll probably do so and you'll be able to slide the jumper or jacket on without having to draw her hand through yourself.

Always name the clothes as you put them on or take them off, and make a game out of the whole procedure. For example, make it into a kind of hide and seek, peek-bo game: "Where's your arm gone, then?" "Oh, look, here it comes now." Other tips which will make dressing your baby slightly easier are as follows:

☐ Pull up trousers, tights or even trainer pants while your baby stands between your legs so that she's immobilized.

☐ Put your baby's shoes on while she's sitting in her high chair and can't squirm out of the way.

☐ Put on Wellingtons or overshoes when your child's sitting on the bottom step of the stairs. You can make a game out of her stepping down into her shoes.

☐ Always try to undress your baby when she's occupied with something else like doing a puzzle or listening to a song.

☐ If your baby has a favourite song that she likes joining in with, always sing it while dressing or undressing her.

DRESSING AND UNDRESSING 1–3

It'll take a while for your child to develop the co-ordination required to dress successfully, but by the time she's 18 months she'll be attempting it with various items of clothing, even if it's just pulling off skirts or wriggling into cardigans. Any attempts at dressing or undressing should be encouraged. They're a sign of growing independence and maturity, not to mention co-ordination.

Try laying out the clothes in such a way that your child can go up to them and manoeuvre them on easily. Even if she seems to be fumbling, don't step in until it's really necessary. You will, however, have to deal with most of the fastenings until your child has adequate dexterity to cope with them.

DRESSING TIPS

● Stop your toddler's overall straps slipping down by pinning them together with a large safety pin where they cross over at the back.

● When you are teaching your child to handle buttons show her how to button from the bottom upwards.

● Wherever appropriate use Velcro but don't use this near the neck as it may rub and cause sore patches.

● Tiny hands find zip fasteners difficult to manage so put a key ring through the zip fastener for easy handling.

● When your child is learning to use a zip fastener, teach her to pull the zip away from both skin and clothes to prevent the zip fastener catching.

● Until your child is toilet-trained buy trousers with elasticated waists to avoid hooks and zip fasteners.

● Put a badge or clear marking on the front of a garment so that your child can tell front from back.

● Mark the hole in a belt that your child should use with a stick-on gold star or a piece of tape.

● Until your child learns to hold a sweater when she is putting on a coat, sew elastic loops inside the cuffs so that the child can hang onto those and stop the sleeves being dragged up as the coat is being put on.

● If the zipper is sticking run a soft lead pencil or a bar of soap over the zipper to make it run smoothly.
● If your child is unwilling to make a fist when you're putting on a jumper, put a small treat such as a raisin or a potato crisp into your child's hand. She will grasp it and make a fist allowing you to push the sleeve on.
● Attach gloves or mittens to a long piece of tape which you can thread through the arms of the coat.
● Wet shoe laces before tying – the bows won't slip and they will stay tied.

● When you first put on your baby's shoes cover the slippery soles with a piece of adhesive tape so that she won't slide on a slippery floor; alternatively, score the soles with scissors so that they grip.

● If the ends of shoe laces become frayed, coat the ends with clear nail polish or wrap some sticky tape around them.
● Always buy boots large enough to accommodate an extra pair of socks. Wellingtons aren't very warm so put a pair of thick socks over your child's usual socks to keep her feet warm.
● When your child first starts to use buttons, sew large buttons on to clothes so that she can handle them easily and, if you can, sew them on with elastic thread.

Holding and handling

In the first few weeks of life your baby will seem very vulnerable, and many parents are rather scared of picking up their newborns, fearful that they may somehow damage their child. However, you have to come to terms with holding your baby properly, not just for the baby's comfort but for your own sake; you'll never feed or bath her successfully if you are unsure about how to hold her.

HANDLING YOUR BABY   0-1

Most babies like to be handled in a firm way, especially in the early weeks when the sensation of being tightly enclosed (whether by your arms, by clothing or by a swaddling shawl), gives a great sense of security. When it comes to actually moving your baby, do it as slowly, as gently and as quietly as you can.

It's an instinctive reaction to hold your baby close to you, to talk soothingly and lovingly as you look into her face and eyes, and many experiments have shown that children do in fact need and benefit from this physical contact. For example, premature babies gain more weight when they are laid on soft, downy sheets simply because the fluffy sheets give them the impression of being touched. Your newborn baby will be comforted by any kind of holding, cuddling or caressing, and skin-to-skin contact, with both of you lying naked in bed, is probably the best of all. In this way she can smell your skin, feel its touch and warmth and hear your heart beating clearly.

Picking up your newborn baby

Don't worry about picking your baby up; she's much tougher than you think. The only thing that you really have to take care of is her lolling head. Until she is about four weeks old she'll have little control over it so whenever you pick her up do it in a way that supports the head.

PICKING UP YOUR BABY
Slide one hand under your baby's neck to support the head. Slide the other underneath her back and bottom to support the lower half of the baby securely. Held in this way, the baby can easily be transferred to any of the carrying positions. Make sure that you pick the baby up gently and smoothly.

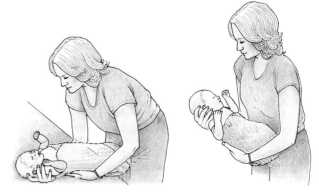

Putting down your newborn baby

When you lay your baby down you must make sure that her head is supported. Unless you do, her head will flop back and may give your baby the sensation that she is going to fall; her body will jerk and she'll stretch out both arms and legs in the "startle" reflex (see p. 30). Either put your baby down in the way I suggested for picking up, so that the whole arm supports spine, neck and head, or wrap your baby fairly tightly in a shawl (see Using Shawls, right) so that the head is supported until she is down in the cot when you can gently unwrap it.

Newborn and very young babies should be placed on their backs to sleep. The latest medical opinion and research suggests that this is the best and safest position in which to minimise the risk of cot death, and it is no longer believed that in this position there is an increased risk of the baby bringing up his feed and possibly choking. After four or five months, the baby will instinctively choose the position he finds suits him best.

Whenever you put your baby down to sleep, remember that her head must always be carefully supported to prevent it from flopping back.

Carrying your newborn baby

In your arms
There are two main positions for carrying your baby in your arms. The first is with the baby's head in the crook of either arm, slightly higher than the rest of the body which rests on the lower part of your arm and is encircled by the wrist and the hand which support the back and bottom. The other arm provides additional support, to the baby's bottom and legs. This is a good position because it allows you to talk to and smile at your baby.

The second way is to hold your baby against the upper part of your chest, with your forearm across her back and her head resting on your shoulder supported by your hand. This position leaves the other hand free, which is useful if you need to pick something up. Otherwise it can provide support to the baby's bottom

Gently support your baby's head in the crook of your arm.

Cradle your baby so that her head rests on your shoulder.

In a sling
There is no reason at all why your newborn shouldn't be carried in a sling (see p. 44), as long as it provides adequate support for the baby's neck and head, and as long as it comfortably envelops the baby's body so that she can't slip out of either side. The best kinds of sling are the very soft, pouch-like ones which allow the baby to take up her curled form. Most parents feel happiest with the sling worn on their chest because there they can see and cuddle the baby easily and generally protect her more efficiently.

Using shawls

Tight swaddling (see p. 166), has been shown to comfort a child not only because it simulates a caress, but also because the tightness of the wrapping makes the baby feel secure. Because most babies go to sleep when they are swaddled it is a useful way of calming an otherwise distressed baby. You can either put the baby down to sleep in the shawl or use it as a kind of sling.

PROPPING

Instead of leaving your baby staring up at the ceiling prop her up with pillows so that she can see what's going on; you can do this as early as six weeks (see p. 206). Wherever you prop the baby, make sure that she can't topple forwards or sideways.

USING A SHAWL AS A SLING

1 *Drape a long shawl around your shoulders, with a slightly shorter length on the side where you'll hold the baby. Pick up the baby in the crook of your arm.*

2 *Fold the shorter edge over her body, leaving the feet free. Wrap the fabric securely around the baby.*

3 *Bring the other length of fabric over and under the baby, then pull the fabric up between your chest and the baby.*

4 *Tuck the remaining fabric neatly inside the "pocket" you've just folded. The shawl will leave you with both hands free if you want.*

Picking up your older baby

Once your baby has control of her head there is no need to take the kind of care you did when she was newborn because the head and body will now stay aligned when the baby's picked up. When she reaches this stage the best way to pick up your baby is to put your hands under her armpits and to lift her forward towards you. Once she's been picked up you can then carry her in the crook of your arm or against your shoulder or, as the back, neck and head muscles become stronger, she can be placed astride one hip with your arm going diagonally across her back and holding on to a thigh.

Carrying your older baby

By the age of four or five months, most parents carry their baby on one of their hips; which one is determined by whether the parent is right-or left-handed. You'll inevitably develop your own methods of carrying your baby and these may well vary according to her mood. For longer journeys you can also carry your baby in a front sling or in a backpack.

Once your baby can support her head she can be lifted up under the armpits. As she gets heavier, take the strain on your legs not on your back.

Avoiding back strain

Babies and toddlers inevitably require constant lifting and carrying, not to mention the prams, pushchairs and other equipment that go along with them, so it is important for the protection of your back that you learn a lifting technique that avoids injury and strain. Don't lift with straight legs and curved back, as this puts strain on the back. Instead, keep the back straight, bend the knees and lift, using the powerful thigh muscles to take the weight.

CARRYING THE OLDER BABY

Sitting astride your hip, your baby has the advantage of being able to look all around her, but she'll still feel secure and close to you; one hand is left free.

Many parents slip comfortably into holding their baby this way. It allows them one hand free if necessary as the baby is securely held around the waist.

Once your baby can support her head she may find this position soothing, especially if you gently swing from side to side. The game can be made more boisterous by swinging her higher and higher.

Putting down your older baby

You don't have to be as careful putting down an older baby as a newborn one. She can be put down in exactly the same way as she was picked up. Alternatively you can support the upper part of the baby's body with one hand curved diagon- ally across her back with the other hand supporting her bottom. If you are putting your child into a high chair support her under the armpits and let both legs dangle so that she can place them easily between tray and seat.

HANDLING YOUR CHILD 1–3

Cuddling and security

A toddler needs much less holding and carrying than a young baby but there will still be times when she'll signal that she wants to be carried, just like she used to be. If you ignore these signals she'll probably cry. You may find that she wants to be carried when she's tired; when you've been out for a long walk; when your toddler's cutting a tooth; if she isn't feeling well; if she's fearful or if you have been away. Don't hesitate to give this kind of physical support and affection. She will give you a clear signal when she is reassured and has had enough, and will wriggle down and run off.

We never outgrow the need for physical affection. Always recognize this in your children; never scoff at it and always give it. My son of eleven-and-a-half still likes a cuddle every now and then, especially when he is tired or if he has had a telling-off from a teacher at school, if he is fearful about my departure or absence or if, as he puts it, "The world doesn't feel right". Even when children are quite old they may still want to sit on your knee occasionally. In strange circumstances they may even like to sit on your knee while eating, particularly if strangers are present and they feel that they are under observation. Don't ridicule your child for wanting this. If it is convenient, let her sit on your knee; there is absolutely nothing wrong with it and a few moments of your touch will give your child the confidence to handle the situation in her own way. To my mind, a child should never have to go to bed without some cuddling to provide a sense of security and the reassuring feeling that you really do care. When your small child is hurt, worried, puzzled or frightened, always be there with an encircling, comforting arm and a sympathetic word. But do give such reassurances as these in the form that your child wants and don't overpower her with your physical affection when she makes obvious signs that she doesn't require it.

Of course there are some children who don't like to be handled or cuddled very much. They usually show this from a very early age by stiffening their bodies and crying when you hold them. This can be quite difficult for a parent to cope with because it seems like rejection (see p. 261). These babies usually grow up to be children who avoid physical contact and usually turn their heads away if you lean to kiss them. They make no physical overtures themselves and can be really quite difficult children to show affection to and to love in an overt way. They may never learn how to accept physical affection nor to be comfortable with it. If your child is like this, the only way for you to treat her is to not make the discomfort worse by thrusting physical affection on her. Respect your child's diffidence. Wait for her to come to you and only give your physical affection when she shows you by her actions that she wants it.

HOLDING AND HANDLING OLDER CHILDREN

As children get older they become more independent and we may think of them as needing less touching, stroking, holding, and cuddling. This is true, up to a point, but don't make the mistake of thinking that they don't need physical affection at all – especially boys, who may be expected to keep a stiff upper lip much younger than they are capable of doing so.

I personally make it a rule to tell my children every day that I love them, whenever the whim takes me, and I think that parents should make similar resolutions about holding and touching their children even if it's just letting them sit on your knee at the breakfast table, or your putting an arm around your child when you read a book or look at the paper, or your giving them a cuddle as you talk over what's happened during the day when you put them to bed.
As children get older, they often become somewhat shy about public demonstrations of affection, and even more so about the need for it, so choose private moments and they'll not feel they're being soppy when they luxuriate in your care, attention, and love.

If you have several young children it can be very difficult to spread yourself out evenly between them. I remember a friend of mine who had twins; from necessity, she adopted a pragmatic approach to the problem: instead of trying to ensure that each twin had an equal share of her time and attention at all times, she concentrated instead on attending to whichever twin needed her at any one moment, and assumed that over the months and years it would all even out.

This is the attitude I have tried to pursue with my own children, and it is an invaluable one for a mother of twins. Of course, for much of the time you will give them equal attention, but if one demands more than the other, give it.

All about nappies

Until your child is toilet trained, probably some time during the third year, she will have to wear nappies both day and night. During the first few months life may seem like an endless round of nappy changing. But don't despair. As your child grows and gains more control over bowel and

bladder muscles she will go for longer without excreting and urinating and the number of nappies you need to change will decrease. By about two and a half she will probably become aware of wanting to go to the lavatory. It is at this point that you should start toilet training.

NAPPIES AND CHANGING 0–1

Nappies are now produced in a wide variety of styles and sizes, but your basic choice will be between disposable and fabric makes. Whichever method you choose you'll still use the same changing equipment, and the general techniques for cleaning and caring for your baby's bottom will be the same.

Changing a nappy
You should change a nappy whenever you notice that it is soiled or wet. The number of times the nappy needs to be changed will vary from baby to baby and from day to day. However, you will probably always change the nappy when your baby wakes in the morning, when she is put to bed at night, and when she's been given a bath. In addition, you'll find that your baby will need to be changed after every feed. This is because of the gastrocolic reflex which stimulates the elimination of faeces when food is taken in.

Where to change a nappy
Always change your baby on a soft, warm, waterproof surface; padded changing mats are ideal for this. Usually made of a foam-filled, waterproof material, they have a slightly raised edge to prevent the

baby from rolling off. They can be placed on whatever surface suits you best – floor, table or bed. As your baby gets older and starts to roll and wriggle while you change the nappy, you may find it safer to change the baby on the floor or on a low bed, whether or not you use a mat.

Putting on a nappy
Putting on nappies, even your first ones, will be easier if you are well prepared. Make sure that you have everything that you need within easy reach. The last thing you want to discover halfway through changing the nappy is that you've left the baby lotion in the bathroom and the clean nappies downstairs.

There is no need to wash your baby's bottom with soap each change: just gently wipe away most of the faeces with a nappy corner then clean the baby's bottom with oil or lotion. If your baby has only wet the nappy, use a water-soaked flannel or cotton wool. You don't need to use talcum powder; in fact, I disapprove of it. Powder can become caked and irritating in the skin creases, increasing the risk of nappy rash. When you change your baby, watch out for any redness and take the appropriate action immediately (see p. 80).

75

DISPOSABLE NAPPIES 0–1

If you can afford them, disposable nappies are the answer to every parent's prayers. There is no cleaning, washing or drying involved – you simply put on the nappy and then discard it when it is wet or dirty. A disposable nappy is also much easier to put on the baby as it needs no elaborate folding, nappy pins or plastic pants. In fact, even from the beginning you'll feel more at ease using them because there will be no risk of hurting the baby with a pin.

Even if you've chosen to use the fabric variety, keep a stock of disposables in the house. They're a useful back-up if you've run out of your usual nappy, or if your baby develops a rash because of your washing methods. They are much more practical than fabric nappies if you're travelling – they are easier to change when you have little room, and you don't have to carry as many accessories with you. Also, if you go visiting, used disposables can be thrown away in a suitable receptacle; fabric nappies, which may be both sodden and smelly, will have to be taken home

with you to be washed. Disposables are also practical for toddlers as they are less bulky for them to walk with and are neater looking than fabric nappies.

However, certain factors have to be balanced against their time-saving practicability. Because they can only be used once, you have to make sure that you have a constant supply at home. To save your energy, buy them in as large a batch as possible: wholesalers and discount warehouses are ideal for this, especially as their prices for bulk purchases are cheaper. Alternatively you could find a firm which delivers disposables to you. Disposable nappies are available in a variety of sizes, suitable for newborns to toddlers, and in a range of styles. The best have elasticated legs for added protection against leaks. They all have a plastic outer covering and an absorbent inner layer, sometimes topped with a one-way nappy liner, and are secured with adjustable adhesive tabs.

DISPOSABLE NAPPIES

Disposable nappies are increasingly sophisticated in design; they come in a range of sizes with different features to cover different problems. More efficient leg elastication ensures a good fit with less chance of leaks. The clever "wetness indicator" changes colour to tell you when the nappy needs changing.

Boys and girls have different needs as far as nappies are concerned and disposables are now available with extra padding strategically placed where it is most needed – at the front for boys and in the centre for girls.

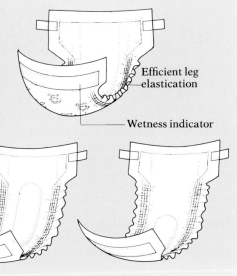

Efficient leg elastication

Wetness indicator

Girl's nappy   Boy's nappy

CHANGING TIPS

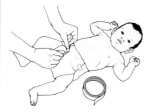

• If you've torn the adhesive strip to remove a nappy, only to find that the nappy is clean, you can use a strip of household masking tape to re-seal that nappy. The same applies if the tape fails to stick.
• If your baby has a stomach upset or a very sore bottom and you're therefore having to change the nappy very regularly, use disposable pads. This works out cheaper.

• Even although they have a one-way liner, it's useful to put a paper liner in, too. This means that any faeces can easily be lifted out with the liner and put down the lavatory.

• If you use all-in-ones without elasticated legs, you can gently pull out the leg area for a better fit.
• Keep a supply of fabric nappies just in case you run out of disposables.

• At night try putting a standard pad inside an all-in-one disposable for extra absorbency.
• If you split open the back of an all-in-one disposable, you will be able to slip a disposable pad between the padding and the plastic layer for extra absorbency.
• If you're really worried about leaks and you're going out, you could put a pair of tie-ons over the all-in-one.

Disposing of a disposable

All disposable nappies are designed to be thrown away: the whole of an all-in-one nappy, plastic backing included, can be discarded; in a two-piece nappy the pants are retained and the pad is replaced. However, despite many manufacturers' claims to the contrary, you will have to find an hygienic alternative to flushing them down the lavatory – they have a 100% success rate of getting stuck at the S-bend. I suggest that you flush off as much faeces as possible under the lavatory spray, wring out the excess water and put the nappy in a strong plastic bag. Garden refuse bags are ideal. When it comes to throwing the bag out make sure that it is firmly secured at the neck.

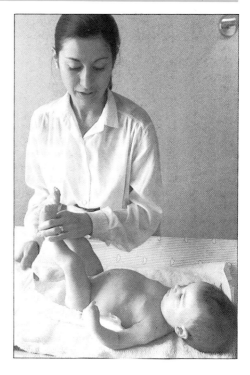

Nappy changing sequence

1 Remove the baby's dirty nappy. Use the front to clear any faeces off the baby (see below). Fold it over so that the faeces can't fall out, and place the nappy to one side of the changing mat.

2 Clean the baby's genital area, bottom and top of the legs, as shown below.

3 Put on a clean nappy using one of the techniques described on pages 79 to 83.

4 Dress the baby.

5 Put the baby somewhere safe (like a cot or a baby bouncer), then deal with the dirty nappy (see p. 77 or p. 84). Wash your hands.

- Changing mat
- Clean fabric nappy, nappy liner, pins and plastic pants or a disposable nappy
- Baby lotion or oil and cotton wool or baby wipes
- Tissues
- Facecloth or flannel
- Bowl of water
- Nappy rash cream, if necessary
- Clean clothes
- Pedal bin
- Distracting toy

CLEANING A BOY

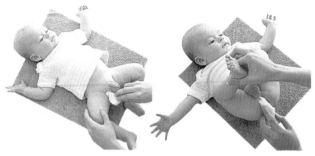

1 If the nappy is soiled, remove as much faeces as possible with the front of the nappy. Use lotion or oil with cotton wool, and use a different piece for each wipe. Wash your hands.

2 Using a wet cloth or cotton wool to remove urine, work from the leg creases in towards the penis. Don't pull the foreskin back.

3 Clean his bottom by lifting up his legs, holding both ankles in one hand with your fingers in between his heels to stop his ankles grinding together. Dry thoroughly.

CLEANING A GIRL

1 If the nappy is soiled, clean with lotion or oil and cotton wool. Use a new piece for each wipe. Wipe from legs and bottom inwards. Wash hands.

2 Using a wet cloth or cotton wool to remove urine, clean the genitals and surrounding skin. Never pull back the labia to clean inside.

3 Lift up her legs, holding them as shown, and clean her bottom. Wipe from the vagina back towards the rectum to prevent the spread of bacteria.

HOW TO PUT ON A DISPOSABLE NAPPY

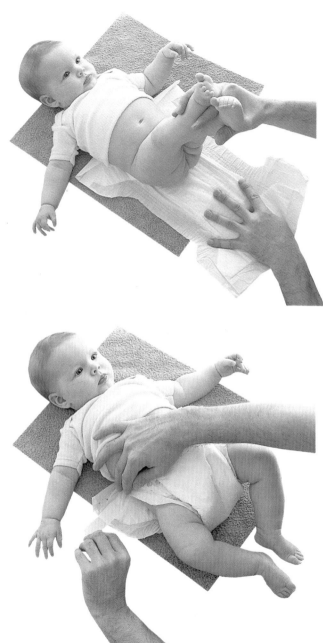

1 *Open out the nappy with the adhesive tabs at the top. Lift the baby's legs and slide the nappy under so that the top aligns with the baby's waist.*

2 *Bring the front up between the baby's legs and smooth the sides of the nappy round the baby's tummy so that they tuck under neatly.*

3 *Unpeel the adhesive tabs and pull them firmly over the front flap to secure the nappy. They should be quite taut.*

Nappy rash

Because passing urine is automatic, your baby's bottom will often be in contact with a damp nappy. Urine, if left for any length of time in a nappy or on the skin, is broken down to ammonia by bacteria from the baby's stools. Ammonia is an irritant: it burns the skin and results in nappy rash. Nappy rash can range from a mild redness to an inflamed area of broken skin and pussy spots. The bacteria which produce nappy rash thrive in an alkaline medium. The stools of bottle-fed babies are alkaline, unlike those of breast-fed babies which are acid. For this reason, bottle-fed babies are more prone to nappy rash. To minimize the possibility of nappy rash occurring:

☐ Change your baby's nappy regularly; never leave your baby lying in a wet nappy.
☐ Put a one-way disposable nappy liner next to your baby's skin. This allows urine to pass straight through to be absorbed by the nappy below, and so keeps the skin dry.
☐ Use a fairly thick barrier cream. There is no need to buy an expensive one. Simple zinc oxide or a proprietary nappy cream are usually good enough if applied generously.
☐ Leave the baby's bottom open to the air whenever you can. Let the baby kick happily without a nappy after a bath or at feeding time. Just slide a nappy underneath her bottom to catch any mess.
☐ Pay particular attention to washing nappies. Make sure they are well washed and rinsed to remove all the ammonia (see p.84).
☐ At the first sign of broken skin start using a special cream for the prevention of nappy rash. I always found one which included titanium salts especially good.
☐ At the first hint of nappy rash stop using plastic pants. These help to keep the urine close to the skin and promote the formation of ammonia.
☐ Stop washing the baby's bottom with soap and water. They are drying to the skin and can cause it to become cracked.

Treatment of nappy rash

You may find, despite your precautions, that your baby develops a sore bottom. If you are satisfied that your baby doesn't require specific treatment (see chart below), then the most successful remedy will be a combination of the tips listed above, plus a few more, below.
☐ Change the nappy more frequently.
☐ At night, use a disposable pad inside a towelling one for extra absorbency. This is especially useful for older babies who are sleeping through the night and will therefore not be changed from evening until morning.
☐ Do not apply barrier creams when changing the nappy as this prevents air getting to the skin. Although it also keeps the skin dry it is more important that the skin be well aired when your baby has nappy rash.

NAPPY RASH CHART

Appearance	Cause	Treatment
Redness and broken skin in the leg folds.	Inadequate drying after bathing.	Meticulous and thorough drying. Do not use powder.
Rash which starts around the genitals rather than the anus. Strong smell of ammonia.	Ammonia dermatitis.	General nappy rash treatment, above. If this doesn't work, check with your doctor.
Spotty rash all over the genitals, bottom, groin and thighs, which eventually leads to thick and wrinkled skin.	Extreme form of ammonia dermatitis.	Check with doctor for advice after trying general treatment, above, first.
Rash which starts around the anus and moves on to the buttocks.	Thrush.	Check with your doctor. You will probably be given nystatin cream and medicine.
Brownish-red scaly rash on the genitals and buttocks and anywhere the skin is greasy.	Seborrhoeic dermatitis.	Ointment for rash, prescribed by your doctor. You might also get a special lotion if the scalp is very scaly and sore.
Small blisters all over the nappy area.	Heat rash.	Don't use plastic pants, and leave off the nappy as much as possible.

FABRIC NAPPIES   0–1

Although initially more expensive to buy than all-in-one disposables, fabric nappies work out cheaper over the years. Made of terry towelling or muslin, in a variety of styles, they have to be rinsed, sterilized, washed out and dried after use and therefore involve much more labour than disposables. Because they have to be washed regularly you will need a minimum of 24 nappies. Obviously, the more nappies that you can afford to buy the less frequently you'll have to do the washing (and the larger and therefore more economical your batches will be). Buy the best quality that you can afford. They'll last longer and be more absorbent.

Types available

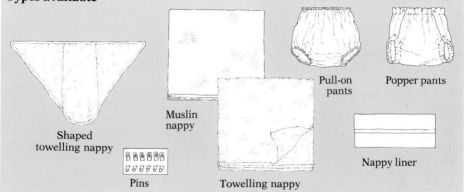

Shaped towelling nappy

Pins

Muslin nappy

Towelling nappy

Pull-on pants

Popper pants

Nappy liner

Towelling squares
These traditional nappies are thick and absorbent and will fold into a variety of shapes according to your baby's size and needs (see p. 82–83). Buy them ready-hemmed to avoid fraying when they are washed. They are more absorbent than the majority of disposables and are therefore very suitable at night. They can be bulky on very small babies and newborns.
Shaped terry towelling
These T-shaped nappies are made of a softer, finer towelling than ordinary squares and have a triple-layered central panel for added absorbency. They are shaped to fit neatly around the baby's legs and are more straightforward to put on.
Muslin squares
These are about the same size as towelling squares but they are soft and filmy. They are ideal for newborns because they are so comfortable against their skin. However, they are not very absorbent, and have to be changed frequently.

Nappy liners
These are placed inside the nappy and go next to the baby's skin. The best variety is made of a special material which lets urine pass through but remains dry next to the baby's skin. This minimizes the risk of a sore bottom due to friction or moisture. They also catch most of the faeces and prevent the nappy from getting badly soiled. When it comes to changing the nappy, the liner can be lifted out with any faeces and dropped down the lavatory.
Nappy pins
Specially-designed for fabric nappies, these pins have a self-locking head which makes it impossible for them to come undone accidently. Buy at least twelve.
Plastic pants
These pants, which come in several designs, are used over fabric nappies to prevent wet or dirty nappies soiling clothes or bedding. Buy six initially. You'll need to replace them as they get old and unusable.

81

Folding nappies

Not long ago, most parents were taught to use the simple triangle or rectangle methods. Although these methods were easy to fold they were not very efficient. The triangle was baggy around the legs, and the rectangle, although absorbent, was very bulky and was only suitable for small babies. I therefore suggest that you use the methods which I consider to be the best. By best I mean the most absorbent and the neatest. I suggest that you use the triple absorbent fold for your newborn. It has good absorbency because of its central panel and it is also very small and neat when on. Another method you could use for a newborn baby is the nappy skirt. Put a muslin nappy on the baby then lay the baby on an open towelling square. Fold it around the baby like a skirt and secure it at one side with a nappy pin.

When she grows too large for the triple fold use either the kite or the parallel method – whichever suits you best. The kite is probably easier to adapt to your growing baby as you can adjust how much you fold in to the centre to give the depth of the nappy.

TRIPLE ABSORBENT FOLD

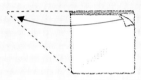
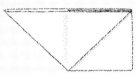

1 *Take a nappy folded in four with the open edges to the top and right. Pick up the top layer by right-hand edge.*

2 *Pull out the top layer to form an inverted triangle.*

3 *Carefully turn the whole nappy over so that the pointed edge is at the top right-hand side.*

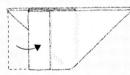
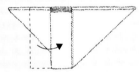
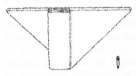

4 *Fold the two middle layers into the centre by one third.*

5 *Fold in another third to form a thick central panel.*

6 *Put a nappy liner in the middle and have a pin ready.*

PARALLEL FOLD

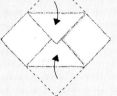

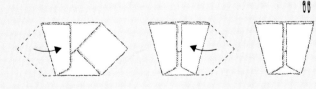

1 *Lay out nappy in a diamond shape. Fold top point in to the centre; fold bottom up and over the centre.*

2 *Pick up the left-hand point and align it with the top edge.*

3 & 4 *Fold in the right-hand edge in the same way. Place a nappy liner in the middle and have two pins ready.*

KITE FOLD

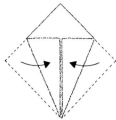 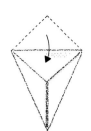 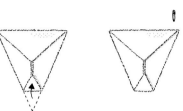

1 *Lay out nappy in a diamond shape. Fold sides in to the centre to form a kite shape.*

2 *Fold the top point down to the centre, leaving a straight edge at the top.*

3 & 4 *Fold the bottom edge up to the centre, according to the baby's size. Place a nappy liner in the middle and have a pin ready.*

HOW TO PUT ON A FABRIC NAPPY

 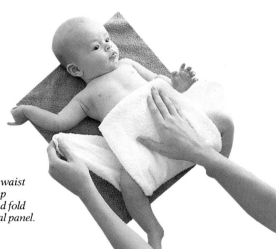

1 *Slide the nappy under so that the baby's waist aligns with the top edge. Bring the nappy up between the baby's legs. Hold it in place and fold first one side, then the other, over the central panel.*

2 *Secure the nappy for a small baby with one pin in the middle; use two side pins for bigger babies. Keep your fingers between the nappy and the skin when inserting a pin.*

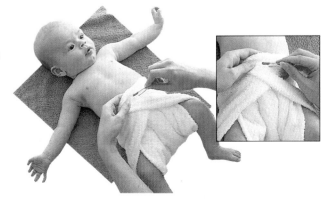

83

CHANGING TIPS

● If your baby is very wriggly have a toy handy to act as a distraction. Involve an older baby by letting her hold the cream, or read or look at a book.

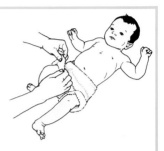

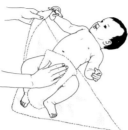

● Use a disposable inside a towelling nappy for extra absorbency at night. Also use this method if you're travelling and want to avoid a difficult change.
● Use stretch towelling pants over plastic pants – they look neater than plastic pants on their own. Frilly and patterned plastic pants are also available if you want something fancier.

● Boys often urinate when changed, so cover penis with a clean nappy as you take old one off.
● Always keep your fingers between the nappy and the skin when inserting a pin.

● When you've put on the nappy run your fingers round the legs to make sure that they are not too tight.
● To save time, fold all the nappies ready for use and put the nappy liners in position.
● Make sure that the nappy fits snugly around the baby's body. It will gradually give as the baby wears it so if you've pinned it too loosely it will slide down.

Nappy washing and sterilization

Nappies must be thoroughly washed to remove all traces of ammonia and faecal bacteria which would otherwise cause irritation and possible infection (see p.80). Special nappy sterilants are now available which make this process much easier and less time-consuming. With this method the nappies are soaked in a sterilizing solution for a specified length of time and then only the soiled nappies are washed with powder; the wet nappies are thoroughly rinsed. Whenever you wash nappies use pure soap flakes or powders. Avoid strong detergents and biological enzyme powders as these will irritate the baby's tender skin. If you have to use a fabric conditioner because the towelling has become stiff make sure that you rinse it all out; despite manufacturers' instructions to the contrary, this too can cause irritation. Unless the nappies are very stained, or have become rather grey, there is no need to boil them. Hot water is sufficient for both rinsing and washing after using sterilizing tablets. Never add

coloured clothing to the sterilizing solution – the colour will run. Even if the clothing has been soiled, just remove the worst of the mess, rinse the item and then wash as normal.

Nappy washing routine

To balance the chores of feeding, changing and nappy washing, try to develop a routine whereby you wash the nappies in sufficiently large loads. The prerequisite of this routine is a large supply of nappies – I suggest no less than 24. In order to sterilize the nappies you will need two plastic bins: one for soiled nappies, one for wet ones. They should be large enough to hold at least six nappies, plus solution, and they must have lids and strong, reliable handles. Don't, however, buy such a large bin that you can't carry it fully loaded to the washing machine or bath. Special nappy bins are sold but any bin of a decent size with a lid is suitable. Bins designed for beer-making are ideal and they are also quite cheap.

Each morning fill the bins with the

required amounts of water and solution. Rinse a urine-soaked nappy in cold water, squeeze out the excess moisture and put it into the bin. Remove as much faeces as possible down the lavatory then hold the soiled nappy under the water as you flush it to remove the excess. Wring out the nappy and submerge it in the solution. After the required time, wring out both sets of nappies. Rinse the urine-soaked ones thoroughly in hot water before drying them. Put the soiled ones through the hot programme of a washing machine then rinse and dry them. Alternatively, wash them out in a bath with hot water.

Washing plastic pants

If they become soiled or wet they should be washed in warm water with a little washing-up liquid. If the water is either too hot or too cold the plastic hardens and becomes unusable. Pat the pants dry after washing and leave them to air before using. One way of softening them is to tumble dry them with a load of towels.

WASHING TIPS
- Some buckets have special holders for air-fresheners. If yours doesn't, hook a piece of wire through a freshener and attach above water line.
- Keep plastic gloves near the bucket for lifting nappies out. Alternatively use plastic tongs.
- If you use powder sterilant always put the water in before the powder. The powder otherwise spreads through the air and you inhale it.
- Both drying in the open air and in a tumble drier keep the fabric softer. If you use radiators to dry nappies they tend to harden the fabric. It's better to invest in a rack which can be placed over the bath or to use a pull-out line if you don't dry outdoors or with a tumble drier.
- Keep any nappies changed at night in another bucket, or in a large plastic bag, and add them to the new day's solution the following morning.

USING NAPPIES

A one-year-old child still urinates automatically but because the bladder can hold an increasing amount of urine she'll be dry for longer periods. You will therefore use fewer nappies – on average 50 per week as opposed to the 80 used on a newborn. If you hesitated to use disposables before because of the price you may consider them now. Another reason why they become more practical now is that they're neater and less bulky than fabric nappies. This is important because your increasingly mobile child will find it difficult to walk with a cumbersome wad of nappy between her legs. If you use fabric nappies, fold them in the least bulky way – use either the kite fold or a shaped terry. When it comes to changing the nappy you'll find your toddler far less willing to lie still. Make sure that you've got some books or toys as distractions (see p. 296) or you'll find that each change becomes a battle ground. Clothes which

give easy access to the nappy save your time and energy, so buy overalls which have poppers or zips in the crotch, or use pants which you can just pull down quickly.

At some time during the third year your child will probably gain conscious control over the bowel and bladder muscles and your days of frequent nappy changes should be over. When your child stays dry during naps you can start leaving off that nappy (see p. 158). Once again, I'd suggest that you use disposables. As part of your toilet training you may also want to use trainer pants which can be pulled down quickly when your child tells you that she wants to go to the lavatory. These are basically plastic knickers lined with towelling. They're comfortable to wear and provide some protection against the inevitable accidents which will occur. Buy at least six to begin with, because they're not absorbent.

7 Bathing and hygiene

Part of your daily routine will be to keep your baby clean. This will be reasonably easy when she's very small, but as your baby becomes more active you'll find that you will not only have to clean her more often, but that it will require a bit more effort to manage the daily bath. However, by the time she's two she will increasingly try to take control over washing her own body.

WASHING YOUR BABY   0–1

Most young babies don't need bathing very often because, apart from their bottoms, faces, necks and skin creases, they don't get very dirty. There is no reason why you shouldn't go for two or three days without bathing her as long as you clean the baby's face, hands and bottom every day. You can do this without even putting the baby in the bath by topping and tailing, (see p. 88). It is also advisable to wash her hair regularly to prevent cradle cap forming (see p. 93).

Some parents feel apprehensive the first few times they bath their baby. However, if you set aside half an hour, have everything you need around you and try to relax you will probably enjoy it. After the first two or three times it will become fairly routine and you'll wonder what your first bathtime nerves were all about.

Where to bath your baby

Until she's big enough to go into an adult bath you don't have to use a bathroom to wash your baby. You can use the baby's room, the kitchen or any other room that is warm and has enough space to lay out all that you need to bath your baby in comfort. The baby's bath can be filled in the bathroom and then carried to the chosen room (make sure you don't fill it too full or the water will splash out as you walk from room to room).

A small baby can be washed in a specially designed, sculpted plastic bath with a non-slip surface (see p. 37). As it is most comfortable for you if you don't have to bend too much, the bath should be placed on a table or worktop of a convenient height. Alternatively, you could place it on an adjustable stand (although they tend to be rather flimsy) or on a rack which straddles the bath.

If, however, you don't have a baby bath there are some inexpensive, practical alternatives that you can use until your baby can go into the big bath. For example, a plastic household basin functions in exactly the same way as a baby bath and is useful because, like a baby bath, it can be carried anywhere you choose. Kitchen or bathroom sinks are also practical because they are generally at a comfortable height and they often have additional counter space to the side. However, you must make sure that the taps are well out of reach of your baby's kicking legs. If they aren't, they should be bound up with cloths or towels so that they can cause no harm. If the "bath" surface is too slippery, either use a plastic suction mat or line the bath with a small towel or nappy to provide a non-slip surface for your baby's bottom.

Topping and tailing

This method allows you to wash the parts of your newborn baby that really need it, with the minimum of disturbance and distress to the baby. As your baby gets older, you need not use boiled water; warm water will do.

- Water boiled then cooled
- Cotton wool
- Facecloth
- Towel
- Clean nappy
- Nappy liner
- Plastic pants, if used
- Nappy changing equipment
- Clean clothes

 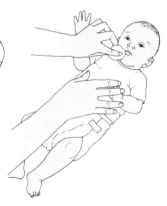

1 *Lay your baby on a firm surface. Taking a moist piece of cotton wool for each eye, gently wipe from the bridge of the nose outwards.*

2 *Wipe outside and behind the ears with moist cotton wool. Do not poke about or clean inside them.*

3 *Wipe your baby's face with moist cotton wool to remove any milk or spittle. If left, this will irritate the baby's skin.*

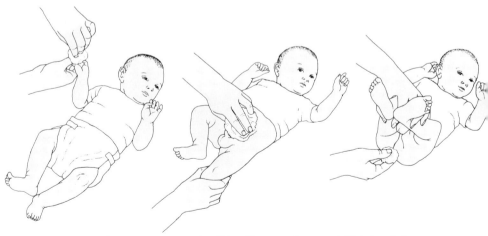

4 *Use a new piece of cotton wool to clean her hands. When she's older you can use a facecloth. Dry with a towel.*

5 *Take off the old nappy. If she's just wet, wipe the area with damp cotton wool or a facecloth.*

6 *If she's soiled, remove as much as you can with the nappy, then use baby lotion and cotton wool to clean the nappy area (see p. 90).*

Giving a sponge bath

If you're a bit scared of giving your new baby a bath, or if she really hates being undressed, you can use the sponge bath method of washing. This way, the baby is held securely in your lap and only the minimum amount of clothing is removed. You could alternatively wash your baby on a mat, using the same techniques.

- Bowl of water
- Cotton wool
- Facecloth or sponge
- Towel
- Soap
- Baby shampoo
- Clean nappy
- Nappy liner
- Plastic pants, if used
- Nappy changing equipment
- Clean clothes

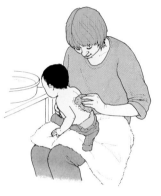

1 *Have a bowl of warm water on a table near your chair and put a towel across your knees. Remove the top half of your baby's clothing but keep the legs covered. Gently soap the baby's front.*

2 *Rinse off soap using squeezed out cloth, making sure all the soap is removed from the skin creases. Pat your baby's skin dry, paying special attention to the skin folds.*

3 *Lean your baby forwards over your arm so that you can wash her back. Rinse and pat dry. Put on a clean vest.*

4 *If you want to clean your baby's hair do so before you put on the vest. Sponge the head gently with water and then use a non-sting baby shampoo. Rinse carefully.*

5 *Remove the bottom half of your baby's clothing and then take off your baby's nappy. Use baby lotion to clean the nappy area (see p. 78).*

6 *Wash the legs and feet using a damp cloth. Rinse and pat dry. Put on a clean nappy and dress your baby.*

Giving your baby a bath

It is important that your baby doesn't get cold, so make sure the room is warm with no draughts, and that you have everything you need ready and at hand: bath, large towel, soap (if used), facecloth, cotton wool, clean nappy, nappy liner, nappy changing equipment, and clean clothes.

1 *Always pour cold water into the bath first. Before putting your baby in the bath, test the temperature of the water with your elbow, or the inner side of your wrist. It should feel neither hot nor cold, just warm. If you are unsure, use a bath thermometer.*

2 *Undress your baby on a flat surface, but leave his vest on so he doesn't get cold. Clean the nappy area with baby lotion (see p. 78). Once in the bath all he'll need will be a good rinse with water.*

3 *Remove the baby's vest and wrap him securely in a towel so that he doesn't panic at being undressed. Clean the eyes, ears and nose (see p. 88).*

4 *Using the football carry (see p. 93), lean over the bath and wash the baby's head. Rinse well and pat dry. (For prevention of cradle cap, see Care of the hair, p. 93.)*

5 Remove the towel. Support your baby's shoulders with your left forearm and hook your hand over the baby's shoulder and under his armpit. Cradle the baby's legs with your right arm, holding onto one thigh. Gently place the baby in the bath so that you are facing him.

6 Keep your baby in a semi-upright position so that the lower half of his body is immersed and his head and shoulders are clear of water. Use your free hand to wash the baby. Chat and smile all the time you are bathing him. When he is clean and well rinsed put your free hand under his bottom and, gently lift your baby on to the towel.

7 Place your baby diagonally across the towel. Fold the bottom corner over the feet, followed by the two sides. Pick your baby up for a cuddle while you dry him. Pay particular attention to the skin creases, drying them gently but thoroughly.

TIPS

● Make sure that you have everything that you need for washing, drying and dressing close by.
● Wear a waterproof apron to protect your own clothing but also lay a large, soft towel across your lap and up your front so that when you cuddle up your baby after the bath she will feel warm and comfortable.
● Very young babies can't regulate their own temperatures very efficiently, so keep the time she's undressed to a minimum.

● Baby bathcare liquid added to the bath water is easier to use than soap.
● For an older baby try using one of those towels with hoods: she will feel even more secure and snuggly, especially if you've had it over a radiator to warm.
● Only fill the bath with a couple of inches of water until you get used to bathing your baby.
● Never use baby powders. They are unnecessarily drying to a baby's skin and may cake in the creases, causing irritation and rashes.

91

Using a bathtub

Between three and six months old your baby will outgrow most small baths and you will have to start using an adult one. If you think that your baby may be frightened by the size of this new bath, continue to use the small bath but place it inside the large, empty one until she gets used to it.

It is much more awkward to wash a baby in a big bath but you must still hold on to the baby's arm until she can support herself. Don't bend over the bath or you'll strain your back. Instead, kneel by the bath and have everything that you need next to you on the floor. Use a plastic suction mat on the bottom of the bath to prevent the baby sliding about and keep the water shallow (no deeper than 10–13 cm [4–5 in]). It doesn't take much for a wriggly, kicking baby to slip under the water so you must be vigilant at all times. Never, ever, leave your baby alone in the bath, even for a moment; don't even turn away to attend to something else in the same room. If the phone rings either ignore it or take your wet baby with you. Leaving your baby, even for a second, is just not worth the risk.

As your baby gets older she'll spend more and more time crawling about on the floor and, as a result, will need to be washed more often; baths will become a regular feature of the day. By this time she will no longer be scared of being undressed and will feel quite secure in the water. In fact, she will almost certainly have begun to enjoy bathtimes. It is therefore your job to make them fun and as trouble-free as possible.

As soon as your baby can sit up, always have a period at the end of the bath when she can enjoy splashing and playing with toys. Have some boats, ducks, sponges or mugs on hand so that she can experiment with them and see what they do. If you have two children, try occasionally bathing them together so that your older child can share games and can teach your baby about the things that water does. It's exciting for your baby to see how containers can be filled and emptied or water poured from one to the other, and she'll love watching how some toys float and others sink slowly to the bottom of the bath.

BATH TOYS

Many household items can be adapted for bathtime. Babies love seeing water pour out of objects and this makes plastic fruit boxes with their air holes, ideal. Other good toys include measuring spoons, small watering cans, ice cube trays and colanders.

Even if your baby can sit unsupported it's sensible to keep a light grip on her thigh, just in case she should slip

BATHING TIPS

● Never, ever, leave your baby alone in the bath. Even if you turn around for a moment she could slip under the water and drown.

● Don't let the baby stand up in the bath without your support – she could fall.

● If your child starts to jump up and down – no doubt rejoicing in a newly found skill – be very firm about making her sit still; she could easily topple without your support.

● Cover up hot taps with a flannel or towel so that she won't get scalded.

● Don't pour more hot water into the bath with the baby in it – she may get scalded.

● Don't see if she can sit unsupported. She could easily tumble under the water and get a bad fright – bad enough to go off bathing for a while.

● Don't pull the plug out when the baby's in the bath. She may be both frightened by the disappearing water and the noise.

● Don't dust your baby with talcum powder after a bath – it's very drying to the skin.

● If you're at work during the day, make the most of bathtime – it can be a great time to play and relax with your baby.

● Make sure that you pick your baby out of the bath with your back straight, taking the strain with your thighs.

Care of the hair

To prevent cradle cap from forming you should wash your newborn's head every day with a soft bristle brush and a little baby shampoo. To prevent any scales forming you should comb through the hair, even if she has very little. If cradle cap does appear, smear a little baby oil on her scalp and wash it off the following morning. This will dissolve the scales, making them soft, loose and easy to wash away. Don't be tempted to pick them off with your fingers.

After about twelve to sixteen weeks wash your baby's head with water every day and once or twice a week with baby shampoo. You can either use a football carry (if the baby is quite light) or you can sit on the edge of the bath with the baby across your legs, facing you. (This method is especially useful if she's scared of the water.) Make sure that you use a non-sting variety of baby shampoo, but nevertheless take care to avoid getting it near her eyes. Don't worry about the newborn's fontanelles. They are covered with a very sturdy membrane and you can do no harm if you are gentle. You need not scrub the hair. Modern detergents get dirt and oil off hair within seconds, so you just have to bring the shampoo to a lather, count to twenty and then rinse it off again. One

wash is quite enough, and your baby's hair will be absolutely clean at the end of this operation. Rinse your baby's hair by simply dipping the flannel into the basin of warm water and wiping it over her head. Try and get as much off as possible, but if your child is complaining it really doesn't matter if you leave slight traces on the hair. Dry her head with the end of the towel, taking care not to cover the baby's face or she will become very distressed and panicky.

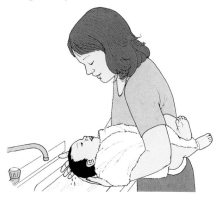

Pick up the baby in a football carry by tucking her legs under your armpit and supporting the baby's back along your arm. Fan out your fingers to cradle the baby's head. Wash the hair using mild, non-sting shampoo.

93

Care of the skin

A newborn has no need of soap. It is a de-fatting agent and your baby's skin is delicate. She needs to preserve all the natural oils so use only water until about six weeks. After then, any soap you choose can be used – you may want to try a special liquid soap which is simply added to the bath water and needs no rinsing off. Make sure that you wash any folds and creases properly by running a soapy finger along them then rinsing well. Dry the skin thoroughly – any moist creases will lead to irritations; never use talcum powders.

Care of the eyes

When you wash your baby's eyes, squeeze a couple of cotton wool balls in the warm water, and use a different one to wash each closed eye, starting from the inner part of the eye and working to the outer.

Care of the nose and ears

The nose and ears are self-cleaning organs so you should never try to push anything up them or in them or interfere with them in any way. Pushing something the size of a cotton bud up a baby's nose or into a baby's ears, will only push whatever is there further in. It is much better to let whatever is in the nose come down naturally. Never put drops into the ears or nose except under a doctor's instruction (see p. 116). Never try to scrape wax out of a baby's ears even though you can see it. Wax is the natural secretion of the skin lining the canal of the outer ear. It is antiseptic and it prevents dust and grit getting near the ear drum. Some babies make more than others, but removing it will only result in the production of even more. Removing wax irritates the skin, so leave it alone and consult your doctor if you are concerned about it. Wash your baby's ears and nose using moist cotton wool (see p. 88).

Care of the nails

There is no need to cut a newborn baby's nails for about three or four weeks, unless your baby is scratching her skin. Nails are easiest to cut when they are soft so have a pair of small, blunt-ended scissors nearby when you take your baby out of the bath. If you do them immediately you'll be able to cut the nails of both hands and toes in less than half a minute. If, however, you are worried about cutting your baby's nails try doing it when she is asleep. Or bite them off yourself – your mouth will be sensitive to every move she makes and it will be impossible to hurt her.

If you're going to use scissors lay your baby on a flat surface, talk soothingly to her, and then gently cut the nails following the shape of the fingertips.

Care of the navel

The umbilical cord will have been clamped and cut immediately after delivery, leaving a 5–8 cm (2–3 in) stump protruding from your baby's abdomen. This may be clamped by a plastic clip. Over the next few days the cord dries and shrivels, and will then drop off.

You will probably be advised to gently wipe the umbilical stump daily with surgical spirit and sterile cotton wool, and then to cover the area with sterile gauze. Let the area stay open to the air as much as possible as this will help to speed up the shrinking and healing process. If you notice any redness, discharge or other signs of infection, ask your health visitor or doctor for advice. You don't have to wait for the navel to heal before you give your baby a bath, as long as you dry it thoroughly afterwards.

Some babies develop umbilical hernias but they nearly always clear up within a year or two. If your baby has one and it enlarges or persists, see your doctor for

Care of the genitals

You should never try to open the lips of your baby girl's vulva to clean inside; there is no need. Just wash the exterior nappy area (see p. 78). However, you should take care to wipe from the front back towards the anus whenever you are cleaning the nappy area. This minimizes the risk of bacteria spreading from the bowels to the bladder, causing infection.

An uncircumcised baby boy should not have his foreskin pulled back for cleaning. Just wash the exterior of the nappy area as normal; the foreskin will retract naturally at about 3 or 4 years of age.

If your baby has been circumcised, it is important to keep a careful watch to make sure that the penis is not bleeding. A dressing may or may not be applied, but in either case you will be given advice about bathing your baby and special care of the penis. Following circumcision, the penis is nearly always swollen and slightly inflamed for a few days, and occasionally there may be a few drops of blood: this is normal and will gradually settle down. However, if bleeding persists or there is any sign of infection, consult your doctor.

POSSIBLE PROBLEMS 0–1

Fear of undressing

Many young babies become extremely distressed when they are undressed. They hate the feeling of air on their bodies, preferring instead the security of being fully clothed or wrapped tightly. When your baby's very small you can get around this by giving sponge baths or by topping and tailing (see pp. 88–89).

Fear of bathing

If your baby is absolutely terrified of having a bath, skip it for a couple of days and then try again, very gently, using only a little water in the bath. Until your baby is ready to go back into the bath give sponge baths or top and tail.

If, after some time, she still doesn't like being bathed and remains frightened of water, try to overcome it by introducing bathtime in a play context. In a warm room (but not the bathroom), lay out a towel with a large plastic bowl full of

water next to it. Put some floatable toys and plastic beakers into the bowl, undress your baby and encourage her to play with the toys. She'll gradually get used to the idea of being near the water.

When she seems happy and confident help your baby to paddle in the water: if your kitchen is warm put a towel on the draining board, fill the sink with warm water and let your baby dangle her feet while sitting on the towel. Make sure that you keep a firm grip on your baby with one hand while you play with toys and beakers with the other, and that all the taps are bound up with a cloth.

Do this a couple of times then swap the bowl or kitchen sink for a baby bath and let your baby play in the same way as before. You'll know she's overcome any fear when she struggles to get into the water with the toys. Let your baby do this a couple of times before you turn it into an occasion for washing as well.

Fear of the big bath

Once your baby is splashing about and making a mess in the small baby bath, she is ready to go into a big bath. However, if your child is frightened of getting into a big bath, you'll have to build up to it gradually. Place the baby bath inside the big bath and put a towel or a rubber mat next to it so that she can't slip. Sit her in the big bath along with some toys and fill up the baby bath with warm water as usual. Then let her climb into the baby bath. Once she is happy doing this, you can introduce a few centimetres of water into the big bath, with the towel or rubber mat in the bottom and all the toys, as before, and the baby bath full of warm water. She will then probably climb in and out of the baby bath and quickly get used to sitting in the big bath in just a few centimetres of water. You can then increase the amount of water in the big bath, leaving the baby bath there until she is no longer interested in it. This makes the transition fairly painless, and does quite a lot to increase your child's confidence.

Dislike of hair washing

A baby who thoroughly enjoys having a bath, may hate hair washing and she will probably develop this dislike around eight or nine months old. Even though you may be gentle and take every precaution to make sure that your child isn't frightened by hair washing, you may find that it remains a problem until your child is of school age, so it is worth getting the technique right from the start.

☐ Young children hate to get water in the eyes, let alone soap, so do everything you can to keep your baby's face and eyes dry throughout the whole operation of hair washing.

☐ Never pour water over your child's head just to prove that it won't hurt. Few children under the age of six can stand this, and if it is done suddenly to them they find it extremely unpleasant. Don't continue the washing operation if she screams or struggles and *never* forcibly hold your child so that you can get her hair washed. You may have an accident, like getting some soap into her eyes, which will make the whole incident much worse. It will also make all future attempts to wash your child's hair very difficult and fraught experiences for both of you.

☐ Once your child strenuously objects to hair washing, give up and don't try again for three or four weeks. Bathtimes are generally happy for most children, so it is better to dissociate hair washing from bathtimes if it's unpleasant. If you find bits of food in your child's hair, simply sponge them out or wait until they are dry before brushing them out with a soft, damp brush. It really doesn't matter if your child's hair is greasy; it will come to no harm.

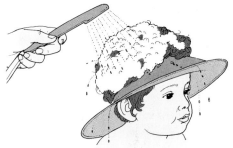

☐ Another way of keeping the water from your baby's face is to use a specially-designed shield. This fits like a halo around the hairline and allows you to rinse off any shampoo without getting soapy water all over your baby's face.

☐ You may find that your baby will let you wash her hair as long as she's being held by you. Sit with the baby on your lap next to a basin of warm water, and use a flannel to wet the baby's head before you use a non-sting shampoo. So that no water gets onto the baby's face, rinse the water off with a damp facecloth, *not* by pouring water over the head. She won't be disturbed by this because she'll feel no water trickling over either her head or her body.

97

WASHING YOUR TODDLER   1–3

As your child gets older she will probably regard bathtime primarily as playtime. Most children love playing with water and the bath is one of the most convenient places for them to do it, so provide plastic cups, beakers, boats and ducks, allow plenty of time, relax, and let bathtime be fun. Encourage your child to wash herself by having a special sponge that she can use. Until she's developed adequate co-ordination she won't make a perfect job of it so be prepared to go over the same areas with another facecloth. Soap both your child's hands by holding a bar of soap between them, and show her how to spread the soap over her body and arms.

Daily routine

Most children need a wash in the morning but it's probably best to leave it until after breakfast. A child is often ravenously hungry when she wakes up, and you'll only have time to change the soggy nappy before food becomes imperative. After your child has eaten she'll be more willing to stand still to have her face and hands washed, teeth brushed (see p. 227), and hair combed. By the time she's about one and a half she'll be able to rinse both

hands under water and, with improving co-ordination, will learn to soap them. Do remember, though, that she'll not always remember the routine of hand washing: sleeves may not be rolled up, jumpers may get wet and soap may slip out of tiny fingers. So always be close by to lend a hand should she need it.

Hygiene

Start hygiene routines young and, where possible, teach by example. For instance, from the time that your child starts to crawl and get her hands dirty, washing before eating should become automatic. If you start by washing your hands with your child (and I mean *with*), by getting your hands soapy together and washing each others hands, it can become fun. While you're teaching your child how to wash you can make a game of it by trying to blow bubbles with the soap film that forms between your forefinger and thumb when you make a circle. Afterwards, let your child inspect yours and then you look at your child's.

If you start like this it makes it easier to apply hygiene rules at other times. For example, hand washing should always

DAILY HYGIENE
Encourage your toddler to wash her hands from an early age. She may find it easier to rub both hands with a soapy facecloth.

If your child objects to washing her face, suggest that she use a sponge. This is more fun, and much softer on the skin.

Give your child a soft toothbrush and encourage her to use it after meals, especially once the molars are through (see p. 228).

follow visits to the lavatory. But you should start at the potty stage and do it with your child every single time.

You can help your child to become more independent by providing a stable, non-slip standing block in the bathroom, so she can reach the basin and toilet easily and safely by herself.

Pets and hygiene

There are important advantages for your toddler in having a pet, but you may be concerned about the possible health risks involved. However, if you follow a few simple rules about handling pets, you should have no cause for concern.

Encourage your child to wash her hands after playing with her pet – especially before touching or eating food. Also, you should stop your child from kissing her pet, especially near its nose and mouth.

The most common problems caused by pets are infestations of fleas and worms. Both of these are easily avoided by regular use of the appropriate preventative treatments. If infestations do occur, treat promptly and stop your child from playing with the pet until treatment has worked.

Ringworm is a contagious skin condition which can be caught from pets, and is commonly seen in children. If you suspect ringworm, consult your doctor.

POSSIBLE PROBLEMS   1–3

Fear of hair washing
If your child really hates having her hair washed, keep the hair very short so that it needs only sponging to keep it clean (see p. 97). One of the major reasons why children hate having their hair washed is that they don't like water going over their faces. To overcome this you'll have to encourage your child to believe that hair washing won't hurt and that it won't feel nasty when water is rinsed over her head.
□ Another problem that can make hair washing unpleasant is when your child has the kind of fine, curly hair that gets very tangled; combing through the tangles after hair washing can become a

nightmare. If you don't want to cut her hair really short – which is the simplest solution to the problem – try using conditioner: after rinsing off the shampoo, work some conditioner through the hair, gently comb through with a wide-toothed comb, then rinse off the conditioner with a spray attachment. Don't rough-towel her hair dry – just pat it gently with the towel to absorb the excess water.
□ Make a game out of hair washing. It will become much more fun from your child's point of view if you get into the bath as well and wash your own hair. Rinse it with a plastic jug of water and make out that it's great fun pouring water over your head.

□ If you have an older child you could prove that it doesn't hurt by letting the smaller child help you wash the elder's hair. Once you've lathered up the shampoo, hold the frightened child and let her rub both her hands through the bubbles. If possible, get the child to help pour the rinsing water over, too. Alternatively, wash a doll's hair in the bath with your toddler's assistance. Let your child help with the rinsing and then suggest that you do it to her hair. With any luck she'll just take this as part of the game. Alternatively, encourage your child to wet her own hair with a facecloth and put a tiny bit of shampoo into both hands so that she can participate.

□ An older child is also useful in proving that a wet face isn't unpleasant. For example, the elder child may well be proud of holding her breath under water and once your child is about three she might want to join in with this game, even if it means only putting nose and mouth under the surface for a count of five.

□ Another way of getting your child used to water on the face is to take her swimming. Once she's got used to splashing and getting wet hair you'll be able to start hair washing. This is especially easy if you have a shower after swimming. You can then gently and deftly introduce the idea of having a shampoo in the shower using a non-sting baby shampoo: a quick shampoo should take no longer than a couple of minutes. You can also use the shower attachment at home, encouraging the child to play with the spray, playing it up to her shoulders and eventually on to her hair and face. Once again, when she's used to wet hair, you can quickly shampoo and rinse it.

Fear of water

A few children hate water and bathtimes and for these children and their parents will be very distressing. Probably the easiest way of overcoming this fear is to make bathtimes as happy and relaxing as possible, with plenty of playtime included. Try to find out what is frightening your

child: is it the size of the bath; is it the amount of water in it; is it related to an incident, for example slipping and suddenly being ducked under the water? If it is the size of the bath that causes the worry, introduce alternatives, like the kitchen sink or a large washing-up bowl. Your child will probably sit quite happily on a towel on the draining board, playing and dipping her feet into the water (see p. 96). This should also help if she's scared of the volume of water, as will playing with a shower attachment or a garden hose (as long as the flow is gentle).

Ironically, swimming can be used to overcome your child's fear of water although you'll have to introduce the subject gently. Once you've tried the methods above, and your child has shown signs of progress, you can think about going swimming. If you can, take advantage of swimming classes which you can attend with your child and where you do most of the teaching (with help from an instructor if you need it). Being able to swim may save your child's life and, if possible, you should make sure that she can swim before she goes to school.

Feeding

The main aim of infant feeding is to *provide adequate nutrition*. It helps to bear in mind also that while breast-feeding is undoubtedly best if, for whatever reason, you don't breast-feed your baby, she will be perfectly all right fed from a bottle. Don't feel guilty if you make this decision; concentrate on the needs of your baby.

As important as any milk is the love and affection that you give your baby. The important rule to remember is to take your lead from your child; as long as you offer a wide variety of foods she doesn't have to have "essential" foods every day. Remember, above all, that food is a pleasure.

NUTRITIONAL REQUIREMENTS   0-1

A baby's growth is more rapid during the first six months than at any other time in its life. The majority of babies double their birth weight in around four months and have tripled it by the time they are about one year old. All parts of the body develop quickly and gain tremendously in size, and your baby may grow from 50–80 cm (19–31 in) during the year. Your baby's nutritional needs run parallel with this.

In order to grow, your baby needs to take food; for your baby to be healthy that food has to contain adequate amounts of protein, vitamins, carbohydrates and minerals, whatever age she is. Until she's at least four months old your baby will receive these supplies in the form of milk. After this, when she's started on a solid diet, she will get all she needs if you provide a sensible, well-balanced diet.

Calories

The energy needed to perform all bodily functions comes from food. The energy content of food is usually expressed in calories, and in an infant the calorie requirements are about two-and-a-half to three times those of an adult. During the first six months slightly more than 100 calories per kilo are needed, and from six months to one year slightly less than 100 per kilo.

A baby weighing 3500 g at birth will therefore need in the region of 400 calories a day. If the same baby doubles its weight in approximately six months, to 7000 g, she will need 667 calories a day. At twelve months, if the baby has tripled its birth weight to 10.5 kilos, she will need about 1000 calories a day.

Protein

Most of the protein that a baby takes in is used for growth, and the protein requirements during the first twelve months are correspondingly higher than at any other time of life; they are three times as great as those for adults. Milk, as long as it is given in adequate amounts, provides all the protein that a newborn infant needs.

Vitamins

Breast milk is short of nothing except vitamin D. The main source of this is the sun, which stimulates the skin to manufacture it. If you live in a poor climate, or if your child has a very dark skin, you may need to give vitamin D supplements; ask your doctor for advice. If you bottle-feed your baby all vitamin requirements will be satisfied by the formula, to which the manufacturer adds supplements.

Minerals

The rapid growth of bone and muscle during the first year means that babies have a greater need for minerals like calcium, phosphorous and magnesium than adults. All babies are born with a supply of iron that will last for up to four months; after this, iron has to be added to the diet, usually in the form of solids, but possibly as iron supplements. Breast milk and cow's milk are both pretty low on iron; formula milk usually has iron added to it by the manufacturer, and you can check this on the contents label.

Trace elements

Your baby needs traces of certain minerals like zinc, copper and fluoride. The first two are present in both breast and formula milk. Fluoride, however, is not. As infants need fluoride to protect them against dental decay in infancy and childhood, you should check with your midwife or doctor about giving your baby a fluoride supplement (of about 0.5 milligrams per day). You can give it as drops until your baby is old enough to take a tablet each morning (incidentally, this is better chewed as the teeth become coated with fluoride, giving protection). If fluoride is added to the drinking water in your area you won't have to give fluoride supplements to your children. If you're in doubt, contact your water authority.

Fats

The body needs minute traces of fatty acids for growth and repair. The fat content of both breast and formula milk is about the same, but in human milk the droplets of fat are smaller and therefore more digestible.

Carbohydrates

These are major energy providers. Both breast and formula milk contain the same carbohydrates, although the carbohydrate level is slightly higher in breast milk.

BREAST-FEEDING   0–1

Human breast milk is tailor-made for a baby: it contains just the right amount of protein, carbohydrates, minerals and vitamins to sustain your growing baby. Don't be put off by the bluish, watery appearance, or worry that it can't possibly be "good enough" because it's not as creamy as cow's milk: your milk is rich in every foodstuff that your baby needs.

Apart from its nutritional worth, breast-feeding makes sound sense for the following reasons:

☐ Breast-fed babies are less prone to illness than bottle-fed babies. There are fewer cases of gastroenteritis, chest infection, and measles and this is directly attributable to the antibodies that the baby receives. All babies receive some antibodies from their mother's placental blood, via the umbilical cord, but in the case of breast-fed babies these are supplemented by antibodies in both the colostrum (see p.106) and in the mother's milk. In your baby's first few days of life

they exert a protective influence on the intestine (reducing the likelihood of intestinal disturbance), and because they are also absorbed into the bloodstream they form part of the body's protection against infections. Some antibodies, such as those against poliomyelitis, are in the breast milk, so the mother can actively protect her newborn while she is breast-feeding. (The baby will still have to be immunized herself, however, at 3–9 months of age.)

☐ Breast milk is more easily, and quickly, digested than cow's milk. Breast-fed babies don't get constipated: they may pass stools infrequently but this is because the food is so efficiently and completely used up. The stools that they do pass are always soft and comparatively odourless, and don't contain the bacteria which generally cause ammonia dermatitis, so your baby is less prone to nappy rash.

☐ Breast-fed babies rarely become over-weight. Each baby has its own appetite and metabolic rate – it won't be the same as the baby next door, so don't worry if your baby is fatter or thinner than your neighbour's. She'll be the right weight for her own body.

☐ Breast-feeding is the most convenient method. The milk is always at the right temperature, you don't have to waste your time sterilizing bottles and making up formula, and you save money by not having to buy all the equipment. Breast-fed babies have less wind, sleep longer, posset less and the posset smells less unpleasant.

☐ Breast-feeding is good for your figure. Research has shown that most of the fat that is gained in pregnancy is shed if a woman breast-feeds. During breast-feeding a hormone called oxytocin is released and this encourages the uterus to return to its normal size, as well as stimulating the production of milk (see p.106). Your pelvis returns to normal more quickly and so does your waistline. Contrary to popular belief, breast-feeding does not affect the shape or size of your breasts. Breasts may get bigger, smaller, or sag after pregnancy, but none of these changes is contingent upon breast-feeding; they are due to being pregnant.

☐ Breast cancer is rarer in parts of the world where breast-feeding is traditional. Breast-feeding may provide some pro-tection against the disease.

Breast-feeding and contraception

Because the hormone which activates milk production also suppresses ovulation, it is unlikely that you will conceive while breast-feeding. However, you should *never* rely on this as a means of contraception. See your doctor for advice.

Milk supply and demand feeding

All mothers are anatomically equipped to feed their babies and there is no such thing as mother's milk which does not suit a baby: the milk the breasts produce is the baby's natural food and she will not reject it. Nor is there such a thing as a mother physically incapable of feeding her baby:

the size of your breasts bears no relation to the amount of milk that you can produce. Milk is produced in deeply buried glands, not in the fatty tissue of the breasts, so don't worry if your breasts are rather small: they *are* adequate. The actual amount of milk that you produce is dependent on how much your baby takes, hence the expression supply and demand. For example, if your baby's appetite is not very great then your breasts will not produce very much milk because they're not being stimulated by your baby to do so. If, however, your baby is an eager feeder, your breasts will respond and produce more. The amount of milk available for your baby will fluctuate throughout the whole time that you breast-feed, according to how much your baby takes. Even if your baby is hungry half an hour after being fed, don't worry. Your breasts will have produced some milk for your baby to feed on, and they'll soon build up a supply for her new needs. When the need for more feeds slows down the breasts will correspondingly produce less.

A newborn baby requires between 60 and 100 ml of milk per 500 g of body weight, so a 3500 g baby will need between 400 and 650 ml per day. Your breasts can manufacture 40 to 60 ml of milk in three hours, in each breast, so your daily output of 700–1000 ml is ample and will continue to be throughout nursing.

Preparing to breast-feed

You should make the decision whether or not to breast-feed your baby well before delivery so that you can prepare and plan for it. At one time women were advised to harden their nipples by, among other things, rolling them between their fingertips or even scrubbing them with a nail brush. Hardening up is no longer considered essential. The only time you have to take special action is if you have an inverted nipple. In such cases the nipple is completely flat so the baby has nothing to latch on to. This condition is quite rare but if you do have an inverted nipple you will be encouraged to wear breast shells to make the nipple protrude more. Most women, no matter how small their nipples, are perfectly able to feed their babies.

If you are having your baby in hospital, tell the nursing staff as soon as you are admitted that you intend to breast-feed. Be very firm about asking for help from them. Don't be intimidated by busy nurses who seem to have no time for you. Demand to see the staff nurse or sister if necessary. Ask her to sit with you for an entire feed, and to give a running commentary of what you should and shouldn't be doing. The best way to learn is to have someone who knows a lot about breast-feeding watching and encouraging you. With the restricted family size that we tend to have now very few girls see anybody breast-feed.

The first contact

It is good for both you and your baby to try suckling as soon as the baby is born. If you are in hospital you can ask for the baby to be put to your breast in the delivery room and there are two important reasons for doing so: suckling naturally stimulates the production of oxytocin, a hormone which, among other things (see p.105), makes the uterus contract and expel the placenta soon after birth. Suckling also helps to form a very strong bond between mother and baby immediately after birth. Incidentally, you needn't worry about your baby choking. The natural reflex to suck is very strong, and she is able to swallow at birth.

Colostrum

During the seventy-two hours after delivery the breasts don't produce milk. Instead they manufacture a thin, yellow fluid called colostrum. This is made up of water, protein and minerals and it takes care of all your baby's nutritional needs during the first days of life before the milk comes in. Colostrum also contains invaluable antibodies which protect the baby against diseases like polio and influenza, and intestinal and respiratory infections. It has an additional laxative effect which stimulates the excretion of meconium (see p. 26). Your baby should be put regularly to the breast in the first days, both to feed on the colostrum and to get used to fixing on the breast (see p.109). If you're in a hospital where they have "rooming in" (where the baby is left with the mother all the time), and where they actually encourage demand feeding (see p.105), so much the better. Every time your baby cries you can put her to the breast but for only a couple of minutes each side at first so that the nipples don't get sore. If your baby is automatically put into the hospital nursery tell the staff that you want your baby brought to you for feeding and that she's not to be bottle-fed.

The let-down reflex

When your baby suckles at the breast the pituitary gland in the brain is stimulated to release two hormones: prolactin and oxytocin. Prolactin activates the actual manufacture of milk in the milk glands; oxytocin is responsible for the milk being passed from the milk glands to the milk reservoirs behind the areola. This process happens within seconds and is known as the let-down or draught reflex. You may feel this reflex very powerfully: in fact, the very sight or sound of your baby may trigger it off, and milk may actually shoot out of your nipples in anticipation of feeding.

How to hold the baby

Cradle your baby in your arm, with her head in the crook of your elbow, and her back and bottom supported by your hand. Never bend or strain forward to lower the nipple into your baby's mouth. If she's too far away from the nipple when held in your arm try laying your baby on a pillow on your lap, still supporting the head in the crook of your arm. Alternatively, cross your legs and use your knee as a prop for the arm that's holding the baby. Leave your baby's arm free to touch your breast – she'll enjoy the sensation of your warmth and closeness.

The rooting reflex

The first few times you put your baby to the breast she may need some encouragement and help to actually find the nipple. Cradle your baby in your arms and gently stroke the cheek nearest the breast. This will elicit the rooting reflex. Your baby will immediately turn towards your breast, mouth open and ready. If you put your nipple in now she will happily clamp both lips around the areola and settle down to suckle. Many babies lick the nipple before they take it into their mouths and it sometimes helps to express some colostrum as an added incentive.

Gently stroke the cheek nearest to you, so that your baby turns to your breast.

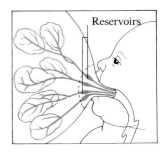

She will turn to your touch, open-mouthed, searching for your nipple.

Cradled in your arm, mouth surrounding the areola, your baby settles down to suckle. As you can see, above, your baby squeezes down on the reservoirs while at the same time sucking so that the nipple elongates and milk comes out.

After a few days your baby will need no artificial stimulation and will happily turn and latch on to the breast as soon as she is picked up and held close to your body.

Never try to guide your baby's head to the nipple by holding both her cheeks between your fingers, or by squeezing the mouth open. The baby will become very confused by the conflicting stimuli of both cheeks being touched and will turn from side-to-side in a desperate bid to find the nipple.

Putting the baby to the breast

Each time you put your baby to the breast (also called "fixing") try to get your nipple well inside the baby's mouth. This is important for two reasons. Firstly, unless she takes a good proportion of the areola into the mouth the milk will not be successfully sucked from your breast. Your baby extracts milk from the breast in a kind of chomping, sucking motion: the baby's mouth forms a seal around the areola, and as she sucks, the tongue pushes the nipple up against the roof of the mouth. The milk is then drawn out in a rhythmic combination of sucking and squeezing. It can only be successful if the baby can exert pressure on the milk ducts behind the areola. Secondly, if you position the nipple well into the baby's mouth, you minimize the chances of developing sore or cracked nipples (see p.119). Your baby has a very strong sucking action and if only the nipple is in her mouth she will effectively shut off the openings of the milk ducts and little milk will get out. Your nipples will become extremely sore and your milk supply will eventually be reduced because the milk is not being drawn off (see p.105). The baby will quite naturally become frustrated and bad-tempered with hunger.

Bonding

Once your baby is happily sucking at your breast, settle down and *look* at your baby. If the baby's eyes are open make eye contact. Smile, talk and chat softly while she is feeding so that she associates the pleasure of feeding with the sight of your face, the sound of your voice and the smell of your skin.

BREAST-FEEDING TIPS

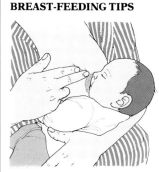

● You may find that because your let-down reflex is too efficient your milk pours out too quickly and chokes the baby as soon as she sucks. You can slow the flow down by expressing a little milk first, see p.114. If you have a lot of milk you can reduce the flow by applying pressure above and below the areola.

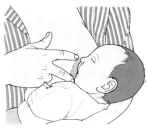

● Your baby must be free to breathe while she feeds. If you have very large or full breasts, or if there is any risk of smothering the baby, gently pull your breast back from the baby's face, just above the areola.

● If your milk is gushing out of the breast that you're not feeding from, press the heel or palm of your hand over the areola. This should stop it.

How long on each breast

Your baby's sucking will be strongest in the first five minutes when she will take eighty per cent of the feed. As a general rule, keep your baby on the breast for as long as she shows interest in sucking, but not usually longer than ten minutes or so on each breast. Your breast will probably have emptied by this time, and your baby may just be enjoying the sensation of sucking. You'll find that your baby will lose interest in her own individual way: it may be that she starts to play with your breast, slipping her mouth on and off the nipple; she may turn away; she may fall asleep. When she appears to have had enough of one breast gently take the baby off your nipple (see right) and put her on to the other breast. If your baby does fall asleep after feeding from both breasts she's probably had enough: you'll soon learn whether this is the case or whether she's going to wake, hungry again, after ten minutes, or so. Similarly, if your baby appears to have taken all she wants from just one breast, don't worry. You can start the next feed off on the breast she didn't drink from.

Removing the baby from the breast

Never pull your baby off the breast – you'll only hurt your nipple. To get the baby off loosen her mouth by pressing gently but firmly on her chin. Alternatively, slip your finger down between the areola and your baby's cheek and put your little finger into the corner of the baby's mouth. Both these techniques will make her mouth open, breaking the suction, and your breast will slip out easily instead of being dragged off. In the first few days this is very important because the nipple is rather soft and needs a chance to harden.

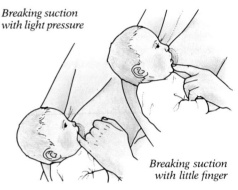

Breaking suction with light pressure

Breaking suction with little finger

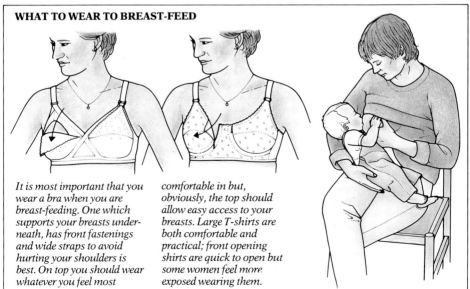

WHAT TO WEAR TO BREAST-FEED

It is most important that you wear a bra when you are breast-feeding. One which supports your breasts underneath, has front fastenings and wide straps to avoid hurting your shoulders is best. On top you should wear whatever you feel most *comfortable in but, obviously, the top should allow easy access to your breasts. Large T-shirts are both comfortable and practical; front opening shirts are quick to open but some women feel more exposed wearing them.*

Breast-feeding positions

You can feed your baby in whatever position you choose, as long as your baby can fix on to the nipple and as long as you are comfortable and relaxed. Some of the most popular methods are shown right. Experiment with them and use whichever feels most natural. Do try to change positions throughout the day – this will ensure that your baby doesn't only exert pressure on one part of the areola, and minimizes the risk of a blocked milk duct.

If you are going to sit down and feed your baby, make sure that you are in a comfortable position, with your arms and back supported with cushions or pillows if necessary.

It's also quite nice to lie in bed to feed your baby, especially in the first few weeks and at night, and there's no reason why you shouldn't do this. Lie on your side, propped with pillows if that's more comfortable, and gently cradle the baby's head and body alongside you. You may need to lay a small baby on a pillow so that she's at the right height for your nipple, but a larger baby should be able to lie on the bed next to you. Make sure that the muscles under your arm aren't strained or taut as this will slow down the flow of milk. An alternative method is to lay your baby on a pillow under your arm, with her feet tucked behind you. Your hand can support your baby's head as she faces your breast.

The position you choose initially may be affected by the delivery you have. For example, if you've had an episiotomy you'll probably find it extremely uncomfortable sitting down, so any position feeding on your side will be more suitable. Similarly, if you've had a Caesarian section your stomach may be too tender for your baby to lie on so try the position with your baby's feet tucked under your arm. Alternatively, use the position with your baby lying on the bed alongside you.

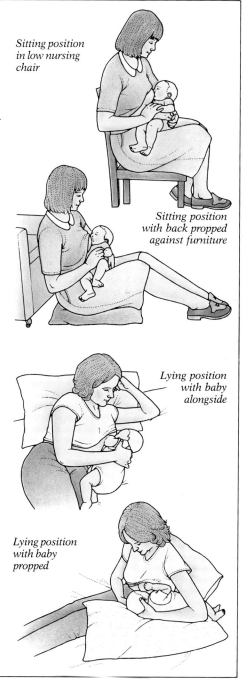

Sitting position in low nursing chair

Sitting position with back propped against furniture

Lying position with baby alongside

Lying position with baby propped

111

Ensuring a good milk supply

☐ Rest as much as you can, particularly during the first weeks. This really is a situation where you should sit rather than stand, and lie rather than sit.

☐ Your milk flow will be affected if you are tense so go through your ante-natal relaxation routines and make sure that you have a period to yourself every day when you can lie down.

☐ Go to bed as early as you can. You will be quite tired anyway and your sleep patterns will probably be broken by your baby.

☐ As far as the house is concerned, let the housework go. Don't do anything but the most urgent things.

☐ Whenever you can, give yourself a few treats; have a glass of wine to relax with at the end of the day.

☐ Make sure that your diet is well-balanced and fairly rich in protein. Don't eat a lot of highly refined and processed carbohydrates (cakes, biscuits, sweets, chocolates, etc.).

☐ You may need some iron supplements and possibly some vitamin supplements, so ask your doctor about this.

☐ You should drink about three litres of fluid every day that you are breast-feeding; some women find that they even need a drink by them while they are actually feeding.

☐ Most of your milk is produced in the morning when you are rested so if you consistently rush about or become tense during the day you'll find by evening that your supply is poor.

☐ If your baby doesn't take all the milk available in the early feeds of the day express the remainder off. This will ensure that the supply is topped up throughout the day.

☐ Get help and support from everyone around you who is positive and optimistic. Use your midwife and health visitor; speak to friends who have had babies and get reassuring advice from them.

☐ If you are unable to give your baby a feed because you're away or because you're ill, express the milk off to keep the supply going.

☐ Avoid using the contraceptive pill for the first five months after delivery as it decreases the supply of milk. Discuss the alternative methods with your doctor.

Frequency of feeds

Babies need frequent feeding because of their body size. Breast-fed babies may need more feeds than bottle-fed babies because they absorb their milk more quickly.

Babies should be fed on demand (see p. 105), and parents will quickly learn to recognize the cries that mean their baby is hungry (see p. 179). Newborn babies may need to be fed every two hours, having as many as eight to ten feeds a day. By about one month, babies are usually taking food every three hours, and at two to three months approximately every four hours. However, every baby is different because each has its own needs and appetites.

Most babies sleep through the night after their late evening feed by the time they are three months old, but you shouldn't even consider dropping the night feed unless your baby indicates willingness by sleeping through.

FREQUENCY OF FEEDS   ✳ = feed

	12	2 AM	4	6	8	10	12	2 PM	4	6	8	10	12
2-week-old baby		✳		✳	✳		✳	✳	✳	✳	✳	✳	✳
2-month-old baby		✳			✳	✳		✳		✳		✳	
	12	2 AM	4	6	8	10	12	2 PM	4	6	8	10	12

Supplementary bottles

We have all heard tales about women not having enough milk to feed their babies and, even though the fear may be only subconscious, when problems arise during early feeding a woman may use this as an excuse to justify giving up on breast-feeding. Please don't succumb to this pressure; resist it even when a midwife may mention it to you, and certainly when friends and relatives do.

Every woman comes equipped with the means and capacity to feed her baby. Breasts respond to the demand for milk by producing it, so if your baby is not taking off all your milk in the initial stages you should try to express the rest so that the demand for milk from your breasts is kept up. Most breasts respond to this approach with a good flow of milk.

As your child gets older and perhaps has bouts of crying, someone will nudge you and say the baby is hungry. You may have just fed your baby, in which case she may be simply thirsty. This occurs, of course, as soon as you start mixed feeding because food needs liquid to dilute it and to be digested. So initially you can try your baby with 15 ml of plain, boiled water to quench her thirst.

Every new mother is worried about how well she can feed her baby and may feel a pressure to go onto supplementary bottles. The attraction of the bottle to an anxious mother is that she can see instantly how much milk the baby has taken – an assurance not available when breastfeeding. But try to be logical and rational about it, and above all have confidence in your ability to feed your baby. Remember that a baby takes ninety per cent of the feed in the first two to three minutes on each breast. So although the baby may become rather bored with being on the breast, if she has been sucking for five minutes, she has almost certainly had enough.

However, even although you are committed to demand feeding there are occasions when you may have to give supplementary bottles; for example, if you

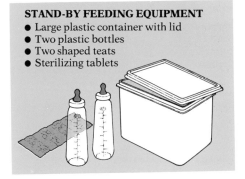

STAND-BY FEEDING EQUIPMENT
● Large plastic container with lid
● Two plastic bottles
● Two shaped teats
● Sterilizing tablets

have a very sore nipple or a blocked duct (see p.119). If this does occur, feed your baby from the unaffected breast first to satisfy some of the hunger and then give the bottle. You will also have to give supplementary bottles if there is any risk of the baby being underfed (see p.117), but if you are demand feeding this is unlikely.

Whenever you have to give a bottle make sure that you sterilize all the equipment and make up the formula according to the instructions given on page 120. The amount of formula you should use will be specified on the container, according to your baby's weight.

There are certain disadvantages related to supplementary bottles. Babies used to the nipple tend to dislike plastic teats. Unfortunately, if she rejects the bottle you won't know if your baby just dislikes the teat, or if she's not hungry. However, if you persist, she'll eventually get used to the bottle, especially if she's hungry, but by this time you may well find that she doesn't want to go back to the breast. If you're worried about this, try giving the milk from a sterilized spoon.

Relief bottles

These are bottles of your own expressed milk which can be given to your baby when you are ill, extremely tired, or are leaving the baby with someone else. Expressed milk can be frozen and kept for up to six months (see p.114).
Milk can be expressed by hand or with a breast pump (see p.114).

Expressing milk

There is no need to feel tied down with breast-feeding as you can express milk from your breasts and keep it either in sterile containers in the refrigerator or in the freezer. This will enable your partner or child-minder to feed your baby in your absence, but with the bonus of it being your milk.

You can express milk from your breasts with your hands or with a breast pump. Most women find hand expression easier and more convenient than using a pump. Before you start, get a bowl, a funnel and a container that can be sealed, and sterilize all of them, either in a sterilizing solution or with boiling water. Hand expressing is nearly always a bit difficult in the first six weeks as the breasts have not reached full production, but do persevere. The best time to express milk is in the morning, when you'll have the most milk, although when your baby drops the night feed you may find the evening the best time. You will be able to take off 30–60 ml without too much trouble then. If your baby is premature you'll need to express your milk at least four times a day to maintain your milk supply.

EXPRESSING TIPS
● Expressing can be quite back-breaking if you have to lean over a low surface. If you haven't got a high enough table or work surface try putting the container on a pile of books.
● Expressing milk should never hurt. If it does you're not doing it correctly; stop immediately.
● Every piece of equipment and all containers should be sterile; your hands must be clean.
● If you're worried about your baby not going back to breast-feeding having got used to the bottle, try giving the expressed milk from a cup, with a spoon. They should both be sterilized before use.
● Milk must be stored correctly otherwise it will go off just like bottled cow's milk. If you feed your baby such milk she'll become ill. As soon as you've collected your milk put it straight into the refrigerator until it is needed; it will keep for 48 hours. You can also freeze the milk for up to six months; the expressed milk should be put into sterile plastic containers which can be sealed. Don't use glass – it might crack.

EXPRESSING BY HAND

1 Wash your hands. Cup your breast in both hands with the fingers underneath and the thumbs above.

2 Squeeze the outer part of your breast between your fingers and thumbs, gently and firmly. Repeat this ten times, moving around the breast as you do so.

3 Repeat the squeezing movement ten times between the outer part of your breast and the nipple area. This stimulates the flow of milk down the ducts to the milk reservoirs in the

EXPRESSING BY PUMP

Bulb pump

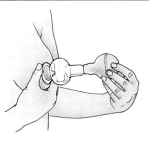

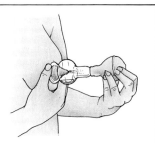

1 *Place the opening firmly over your nipple to form an airtight seal.*

2 *Squeeze the bulb rhythmically until the milk comes out to fill the reservoir. Empty the bulb when the reservoir fills and start again.*

Syringe pump

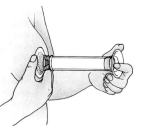

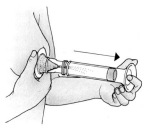

1 *Assemble the cylinders according to the instructions and place the opening firmly over the nipple to form an airtight seal.*

2 *Hold the end against your breast and gently pull the cylinder away from you with a downward movement.*

4 *While holding your breast in one hand, place the tips of your thumb and forefinger of your other hand on either side of the areola.*

5 *Press your thumb and fingers **back** into your ribs then squeeze them together gently and rhythmically. If milk doesn't flow immediately keep on trying*

6 *Move your hand around the areola, so that all parts are compressed, and keep going for five minutes or so. Repeat on the second breast, then go back to the first breast and repeat the whole procedure.*

115

POSSIBLE PROBLEMS   0–1

All will probably go without a hitch from the beginning but you should be prepared to be a bit clumsy for the first few times, for your baby not to suck very vigorously or for very long during the first twenty-four to thirty-six hours, and for your breasts to be a bit sore.

Refusing the breast

One of the most common reasons for a baby having problems taking the breast is that she has difficulty breathing. Your baby can't breathe through her nose and swallow at the same time, so make sure that your breast is not covering her nostrils (see p.109). Another reason your baby may not be able to breathe properly is because she has a snuffly or blocked nose. Your doctor can prescribe nose drops which should be used to clear the nostrils before every feed.

Your baby may be reluctant to take the breast if there has been a delay in starting to breast-feed after birth. For both you and your baby, the sooner you start the better. Babies learn to take the breast quickly in the first forty-eight hours but find it increasingly difficult the longer it is left. This does not mean, however, that your baby will never take to the breast. It just means that you will have to be patient and persevering. If, for example, your baby is premature, you could ask that she be given your expressed milk (so that your supplies of milk continue), and when you get home introduce the breast.

Another reason for your baby refusing to take the breast may be that she's fretful. If she's woken up, keen to feed, only to find that she's either ignored, fussed over, or changed, you may well find that she's too distressed to take your breast. If this happens you'll have to hold your baby firmly and talk soothingly and not even try to give the feed until she's calmed down.

"Sucky" babies

For many babies, sucking on their mother's breast is the most pleasant experience of the day. You'll soon learn to distinguish between sucking for food and sucking for comfort. During a feed you may see and feel your baby making strong, rhythmic sucking movements but if you look closely, you'll see that she isn't swallowing. There's no reason, however, why your baby shouldn't suck as long as she wants, as long as you are happy, and as long as your nipples aren't sore.

Sleeping through feeds

During the first few days your baby may not be all that interested in feeding. Don't be put off. Still try suckling your baby for about five minutes on each breast, at each feed. If your baby goes to sleep at the breast don't worry; it is a very good sign that your baby is contented and doing well. (This is not the case, however, with premature babies who sleep a lot and need to be awakened and fed frequently.)

Don't stick to a rigid routine. If your baby sleeps through a feed, leave it for half an hour and then wake her up gently and try the breast. If she wants to go on sleeping, let her do so: just give the feed when she wakes. If she is hungry she will perk up when food is offered.

Startled babies

Most babies are easily startled by any sudden, loud noise or violent movements in their first few weeks. When you pick your baby up for a feed, hold her firmly and talk soothingly all the time. Lower your head towards your baby so that your face and eyes are all that she sees. Make sure that there are no disturbing noises around you and, if possible, pick your baby up before she starts to cry.

If your breast is engorged (a) as opposed to just being full (b), your baby won't be able to latch on successfully so gently express some milk before feeding.

a   b

Biting

This is a natural impulse and your baby may well bite you even before her teeth have come in. When it happens you will automatically jerk back and may even let out a cry. Your baby will be startled by this and if you say "NO", quite firmly but without shouting, she will soon learn not to do it – even at a very early age.

If you become ill

As long as you feel like breast-feeding you should continue to do so – even if you have to be hospitalized. You may have to make special arrangements with the nursing staff, but if this is what you want you should argue firmly for it, and not be dissuaded. However, if you have to have an anaesthetic you will not be able to breast-feed – not only will you be too groggy afterwards, but the drugs you will have been given will have passed into your milk. So if you have an advance warning of an operation, try to express and freeze your milk. This way the baby will not miss your milk, even if she misses the pleasure of feeding from you.

If you are just confined to bed with a bad cold or 'flu, you can still express your milk so that your partner can feed the baby when you feel too weak or tired. If, however, you are too ill even to express your milk your baby will have to be given formula milk by bottle or by spoon. She'll probably protest at first but will acquiesce as she becomes hungier.

Anxiousness on your part

If you meet a minor obstacle such as your baby refusing to have a feed, try not to get worked up about it. Nervousness may lead to more difficulties which will make you more discouraged and may even put you permanently off breast-feeding. Nervousness may also affect your milk. As far as your baby's health is concerned, even a few days of colostrum and breast milk give a good start to life and are better than none at all. You should never get worried about your baby going without food because you can always fall back on

bottle-feeding. Don't let small problems lead you to hasty decisions. You may be feeling quite tearful and easily upset during the first week or so after delivery anyway, and it would be wrong to give up breast-feeding when you are in this rather unsettled state. Try and persevere and ask your midwife or health visitor for advice and suggestions.

If you are worried about breast-feeding, make it as easy on yourself as you can. If you are embarrassed about it, make sure that you are not in a public place when feeding time comes around. Don't invite visitors to the house at feeding time, unless you are prepared to feed your baby in front of them if she wants food in a hurry.

Overfeeding

You cannot overfeed a breast-fed baby. She regulates how much she wants (see p.105), so unless you give something other than breast milk (like badly made-up supplementary bottles), her weight will be correct.

Underfeeding

Although it is highly unlikely, it is possible to underfeed a breast-fed baby. The first sign of this will probably be your baby wanting to continue sucking even although she's finished feeding from both breasts. The difficulty for you is that this doesn't always signify hunger; it could mean that your child is thirsty or simply likes sucking. After a feed try giving about 30 ml of cooled, boiled water (off a sterilized spoon) in case she is thirsty. If she's still fretful or seems to cry a lot, go to your clinic to have the baby weighed. If she has not gained weight as quickly as expected you'll know that you've not been producing enough milk. This can happen if you start doing too much and get tired and run down. It's possible to build up your milk supply (see p.112), but it will probably take a couple of weeks to get full milk production, and you may have to give supplementary bottles (see p.113) meanwhile. If you are at all worried you should contact your doctor.

CARE OF THE BREASTS 0-1

Take good care of your breasts: they are going to be working quite hard for the next few months. The first step is to buy yourself a couple of the best maternity bras that you can afford. Ask the assistant to measure you and make sure that the bra gives you good support both below your breasts and on your shoulders. The drop-front kind (see p. 110), is very good because it makes feeding quick, convenient and hygienic and your breasts are never left to sag. Towards the end of the first week when lactation becomes well established, your breasts may become full, sore, tender to the touch and quite hard because there is so much milk. A good bra will minimize discomfort; so will expressing (see p. 114).

Pay attention to the daily hygiene of your breasts and nipples. You should cleanse them every day with water or baby lotion. Don't use soap because it is drying

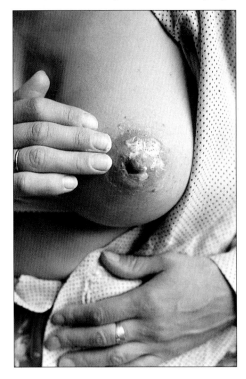

to the skin and can aggravate a sore or cracked nipple. Always handle your breasts carefully: pat them dry gently after both feeding and washing. Leave your nipples open to the air whenever you can: still wear your bra for support, but leave the front flaps down. Use a proprietary spray or cream on your nipples if you find that it helps you.

Once the milk really starts to flow it may leak out quite a lot during the day. Put breast pads or clean handkerchiefs inside your bra to soak up the leaking milk. Change the pad frequently for cleanliness.

While there are no muscles in the breasts themselves, exercise can help keep them in good shape. By shortening the connecting fibres that attach your breasts to your chest muscles, you draw them up and maintain their firmness. The following "top-lift" exercise is most beneficial once you've weaned your baby, but you can use it, too, once breast-feeding is well established. You can do the exercise either sitting or standing. Raise your arms to shoulder level; grasp the left forearm with your right hand and *vice versa*, and simultaneously, press and push with each hand towards the elbow with a jerky movement. Repeat for as long as feels comfortable. Do the exercise as often as you feel like it but for a minimum of six weeks for the best results.

If you can, avoid all drugs when breast-feeding; many medications pass into the breast milk and can affect your baby. If you are already taking medications, or if you consult your doctor for any new problem, make certain he or she knows that you are breast-feeding. Even if you must take drugs, there may be more appropriate ones that can be prescribed. If you want to use oral contraceptives, ask for something other than the combined oestrogen-progestogen pill. If the pills reduce your milk supply when you first take them, feed more frequently until the supply is as desired.

Sore nipples

The new stimulation of your nipples by your baby may make your nipples sore, especially if you are very fair-skinned. However, if you always make sure that the baby has the nipple and areola well into her mouth, if you always take the baby off gently, and if you try to keep your nipples as dry as possible between feeds, you will minimize the possibility of any problems.

If you do notice that a nipple is becoming sore give that breast a rest from feeding for twenty-four hours or until the soreness has gone, and avoid comfort sucks. Feed your baby from the other breast and express milk from the affected one. Smear a recommended cream on to the sore nipple two or three times a day to prevent the nipple from becoming cracked. You could also try using a nipple shield when you feed your baby. Made of soft rubber, it fits over your nipple but allows the baby to suck through a small teat on the front. It should be left in sterilant before use.

If you suddenly experience a sharp pain darting through your nipple as you put your baby to the breast you probably have a cracked nipple. This arises if a sore nipple is not dealt with properly.

BREAST PROBLEMS

	Description	Prevention	Cure
Cracked nipples	Shooting pain when the baby suckles.	Feed little and often in the first days. Keep the nipples dry by using disposable breast pads or clean hankies.	Don't feed from the affected breast until the crack heals. Express the milk by hand (not by pump), and feed the baby by bottle or by spoon.
Engorgement	Extremely full and painful breasts with a swollen areola.	Feed your baby frequently and try to encourage her to empty your breasts regularly.	Have a hot bath and gently express some milk, or encourage it to flow by massaging towards the nipple.
Blocked duct	A hard red patch on the outside of the breast where the duct lies. This can often occur as a result of engorgement, or when your bra or clothes are too tight.	As for engorgement. Wear a properly fitting bra and feed the baby in different positions throughout the day.	Frequent feeding, offering the breast with the blocked duct first so that it is properly emptied. Express the breast if necessary.
Mastitis	Acute infection of the milk ducts resulting in a pus-filled lump.	As for a blocked duct.	Antibiotics prescribed by your doctor. If this fails it will have to be drained surgically. You can, however, continue to feed, even if you need an operation.
Breast abscesses	This infection, which results from an untreated blocked duct, often makes you feel feverish, as if you're going down with 'flu; you may have a shiny red patch on your breast.	As for a blocked duct.	As for a blocked duct, although you will probably be prescribed antibiotics by your doctor. Unless instructed otherwise, you can continue to feed your baby from the affected breast.

BOTTLE-FEEDING 0–1

Once you make the decision to bottle-feed, stick to it and don't feel guilty about it. The majority of babies are bottle-fed, including those who started out on the breast. All of them thrive. Your baby will be just as happy and will do just as well on infant formula (powdered cow's milk). Just make sure that your child has the same attention and closeness at feeding times as she would have if you were breast-feeding.

Mother's milk is important to your baby, but it is not as important as your love. Fill the hours you spend with your baby, particularly feeding times, with your love, affection and care. These are just as important to your baby's physical and emotional well-being as your milk.

Most women feel pressure to breast-feed their babies, and worry quite a lot if they decide not to, but there are some good reasons for deciding that breast-feeding is not for you. Despite your best efforts you may simply not be successful at it. In that case, the best thing is to forget about it and concentrate on giving your baby a good bottle-fed diet: she will do just as well. Other women find it emotionally or psychologically difficult, some feel that they may be too tied down by a breast-feeding routine and that it will curtail many of their activities, including return to work. Some couples are opposed to breast-feeding because it excludes the father. (If you decide not to breast-feed you will probably need to have your milk suppressed by hormones).

One of the good things about bottle-feeding is that the new father can be just as involved as a new mother at feeding times. Make sure that your partner feeds the baby very soon after you get home from the hospital, so that he gets used to the technique and isn't afraid to handle the baby. The sooner he learns to do all the things that your baby needs the better. If possible your partner should share the feeding equally with you. If not, he should give at least two out of the six feeds a day.

Choosing the bottles

You should choose unbreakable bottles which have a wide neck so that they're easy to fill and to clean; the 250 ml size is most suitable. The teat should ideally be one shaped to fit the baby's mouth. Disposable bottles are useful for travelling, and for when you accidentally run out of sterilized bottles.

Sterilizing the bottles

Buy your feeding equipment well in advance of having your baby so that you can practise with it before you go into hospital. Major department stores and chemists sell bottle-feeding packs which contain all the essential equipment.

Keep your sterilizing equipment in the kitchen, preferably near the sink. You'll soon develop your own routine of sterilizing and making up bottles but I would suggest that you always sterilize and make up a full batch (see p.121), keeping the bottles in the fridge until they're needed. Once you've given the feed, rinse the bottle in warm water and then put it to one side. When your stock of made-up bottles is down to two, sterilize more bottles. You should continue to sterilize all feeding equipment until your baby is at least 4 months old.

Sterilizing units usually hold only 4–6 bottles. Because your newborn baby will be taking around seven feeds over twenty-four hours you'll have to sterilize and prepare the bottles twice a day – morning and evening – so that you have enough feed ready whenever she wants it. As your baby grows, the number of feeds will decline and you'll be able to make up all the feeds she needs in a single batch.

EQUIPMENT	
● Sterilizing unit	● Bottle brush
● Sterilizing tablets	● Measuring jug
● 6–8 bottles	● Long-handled spoon
● 1 dozen teats	● Salt
	● Knife

Sterilizing the bottles

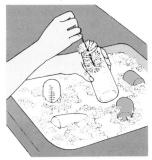

1 *Put all the bottles into warm, soapy water. Use the bottle brush to remove all traces of milk from the bottles.*

2 *Rub the inside of the teats with salt to remove any milk that might have got trapped.*

3 *Rinse the bottles and teats thoroughly in warm water.*

4 *Half-fill the sterilizing unit with cold water. Add a sterilizing tablet and wait for it to dissolve.*

5 *Put the bottles, teats, measuring jug, and spoon into the unit. Fill the bottles with water as you put them in so that they don't bob about. Pour in enough cold water to fill unit.*

6 *Make sure that all the equipment is submerged and leave for the required time. Leave the feeding equipment in the solution until you need it.*

ALTERNATIVE STERILIZING METHODS

● Put all the equipment into a large plastic container, with a lid, and use sterilizing tablets and water as above.
● If available, use the terminal method which sterilizes milk and bottles at the same time. Wash out and rinse the bottles as before. Mix up the formula with cold water, put it into the bottles and screw on the lids loosely, so that steam can get in. Stand them in a large pan with about three inches of water, cover and boil for 20 minutes. Leave to cool down for two hours. Tighten up lids before storing in the fridge.
● Put the equipment into a steam sterilizing unit which quickly and effectively destroys bacteria.

● Boil all the equipment for at least twenty-five minutes in a large, covered pot. This does, however, cause rubber teats to disintegrate rather quickly.
● Put the bottles, jug and knife into the dishwasher on the normal cycle. Boil up the teats separately in a covered pan.

Making up a powder formula

The most commonly used formula for bottle-feeding is powdered cows' milk, which comes in vacuum-sealed tins or cartons. It must be made up strictly in accordance with the proportions of powder to water recommended by the manufacturer or by your health visitor or doctor.

Remove bottles, teats, lids and caps, plus any other equipment to be used in making up the feed, from the sterilizer and drain. Boil water, let cool slightly, then pour the required amount into a jug.

With the plastic measuring scoop provided with the formula, measure out the required amount of powdered milk, levelling off each scoopful with the back of a knife. Do not pack the powder down into the scoop.

Put the required number of scoops of powdered milk into the mixing jug with the boiled and cooled water. Never add any extra milk powder to the formula as it would make the mixture too concentrated and possibly dangerous.

With a sterilized plastic spoon, stir the powdered milk and water mixture thoroughly until all the powder has dissolved in the water, checking to make sure there are no lumps or residue at the bottom of the jug.

Fill the bottles with the made-up formula according to how much has been calculated for each feed. Use a sterilized funnel if necessary.

Put the sterilized teats, upside-down, into the bottles; secure with the screw-on lids and cover the tops of the bottles with the plastic caps provided.

Put the filled bottles into the fridge immediately, placing them on a tray to prevent them falling over. When a feed is due, remove one bottle and heat it for a few minutes in a bowl of hot water.

HYGIENE AND PREPARATION TIPS

● Always wash your hands before sterilizing, preparing and giving feeds.
● Follow all sterilizing instructions to the letter.
● Sterilize every piece of equipment that you use.
● Once you've opened a packet of formula, keep it in the fridge.
● Make up the feed according to the instructions. *Never* add any extra feed.

● Once the formula has been made up, cool it immediately by putting it in the fridge. Never put warm milk into a vacuum flask – it will breed germs.
● Keep all bottles in the fridge until required.
● Give warmed-up milk to a baby immediately.
● Throw away any milk that's left after a feed.

Warming the bottle

When you want a bottle simply bring it out of the fridge half an hour before you need it and allow it to come up to room temperature, with the top still on; there is no need to heat it up.

However, many parents feel that they want their baby to have milk that is as similar to breast milk as possible. If you want to warm your baby's bottle up quickly, run it under the hot tap or stand it in a bowl of hot water for a few minutes. You can heat a bottle up even more quickly by putting it in the microwave for half a minute or by using a bottle warmer. *Never* keep warm milk in a vacuum flask and never leave a bottle standing overnight in a bottle warmer. This will only encourage any germs which are present to multiply. Test the temperature on your wrist before feeding the baby: it should be neither hot nor cold to the touch.

The flow of milk

Milk simply runs out of the breast at the beginning of a feed so there is hardly any need for exertion when your baby is sucking. I feel that bottle-fed babies should find feeding just as easy. To make this possible for them the hole in the teat should be large enough to let drops fall in a steady stream when the bottle is inverted. If it takes a few seconds for a drop to form, then the hole is too small; if the stream is continuous, it is too big.

□ To make a hole bigger you need a fine, red-hot needle. Simply insert it gently through the hole in the teat and the rubber will melt. Have a few spare teats around as it is not as easy as it sounds, and you may end up with half a dozen with holes that

are much too large. I certainly did the first time I tried it.

□ It is worth spending a little time getting the size of the hole just right, because if it is too large your baby will get too much too fast and cough and splutter. If the hole is too small, your baby will get tired from sucking before she has taken a full meal, and she may also swallow too much air.

□ Buy sculpted teats if possible. These are shaped to fit the baby's palate and allow the baby more control over the flow.

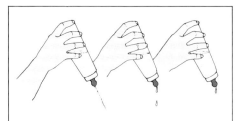

Check the flow of milk by inverting the bottles. The hole is too big if it comes in a steady stream; it is just right when it comes out at several drops per second.

The first feed

There is no artificial equivalent to colostrum. Even if you're not going to continue to breast-feed you will be giving your baby a great head-start if you put her regularly to the breast in the first few days (see p.106). However, if you choose not to do this your baby will be given some sugared water four to eight hours after delivery and then a formula feed after about 48 hours; this will be organized by the medical staff.

Don't worry if your baby doesn't gulp down all that's in the bottle. It's perfectly normal for all babies, breast- or bottle-fed, not to take too much in their first forty-eight hours and they take a while to get into the swing of feeding. Like a breast-fed baby, yours will let you know with a cry when she wants to be fed. Follow your baby's lead and develop the supply and demand system explained on p.105, just as for a breast-fed baby.

Giving a bottle feed

Make sure that you have a quiet, comfortable place to sit and that your arms are well supported with cushions or pillows if necessary (see p.111). Lay the baby in your lap with the head in the crook of your elbow and the back supported along your forearm. Make sure that your baby is not lying horizontally. She should be half-sitting so that breathing and swallowing are both safe and easy and there's no risk of her choking.

Just before you start feeding, test the heat of the milk by letting a couple of drops fall on to the inside of your wrist. The milk should feel neither too hot nor too cold. You should already have tested the flow of milk (see p.124). Loosen the cap of the bottle a very little so that air can enter to take the place of the milk that your baby sucks out. If you don't do this quite a lot of negative pressure can build up inside the bottle which will flatten the teat and make sucking very hard work. Your baby will become bad-tempered and angry and refuse the rest of the feed. If this happens, gently pull the bottle out of your baby's mouth so that the air can get in and then

Always check that the milk's not too hot by letting a few drops fall on to your wrist.

To ensure that the milk comes out and there's no vacuum inside the bottle, loosen the cap slightly before the feed.

Settle down comfortably with your baby and prepare her for the feed by evoking the sucking reflex. Gently stroke the cheek nearest to you and she'll turn to you and the bottle.

125

continue feeding, as before.

To elicit the baby's sucking reflex, so that she takes the bottle, gently stroke the cheek nearest to you. As your baby turns to your touch you can gently insert the teat into her mouth. She should latch on to a fair amount of teat so that the tip is far back into her mouth, like a nipple would be. You should, however, be careful not to push it so far back that she gags on it.

Let your baby set the pace of feeding. She might want to pause mid-feed to look around or play with the bottle and she should be allowed this pleasure. From the very beginning make feeding times as pleasant as possible. Face your baby and make eye contact. Don't sit in silence: talk, sing, chatter, make any kind of sound you like. Just make sure that your voice sounds pleasant, happy and responsive. This is the first conversation that your baby will enjoy, so react to movements, gestures and smiles.

Half-way through the feed, change your baby on to the other arm. This will give your baby a new view to look at and your arm a rest; you may also want to burp your baby at this point (see p.128).

Removing the bottle

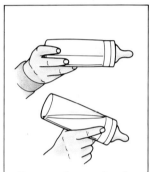

Always make sure that the teat is full of milk by holding the bottle at an angle. Unless you do, the baby will swallow air with the feed.

When the feed is finished, and before she can suck in any air, just pull the teat away gently but firmly and your baby will release the bottle.

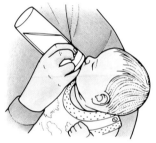

If she doesn't release the bottle, gently slide your little finger into the corner of her mouth to break the suction.

BOTTLE-FEEDING TIPS
● Don't feed your baby lying flat; it is very difficult to swallow in this position and your baby may gag or even be sick.
● Never leave your baby with the bottle propped up on a pillow or cushion. Not only is it very dangerous because your baby could choke, but she could become very uncomfortable if she has to swallow a lot of air along with the feed because of the angle at which the bottle's been propped. Moreover, your baby misses out on the cuddling and affection that she should enjoy while she feeds.
● Don't try to force your baby to finish the bottle after she has stopped sucking: she knows when she's had enough.
● Don't try feeding your baby if her nose is blocked. She can't swallow and breathe at the same time, so ask your doctor for nose drops which can be used before each feed.
● Even if you think the milk formula doesn't suit your baby don't change it without first consulting your midwife or health visitor. It is very rare for a brand of milk to be responsible for a baby not feeding well; very rarely a baby is allergic to cow's milk, and you may then have to use a soya formula, but take medical advice first.

Bottle-feeding patterns

Bottle-fed babies tend to feed less frequently than breast-fed ones. This is because formula milk takes longer to digest; it also contains slightly more protein which therefore provides more calories and delays hunger for longer. After the first two or three days bottle-fed babies usually settle on a four-hourly regime. They will therefore be having six feeds, probably one less than if they were being breast-fed. When your baby is first born she will probably not take much over 60 ml at each feed but as she gets older the feeds will get bigger and the number, per day, will get less.

Let your baby determine when she's to be fed; never, ever, feed your baby according to the clock. Feed her when she tells you with cries that she is hungry, not when you think she should be.

Don't feel that your baby has to finish the bottle at each feed. Like everybody

Approximate age of baby	Mixture for a single feed			Feeds in 24 hours
	Level scoops	Warm water ml	fl oz	
0–14 days	3	85	3	7
2–6 weeks	4	115	4	6
2 months	5	140	5	6
3 months	6	170	6	5
4 months	7	200	7	5
6 months and over	8	225	8	4

else, your baby's appetite will vary, so if she seems satisfied, but there's a little left in the bottle, don't make her take it. She will only get overfull and posset it back (see p.129). What's more, she may become overfed and fat. On the other hand, if your baby seems ravenous, give some extra from another bottle. If she regularly wants more milk start to add the extra amount to every bottle.

POSSIBLE PROBLEMS   0–1

Overfeeding

Fat cells are produced by an infant in response to the amount of fat that is taken in in the food. Once produced these cells can't be removed, so if your baby develops an excessively large number they will still be present when she's an adult. Being fat is not only an embarrassment, it is also a health hazard.

If you overfeed your baby she will become fat; unfortunately, it is easier to overfeed a bottle-fed baby. There are two major reasons for this: firstly, it is tempting to put extra formula into the bottle. You should *always* follow the instructions to the letter (see p. 122), otherwise you'll be giving the baby unseen (and unrequired) calories. Secondly, because you can see the amount of formula she is taking it may be hard to resist encouraging her to finish the last drop. You should always let your baby decide whether she's had enough or not. Other causes of overfeeding include giving sweet, syrupy drinks and introducing solids too early.

Underfeeding

This is rare in bottle-fed babies, but it can happen. Your baby should be fed on demand (see p.105), and not according to the clock. Although most babies will be ready for a feed every four hours by the time that they are 2–3 months old, their individual appetites may vary from day-to-day. Say, for example, your baby's at the age when she can take five 180 ml bottles per day, but at one feed she only takes 115 ml out of the bottle. If you insist on feeding to a schedule, don't give any extra milk in these scheduled bottles and don't allow any of the interim feeds that your baby will be crying for, she will never be able to catch up with the total volume of milk that she needs, and will not gain weight.

You should also be flexible about how much feed you make up. The figures on the packages are given as a general estimate but, for example, if your child consistently drains each bottle you give and also seems fretful and upset, she may well be hungry. Make up an extra 60ml of formula and see if she wants it. If she takes it, without forcing, then she needs it and she won't put on weight.

If you find that your baby is demanding frequent feeds but doesn't take much and remains fretful, check that the teat hole isn't too small. It may well be that she's having a hard time actually sucking the milk out of the bottles and is therefore not getting enough nourishment.

BURPING AND POSSETTING   0–1

Burping

The point of burping is to bring up any wind that has been swallowed during feeding or crying prior to feeding. The point of bringing up wind is to prevent it from causing your baby discomfort. Babies vary a great deal in their reaction to wind, and in my experience the majority of them aren't noticeably happier or more contented for having been burped.

Babies also vary a great deal in the amount of air that they swallow during feeding. Some, including all breast-fed babies, swallow very little. Swallowing air is much more common in bottle-fed babies but even then it doesn't seem to be a problem.

If very small quantities of air are swallowed during feeding they form small bubbles in the stomach which cannot be burped up until they have coalesced into a large bubble, and this can take a great deal of time. Small bubbles in the stomach are very unlikely to give rise to discomfort.

The one point in favour of burping is that it makes *you* pause, relax, take things slowly, hold your baby gently and stroke or pat her in a firm reassuring way. This is very good for your baby and very good for you, too.

My attitude towards burping, therefore, is that by all means do it, even if it is just for your peace of mind, but don't become fanatical about it.

Don't pat or rub your baby too hard as you may jerk your baby and she will bring up some of the feed. A gentle upward stroking movement is usually preferable to firm pats.

Most authorities advise that you stop the feeding half way through to burp the baby. I don't think there is any need to do that. Wait until your baby pauses naturally in the feed and take advantage of this little rest to try burping. As your baby gets older you will probably find that she finishes the whole bottle quite comfortably without needing to burp.

BURPING POSITIONS

Hold your baby upright on your shoulder with a bib or a nappy draped over your shoulder and underneath the baby's chin to catch any dribble. Gently rub or pat the baby's back between the shoulder blades.

Sit your baby up on your knee with the chin supported between your finger and thumb; pat or rub her back.

Lay your baby on your lap, face downwards with the head turned to one side, and gently pat or rub her back.

Possetting

Some babies never posset at all. Others do so with surprising ease, and this can be quite a cause of concern to parents. My youngest son was a child who had a tendency to posset. If he took a little too much feed he would always bring back the last few mouthfuls. If he cried for longer than a few seconds the exertion made him cough and then spit up. Whenever he had a cough he invariably brought back his food. I always knew that he wasn't ill because he was perfectly happy and contented. On the other hand, I worried in case he wasn't getting enough to eat. If he possetted any quantity, I simply followed my own instinct which was to offer him more food. If he took more, I assumed that he needed it. If he refused, I assumed that he had possetted an excess which he didn't

require. In very young babies, the commonest cause of possetting is overfeeding. This is another reason why you should never coerce a bottle-fed baby into finishing the feed.

If your bottle-fed baby shows a tendency to posset, check the hole in the teat. If it is too large she may be taking too much, too quickly. If it is too small she may be sucking in a lot of air because she has to suck very hard.

As an observant parent, you should always be able to tell whether spitting up is serious. Forcible vomiting, especially if it occurs after consecutive feeds or goes on for more than a day, should be reported immediately to your doctor. Vomiting in a very small baby can quickly lead to dehydration, and you should have medical advice as soon as possible.

NIGHT FEEDS   0–1

Because you'll respond to all your baby's demands for food you may find that feeding takes up quite a lot of your time – at least thirty minutes per feed, making more than three hours out of every twenty-four. With night feeding on top of all the other things that you have to do to take care of your baby you may get extremely tired and tense. It won't be so much the number of hours sleep that you lose, but more the way in which your sleep patterns are broken over long periods. It is very important that you get adequate rest both day and night, and this means that your partner has to give you a hand, and do a few chores for you. There should be equality of child-nurturing between you and your partner and as you are doing most of the feeding it is only fair that he takes over some of the other jobs for the baby from you. In fact, even if you've decided to breast-feed, the night feeds shouldn't be your entire responsibility. If the baby sleeps in another room, ask your partner to bring her to you as soon as she cries, and get him to take the baby back and change the nappy after she's been fed, as well.

> **TIPS**
> ● Feed your baby in bed so that you are warm and comfortable.
> ● If you're very tired, express enough milk for the night feed and put it into a sterile bottle, and arrange for your partner to give the baby the bottle.
> ● Keep some nappy-changing equipment in your bedroom so you can feed and change the baby with the minimum of disturbance.
> ● It's easy to get cold sitting up in bed so have a sweater or dressing gown nearby.
> ● Have a drink by your bedside in case you get thirsty while feeding.
> ● If the baby's in another room and you're scared of not hearing the cries, invest in a baby alarm.

Reducing night feeds

Until your baby weighs about 5 kg she won't be able to sleep for more than five hours at a time without waking with hunger. However, once this weight is reached you can try stretching the time between feeds with the aim of giving yourself about six hours of undisturbed sleep, and of painlessly getting your baby to drop the early morning feed. Your baby will have her own routine, but as a general rule, it's sensible to try to juggle your baby's last feed so that it's given at around the time that you go to bed. But *do* be flexible; it may be that your baby doesn't want to drop the early morning feed, and no matter how much you try to alter the feeding routine will still wake up and want feeding. If this is the case you'll just have to make the night feeds as straightforward as possible and look forward to when she drops them.

HOW FEEDING FREQUENCY CHANGES

This chart shows the varying times at which four four-week-old babies wanted to feed.

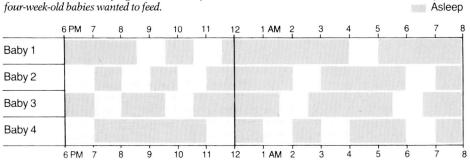

Feed
Asleep

INTRODUCING SOLIDS   4–6m

At some stage during the first year you will have to start to wean your baby off milk and on to solid food. There is quite a lot of pressure on parents to start giving solids before the age of three months, and in the United States many babies are started off as early as six weeks. You should, however, resist *all* such pressure for the following reasons: firstly, breast milk (or its formula equivalent) is the only food that your baby needs in the early months. Secondly, the introduction of solids to too young a baby can lessen the desire to suck. In the case of breast-fed babies this decreases the amount taken from the breasts which respond by producing less milk. Either way, your baby will end up having an unsatisfactory diet for her needs. Thirdly, until your baby is at least three months old the digestive tract is incapable of digesting and absorbing complex foods. If you introduce solids before this time not only will they pass through largely undigested, but you will be putting an increased strain on the baby's immature kidneys.

When to introduce solids
In the early months milk provides all the calories required to make your baby grow: the more she grows, the more milk she'll therefore need to drink. But your baby's stomach can only hold a certain amount of milk at each feed, and she will eventually reach a point when she's drinking to full capacity at each feed, but still won't have enough calories to keep going. This is the point at which you'll have to introduce solids, and you'll recognize the sign when your baby starts to demand more milk and appears very unsatisfied after each feed. She may suddenly start demanding a sixth feed, having been quite content on five for the previous couple of months. In many babies this happens at around four months and it's an ideal time to start solids because it also coincides with a tapering off of your baby's intense desire to suck.

What foods to give
Up until the fourth month your baby will have had a diet of milk. It is therefore only sensible to start with bland, semi-liquid, foods with a smooth, creamy consistency: unsweetened purées of fruit (bananas, dessert apples, ripe pears and peaches) and vegetables (potatoes, carrots and cauliflower), and gluten-free rice cereal are ideal. Although specially-manufactured "first foods" are available, it's better to make up your own. Apart from being cheaper (especially in the small amounts that you'll be using initially), you'll know exactly what is in the food and that it has no additional sugar, salt, or preservatives. Puréed vegetable soups are very quick and easy to make; cook the vegetables in a small amount of water until soft, then purée in a blender or sieve and then thin out with water, milk or yogurt. Of course these can be served hot or cold according to the season. I always use potatoes as the base for a thick soup, but you could use lentils, beans or peas.

Food safety
By the time your baby is ready for weaning you don't have to sterilize all cooking utensils meticulously – but you

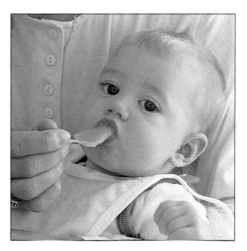

must follow the general principles of good hygiene. Wash your hands before preparing the baby's food and before feeding, make sure that all the utensils are clean and that any made-up food is kept in the refrigerator. Purées of fruit and vegetables will keep safely for two days in the refrigerator; alternatively, they could be frozen in individual portions.

Giving the first solids

Start off by giving your baby one or two teaspoons of food along with a normal milk feed; the one around mid-day is ideal because your baby will be quite alert and not ravenously hungry. Your baby, although ready for the calories that solids provide, will be hungry for what she knows is satisfying – milk – so feed from one breast first, or give half the usual bottle. As she gets more used to solids she may want to be given them before she takes the milk

Having decided which feed to start the solids on, prepare the small amount that you'll need and then settle in your normal position to feed the baby. When you've given half of the milk, sit the baby in an upright position on your lap then, using a small spoon, scoop up some food and place it gently between the baby's lips so that she can suck the food off. Be very careful not to push the spoon in too far or she may gag on the unexpected food on the back of her tongue. She's bound to be messy at first, maybe pushing more food out than she manages to take in. If so, gently scrape the excess off the baby's face and place the spoon on to her lips as before. Your baby will signal that she's had enough by turning away from the spoon with lips shut, maybe even crying. *Never* force your baby to take any more food than she wants. When she's taken the solid food you can give the rest of the milk feed.

TIPS

● Give your baby only one new food at a time and then wait for several days to see if it suits.
● Use dry infant cereals which you have to make up rather than ready-mixed cereals; they contain more iron and are more nutritious.
● Only give cereal once a day.
● If the baby doesn't like taking food from a spoon, try dipping a clean fingertip into the food and let your baby suck it off.
● If you find it awkward to feed the baby on your lap put her in a baby seat on the floor or on a table.
● Keep plenty of kitchen paper nearby to mop up any mess.
● Even early solids can stain clothes, especially banana, so put a small cloth bib on the baby.

SAMPLE WEANING CHART

Stage 1	Around 4 months	Stage 2	Around 4½ months
1st feed		**1st feed**	
Breast or bottle feed, as usual		*Breast or bottle feed, as usual*	
2nd feed		**2nd feed**	
Half breast or bottle feed. Try one or two teaspoons of purée or cereal then give remainder of feed.		*Half breast or bottle feed. Two teaspoons of cereal. Remainder of feed.*	
3rd feed		**3rd feed**	
Breast or bottle feed, as usual		*Half breast or bottle feed. Two teaspoons of vegetable or fruit purée. Remainder of feed.*	
4th feed		**4th feed**	
Breast or bottle feed, as usual		*Breast or bottle feed, as usual*	
5th feed		**5th feed**	
Breast or bottle feed, as usual		*Breast or bottle feed, as usual*	

ESTABLISHING SOLIDS   6m-1

Once your baby happily accepts one or two different solids it's important to introduce a variety of textures and tastes. As the year goes on she'll be able to deal with foods that have only been mashed or chopped and will learn to enjoy chewing and sucking on chunks of food. She'll soon move from the stage of milk feeds with "tastes" of solids to three established solid meals a day with accompanying drinks of water, diluted fruit juice or milk.

The amount of food you give your baby can be gradually increased over the weeks until she takes most of the calories that she requires for growth from solid food and not from milk. As the number of solid meals that she takes increases, the amount of milk needed correspondingly decreases. When your baby is thirsty, give her plain water to diluted fruit juice to drink, rather than milk. It is best to avoid encouraging a taste for sweet drinks, so never give your baby a commercial drink containing sugar and colourings. It's difficult to specify the amount a baby should be eating because every baby has different requirements and appetites. You'll be the best judge of how much your baby wants, but if you have any doubts, make up the food according to the recipes on p.142 and feed as much of each individual portion as your baby wants.

What foods to give

When your baby has got used to taking cereal and fruit or vegetable purées, you can start to introduce other foods – including meat, fish and dairy products – into her diet, until she is eating virtually all the foods that you normally eat. As these gradually replace milk as the main source of her nutritional requirements, you will have to ensure that she has a balanced diet which includes foods from all the main food groups (see p.145).

When first starting on solids, your baby will cope best with foods of a smooth, creamy consistency. After cooking, mash, sieve or purée the food, then thin down with milk, stock or the water that the vegetables were cooked in.

By about 6–7 months of age you can gradually introduce your baby to food of a more lumpy texture. This can be mashed with a fork or finely chopped with a sharp knife. You don't have to wait for your baby's teeth to appear before introducing lumpy food, as she will be able to chew with her gums.

Finger foods will satisfy your baby's desire to feed herself. Start with rusks or other easily held pieces of fruit or vegetables. Never leave your baby alone while she is eating in case she chokes. If she does begin to choke, hold her upside-down by her feet and pat her back until the food is dislodged (see p.332).

Food safety

In the first few months of your baby's life, it is essential that all feeding equipment is sterilized by one of the various methods available (see p.121). By the time she starts eating solids, however, it is no longer necessary to sterilize everything used at feedtimes – though bottles and teats used for milk should still be sterilized as before. For cups, bowls and cutlery, thorough washing in hot, soapy water followed by rinsing with hot water, is adequate. However, as your baby is weaned onto solids and her diet expands to include a wider range of foods, more general questions of food safety become important, especially in the light of recent, much publicized, outbreaks of salmonella and listeria poisoning, as well as other concerns about food safety. As babies – along with old people, pregant women and invalids – are amongst those most vulnerable to the harmful effects of bacteria in food, it is vital to have clear guidelines about the safe preparation, storage and cooking of food for infants, though the advice is equally applicable to the whole family.

Buying food

The rule is to shop often, choosing fresh ingredients wherever possible, and to use it quickly. Avoid bruised or damaged fruit and vegetables, and wash fruit if it is not to be peeled before eating. If buying canned goods, check that there are no dents or signs of leakage on the can, and that seals on jars are unbroken. Check sell-by dates, and avoid cut-price items that have reached their expiry dates.

Storing food

Store food in clean, covered containers in the refrigerator, and use as soon as possible. Don't store cooked and raw foods alongside each other, and take care to put raw meat or fish on a plate so that juices cannot drip down onto food on the shelf below. Don't keep food in the freezer longer than the time recommended by the manufacturer, according to the star rating

of your particular model. Foods that have been frozen must be thoroughly defrosted before cooking, and foods that have been frozen then defrosted must never be refrozen.

Cooking and reheating food

The only safe rule as far as babies' food is concerned is to always cook thoroughly; this is especially true of meat, chicken and eggs. *Never* give raw eggs to babies. Try to avoid giving reheated leftovers to your baby, but if you do, make sure they are thoroughly heated through first. Chilled or frozen food should be heated up once only and any leftovers thrown away. If you're preparing food in advance, don't leave it out to cool before putting it into the refrigerator, as this simply extends the time available for bacteria to multiply; cover and put it straight into the refrigerator or freezer.

Kitchen hygiene

Wash hands with soap and hot water before handling food. Ensure that you and your family wash your hands thoroughly (not at the kitchen sink) after using the toilet and nappy changing, and after playing with pets.

Keep the kitchen scrupulously clean, especially work surfaces, chopping boards and utensils used in food preparation.

Dry dishes with clean tea-towels, or leave to dry in a rack after rinsing with hot water. Wash dish-cloths regularly. Keep waste bins clean and covered and empty them often.

Don't leave any food out without covering it first.

If you are feeding your baby from jars of baby food, it's all right to give it to her straight from the jar if she is going to finish the contents at one meal. Otherwise transfer some to a bowl and leave the remainder in the jar with the lid replaced, and refrigerate until the next meal.

Preparing food for babies

- Blender, liquidizer, food mill or sieve
- Small pan for heating food up
- Steamer or pan with tightly-fitting lid
- Grater

You'll probably already have a liquidizer or food mill; if you haven't, buy a cheap easy-to-use, hand-operated blender. You'll only have to purée food for the initial months of your baby's new diet; thereafter it can be mashed or chopped finely. At the beginning you may find it easier just to sieve the food, especially when you're not making up big batches. If you've frozen portions of food, a small pan is ideal for heating them up quickly.

For thinning down your home-prepared foods simply add water; the water in which you've steamed fruit or vegetables (with no additional salt or sugar), is ideal, but you can also add expressed milk, cow's milk, soup, tomato, orange or apple juice. For thickening, use ground, wholegrain cereals like wheatgerm, cottage cheese, yogurt or mashed potato. If you feel that you need to sweeten foods use naturally sweet fruit juice or dextrose. Never use refined sugar – brown or white. Our bodies don't need it, it's bad for our teeth and it only encourages a sweet tooth which is bad for general health.

PREPARATION TIPS

- Before steaming and puréeing fruit, peel, remove the seeds and any bits which may choke the baby and cut up into fairly small pieces. Do the same for vegetables.
- Give your baby meat, cooked any way you like and then puréed. You need not give red meat more than twice a week. Don't forget fish, chicken and chicken livers which are cheap, quick and easy to prepare. Thin down the meat with vegetable water or soup.
- Always choose the freshest looking vegetables (not wrinkled or dull-looking ones), and cook them as soon as possible.
- Handle fruit and vegetables gently. Don't cut them until you have to and don't crush and bruise them as this destroys any vitamin C present.
- Cook vegetables and fruit in as little water as possible, with a tightly-fitting lid, so that they are cooked by steaming rather than by boiling; this helps to retain the vitamins.
- Cook soft-skinned fruit and vegetables in their skins because this helps to retain the vitamins and it will also give your child fibre. You may have to remove the skin if it's tough and therefore likely to choke the baby.
- Use cast iron cooking pots. A little iron is absorbed into the food and so helps to keep your child's iron supplies topped up.
- Always make the food a suitable consistency for your baby's age. For example, a thick milk for your four-month-old; a thicker cream for your six-month-old and a slightly chunky mash for your nine-month-old.
- Don't use copper pans for green leafy vegetables as copper breaks down vitamin C.
- Don't cook tinned foods for too long – you will destroy the vitamins.
- Don't add salt or sugar to anything you have cooked for a child; the immature kidneys can't handle a heavy salt load and you will be doing your child a favour if you don't encourage a sweet tooth.
- Avoid using too many saturated fats in your cooking – use safflower or corn oil instead.
- Don't prepare vegetables or soak them in water a long time before you cook them or you will destroy the vitamins.
- Don't leave your baby's food to cool down at room temperature. Put it straight into the refrigerator as this will discourage bacteria from growing.

Ready-prepared foods

Whether you make up your baby's foods yourself (see p.136), or buy ready-made foods is up to you. Bought foods are certainly convenient if you are travelling in a hurry, but are more expensive and are not always nutritionally sound. If you are going to use them, especially on a regular basis, follow the guidelines listed below.

SAMPLE LABELS

INGREDIENTS: WATER, BEEF, CARROTS, POTATOES, SWEDES, TOMATOES, MODIFIED CORNFLOUR, PEAS, HYDROLYSED VEGETABLE PROTEIN.

INGREDIENTS: SKIMMED MILK · SUGAR, TAPIOCA · MODIFIED CORNFLOUR COCOA · SUNFLOWER OIL · NATURAL FLAVOURING

INGREDIENTS: WATER, PORK, POTATOES, WHEATFLOUR, HARICOT BEANS, TOMATO PUREE, DRIED ONIONS.

Check the list of ingredients on the tin or jar. They are listed in order of concentration, so never buy anything in which water is listed first.

Make sure that the jar is vacuum sealed when you open it, otherwise it may be contaminated.

If possible, buy meat and vegetables separately and then combine them if you want a "mixed dinner".

Don't keep opened jars in the refrigerator for longer than two days. Throw them away after that.

Don't buy anything which has added salt, sugar, modified starch or monosodium glutamate (MSG).

Don't buy "mixed dinners"; they usually contain a lot of thickener.

Never store food in opened tins; put it into a dish or bowl and keep it covered in the refrigerator.

Don't heat the food up in the jar – it may crack.

It is very unhygienic to feed the baby from the jar then keep the rest for a second meal, as it will have become contaminated with saliva. It's all right to feed your baby from a jar if she's going to eat the lot.

Giving drinks

While you're introducing solids, milk will remain an important part of your baby's diet, and will make up a large part of the daily caloric intake. By the time she's six months old it will be safe for her to have cow's milk, either from a cup or in food. Although the milk doesn't have to be boiled, any containers that it is given in have to be thoroughly cleaned every time the baby's had a drink out of them.

As soon as your baby is having any quantity of solid food she will need water as well as milk to drink. Start her off with 15 ml of water or diluted fruit juice between and after feeds (if you don't want to use a bottle, try giving it from a cup, see p.139). Thereafter she can be given it whenever she's thirsty during the day. Do bear this in mind, especially in summer or in a warm atmosphere. Syrup drinks of blackcurrant or rosehip are traditionally given to babies but they are very high in calories and are also bad for their teeth. Avoid cordials and cola drinks and any that have sugar or saccharin added to them– stick to water or natural, unsweetened fruit juice.

Weaning your baby on to a cup

At around six months you should introduce your baby to drinking from a cup as part of the process of weaning from breast or bottle. The best feeds to use the cup are the lunchtime and late afternoon feeds when she'll probably be keenest to eat solids. Give the solids first and then try the cup.

There is a variety of special cups on the market (see p.39). Beakers with spouts are best at the beginning as they let the liquid drip out and the baby has to half suck and half drink to get anything. Hold the beaker yourself and offer only a few sips of milk at first, but release it as soon as she wants to take it from you. As she gets more dextrous she can use a two-handled cup; the ones with specially slanted lips are ideal because they don't have to be tipped very far before the liquid comes out. Some babies, however, prefer to go straight on to an open cup.

Your baby will gradually wean herself off the breast and by six or seven months will have dropped the morning feed. She'll still want a breast or bottle feed before bedtime until she's at least a year old – more for comfort than for food.

Where to feed your child

Up to six months of age you will probably feed your baby on your lap or in an infant seat, but once the baby's back muscles are strong enough to support her you can consider using a high chair or feeding table (see p.40). Because it is lower on the ground, a feeding table is safer than a high chair, although you do have to bend down to feed the baby until she can do so alone. If it is on wheels it is more convenient for you because you can wheel it around the room to wherever suits you. On the other hand, it does take up more room than a high chair and it may be more expensive.

Initially you may have to prop your baby up with cushions. Many high chairs have harnesses to stop the child slipping or falling out. While they are safety features from this point of view, they could also prevent you from getting to your child quickly if she was choking. Because you should never leave your child alone while she's eating I'd suggest that you leave off the straps and keep a close eye on your baby instead. If she does gag on some food, and she's almost bound to at some stage, pat your child firmly on the back until whatever food is caught dislodges itself. When you give your child a new texture, she may gag out of surprise. Talk soothingly and gently rub the child's back and she'll be able to swallow whatever was worrying her. It is essential that you know how to react quickly in any situation like this. Should the child's choking be severe, and especially if she loses consciousness, you must know how to act accordingly (see p.332).

Feeding your child

Your baby will soon look forward to solids – not only to eat, but to play with. Feeding times will become messier so it's advisable to put newspaper or a plastic sheet below the high chair or table to catch the worst of the mess. Keep your baby well away from expensively covered walls – remember, she can throw food now.

After a month on solids your baby will have grasped the technique of getting food successfully off the spoon, and by the time she's taking two solid meals a day she will be prepared to open her mouth ready to take the food.

139

Self-feeding

Your baby will leave you in no doubt when she wants to feed herself: she will simply take the spoon from you. Let your baby experiment and be prepared to put up with the mess. Encourage all attempts at self-feeding because it is such a huge step forward in your baby's development, both physically and intellectually, and also because it will give your baby a feeling of accomplishment and confidence. It will help your baby to become manually dextrous and to co-ordinate muscles and movements. There is nothing that will speed up the co-ordination of eye and hand faster than getting a spoonful of food to the mouth.

□ Your baby will take several months to become proficient at self-feeding. Food will be a plaything and you may also worry because most of the food seems to be on the floor and not in your baby's stomach. Nature has taken care of this. At a time when a baby starts to self-feed, the initial growth spurt is beginning to slacken off and so she needs less.

□ Until she can manage to get the food successfully into her mouth, have a spoon each. When she can't scoop the food up, swap your full spoon for the empty one.

At six months this baby tries to get the food to his mouth more quickly by trying to grab the spoon, although he can't hold it himself.

By the time the baby's eight months old he's using the spoon himself with reasonable, if messy, success. He can also handle a mug.

Finger foods

If self-feeding with a spoon seems to frustrate your baby, but the appetite is good, try finger foods. Your baby will be able to handle them easily, and even if the food is hard your baby will suck it.

Fruit and vegetables	Grains and cereals	Protein	
Any fresh fruit that is easy to hold, cut into a slice minus the skin or pips, eg bananas Any vegetable that you can make into a stick or shape that is easy to grasp, eg carrots Mashed potato	Small pieces of sugarless dried cereal Little balls of cooked rice Wholemeal bread (without the complete grains) Wholemeal rusks (without the complete grains)	Smooth peanut butter on bread Cubes of soft cheese Macaroni and cheese Fingers of cheese on toast Hamburgers and patties cut into small pieces Scrambled eggs	Cottage cheese Any kind of meat in pieces that are easy to get hold of Chunks of firm fish, taken off the bone Hard boiled eggs in slices

RECIPES FOR ONE- TO THREE-YEAR-OLDS

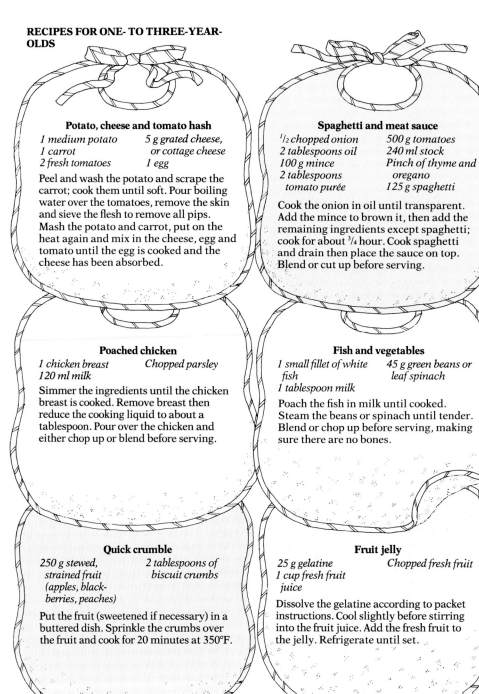

Potato, cheese and tomato hash

1 medium potato
1 carrot
2 fresh tomatoes

5 g grated cheese, or cottage cheese
1 egg

Peel and wash the potato and scrape the carrot; cook them until soft. Pour boiling water over the tomatoes, remove the skin and sieve the flesh to remove all pips. Mash the potato and carrot, put on the heat again and mix in the cheese, egg and tomato until the egg is cooked and the cheese has been absorbed.

Spaghetti and meat sauce

$^1/_2$ chopped onion
2 tablespoons oil
100 g mince
2 tablespoons tomato purée

500 g tomatoes
240 ml stock
Pinch of thyme and oregano
125 g spaghetti

Cook the onion in oil until transparent. Add the mince to brown it, then add the remaining ingredients except spaghetti; cook for about $^3/_4$ hour. Cook spaghetti and drain then place the sauce on top. Blend or cut up before serving.

Poached chicken

1 chicken breast
120 ml milk

Chopped parsley

Simmer the ingredients until the chicken breast is cooked. Remove breast then reduce the cooking liquid to about a tablespoon. Pour over the chicken and either chop up or blend before serving.

Fish and vegetables

1 small fillet of white fish
1 tablespoon milk

45 g green beans or leaf spinach

Poach the fish in milk until cooked. Steam the beans or spinach until tender. Blend or chop up before serving, making sure there are no bones.

Quick crumble

250 g stewed, strained fruit (apples, blackberries, peaches)

2 tablespoons of biscuit crumbs

Put the fruit (sweetened if necessary) in a buttered dish. Sprinkle the crumbs over the fruit and cook for 20 minutes at 350°F.

Fruit jelly

25 g gelatine
1 cup fresh fruit juice

Chopped fresh fruit

Dissolve the gelatine according to packet instructions. Cool slightly before stirring into the fruit juice. Add the fresh fruit to the jelly. Refrigerate until set.

Beef stew

250 g stewing beef, cubed	Garlic
Flour	Mixed herbs
Oil	2 medium potatoes
250 ml stock	1 stick celery
	2 carrots, chopped

Roll the meat in flour and brown in hot oil. Add the stock and bring to the boil. Add the garlic, if desired, and the herbs; simmer for an hour. Add the vegetables and continue cooking until both meat and vegetables are tender. Blend or chop up.

Liver and vegetables

250 g liver	1 chopped onion
2 tomatoes	240 ml stock
250 g carrots	

Slice the liver and put into a casserole. Pour boiling water over the tomatoes, remove the skin and pips; chop them up. Scrape the carrots and chop them. Add all the ingredients to the casserole, pour on the stock and cook on top of the stove for 40 minutes, or until tender. Blend or chop up before serving.

Tuna salad

1 small tin tuna (preferably in brine)	Finely chopped onion, if desired
50 g cottage cheese	Grated lemon
Finely chopped cucumber	

Drain then flake the tuna fish and mix in all the remaining ingredients.

Hamburgers

125 g minced beef	Pinch each of cumin and oregano
1 egg yolk	
½ finely chopped onion	
1 tablespoon tomato purée	

Mix all the ingredients. Form the meat into patties and grill them. Chop up or mash before serving.

Baked egg custard

2 eggs	2 tablespoons clear honey
500 ml milk	

Beat the eggs together then add the milk and honey. Pour into a baking dish and place this in a pan of water (the water should come about half way up the side). Bake at 325°F for an hour, or until set.

Apricot mousse

250 g apricots	1 tablespoon plain yogurt
1 egg yolk	
Lemon juice	

Cook and purée the apricots. Beat the egg yolk into 2 to 3 tablespoons of purée, add a few drops of lemon juice and then bring the mixture to the boil, stirring carefully. Let it cool slightly before stirring in the yogurt. Cool in the refrigerator before serving.

143

SAFETY TIPS
- You should still take care not to give your child food of a size that might stick in her throat or be inhaled, so you should avoid peanuts, fruit with pips and seeds and unpeeled fruit with tough skins.
- Don't ever leave your child eating or drinking alone in a room. If she gags, chokes or vomits, she needs immediate help (see p.332).
- Don't be obsessive, but be careful with mealtime hygiene. Have clean utensils, a clean high chair and a clean bib.
- When you are storing food in the refrigerator, cover containers with film, and never put cooked with uncooked meat.

FEEDING TIPS
- Tuck a pile of tissues under the neckline of the bib to stop the baby's neck getting wet as she practises drinking.
- If a baby won't wear a bib, put a coloured scarf round her neck so that the clothes are protected.
- If your baby is going to sneeze get out of the way or you will be covered in food.
- Fit a paper towel holder on the back of the high chair or near it.
- Keep the high chair well away from any walls – your baby will be quite capable of throwing food by now.
- A non-slip bowl is useful as it will stay in place while your baby is getting the food on to her spoon.

Be flexible about feeding

Try not to get tense at mealtimes. This will be easier to do if you don't spend too much time preparing the food and then feel resentful if it isn't eaten, and if you take a few precautions so you don't have a lot of clearing up to do. The most important rule of all is not to pit your will against your baby's. In the end there is no way that you can force a baby to take food and you should never reach that point. Even if you are worried that your baby isn't taking enough food – she is. If she doesn't want to eat then her needs have temporarily shrunk. A child will always eat if it is hungry, and will always eat to satisfy its needs. And this period of eating very little will probably be followed by a period of eating a lot.

Think in the long-term. Don't think of your baby's nutritional intake as what has been eaten that day but rather what has been eaten that week, and try to balance it out in this time scale. You may find that for a couple of days your baby will refuse everything but cereal and then on the third day go on a fruit-eating binge, or want only cheese. A baby, like most animals, is self-regulating. She knows what she wants and when she wants it. Like many things in child-rearing you should take your lead from your baby. As a

note of reassurance, a baby's chosen diet is a balanced diet, short of nothing as long as she is given the correct food to choose from.

Regardless of the guidelines already given, or what some baby books say about nutrition, your baby doesn't have to have every kind of food at each meal. She can take a whole day's ration of protein at one meal, and a whole day's ration of carbohydrate at the next. Try to let go of the urge to control your baby's diet, and not to think that being a good mother means that she has to eat "good" food at every meal.

Your baby won't need more than one or two big meals a day. In between times she'll simply need a snack. Don't confine eating to meal times; with a stubborn baby they will become pitched battle-grounds. Of course you should encourage your baby to have regular feeding times, but if she is going through a difficult phase, bend a little and supplement a small meal with a snack later on.

If she stands up or tries to get out of the high chair take your baby out and forget about the feeding. She will come back to the food or ask for it when she is hungry. If you argue you will get upset, your baby will get upset and mealtimes will become unpleasant. Your baby will come to associate mealtimes with unhappiness and this will lead to feeding difficulties.

FOOD AND EATING   1-2

For your toddler to be strong and healthy she must have a diet with sufficient amounts of protein, carbohydrate, fats, vitamins and minerals (see below). She will get this if you provide a wide variety of foods from which to choose. The amount your child eats will largely be determined by how active she is and whether the body is going through a growth spurt: for example, the body slows down around the first birthday, but speeds up again when the child learns to walk. Thus, by the time she's eighteen months old she'll need about three times the number of calories per day that an adult does because of the speed of growth. To provide enough energy for this your child should have roughly 45 calories for half a kilo of weight. She'll also need 25 g of protein a day which, although less than for infants, is still twice that of adults.

What foods to give

By the second year your child will be able to eat more or less the same diet as you. There is no one essential food that your child *has* to eat in order to be healthy – she just has to have a plentiful supply of sensibly-cooked, fresh foods from which to build up a balanced diet. Milk will remain an important part of the diet as it is a useful source of protein (one cup of milk =

8 g of protein) but, as before, drinks of water and diluted fruit juice should also be given when she's thirsty.

Give your child at least one nutritious protein dish at each meal, and at least four servings of fruit and vegetables a day. She'll be able to eat an increasingly large amount of food at each meal; exactly how much will depend on appetite, but she'll probably be able to take a third to half a standard adult portion each time.

Help your child to develop good eating habits by not sugaring or salting the food and by not giving "empty" calories in the form of cakes, biscuits and sweets. Don't give your child sweet puddings – fruits, yogurts or fruit purées are much better.

Don't give your child:
Whole nuts
Popcorn
Very rough wholemeal bread, with pieces of whole grain
Small pieces of raw fruit or vegetable
Fruits with stones or pips e.g. orange
Unpeeled fruit with thick skins
Highly spiced dishes, unless child really enjoys them and specifically requests them
Excessively salty dishes
Sugary drinks

FOOD GROUPS	Food	Content
High protein	Chicken, fish, lamb, beef, pork, offal, eggs, cheese, nuts, legumes	*Protein, fat, iron, vitamins A, D, B*
Milk and dairy products	Milk, cream, yogurt, ice cream, cheese	*Protein, fat, calcium, vitamins A, D, B2*
Green and yellow vegetables	Cabbage, sprouts, spinach, kale, green beans, squash, lettuce, celery, courgettes	*Minerals, including calcium, chlorine, chromium, cobalt, copper, manganese, potassium and sodium*
Citrus fruits	Oranges, grapefruit, lemons	*Vitamin C*
Other vegetables and fruits	Potatoes, beetroot, corn, carrots, cauliflower, pineapples, apricots	*Carbohydrates, vitamins A, B, C*
Breads and cereals	Wholemeal bread, noodles, rice	*Protein, carbohydrates, B vitamins, iron and calcium*
Fats	Butter, margarine, vegetable oils	*Vitamins A, D*

145

SAMPLE DIET FOR A 14 MONTH-OLD TODDLER

Day 1

Breakfast	Mid-morning	Lunch	Dinner
1 scrambled egg	1 cup diluted	50 g white fish	150 g baked beans
½ slice buttered	orange juice	½ brown bread roll	50–75 g potatoes
brown toast	1 apple	1 tablespoon green	50 g grated cheese
		beans	on top
		1 cup diluted fruit	½ banana
		juice	1 cup milk

Day 2

Breakfast	Mid-morning	Lunch	Mid-afternoon
1 cup diluted fresh	1 cup diluted fruit	1 cup milk	1 cup water
orange juice	juice	1 cup water	
125 g yogurt	1 biscuit	2 fish fingers	**Dinner**
1 tablespoon baby		1 tablespoon peas	1 egg omelette with
muesli			25 g cheese
½ tablespoon			1 tablespoon fresh
wheatgerm			green beans
Small amount of			1 cup milk
milk (50 ml)			¼ slice brown
½ mashed banana			bread

Day 3

Breakfast	Lunch	Mid-afternoon	Dinner
2oz cereal plus milk	Egg florentine	2 cups diluted	Ham sandwich
1 cup diluted fresh	(2 tablespoons	apple juice	with wholemeal
orange juice	spinach	1 oat cookie	bread
½ banana	1 poached egg		Cubes of cheese
	25–50 g cheese)		Raw carrot
Mid-morning	1 pear yoghurt		Cubes of melon
1 cup water	(without sugar)		
1 apple	1 cup milk		

Eating patterns

By the time your child is toddling she will eat three smallish meals a day with a snack in the morning and the afternoon. Be prepared for your child's appetite to be a bit erratic during this year: she may be starving one day and eat everything that you serve, but the next day eat hardly anything. And don't worry if your child goes on food binges, eating only one food and refusing all others; it is a perfectly normal occurrence at this age (see p.148). Similarly, don't be alarmed when she goes through periods of little appetite – your child knows exactly what she needs and will eat to keep pace with herself.

Giving sweets

I believe that it is wrong to deprive children of sweets. Deprivation very often leads to furtiveness and dishonesty. I believe, however, in sweet rationing. But I am not beyond giving sweets as a reward as this kind of reward is immediately understood by your child. With regard to my own children I ration them to one sweet after lunch and supper. This scheme has worked with all four of them and it has encouraged self-control and good eating habits. They should always brush their teeth afterwards.

Eating at the table

Introduce your toddler to family mealtimes by pulling the high chair up to the
table when you have a meal. She'll be
able to see everything that is going on and
will gradually become more accustomed
to family meals and to mealtime
behaviour and good manners. To make
sure that she feels included give your
toddler the same food that you are eating
but prepare it in a way that she can
manage to spoon or pick up without your
help. This process will be much easier if
your child is quite neat and able to eat
without much mess. However, if your
child is very messy you may find it more
successful to feed her before the rest
of the family and to then bring the child to
the table with a few favourite finger foods.

Don't expect your child to automatically
adopt adult behaviour, especially at the
beginning. Around the age of twelve
months she'll be used to crawling and
"cruising" and will probably not be far off
walking, so don't be surprised if your child
is unwilling to sit still for long. If she
insists on getting down, let her do so; she'll
probably come back for more food in a few
minutes and will soon learn that food
means sitting still and eating. If, however,
she shows no signs of wanting to come
back don't insist that the food is eaten.
She'll make up for it at the next meal.

Messy eaters

Some children take so much pleasure in
the experience of eating that they find it
hard to concentrate on the job of getting
food successfully from plate to mouth. Try
to be philosophical about the mess your
toddler makes at mealtimes. It is a
transient phase during which she will be
learning how to co-ordinate. You may
think that she's learning this at your

expense, but do try to stay cool and calm. Make mealtimes pleasant and minimize the amount of work you have to do by following the tips below. And remember, being tidy is nowhere near as important as your child being happy and eating the way she wants to.

□ Stand the high chair on a plastic table cloth so that you can mop up spillages easily; otherwise just surround the high chair with newspaper which can be gathered up after each meal.

□ Draw a circle some distance from the edge of the high chair tray to show your baby where the cup should go. Make the positioning of the mug into a game.

□ Most toddlers don't like having their faces wiped with a cloth. Use your own hand dipped into water; for some reason, this is much more acceptable and will do the job just as well.

□ If your child is very messy, take her over to the sink to be washed. Make a game out of washing hands and let your child play some water games while you're at the sink.

□ Let your child dip both hands into a bowl of water when she's still sitting in the high chair and then just wipe them dry with a towel.

POSSIBLE PROBLEMS   1–2

Food fads

Between one and two your child will begin to show pronounced preferences for certain foods. It is very common for children to have these food fads, eating one food and refusing everything else. She may, for example, go right off meat and want to eat only yogurt and fruit. A week of this may be followed by a dislike of yogurt and desire to eat cheese and fruit. Being a good parent means not making a fuss about any of this. There is nothing magical about any one food and there is always a nutritious alternative to the one that your baby rejects. Don't spend time cooking food that you think your toddler will refuse and then feel resentful when she does. Take the easy way out and cook food that you know she really wants, even if it's something of which you disapprove. Research has shown that as long as you offer your child a wide variety of foods, the diet that she chooses will be a balanced one. There is, after all, no reason on earth why your toddler should eat the food that you choose. Her tastes are not necessarily yours and, if it is your baby's happiness and well-being that you are concerned about, you will soon realize that it is more important that she eats something that she likes than that she doesn't eat at all. Do be flexible about what you give your toddler to eat.

Disliked foods

I really don't believe in camouflaging a disliked food, of mixing it with a food that is well-liked, or of bribing a child to have a spoonful of a disliked food with a spoonful of one that is liked.

If your child dislikes one food, give an alternative that provides the same nourishment and which you know she likes. If your baby shows a profound dislike for one food, trying to trick or bribe her into eating it may well result in the child refusing other foods as well. When you introduce a new food do it when you know your baby is hungry and she's more likely to take it. The only thing that

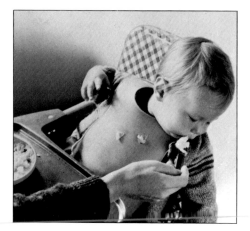

you must actually be on your guard against is that your child excludes all of one food group. If this happens the diet will become unbalanced. Other than that there is absolutely nothing wrong with odd fads, and don't forget, the more worked up you get about them the more your toddler will display them because she'll very quickly learn that it is a way of manipulating you. So play them down.

Weight problems

If a baby is offered the right kind of food she can be neither underweight nor overweight. She will regulate the food and will take in just enough to supply her needs at any particular time. An underweight or overweight baby is, therefore, the fault of the parent in offering the wrong kind of food.
Overweight
Excess weight in a baby is nearly always due to too much fatty meat, too many sweetened drinks and refined carbo-hydrates (cakes, biscuits, jams and sweet foods) in the diet. It may also be because you curb your toddler's activity by keeping her in a pram or play pen and not allowing the child to use up energy by crawling and walking. Always encourage your child to be active by playing games with her yourself – the livelier the better.
Underweight
Unless purposely deprived of food, very few toddlers are underweight for *themselves*. They may be underweight compared to another baby of the same age and sex, but rarely are they underweight for their own physique and size. Many parents worry unnecessarily about having a small, thin toddler but some babies are naturally and healthily small and thin, just as there are small, thin adults. If you are giving your baby a balanced diet and she is happy, contented and developing normally (see p.212) then you probably have nothing to worry about. However, if you are anxious, check with your doctor.

FOOD AND EATING

Your child's daily caloric requirements will continue to increase as she grows, and during the third year she'll need roughly 50 calories for every half kilo that she weighs. Her nutritional requirements will remain the same and she'll need a variety of well-prepared foods.

What foods to give

Between the ages of two and three, children tend to prefer dairy products like milk, yogurt, ice cream and cottage cheese as well as breads and cereals. They dislike, and may even reject, meat, fruit and vegetables. Don't get worked up about this; try, instead, to find a couple of meats and some fruits and vegetables that she does like and stick to them until your child signals that she wants a change.

Give your child two or three servings of protein, and four or more servings of fruit and vegetables a day. Provide four or more servings of bread and cereal – a serving of bread being ½ a slice, and one or two tablespoons of cereal. Always serve whole-grain bread and avoid high calorie, starchy foods.

Eating patterns

Your child may continue to have food fads (see p.148) throughout this year, and may also demand rituals at meal-times. A ritual is something that your child has to have repeated. For instance, it may become a ritual to have a sandwich cut on the diagonal: your child will refuse a sandwich which is cut in any other way. Some children want their plate set in a certain way and will throw a temper tantrum if it is not. The best way to approach both of these rituals is with patience. After all, adults have food rituals, too: we sit in certain positions at the table, and may prefer our tables set in a certain way. As long as it is reasonable, you should indulge your child's ritual. On the other hand, if it interferes seriously with the intake of food or disrupts the family, try to reason with your child and explain that such behaviour is not fair on others. Be firm, but be prepared for it to take several attempts to break an undesirable ritual.

Organising mealtimes

Your child should be getting quite familiar with the social aspects of eating but don't expect too much from her. It is very difficult for a child to concentrate on eating with a spoon, not spilling the drink, not making a mess and being quiet while eating at the table. She is trying to listen to what you are all saying, to participate in the conversation, and to concentrate on the food. She is trying to learn a great many new skills all at once, and viewed like this it is not surprising she can get a bit excitable, just to break the tension, and there are bound to be accidents. Again, be understanding and flexible.

TIPS
● Always make sure that a meal contains at least one food that you know your youngster likes.
● Always serve small amounts and allow second helpings. A large piled-up plate is intimidating for a child.
● Keep foods simple. Children like to see what they are eating: they don't like messy foods.
● Always offer a variety of foods to guarantee a balanced diet.
● Liven up your toddler's meal by using brightly-coloured food.
● Until your child is going to school, include a finger food in a meal where possible.
● Include foods that are fun to eat like jelly, potato chips, or ice cream from a cone.

MAKING MEALTIMES FUN
As with all feeding, the key word is flexibility. You and your child should enjoy yourselves, so give a little thought to making meal-times entertaining for all of you

● If she wants to use a knife, give your child a plastic or blunt-ended one.

● Ice cream cones don't have to be used just for ice cream. Fill one with cheese and tomato chopped together or a tuna fish salad. This means that you can give your three-year-old a snack on the move.

● Encourage your child to sometimes "build" her meal from sandwiches, cubes of cheese, vegetables and dried fruit. She could build a house or a car or a boat, and when it is finished eat it.

● Let your child use a straw for drinking sometimes. So that she won't tip the drink over cut it off so that there is no more than two inches above the cup.

● Be open to innovation and occasionally serve your child's meal on a doll's plate or on a flat toy.

● Fill a cake tin with lots of different finger foods such as cheese cut into cubes, bits of cold meat, raw vegetables, fruit, potato chips and tiny peanut butter sandwiches and let your child pick out what she wants.

POSSIBLE PROBLEMS 2-3

The overweight toddler

Obesity in a young child is nearly always caused by lack of exercise combined with a poor diet which is high in "empty" calories, for example highly refined starches and carbohydrates such as those found in cakes, biscuits, sweets, chocolate, ice cream and sweet drinks. If your toddler is overweight consider doing some of the following things:

☐ Look at the amount of sugar your child is consuming. There is absolutely no need for your child to take in any sugar in any form.

☐ If you have been adding sugar to food, stop now. If necessary, use an artificial sweetener for a short time.

☐ Look at the amount of food your child is eating as snacks. Try cutting them down and changing them to some of the low-calorie, safe snacks (see below).

☐ Cut down on the amount of fat you use: for example, stop using butter and don't even use margarine. Your child will probably not even notice. Don't fry in fat but grill; buy the leanest meat that you can and trim off any fat; cut down on cheese.

☐ Make sure your child is getting every opportunity to be active and to play. Encourage active sports. Have friends to the house for a game of football or go outside with your child and play an active game with her.

☐ Look at the amount of milk your child is consuming. If she is taking a lot of protein, plus a lot of milk, she is probably getting too much. Cut down.

☐ Try giving your child more homemade and uncooked food. Pre-packaged foods, especially snacks, are often high in calories.

Refusing to eat

Refusal to eat is one of the first signs that your child is off colour, so observe her carefully. Is she more clumsy than normal, rather pale and fretful? If so check her temperature and get medical advice if you're worried. At other times your child may simply not be hungry at mealtime. She may have had a lot of snacks before the meal – for example, if she's had a snack or a drink of milk in the hour before the meal it's not fair to expect your child to eat with her normal enthusiasm.

Sometimes your child may appear to refuse food for no reason at all. What you must never do in a case like this is force your child to eat, so don't be taken in by your child's capricious behaviour. Try to be casual about it and get on with something else. If you insist, mealtimes can quickly become a battleground and in the end you always lose. If you ignore your child she'll eat when she's hungry; if she doesn't, don't worry. She'll make it up at the next meal.

Food allergy

Food allergy should not be confused with food intolerence. Food intolerence simply means that some food doesn't suit you as well as others. Food allergy, however, is quite specific and quite rare. Most cases of suspected food allergy turn out to be simple intolerence, or the combination of a fussy child and a fussy mother.

Allergy is the body's reaction to a foreign protein or chemical. It is a

151

protective mechanism and produces symptoms ranging from a headache, a slight rash, a feeling of indigestion, to profuse vomiting, swelling of the mouth, tongue, face and eyes, widespread red blotches in the skin, diarrhoea and an extremely ill child. When first exposed to the allergen the reaction may be very slight but, if exposure is repeated, the allergic response may get worse and worse.

One of the reasons why food allergies have attracted so much attention recently is that they have been blamed for behavioural disturbances in children, but the number of cases where this can be proven is infinitessimal. The only proof of a true allergy as the cause of behavioural problems is when the food is withdrawn and the child's behaviour changes markedly, then when the offending substance is reintroduced the child reverts to the previous bad behaviour. Nothing else counts as proof; improvement on its own is not proof, there has to be confirmation by the reappearance of symptoms after the reintroduction of the allergic substance.

In a very small number of cases there is such proof, although even then it is very difficult to decide whether the child is responding to the removal of the food or the added attention she has received from parents, doctors, nurses and relatives. It may be, and in many cases it undoubtedly is the case, that bad behaviour is a cry for attention, love and affection and if this were given the behaviour would improve anyway. Parents should not sidestep this issue, and should perhaps try changing their ways before any food is withdrawn from a child's diet.

The reason I am so concerned about this problem is that many a child has needlessly had her diet seriously curtailed and robbed of nutritious foodstuffs in the name of this unproven association. Parents should never attempt to isolate a food allergy on their own, without a doctor's advice: a clear diagnosis from a paediatric allergist should always be the first step.

SNACKS 1–3

Studies performed on the eating habits of children show that under the age of four to five children prefer to eat, indeed their bodies require them to eat, frequently throughout the day. This is largely because their stomachs can't cope with three adult-sized meals a day, and we shouldn't try to impose an adult eating pattern on them. The actual range of how often a child eats is quite wide – from three to fourteen times a day, with the average being around five to seven times. The size of the meal she'll want will vary throughout the day, but as a general rule the more often a child eats, the smaller the meals will be. On average, children take in the same amount of nutrients, regardless of the number of times they eat in the day. What is important is not the number of times that your child eats but what she eats.

Sensible snacks are those which provide adequate calories in a nutritious form but contribute little to tooth decay. They include fresh fruits and vegetables, cubes of cheese, peanut butter and cheese sandwiches with wholemeal bread and fruit juice.

Most commercial snack foods, especially those bought from vending machines and fast food stores are highly refined and processed, contain a lot of calories and very few nutrients. Avoid foods like biscuits, sweets, cakes, ice cream sundaes, raisins and other dried foods.

Planning out snacks

Snack food should contribute to the whole day's nutrition, so don't leave them to chance; plan them out carefully. It is important to introduce variety as snacks can become boring to children just as meals can. Some of the ways in which you can do this are as follows:

☐ Try to co-ordinate meals and snacks so

that you serve different foods in the snacks and in the meals.

☐ Try to make the snacks amusing. Place a tomato on top of an open wholemeal sandwich so that it looks like a smiling face, for instance, or cut up pieces of fruit in unusual shapes.

☐ Try to involve your child in planning and, more importantly, preparing part of the snack.

☐ Take advantage of the activity to make the snack exciting and even educational. For example, have your child help you shell peas or make bread and then use whatever you've prepared as part of the snack.

☐ You could think about serving an ordinary food in a different form: yogurt, which may be unpalatable straight out of the tub, becomes more like ice cream if you freeze it.

☐ Drinks are one of the best kinds of snacks, particularly if they are milk-based – though you should use low fat or skimmed milk. These are very nutritious because they contain protein, calcium, iron and many of the B vitamins.

☐ Raw fruit juice drinks are also very nutritious in that they contain natural sugars as well as a lot of vitamin C but don't promote tooth decay.

Snacks and tooth decay

Food encourages the development of tooth decay. Every time we eat, small amounts of food are left on and between the teeth, and these particles, particularly if they are starches, are broken down to acid by bacteria. It is these acids which dissolve the outer enamel layer of the tooth and cause tooth decay.

Carbohydrates and starches form the major food source for bacteria in the mouth. Refined sugar (sucrose) found in sweetened drinks, cakes and sweets is more easily converted to acid by bacteria than any other form of food. It has been shown that the higher the sugar content of the food the more acid can be made by the bacteria and the greater the likelihood of tooth decay.

Not surprisingly, sticky foods stay on the teeth longer so that the bacteria are given a longer time to convert the starches into acid. Sticky foods, therefore, give rise to more tooth decay than sweet foods which don't remain in the mouth for long, getting trapped between, or coating, the teeth. A sticky toffee, for example, will lead to tooth decay more easily than the same amount of sugar taken in a drink. The same applies to other chewy foods.

In considering the snacks that you give your child you must consider the effect they will have on tooth decay. You can start early in your baby's life by never adding sugar to the food. No person needs white sugar; the body can manage perfectly well without it, so do your children a favour and don't encourage a sweet tooth.

Another precaution you can take is to encourage your child to brush her teeth after eating any food (see p. 227). In addition, you can avoid ending a meal with a sweet dessert. It is much better to finish off with fruit or, best of all, a piece of cheese. Cheese is alkaline and neutralizes the acid in the mouth, therefore helping to prevent tooth decay.

Bowel and bladder function

The most important event that will occur in relation to the passing of urine and stools will be when your child manages to stay dry and clean both day and night. However, this won't happen until she's physiologically and mentally mature enough to co-operate. You can't speed up this process – you can only help your child as she gradually gains control over her own body.

PASSING URINE 0–1

In young babies, the bladder empties itself automatically , and a baby will pass urine frequently during the day and night. This is because the bladder is unable to hold urine for any length of time and as soon as it contains a little the bladder wall is stretched and stimulates emptying. This is perfectly normal, and you cannot expect your baby to behave any differently until the bladder has developed enough to hold urine. This rarely happens before the age of fifteen months.

BOWEL MOVEMENTS 0–1

For the twenty-four hours after delivery your baby will excrete a sticky black substance called meconium. This filled the intestines when the baby was in the womb and has to be eliminated before normal digestion can take place.

Your baby will soon settle into a regular routine, and the stools will become firmer. As long as your baby is healthy, happy and gaining weight, you should pay very little attention to the bowel movements. Don't become obsessive about them and don't worry about them.

Though babies vary a great deal in the number of stools that they pass, there is a tendency for them to become fewer as the baby grows older. At the beginning your baby may pass three or four a day, but at the end of a couple of weeks she may only have a bowel movement every other day. This is perfectly normal. In fact, all the following are normal: loose, unformed stools; a totally green stool; a bowel movement after every meal or up to six stools in the first few days.

Stools of the breast-fed baby

During the first day or so, the stools will be greenish-black, smooth, sticky, meconium ones; afterwards, the light yellow stools typical of the breast-fed baby will first appear. The number of stools per day is quite unimportant. Some babies have several, some have few, and some may have a bowel movement every time they feed. The stools may be pasty or they may be no thicker than cream soup but they are rarely hard or smelly. Breast-fed babies hardly ever suffer from constipation; they absorb practically all of the milk so there is very little waste. It is therefore quite logical that they might not move their bowels more than once every third day. Remember that your baby will be affected by the food that you eat and that anything very spicy, could upset digestion.

155

Stools of the bottle-fed baby

Once the digestion has settled down, a baby fed on formula tends to have more frequent stools and the stools tend to be firmer, browner and smellier than those of a breast-fed baby.

You will sometimes find that your baby's stools are soft, like scrambled eggs, but the commonest tendency is for the stools to be rather hard. The easiest way to put this right is to give your baby more water to drink: a good tip is to add a little more water to the normal number of scoops of powder when you are making up the bottles. Also try giving your baby a little cooled, boiled water to drink in between feeds, tipping it gently into the mouth with a spoon. When your baby gets to several months old you can soften the stools by adding a little prune juice to your baby's drink, or by giving a few teaspoonfuls of sieved fruit thinned down with water.

There is absolutely no need to add sugar to your baby's bottles, but if for some reason you have, or the formula has a high sugar content, the stools may have a tendency to be loose, green and curdy. The first thing you should do is to stop putting sugar in the feeds. If it goes on, however, contact your doctor.

Changes in bowel movements

As long as your baby is doing well, it really doesn't matter if the stools change in appearance from one day to the next. A slightly lighter or a slightly darker colour doesn't mean anything serious. A slightly less well-formed or a harder stool doesn't mean to say that there is anything wrong. If you are ever worried, however, do consult your midwife, community nurse or doctor who will be glad to give you advice. Looseness of the stools *per se* doesn't indicate an abnormality or an infection. On the other hand, watery stools which are accompanied by a sudden change in colour, a sudden change in the frequency of passing stools, plus a change in the smell of the stools, should be mentioned to your doctor, especially if you feel that your baby is "off colour" (see p. 339). As a general rule, changes in the number and colour of the movements are much less important than changes in the smell and the amount of water in the stools.

As your baby gets older be prepared for the stools to change whenever you add a new food, particularly fruits and vegetables. If the stools become very loose after introducing a new food don't give it again for several days and then try it again in a very small quantity.

Don't forget that beetroot can turn the stools red and that it is quite normal for a stool to turn brown or green if left exposed to the air.

Streaks of blood in the stools are never normal. Even though the cause may be quite minor, like a tiny crack in the skin around the anus, you should consult your doctor. Large amounts of blood, pus or mucus may herald an intestinal infection, so contact your doctor immediately.

POSSIBLE PROBLEMS 0–1

Constipation

Constipation is hard, infrequent stools. Infrequent means less often than every three or four days, and hard means hard enough to cause discomfort or pain. Constipation itself cannot make a child ill, and old theories that constipation poisoned the system were discarded long ago. Constipation without any other signs of illness is nothing to worry about. However, if your baby is straining a great deal to pass a hard stool and it causes discomfort, you should consult your doctor to see if it is necessary to get any medicine to soften the stool. Doctors are loath to use laxatives or purgatives for a small child, and it is hardly ever necessary to resort to such treatments. In a very small baby constipation is rare and it is nearly always due to not giving the baby enough water. It can, therefore, nearly always be corrected by giving your baby more drinks or by adding a little extra water to each bottle. Don't try the old-fashioned remedy of adding a little more sugar to your baby's feeds – your baby doesn't need sugar, and it will only encourage a sweet tooth.

By far the best way to soften the stools is to alter the diet and to add a little more fibre and roughage. A couple of teaspoons of prune juice added to your baby's water drink will help, and when she's on solids, two teaspoons of sieved stewed prunes with the evening feed should bring results.

Once your child is on a varied diet, constipation should never occur, unless you are giving your child a diet which is inadequate in fresh fruit, vegetables, whole wheat breads and whole grains (see p. 145). It is very easy to correct constipation once your child is on solids: you simply add more of these to the diet. In a small child, the bowel always responds to the addition of complex carbohydrates (which are contained in root and green vegetables), because the cellulose within them holds water in the stools and makes them more bulky and soft. There are really only two reasons why a child should become chronically constipated. The first is due to an over-fussy parent who has become obsessive about the regularity of the child's bowel motions. The second is if a child has previously felt great discomfort and pain when trying to pass a motion, and retains the stools to prevent that pain recurring.

It is fairly common for your child to have a few days of constipation after having an illness with a high temperature. This is partly because she has taken in very little food so there are no waste products to pass, and partly because of the loss of water due to sweating with the fever. The body conserves all the moisture it can by absorbing it from the stools and this makes the motions hard. This kind of constipation needs no treatment at all and it will correct itself when your child goes back on to a proper diet. Don't use patent medicines, laxatives, suppositories or enemas without consulting your doctor.

Diarrhoea

True diarrhoea – very loose, frequent, watery stools – is a sign that the intestines are irritated and that the food is "hurrying" along. Once your child is on solids, a change of diet, such as the introduction of a new fruit or vegetable, may be enough to cause it.

Diarrhoea in small babies is always dangerous because the intestines are not given sufficient time to absorb the water essential for life, and severe dehydration can develop quite rapidly. There is no need to be concerned about the odd loose stool if your baby remains well, eats normally and is perfectly happy. However, if your baby has very watery stools, if they are green and smelly, if she refuses food, has a fever of 38°C (100°F) or more, has blood or pus in the stools and is listless with dark rings under her eyes, then you should contact your doctor immediately; diarrhoea can be cured quickly if it is treated early.

If your baby is very young (under four months) go directly to your doctor or hospital casualty department as soon as possible. With an older baby, stop all food and just give drinks of water until you can see your doctor. If your baby has mild diarrhoea and no other symptoms, you can start treatment immediately yourself. If you are breast-feeding your baby continue to nurse. Diarrhoea usually clears up well on breast milk. If you are bottle-feeding, make up the next bottle at half-strength, with half the regular formula to the usual amount of water. Let your baby take as much of this mixture as often as she likes. She may be off food, taking only small amounts, and will therefore become hungry more quickly. If a mild diarrhoea doesn't improve within two days, consult your doctor even if your child seems well.

Once the diarrhoea has cleared up you can start re-introducing food. The best foods to start off with are mild, milky ones like jelly or junket; dilute fruit juice and stewed apple; dried cereal made up with milk; sieved vegetables; mashed potatoes; white meat and eggs, mashed banana and other fruit. Start off with a third to a half the usual serving on the first day and on the second day a half to two thirds of the usual amount. On the third day, if all is going well, and she has a good appetite, you can go back to regular servings.

GAINING BOWEL AND BLADDER CONTROL   1–2

To my mind there is only one way to approach the whole subject of bowel and bladder control and that is to take signals from your child and to *help*, not train, your child. Control over the bowel or bladder rarely begins before the age of fifteen or eighteen months; sometimes it is very much later.

Gaining bowel control

It is not uncommon for babies to empty their bowels during a meal or very soon after as early as three months. Some parents take this to be an early sign of readiness for toilet training. It is not at all. It is simply the working of the gastro-colic reflex which stimulates the passage of food down the intestines to the bowels when food is eaten.

Your child will be ready for your help when she can make the connection between inner sensations and the physical reality of passing urine and faeces. You'll notice this awareness when, for example, she suddenly stops what she's doing and points to the nappy, or otherwise attracts your attention with a cry or a shout.

Your child's awareness of having a full rectum and a full bladder will probably occur at the same time, but her ability to deal with them will be different. It's much easier to "hold on" to a full rectum than it is to a full bladder, and your child will probably achieve bowel control first. Because of this it's sensible to help your child use the potty for bowel movements first. It's also sensible from your point of view because bowel movements are more predictable than urination, so you can prepare for them on your child's behalf. When your child makes her special movements or sounds, suggest that she use the potty. Make things easier by deliberately leaving off any clothes or nappies so that nothing hinders your child

getting on to the potty in time.

After she's been on the potty, wipe her bottom (front-to-back in girls) with some toilet paper. Put the wipes in the potty and flush the whole lot down the lavatory. Remove any trace of faeces and rinse out the potty, then wash it with disinfectant, remembering to wash your hands afterwards.

Never force your child to sit on the potty – it will have the reverse effect, so that when you next suggest that she use it you'll be faced with a point-blank refusal or even a tantrum. Instead of causing a confrontation, just forget about the potty for a few days and then re-introduce it in a casual way.

Gaining bladder control

This process will have to be gradual and for it to be successful your child's bladder will have to be capable of holding more than a little urine without spontaneously emptying. One of the first signs of this maturity is your child's nappy being dry after a reasonable length of time (for example, after an afternoon nap). Once your child stays dry regularly throughout this nap you can start to leave off that nappy. Before you put your child down for her nap, encourage her to empty her bladder. If she does, congratulate your child; if she doesn't, don't make a fuss, just try it again another day.

When she can do this successfully and can indicate to you that she wants to go on to the potty, you can start leaving off nappies completely during the day. Never start this until she can wait quite comfortably for a few minutes while you take down her clothes.

There will be accidents so be prepared for them and always be sympathetic. Never scold your toddler: it's not her fault. Initially she probably won't be able to give you a clear signal, so unless you're quick to interpret what she wants, she'll have no alternative but to pass urine without getting to the potty. Just mop up and change any clothing without a fuss.

TIPS

● Do let your child develop at her own pace. There is no way that you can speed up the process, you can only be there to help your child along.

● Let your child decide whether or not to sit on the potty. You can suggest that she does but you should never force the issue.

● Do treat your child's faeces in a sensible manner, and never show any disgust or dislike for them. They're a natural part of your child and initially she'll be very proud of them.

● Do not delay once your child has signalled as control is only possible for a short time.

● Praise your child and treat her control as an accomplishment.

Toilet training

I am whole-heartedly against toilet training. For me there are no arguments in favour of it, there are only arguments against it. I believe that toilet training proceedings and the attitudes which advocate "training" a child's bowel movements and bladder function should be eradicated from child care and child development. The reasons I feel this so strongly are as follows: it is impossible to train a child to do anything unless the body has developed to a point where it is anatomically and physiologically able to perform the tasks that you demand of it. Applied to bowel and bladder function this means that it is impossible for your child to control either of these unless the bowel and the bladder muscles are strong enough to hold urine and faeces, and that, at a given order from the brain, the nerves to the bowel and bladder are mature enough to obey the order and evacuate.

If this level of development has not been reached there is nothing that your child can do to adhere to your training programme. You can see immediately what a dreadful position this puts your child in. She is immediately aware of what you want, but her body is unable to perform the task. Your baby's desire to please you overrides almost all other desires, and in this she is frustrated. She becomes unhappy at not being able to please you and may then feel inadequate, ashamed, guilty and finally resentful.

If you insist on a toilet programme when your child is not ready for it, the end can only be sadness. The relationship with your child will deteriorate. You will become a source of unhappiness, and bowel movements and potty training will become a battle ground of your baby's will against your nerves, and you will always be the loser. You cannot make your baby pass a stool, or keep a nappy dry and if you try to do either of these things you'll make your child suffer every time the inevitable accident occurs.

BOWEL AND BLADDER CONTROL 2-3

While it is likely that your child has already shown signs of both muscle control and an awareness of urination and bowel movements, it is possible that she hasn't. If this is the case, don't worry. The procedure for helping your child to understand her bodily requirements is the same, no matter what age she starts, and is given on the previous page.

If, however, your child *has* gained some control, you'll find that she'll continue to improve during this year. It has been shown that by two-and-a-half years old approximately 90% of girls and 75% of boys have complete bowel control and even go to the lavatory alone. However, the same study showed that more than half the children of that age were still wet at night, although they could go without a nappy during the day.

Staying dry at night

Bladder control at night comes last of all. It is often not possible for a two-and-a-half year old child to hold urine for much longer than four to five hours, and it is often much less than that. The signal to start leaving off the night-time nappy is when she wakes up regularly with a dry nappy. When this happens, leave off the nappy, but take the child to the potty and encourage her to empty her bladder before she goes to sleep. Leave a potty beside the bed and suggest that she use that if necessary during the night. Do leave a night light on so that she can see what she's doing and be prepared to give any assistance if necessary. It's a big step for your child to stop relying on you and to take the responsibility for using the potty herself. Encourage your child as soon as she shows any signs of taking this responsibility because it is important that you help and that she feels a sense of confidence. Be prepared for accidents, but never get upset by them. You can minimize your own work by:

☐ Protecting the mattress with a rubber sheet, putting your usual sheet on top.

☐ Putting a small rubber sheet on top of the child's ordinary sheet, with a half sheet over that. If there's an accident you can quickly remove the half sheet and spare the rest of the undersheet.

☐ Making sure that night wear is free of zips so that your child can take down her clothes without any trouble.

☐ Avoiding any confrontation by not forcing your child in any way. Gentleness and understanding invariably pay off.

Getting used to the lavatory

Once your child is using the potty regularly throughout the day it is sensible to introduce her to the idea of using the lavatory. To help your child adapt to the larger size, and to give a greater feeling of support and security, use a specially-designed seat which fits inside the lavatory rim (see p. 37). Your child should feel comfortable on this but if she's worried, suggest that she holds on to the sides of

the seat, and always stay near at hand. You'll probably need to put a small step or box in front of the lavatory so that she can get up easily. Show your little boy how to stand in front of the lavatory and be very specific in teaching him to aim at the bowl before he passes any urine. You could also put a piece of toilet paper in the bowl for him to aim at.

Your child may become very self-reliant and want to do everything alone, in private. If this is the case you should respect such wishes. However, do teach your child how to wipe her or himself, especially your little girl. She should learn that she must wipe from the front to the back to avoid spreading any bacteria from the rectum to the vagina.

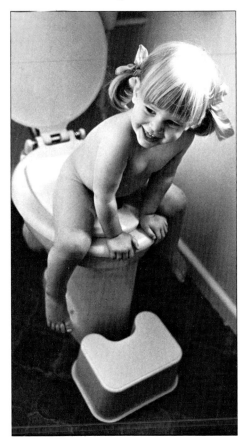

TIPS

● Whenever you travel make sure that you have a potty with you so that your child can go under any circumstances without having to wait. Put the potty on the floor in the back of your car so that you can stop anywhere along the road instead of having to worry about finding a public lavatory in a hurry.
● If she sits down and can't do anything turn on the taps; this works for babies as well as adults.
● If you keep star charts for various accomplishments, keep one for "days without accidents".
● If you have a potty in the bathroom, you and your child could go to the lavatory at the same time.

● Let your child accompany you to the lavatory at an early age so that she can learn from watching you. This works particularly well with boys.
● Tell your child quite firmly and sympathetically that accidents will always be ignored and forgiven, and that she's not to worry about them.
● Get a potty well before you think your child will need it. You can explain why it is there and that when she is old enough she'll be able to use it. This may give your child an incentive to have a go.
● Don't flush the lavatory when your child's with you – many get frightened both by the noise, and by the fact that "part of them" is being taken away.

POSSIBLE PROBLEMS   2–3

Late developers
Some children acquire bowel and bladder control much later than others, and this may present a problem to the parents. In nearly all cases it is wrong to blame the child. Often there is a family history of lateness in acquiring bladder control. If your child is wet during the day and night, most doctors feel that there is no need to investigate this difficulty before your child is three years old, and if she is only wet at night your doctor may feel that these investigations may be put off until she is five years old. Whenever you go along to your doctor about a urinary problem with your child, take along a specimen of urine so that he or she can look at it.

Bed-wetting
Some children, more especially boys, occasionally wet the bed well after the age of four and this is perfectly normal. It is quite likely to be made worse by a change of surroundings or routine, the arrival of another baby, an illness or a spell of unhappiness, such as starting school. If your child has a bed-wetting problem, lightly suggest that she thinks about going for the whole night staying dry – this

positive thinking may help. But don't make a big thing of it – she'll worry and you'll have defeated your purpose. No matter how long bed-wetting goes on, always assure your child that it will eventually stop, because it does. She will just outgrow it, so stay calm and sympathetic at all times.

Regression
If your child suddenly seems to lose bladder and bowel control, and regresses to an earlier stage, the cause could well be a physical illness or an emotional disturbance. Sometimes the cause may be perfectly obvious. A new baby in the house and your child will feel dethroned and rejected. It would be quite normal for her to try all sorts of attention-seeking behaviour to detract from the new baby, including the wetting and soiling of clothes. Starting at nursery school or moving to a new house, or your absence could all stimulate the same pattern of behaviour. If none of these has happened, consult a doctor about investigating your child in case she has an infection or a minor anatomical abnormality in the urinary tract.

161

10 Sleeping

A newborn baby spends most of the time asleep but as she gets older quite regular sleeping patterns will emerge. By the time she's three months old she'll have one main wakeful period a day, usually at the same time and quite often in the late afternoon or early evening. By the time your child's twelve months old she'll probably be having two naps a day, one in the morning and one in the afternoon, and will be sleeping through the night. Although the sleeping patterns will gradually come to resemble those of an adult during the second and third year, your child will still need a brief nap at some time during the day because of the amount of energy being used up both in growing and in play.

ALL ABOUT SLEEPING   0-1

Unless your newborn baby is hungry, cold or otherwise uncomfortable, she'll spend most of the time between feeds asleep. The amount of time she sleeps will depend on individual physiology, but the average is about 60% of the day. Don't, however, *expect* your baby to sleep all the time and don't get worried when she doesn't. Some babies are naturally more wakeful than others right from the start.

Even though your baby will follow her own sleep pattern it is important that she learns to differentiate between day and night and there are several ways of helping your baby to do this. For example, when you put your baby down in the evening make sure that the room is darkened and make an extra effort to see that she is comfortable and contented. When she wakes to be fed in the night simply give the feed but don't play or otherwise distract your baby. As she gets older and more aware of what's going on, develop an evening routine so that she has the evening feed, a bath, a story, games and songs before going to bed happy.

Occasionally a baby is sociable rather than sleepy after a meal and this is something that you should enjoy, although it shouldn't stop you from trying to set up the routine of bed after the evening meal.

If your baby is habitually wakeful after the meal, don't cause unhappiness for all of you by insisting that she stays in the cot. She'll only get upset and you'll end up with a baby who is very hard to pacify and your nerves will be worn to shreds. If, like me, you are a working mother and spend a good deal of your time away from home, your child will naturally see the night time as your mothering time and will want to spend that time with you. The probability is that you will want to spend time with her, too, in which case there is nothing wrong with being flexible about bedtimes. In our house, when we discovered that we had two sleepless young children, we had to abandon the idea of routine bedtimes and the whole household was far happier for having done that. However, we didn't abandon bedtime routines.

Where your baby should sleep

As long as your baby is warm and comfortable she'll be able to sleep almost anywhere. Most parents start their baby off in a basket or carry cot (see p. 42), because that way the baby is portable, and they can therefore keep her close both day and night. However, when the baby outgrows whichever of these you've used, she'll have to be put in a cot - preferably

163

one with drop sides and an adjustable mattress (see p. 43), so that she can be picked up and put down easily.

Whichever room you put the baby to sleep in, it must be warm. Your young baby doesn't have full control over body temperature: she'll lose body heat easily but won't be able to generate it again by moving about or by shivering. For this reason you must keep the room at a constant temperature of about 16-20°C (65-68°F). If you don't want to keep your whole house warm, you could buy a

thermostatically-controlled heater (approved by a recognized safety board), which will maintain your baby's room at a constant temperature.

Whenever you leave your baby to sleep outside, make sure that she's not in direct sunlight. Either put the pram under a shady tree or use a fringed canopy, and if there's a breeze, put the hood up and point the head of the pram into the wind so that there's an effective wind break. Make sure that you put a cat net over the front of the pram, even if you don't have cats yourself.

MAKING UP YOUR BABY'S BED

To cover your baby, use light cellular blankets. (You can use a washable continental quilt when your baby is a year old.) Put the central part of the blanket under the mattress, then fold the sides over the baby when she's lying down.

Lay a muslin nappy where the baby's head is going to be to catch any dribbles or posset.

Use flannelette or terry towelling sheets with elasticated corners for easy bed-making.

Baskets, which may have an oval mattress can still be made up with rectangular sheets but you should make sure that the edges are tucked neatly underneath.

Whatever bed you use, protect the mattress with a thick, waterproof sheet.

Do not use a pillow. Even though your baby will probably roll free if her face gets covered, it's not worth taking the risk of making breathing difficult, should the pillow cover her mouth and nose.

BED MAKING TIPS
● Your baby will be most comfortable wrapped in sheets and blankets made of natural fibre – cotton is ideal.
● Avoid blankets with fringes – she may suck them.
● Avoid lacy, open-work shawls as your baby's fingers might get stuck in the holes.
● Use your own old sheets, cut up to the correct size, in addition to bought ones.

The more you have, the less frequently you'll have to do the washing.
● Use a pillowcase as a sheet – just slide the mattress into it. When one side gets dirty just turn the mattress over.

What your baby should wear

Young babies don't like being changed so in the early weeks, when she's going to need changing quite frequently, you'll want something which gives easy access to the nappy but causes the minimum of disturbance. Nightdresses are therefore most practical initially, but once your baby has settled down, probably within a month, all-in-one stretch suits are equally practical.

When your baby's about four months old you may want to use a sleeping bag, especially in the winter (see p. 57). Your baby will stay snugly warm inside and there will be no risk of the blankets or the quilt being kicked off on a cold night. If the

weather's very cold put the baby in a stretch suit first, otherwise just leave on the vest and nappies. In summer you may not need any covering although you may want to put a vest and nappy on the baby.

Many parents worry about whether their baby's too hot or too cold once she's been put down. You can tell by touching the back of her neck, but do make sure that your hand isn't too hot or too cold when you do this. If the back of the neck feels about the same temperature as your skin then she's at the right temperature; if it feels damp and sweaty she's probably too hot. If you've got blankets on, take one off; if she's got a quilt, take off one layer of clothing. If the neck feels cool, add an extra blanket. Never judge your baby's temperature by feeling the hands. Babies' extremities are often cooler than the rest of their bodies, and are quite often bluish in colour. This is nothing to worry about.

Putting your baby down to sleep

The safest position in which to lay your baby down to sleep is on her back. She will not be more liable to to choke in this position. As a result of research, doctors now believe that the risk of Sudden Infant Death Syndrome (cot death) is reduced when the baby lies on her back. When she is about four or five months, she will be able to roll over to find the most comfortable position, regardless of how you put her down.

Put your baby down with her feet touching, or close to, the bottom of the basket or cot. This makes the baby feel very secure, as does wrapping – but only use a cotton cellular blanket or cotton flannelette sheet, not a woollen shawl, which may make your baby too hot. It's best not to use a cot bumper as it impedes air circulation and later on your baby may use it to try and climb out of the cot. Once your baby has fallen asleep don't change her position or she's bound to wake up. Similarly, don't keep on going in to the room to check that she's all right. However, there's nothing wrong with carrying your baby in a sling while she's asleep; she'll be soothed by your constant closeness.

There's absolutely no need to keep the house quiet when you put your baby to bed. In fact, it's good to encourage her to go to sleep while all the household noises are going on. Steady noises, like a voice on a television set, the sound of a washing machine or spin drier, are quite soothing to a baby and will soon send her off to sleep; it is only sudden changes in the level of noise that are alarming. Over the ensuing months your baby will become an integral part of the family and will therefore have to get used to people living around her with all of their accompanying noise.

WRAPPING

Fold a cotton cellular blanket and lay the baby on top with the head aligning with the longest edge (1). Fold one end across the baby and tuck firmly underneath (2). Repeat with the other edge (3). Tuck the bottom of the blanket under the baby's feet (4).

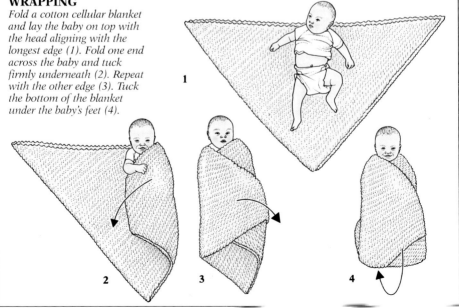

Getting your young baby to sleep

Your newborn baby will undoubtedly fall asleep whenever she's tired, and in almost any situation, but there are a few precautions that you should take to guarantee this:

☐ Wrap your baby before she's put down, at least during the first month. She'll feel much more secure and contented with something firmly wrapped around her.
☐ Darken the room at night.
☐ In the winter leave a hot water bottle in the bed for half an hour before she's put down.
☐ Make sure that the room is warm enough (see p. 164).
☐ Place your hand on your baby's back or on one of the limbs to soothe her; rock the baby slightly.
☐ Use a musical mobile.

SLEEPING TIPS

● Keep pre-bedtimes as happy and pleasant as possible.
● Try giving a comfort suck whether from the breast or the bottle just before she's put to bed.
● Develop a routine and stick to it. Don't just put your baby straight to bed: work out a routine of play, then bath, bed, story, song and then say goodnight. But don't leave the room; quietly tidy up so that your baby learns that she can drift off to sleep without actually "losing" you.
● Let the baby develop comfort habits (see below).

Getting your older baby to sleep

By the time that your baby's about nine months old she'll be able to keep herself awake, even when she's actually quite sleepy. As a result she can become over-tired and so tense that sleep is impossible. The main reason why she does this is attachment to you; you provide love, security and excitement and she doesn't want to lose these, even for a moment. Another reason, which is also linked to the desire for security, is that she doesn't like routines being changed. For example, if you've been on holiday or if your baby has been moved to another room, she may become disturbed by the change. Whatever the cause, this period of clinginess and insecurity will be brief so treat it as calmly and sensibly as possible and remember, yours isn't the only child in the world who refuses to go to sleep.

● Rock the baby's cot if she finds that soothing.
● Play the musical mobile. Many babies are fascinated by the movements they make and are soothed by the sound.
● Don't take the baby out with you in the evenings, even if you used to do this earlier with no problems. She'll be used to her own routine and own room and will be frightened by being moved somewhere else.
● When she does cry, always go back but don't pick the baby up immediately – see what's wrong first – she may just need you to change her position or adjust the temperature.

Security objects

By about nine weeks your baby may be showing signs of becoming attached to a comfort object such as a blanket, a muslin square, a handkerchief, a doll or her own thumb. She may choose to twist a piece of hair, to pull an ear or to rock rhythmically and persistently. There is nothing wrong with *any* of these, although they may previously have been frowned on by child care books. There's no particular age at which comforters should or shouldn't be used and, like bed-wetting, children grow out of them. So, if your baby takes up a security object, don't try to prevent it. If you really feel dubious about letting her use one, look at it in this way: in using one your child is showing self-reliance; she has found a way of coping without you. However, I think the time to question your baby's use of a comforter would be if she used it the whole time,

167

even when you were there. If she clings to it occasionally when she's going down with an illness, or when she's especially tired that's understandable. But if she persistently uses it there's a good chance that you're not providing the kind of comfort and love that you should be, so your baby's having to resort to an artificial source of comfort in place of you.

Naps

Once your baby sleeps through the night she'll need to take one or two naps during the day to revive her energy. What time she takes the naps depends on the individual baby – it may be after breakfast, it may be mid-morning, after lunch or at four o'clock. At the beginning, what's more, the time may change from day-to-day and from week-to-week. By the end of the first year a set pattern will probably emerge. Apart from special occasions (when, for example, you want your baby to be awake at a special time), the length of the nap should be left to your baby – some sleep only twenty minutes a day, others need four hours. However, if

she wants to sleep through the afternoon but then stays up for most of the evening you may want to encourage her to wake up earlier so that she'll go to sleep at a more sociable time for you. This won't harm your baby and it will make life easier for the whole family if the routines of adult and child can dovetail.

Going out at night

Until your baby is about six months old, and really requires a regular routine at bedtime, you can take her with you whenever you go out at night. In fact, it's a very good thing for the parents, and the mother especially, to have some relaxation in the early period, and because your baby will sleep anywhere it's easy to get around.

However, once she starts sleeping through the night, and especially towards the end of the year when sleep isn't always predictable, it's advisable to try to stick to a regular bedtime routine. You can't expect your baby to be as adaptable as an adult, and if you want trouble-free bedtimes you're going to have to follow a consistent routine.

POSSIBLE PROBLEMS   0–1

Early wakers

From the very beginning, try to encourage your baby to be happy alone in bed when she wakes. Put an interesting mobile just above the cot that will swing in the currents of the air and make moving patterns for your baby whenever she's awake. Put a round-edged mirror on one side of the cot so that she can look at her own reflection and not feel lonely and, once your baby can reach up, put a string of objects within arm's reach so that she can move and play with them. These need not be expensive and can be simple household articles, such as a small wooden spoon, an empty bobbin of cotton or clothes pegs strung on to a length of string and attached to the cot. It will also help if you put a few favourite toys in the cot so that there is always something interesting to play with and to distract her

attention without screaming for yours. Make sure that the room isn't too dark in the mornings so that she can at least see what she's playing with. If the room's very dark leave a night light near the cot or consider hanging lighter curtains.

You can help to train your baby to stay happily in bed by training yourself first. Don't lie there waiting for the first wakening murmur and then leap out of bed to see if she is all right. Leave your baby to snuffle and chatter to herself for as long as you possibly can, and only get up if she appears to be getting restless and upset. Always wait to see if she quietens down; you will be teaching your baby self-reliance and independence if you do so, even at this early age. If, however, she becomes fretful, don't delay; go immediately and give all the comfort and affection that you can

KEEPING YOUR BABY AMUSED

Unless your baby is hungry or uncomfortably wet she'll lie quite happily as long as she has something to hold her attention. The shapes within photographs or pictures pinned around the cot or basket stimulate young eyes, as do mobiles which sway and swing in the slightest breeze.

Night wakers

Young babies

It is absolutely essential that you get enough rest. If you have a baby who wakes at night, you and your partner should bear the burden equally from the very beginning and take alternate nights on and off duty. Whatever the cause of the crying, you should always go to your baby immediately. If you don't, she'll become increasingly distressed and the end result will be a baby difficult to pacify and a fraught parent.

Until your baby drops the night feed and sleeps through, you're always going to have to get up at some stage during the night. To cope with this you should try the following:

☐ Work out a routine with your partner so that you can go to bed early at least once or twice a week.

☐ If you are bottle-feeding your baby, make the night feed as little trouble as possible by preparing everything before you go to bed.

☐ If you are bottle-feeding get your partner to give some night feeds.

☐ If you are breast-feeding, and your milk is well-established, make the night feed a bottle of expressed milk which your partner can give. There is absolutely no reason why you shouldn't do this, although your baby may not readily accept the teat (see p. 113).

☐ If you breast-feed your baby, make sure that your partner helps you by collecting the baby if she's in another room, by changing the nappy after feeding and by putting the baby back to sleep.

☐ Many mothers find it difficult to get back to sleep if they have been woken up. Don't lie there fuming with resentment: try some relaxation exercises, read a book that you've been wanting to catch up on, tackle some work, or get up and do something that you've been putting off.

☐ If you've lost sleep during the night, you must make it up the following day. Completely relax your routine and do as little in the house as possible so that you can have a nap when the baby's sleeping.

169

Older babies
In the second half of the year your baby should sleep through the night. However, there may be occasions when, for whatever reason, she wakes up. Try the following:
☐ Make sure that she's not too hot; if she is, remove either some clothing or some bedclothes.
☐ Check that she's not too cold, having kicked off the bedclothes. Either use a sleeping bag (see p. 57), more bedclothes, or leave a safety heater in the baby's room to provide a constant temperature.
☐ Check that she doesn't have nappy rash. If she does, the discomfort of it could wake her up. Deal with the rash immediately (see p. 80).
☐ Don't constantly go into the baby's room to check that she's sleeping well – your anxiety will be more of a disturbance.
☐ If she's had a nightmare, provide comfort and stay until she's asleep again. If it happens on more than one night in succession look for some external reason –

are you getting upset with her rather a lot; is she being looked after by a new baby minder; is she just disturbed by your not being there during the day?

Wakeful babies

Some babies just don't need as much sleep as others and as a result are much more demanding of their parents' time and energy. Such babies should never be left lying alone in their cots with no amusement. They should either have mobiles or activity centres (see p. 169), or should be carried by the parent if they're moving around a lot. For example, you could put your baby in a sling and still move quite easily around the house; alternatively, you could put the baby in a bouncer in the doorway of the room you're in, or have her propped up near you with cushions (see p. 69). Whatever you do, don't fret because your baby sleeps less than anticipated. When she's awake she's learning all the time, and you'll inevitably be rewarded with an eager, bright child.

ALL ABOUT SLEEPING   1–2

Most toddlers will sleep an average of about eleven hours through the night, and will make up any extra sleep that they need in naps. If your baby needed a lot of sleep in the first year she'll probably continue to do so in the second; if she needed little sleep, then this trend will continue, too. Although she sleeps through the night she'll still need two naps a day. How long these naps last will depend, as before, on your baby. What may change this year will be the times at which she wants to take the nap. For example, you may find that the nap that she used to take at around 9–9.30 gets later and later. This means she'll want to sleep immediately after lunch, at around 1.30 or 2. On other days, however, she may take a nap late in the morning but then not want another one until the middle of the afternoon. As far as these changes are concerned, you have to take the lead from your baby; there's no point in trying to make your

baby sleep to order and you'll have to accept that the napping pattern varies from day-to-day. Fit into the baby's routine so that if she establishes a pattern whereby she gets sleepy towards 11.30 and wants to have a nap around noon, you start having lunch around 11.30. She'll then be able to have a satisfying nap after lunch, and you'll have a much less grumpy baby. Alternatively you could wait until she wakes up before having lunch – it depends on your baby.
  Around the age of fifteen months your toddler will reach a period where two naps a day are too many and one nap a day is too little. She'll happily play through the first nap but because she can't last without sleep until the second one she has to have a later nap than usual. This inevitably means that she's alert enough to go through the usual afternoon one, but then because she's too tired to last out until bedtime she has to go to bed early. At with

everything else in child care, you have to be flexible. The period where she has to drop one nap will be brief and she'll soon sort out her own napping routine. By the end of the second year she'll probably take a single nap at the end of the morning, or in the afternoon.

Until she settles into a napping routine do make sure that she is having adequate rest during the day. Even if she doesn't seem to be all that tired and is rushing around, eager to learn new games or play with exciting toys, it's quite easy for her to become over-tired. Keep an eye on your child and if she becomes bad-tempered or fretful, or shows a sudden lack of co-ordination then make sure she rests or plays a quiet game.

Whenever your toddler takes a nap, let her wake up gently from it. It may be a restorative sleep but she's unlikely to wake up perfectly refreshed and active. She'll need a quarter of an hour or so of being cuddled and talked to quietly before she's ready to be active again. If you have to go out immediately after your toddler's nap, make sure that you leave enough time for the recovery of her good humour.

Bedtime routines

Your baby's bedtime routine will change this year in so far as she'll require more diverting games and more of your attention; give your baby both. The essential thing to remember is that bedtimes are play times and happy times, and even although you're worn out, you should try to be calm and relaxed. If you are not, your baby will pick up your anxiety and be fretful, and you may have to spend twice as long trying to put her to sleep than if you had spent an extra five minutes of your undivided attention in a quiet, direct way.

Where your toddler should sleep

At some time during this year your baby may try to get out of her cot to come to you. Obviously a fall from the top of a cot could be dangerous so either lower the mattress and effectively make the top of the rails out of reach, or put your child into a single bed (see p. 43). Specially-designed beds with safety rails are available and this might be advisable if your toddler is quite small when she's first put into a single bed.

171

HELPING YOUR TODDLER TO SLEEP

During the day

• Make up a nap time box for your child with favourite toys and books which she can look at as she gets sleepy before a nap. Don't leave good or expensive books – they may get ripped up. Leave board books or old books. A neat alternative is to make up your own books by pasting interesting pictures from magazines on to board and then covering them with clear acetate.

• Give your child a treat by letting her take a nap in your bed, or on the couch or somewhere else near you.

• If your child won't take a nap, make sure that she has a rest time where she is calm and quiet.

• If your toddler won't go to sleep, put on a long-playing tape. Teach your child that the rest time is not over until the music stops.

HELPING YOUR TODDLER TO SLEEP
In the evening
● Don't put your child to bed immediately after an exciting game or rough-and-tumble – she will have great difficulty settling down which will be frustrating for you. Give her ten to fifteen minutes to quieten down, sitting with you watching TV or looking at a book.
● Even a small child likes looking at a book in bed so, if yours is quite happy, leave her with a favourite, non-scary book.
● Put a dab of your perfume or after-shave on to your child's pillow and suggest that she breathes it in deeply. Deep breathing is relaxing and calming and will help your child go off to sleep.
● Give your toddler a bath before bedtime and follow this with a warm drink and a story in bed.

POSSIBLE PROBLEMS   1–2

Waking in the night

It's been estimated that 15% of two-year-olds wake regularly in the night and this can be a source of great worry to parents who also need their sleep. No matter how often this happens, or how irritating it may be, don't leave your toddler to cry; go to her immediately, provide comfort and try to find out what the problem is. It may be something easily remedied – she may be cold because the blanket or quilt has fallen off; she may be too hot; she may be thirsty; she may be teething. On the other hand, it may be something less tangible: she may have woken up for none of these reasons and may just be afraid after a bad dream. The difficulty is that she can't explain what's upsetting her and you can't tell your toddler that she's got nothing to fear. What you should *always* do is provide love and affection, without any fear of spoiling.

Dealing with a sleepless child

I'm very sympathetic to parents with sleepless children having had two myself, one of whom was sick if he wasn't reached within a minute or so of starting to cry. I would like to give the parents of such children a hopeful message. Neither my husband nor I enjoyed an unbroken night's sleep for six years and on many days we were almost too tired to drag ourselves around; but we got through it and we've forgotten the dawn vigils. When I look at our two loving, outgoing, affectionate children I sometimes think that I wouldn't have had it any other way. We gave them love in the night, they gave us five hundred times as much back every day.

At the time we were so desperate for sleep that it became our over-riding priority; once it did our worries were half over. We decided to do anything to ensure a full night's sleep, at least now and then. I had never believed that taking the baby in to our bed could do him or us any harm. I could not believe staying with my baby when he wanted me could do him any harm, so I followed my instincts and threw any so-called rules to the wind. If you feel it's necessary to try something like this I suggest that you try it sooner rather than later. I'm convinced you're not buying problems, you're only being a good parent to your child.

☐ My husband and I did alternate nights "on duty", the other remaining asleep and undisturbed unless there was an emergency.
☐ We erected a camp bed next to the cot, and later the bed, so that we could put out a reassuring hand to pat him as he started to cry. This way neither of us really woke up at all.
☐ We gave the child fifteen minutes to settle to any of our strategies, then we tried taking him in to our own bed – a sure fire success.
☐ We only ever gave water or fruit juice at night, never milk, so as not to accustom the child to food.

TIPS FOR EARLY WAKERS

● Put a pile of cloth or board books at the bottom of the cot or bed for early morning "reading". Make sure that there is enough light to see by; if there isn't, leave on a low-wattage night light when you put your toddler to bed.

● Put a soft box or plastic bucket at the side of the bed or cot with small toys, crayons, paper, bits of cloth or interesting household articles in it, so she can sort through and play with them.

● Leave a paper bag with some fresh fruit or bread at the bottom of the bed; never put the food in a plastic bag for safety reasons.

● Leave a drink in a beaker or cup within reach of your child.

Refusing to go to bed

According to the correspondence I get, there are more "difficult" babies around than most people realize, and they pose great problems for their parents. The baby who doesn't go to sleep at night is classically intelligent, physically very active, interested in everything that is going on around and openly affectionate. During the day these difficult children are delightful and very rewarding, but you pay the penalty at night.

Two of my four sons were sleepless, demanding babies so I devised a few guiding principles for coping. However, I have to say at the beginning that the standard advice given in the baby books did not work. If you have a difficult baby be prepared for this and you will feel less frustrated and inadequate when it happens. You have to get your priorities right: no one can function properly for long without adequate sleep and you, as a parent, are no exception. The trouble with some baby books is that they shy away from the advice which seems to put parents before the baby, but in the case of a difficult, sleepless child you must think of yourself. Sleep is too important to miss

and you are justified in doing whatever is necessary to get it, so why not adopt a few pragmatic rules as opposed to old-fashioned dogmatic ones:

☐ There is nothing magical about bedrooms. Let your child go to sleep where she is most comfortable: at your feet on the floor, on a couch, in your lap.

☐ Be flexible about bedtimes. Left to themselves, most children go to sleep at around seven or eight o'clock in the evening, whether you put them to bed or not. Why should they be unhappy in a room on their own, instead of happy in your company?

☐ Give your child an early evening bath. This often relaxes and makes them sleepy.

☐ If your child is proving difficult to get to go to bed, still put on her nightclothes before she's brought into the living room. If she falls asleep you won't have to wake her up again, you can just put her straight in to bed.

Sleeping in a strange bed

If you're going to take your child away from home, say on holiday or just to a friend's house for the evening, give a little thought to making the night in a strange bed a happy one. Don't be secretive and spring the holiday or visit on your child at the last minute; this will only increase any feelings of insecurity. Take along a favourite toy and a familiar blanket; be prepared to read her favourite book and play a favourite game once she's in bed. If she does seem rather clingy, stay until she's gone to sleep, leave on a night light and go to her as soon as she starts to cry. For the first few days of a holiday put the cot or bed in your room, or very near it, until she's got used to the surroundings and feels more confident. If your child gets very upset don't force her into bed and don't ever leave her alone or lock the door. If your child's very upset you should keep her on your knee until she falls asleep. However, great distress should make you question if it's a good idea to change the bedtime routine, by taking her out, in the first place.

ALL ABOUT SLEEPING   2–3

By the time your child is two years old she usually needs twelve hours of sleep at night and about one or two hours of napping during the day; once again, the actual amount will depend on the child. In general the nap or rest time will shorten during the year but bedtime will usually stay the same. The amount of time that your child sleeps at night won't decrease until she's around six years old when she'll reduce it half an hour at a time, per year.

Around the age of three many children stop having naps although the majority still need a rest period indoors after lunch until they are about five or six.

Sleep routine

Children around the age of two and three sometimes start delaying tactics at bedtime. There may be the desire to go to the lavatory or to have a drink and, of course, there's the possibility that she may just appear at your side with no excuses, wakeful and charming. In these circumstances I think you have to decide how to act according to what your previous routine has been. If you have been pretty flexible about bedtimes and never insisted that your child went to bed in her room, cot or bed, then you can't suddenly change tactics when your child is two or three: your child will simply not accept the inconsistency, and will quite rightly baulk at the new regime. In these circumstances, I think it is better to be practical and to let your child play in the room with you until she is tired; to let your child fall asleep beside you and to then carry her up to bed.

On the other hand, if the bedtime routine has been carefully set and this new behaviour is a departure, then I think your child will only benefit from your being firm about the re-establishment of routine. No doubt you will get a few whimpers and a few doleful pleas, but you have already established with your child that you are loving and will come if she is in real need,

so you can afford to be firm. You have a lot of credit to draw on and your child will learn this lesson quite quickly, and soon stop repeating it. However, if you give in, then your child will certainly pick it up as a new habit.

The way you handle these situations depends quite a lot on how much energy you have left and how much you are prepared to have your evenings interrupted. If you have been with your children all day, you probably feel with some justification that the night times are your own, and if you've brought your children up to recognize this you can be quite firm in insisting on it.

Keeping bedtimes happy

It is important to keep bedtimes happy. Personally, I am prepared to make quite a lot of concessions to make sure that my children don't go to sleep unhappy. I forgive certain misdemeanours which would normally be punished earlier in the day, so that they won't go to bed with the memory of my angry voice ringing in their ears. I try to avoid them feeling upset or crying with distress. It is worth making pre-bedtime activities especially joyful and friendly: as your child gets older spend the time between supper and bed (about 30 minutes) in their company – even if you are only sitting in the same room reading a newspaper, or getting on with your knitting or doing some work. Having your presence in the room is very comforting and consoling and will calm your child so that she'll be in a happy mood when she makes the transition from the living room to the bedroom. If you can, watch a suitable television programme together, or read a book or play a game before you take your child to the bedroom.

Bedroom rituals

Most children like a bedtime ritual. Mine always had half a dozen favourite songs they liked me to sing, and a story book they liked their father to read. When we

175

were home together we would share the bedtime routine: ten minutes with me on songs and ten minutes with him on a story. We would both stay in the bedroom and, as there were three children going to bed, bedtimes were communal with the children sitting or lying on each other's beds. It was a family time. My husband lay on the bed while I sang the songs. I stayed and lay on a bed while he read a story. When the story and songs were over, it was lights out, except for a low night light, although we often stayed and talked over what had happened during the day. Sometimes we lay under the bedclothes to give our children the extra loving feeling of companionship.

In our house this rather protracted but worthwhile bedtime routine worked. The last thing we did was to switch on the light so the children could see their way to the bathroom during the night or to our room if they needed us. It's quite useful if the light has a dimmer switch so that it gives a suitably low enough light so that no doors have to be shut.

TIPS FOR MAKING BEDTIMES EASY

● Mark the bedtime with an alarm or a timer, so that you can give your children five minutes warning of bedtime.

● For a young child, have a toy clock next to the real clock and set the hands of the toy clock to bedtime. When the hands of the real clock match up with the toy clock, that is the time for bed.

● Keep bedtime as near the same time as you can every night to help establish regular sleeping patterns.

● Children are quite often not sleepy at their bedtimes. They like the time to slow down just lying in bed looking at a new toy, reading a new book, or just

chatting to one another. It is quite often a good idea to have children who are near each other's own age sharing the same bedroom until they require their privacy.

● Once your children get into a proper bed, have a little snuggle down with them before you leave them to go to sleep. It is very nice for them; it warms up the bed, and their last memories are of your closeness. It is also very relaxing for you: I did it with my children and I nearly always found that I dropped off before they did. It was a tradition we started when they were young but continued after they went to school.

POSSIBLE PROBLEMS   2–3

Delaying tactics

Your child may try to stop you leaving by saying that she simply doesn't want you to go. Here again, you have a choice of action. You can stay with your child until any possible fears have gone and she is feeling calm enough to go to sleep, either with you or without you. Or you can call your child's bluff and leave. I think the latter action is dangerous as it can cause your child to get so frightened that she becomes hysterical. This is bad both in the short term – she will have great difficulties in going to sleep that night – and in the long term – you may make your child fearful of going to bed for several years to come. I would never advocate it.

Another way is to say "If you lie still for five minutes I will come back" and then come back in exactly five minutes. Make sure that she is comfortable and say that you will come back in another five minutes and do so again. In your absence, leave some music playing or let your child continue to read the book she has been reading or to enjoy the game she has been playing, so that she is not left alone with fearful thoughts, waiting for you to return. On the third or fourth occasion you will probably find that your child has gone to sleep.

As a last resort you can take your child downstairs with you. Rest assured that there is absolutely no harm in it, although you will have to be prepared for this to become a long-term habit. It makes for some very rewarding family evenings, as long as you don't get too tired and you aren't too jealous of your privacy. Use the method most suitable for you both.

Fear of the dark

If your child delays going to bed because she is fearful of being left alone or of being in the dark, then you yourself can allay both of these fears. If your child is scared of being alone in the dark sit and distract her by reading a story, by playing a game or by singing nursery rhymes. Make sure that she is calm and sleepy, and actually sit and pat her back until she has quietly dropped off. Fear of the dark is perfectly normal and reasonable in a small child so don't insist on the bedroom being dark. Provide a low-voltage night light which will be a comfort to her and will help you to see your way in the child's bedroom late at night.

Bad dreams and sleep walking

Your child probably won't have a nightmare before the age of three, though children sometimes wake up with a scream and a frightened look, which suggest that they have had a bad dream. Many children have the odd nightmare and this is normal, although it can be quite frightening for the parent if the child doesn't become conscious straight away. Nightmares are not abnormal unless they occur frequently or are accompanied by regular sleep walking. This behaviour suggests that the child is having to exercise a great deal of self-control to overcome anxieties when she is awake and only loses this control when she is asleep. If you can, the treatment is to find out the cause of the tension and to remove it. If the cause isn't obvious, like a new baby in the house, or starting at nursery school. talking things over with your doctor may be of help. If nightmares are a real problem, your doctor may recommend a child psychotherapist.

During a nightmare your child's eyes may be open although she won't actually see you. She may shout abuse at you in a strange, garbled language and be extremely rude and angry. Ignore all of these things; she is not in control of herself and, don't forget, during the nightmare she'll be very frightened.

Very often there is little you can do to relieve your child's fear, even though that is your greatest wish. There's no point in trying to speak to her rationally about what is going on. She can't even understand the words you say in many cases. During the nightmare don't ask your child to do anything. This puts further pressure on and only increases her anxiety. The only way for you to behave, even though the nightmare may last as long as half an hour, is to remain by her side, and be entirely sympathetic, calm, softly spoken and caring. Never, ever, leave your child with a night terror. Stay the whole time until it is over. Your nearness and comfort are all that is required. Speak soothingly and quietly about anything you like; don't suggest that she tries to pull herself together; never raise your voice and *never* scold your child as this may make her hysterical.

Locked doors

One of the things you should not do is to lock your child's door to keep her separate from you. This is just admitting to a failure in your ability to handle your child and is quite cruel. Locked doors and barriers shouldn't be used as child care devices. They are no substitute for you teaching your child, even as early as two years old, about respecting other people's privacy, including your own. A three-year-old child is open to reason and you should be able to explain to her that she cannot just get out of bed when she pleases, and that you will put her back no matter how often she does it. If you are firm, but reasonable, your child should respond.

One of the things that you must do, for your child's own safety, if she habitually gets out of bed is to put a guard across the top of the stairs.

11 Crying

A newborn baby can only be in three states – asleep, awake and quiet and awake and crying. Many newborn babies cry quite a lot, so be prepared for it. If you expect your baby to cry, and treat it as normal when she does, you will find it easier to cope with. If your baby is one of the few who doesn't cry much, think of it as a bonus.

In order to understand why your baby is crying, and how you can provide comfort, you have to understand that what upsets a baby and what provides comfort for her changes as the baby develops. A two-week-old baby may cry when she's clumsily undressed for a bath; a one-year-old may cry because she's unhappy when you leave the room. The two-week-old baby will be comforted by being snugly wrapped up in a towel; the one-year-old will be comforted by the sight of you returning.

ALL ABOUT CRYING   0–1

Your newborn baby has a limited repertoire of communication, and crying is almost the only way of telling you that something is wrong. Remember that for six months she's been floating gently in the dark, in a constant temperature with a constant food supply, so a bright light, a hard surface, a cold sensation and hunger are quite a lot to cry about. However, the cry doesn't necessarily mean that your baby is in danger.

Recognizing different cries

Cries can be identified quite accurately by mothers and fathers who become increasingly able to distinguish different kinds of cries from their baby during the weeks following birth. This is not a one-sided distinction; babies become increasingly able to anticipate their mother's responses to their cries. Most parents worry quite a lot about why their baby is crying, and the interpretations seem endless. Is it hunger, boredom, anger, loneliness, overtiredness, stomach pains or colic? Does she want a cuddle or is she just plain miserable? But after the first four weeks mothers pay much less attention to the type of cry than to lots of other information, such as how long is it since the baby was fed? Did she feed well last time?

Responding to crying

The way you respond to your baby's distress can affect how your baby behaves and how your baby grows up. Your response to the crying and the way you have of comforting her can influence the bond that grows between you. This goes beyond the issue of spoiling to the central question of how your child's early experiences with you affect later development.

Some fairly recent work with newborn babies has shown that over the first few days of life a slow response to crying may well lead to more, rather than less, crying. In another study, it was found that babies whose crying was ignored early on tended to cry more frequently and more persistently later in the first year and that after the first six months this persistent crying discouraged the mothers from responding. The same research showed that mothers who had responded quickly to their babies had children who were more likely to be advanced in "communication skills", as measured by comparing the range of facial expressions in each baby.

Further studies give a picture in which the sensitive and prompt response of the mother was found to promote a harmonious relationship with the child who was content, obedient, secure and competent as a result. This research supports the belief that mothers are programmed to respond immediately to their babies. Some psychologists see insensitive mothers, who do not respond promptly, as "going against nature", and they attribute the difficulty mothers have with demanding children largely to the erosion of a natural mother and baby relationship, the erosion being produced by anxiety about spoiling.

Never leave your baby to cry

The factors which prevent a child from forming deep, loving relationships with their parents, are parental apathy and lack of response and they are more important as inhibitors of the child's attachment than even a parent causing distress, say by physical violence.

I have heard mothers say "If she is clean and dry, winded and well fed – let her cry." Or "He needs to cry for an hour, it is the only exercise his lungs get, so leave him alone." I am very strongly against these attitudes. In my opinion a baby should *never* be left to cry. In the first place, a crying baby may swallow air, which will cause discomfort and make feeding difficult. Prolonged crying may make your baby feel very tired, even exhausted, and she will become extremely irritable and difficult to soothe. More important than either of these reasons is that she will quickly learn that pleas for attention go unheeded, and that there is no loving human response when she needs it.

All the research that I have cited supports not letting your baby cry, and suggests that if you do she will very soon stop asking for attention, which may seriously damage her ability ever to form relationships with others while growing up. A baby's pattern of behaviour, first with the mother, then with the father, and later on with family and friends, is

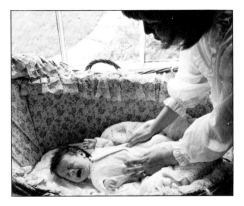

worked out during the first year of life and probably starts as early as the first six weeks. If friendship is denied to a child in these early weeks, she may grow up introverted, withdrawn, shy of displays of affection, and repulsed by physical contact. Don't give your child such an unfair start in life.

Spoiling your baby?

In my opinion a baby cannot be loved too much. I don't share the belief that too much picking up or nursing will spoil a child. A child under one year of age cannot be "spoiled" enough, if picking up, nursing, loving and cuddling mean spoiling. To me, none of this behaviour constitutes spoiling. A child who is picked up and nursed is learning about loving, human behaviour. The model for this behaviour, which she'll retain for life, is the early relationship with her mother.

What we tend to call spoiling is both a natural response of a mother to a distressed child, and the natural need of the baby. A mother's behaviour is "built-in" just as much as the behaviour of the baby. A mother is genetically programmed to respond to her baby's crying, though she may suppress her instinctive response with a learned response which interferes with her natural drives. Her natural drives are to pick up, soothe and nurse her crying baby. Society has suggested that she will spoil her baby if she does this, and so she is torn: she should not be. She should follow

her natural instincts. The protective instinct in a mother (which is what she is displaying when she picks up and tries to soothe her crying child) is the basis of her mothering instinct, and essential to her biological function as a mother. Babies require this physical contact with a soft, warm, loving human being. The need for this is so strong that it almost overrides the need for food.

Undoubtedly crying, and your prompt response to it, play an important part in the way your baby becomes attached to you. Every child in a family will become attached to both parents, but the quality of the attachment depends on the sensitivity of the mother. It is the promptness and appropriateness of the mother's response to the child's distress, in other words how much she is attuned to her child, which is the most important part of this sensitivity, and it is critical for the development of a stable and happy relationship between baby and mother and then between baby and other people as she grows up.

So my unequivocal answer to the question, "Is it possible to spoil a baby?", would be "No."

Crying spells

Spells of crying are likely to go on for three, four or even six weeks, while your baby becomes acclimatized to the outside world. When she has developed a routine which takes account of any likes and dislikes, the frequency of crying usually decreases. Everyone finds it harder to cope with crying during the night. Patience and stamina are much greater during the day when you are feeling strong and sympathetic, but when your sleep is interrupted you will feel, along with every other parent, quite a degree of impatience. Your feelings are not abnormal either; everyone experiences them. Don't panic when your baby starts to cry. It is inevitable that she will, and your tenseness will only make matters worse.

If you feel that your baby seems to be crying rather a lot, you can take comfort from some research which has shown that babies may cry quite independently of any discomfort they may be feeling or of the effectiveness of the comfort you give. For instance, babies whose mothers were given general anaesthesia during delivery took longer to calm down after birth. They were also more easily startled and were less keen on being cuddled. Babies who were born after a long labour, or whose mothers were given drugs during labour, were more likely to cry frequently and sleep in short bouts

Mothers who were highly anxious during pregnancy have more irritable and difficult babies. It is also well-known that male babies are more vulnerable to stress at the time of birth than female babies, and at least one American study has shown that boys are more irritable at the age of three weeks than girls.

There are even cultural differences. Chinese–American babies were found to be calmer, and more passive in their responses to unpleasant stimuli than European–American babies. The Chinese babies were also easier to soothe, and stopped crying immediately they were picked up and spoken to. They were also better at quietening themselves.

One also has to accept that babies are just different. Another study undertaken in America has shown that there are individual differences between babies in the amount that they cry even though they are looked after under the same conditions.

THE CAUSES OF CRYING   0–6m

Hunger

This is the most common cause for crying in young babies, and parents soon learn to recognize the sound. Studies have confirmed what every parent knows – that babies cry more before feeding than after. Experiments have shown that it is the actual feeling of having a full stomach that brings the most comfort, and not being held, sucking or swallowing.

What to do
- Feed on demand. Don't be inflexible about feeding times, and never feed by the clock. Remember, she's very young; she may want feeding every two or three hours and a feed given fifteen or thirty minutes earlier than expected will do your baby no harm.
- If your baby seems only to want to suck give her a little boiled water as a drink between feeds (off a sterilized spoon).
- Use a dummy (see p.38) and hold it in the baby's mouth if necessary so that she can suck on something. You could also use a clean finger.

Temperature

Temperature and humidity both have important effects on the amount of time that a baby sleeps, cries and is active. Young babies sleep more and cry less in relatively warm environments (16-20°C [65-68°F]). Wet or dirty nappies don't in themselves cause crying unless the wet nappy gets cold, too, in which case the drop in temperature is a potent cause of distress.

What to do
- Make sure your baby's room is at the desired temperature.
- Feel the back of your baby's neck to test whether she's too hot or too cold (if it's sweaty; for example, she's too hot [see p.165]). Either add another layer of clothing if she's too cold or take one off if she's too hot.
- Check your baby's nappy to see if it's wet; change it if necessary.

Lack of contact

Some babies cry whenever you put them down in their cots, but stop as soon as you pick them up again. This is a perfectly natural instinct, and means that your baby feels happiest when she is physically close to you. In many cultures babies are constantly swaddled or held in close contact with their mothers' bodies, and these babies rarely cry.

What to do
- Pick your baby up as soon as she cries.
- Carry your baby around with you in a sling or a shawl (see p.69), so that she can hear your heart beat.
- Rock your baby until you get tired then hand over to your partner until the baby's calm again.
- Wrap your baby tightly (see p.166). The texture of the cloth should be warm and fluffy – cool fabrics are far less effective.
- Lay your baby across your lap, tummy downwards, and massage the back and limbs.
- Lay you baby across a *warm* hot water bottle on your lap or on a bed.

Undressing

Most babies hate being undressed, even when the room temperature is controlled and even if they are awake and contented immediately before their clothes are removed. The effect of undressing is consistent and it gets worse over the second and third weeks: as soon as the baby senses that the clothes are being removed she tenses up and finally breaks down when the piece of clothing nearest the skin comes off. The cause is not the cold, but the fact that the skin is no longer in contact with the familiar and reassuring texture of the clothing.

What to do
● Keep undressing to a minimum in the early weeks. Try giving sponge baths (see p. 89), so that you only have to undress the baby a bit at a time.
● Whenever you have to undress the baby fully, lay a towel across her body – the contact with the fabric will help your baby.
● Always talk soothingly and reassuringly and try to get the undressing over as soon as possible.

Pain

This is a very definite cause of crying, but the actual cause of the pain may be hard to determine. It may be the pain of colic (see p.184); it may be something quite obvious like an open nappy pin or a tightly fitting garment. If, for example, it's caused by earache you'll probably see your baby putting her fist against the affected ear.

What to do
● Go to your baby immediately. Hold your baby close, cuddle and talk soothingly to her.
● Remove the source of pain if it's easily discernible.
● Stay with your baby until she's completely calmed down.
● If no amount of comforting on your part works, and your baby seems ill, seek medical advice.

Violent or sudden stimulation

Sudden changes in the level of stimulation of your baby, be it light, noise, jerking movements, being played with too roughly or the sensation of falling, will cause great distress. In the latter case your startled baby will throw out both arms and legs in the Moro reflex (see p. 30), and will invariably begin to cry.

What to do
● Hold your baby close to you and use the general pacifying methods of contact, movement and sound.
● Avoid moving your baby in such a sudden way next time.
● Avoid sudden stimulation with bright lights, loud noises or sudden jerky movements. A baby can stand quite loud noises or quite bright lights over a long period of time but a sudden change will cause immediate distress.

Tiredness

Many babies cry when they are tired. It took me almost two weeks to understand my tired newborn son's message. "Clever baby," I thought, "Dumb mother." Some babies (like adults) twitch or jerk just as they are dropping off to sleep. This may cause a baby to wake up again and, if it continues, will result in a fretful sleep.

What to do
● Lay the baby in a quiet, warm, dimly-lit room.
● If your baby's particularly twitchy, wrap her firmly before she's put down to sleep.

183

Misreading your baby's signals

Not reading your baby's signals to you, whether they be "I'm hungry", "I'm tired", "I want to be cuddled not played with", can all result in tears. For example, if your baby is ready for a feed, but you ignore this and give her a bath first, then your baby is bound to cry. If, while you're breast-feeding, you fail to notice that your baby can't suck properly because she's being smothered by your breast, then she's bound to cry.

What to do
● Be alert. Look at your baby, listen to her gurgles and grumbles and interpret what she's saying to you. She will be saying something to you if you are attentive enough to understand.
● Resolve whatever is causing the alarm immediately.
● Use the general crying cures (right).

Colic

Many young babies have a crying spell sometime during the day; for some this comes around 6 o'clock, just before or after the evening feed. This is quite normal. However, if the cry at this time differs from the usual hungry or lonely cry and is basically a scream; if your baby's face becomes very red, and both legs are drawn up to the stomach as if she's in great pain; if every effort you make to pacify her is unsuccessful – whether it's feeding, burping, wrapping or cuddling – then the likelihood is that it's colic. No one knows why it occurs, but it usually starts in the first three weeks after birth and lasts until the baby's three months old, when it stops as suddenly as it started.

Colic has been attributed to many causes such as underfeeding, overfeeding, allergy, constipation, diarrhoea, too much wind in the bowel, parents picking up their baby too much, parents picking up their baby too little, mild indigestion, intestinal cramps as the intestines start to function properly and, finally, tension.

All paediatricians agree that babies who cry a great deal in the evening seem otherwise healthy. The world-famous paediatrician Ronald Illingworth has commented, "The outstanding impression given by the colicky baby, except in the evening, is that he is a well, happy, thriving, well-fed, well-managed baby with nothing wrong with him."

Although Illingworth found no evidence for the possible causes listed, when he studied 100 babies, he stressed that spoiling was unlikely to be the original cause of regular evening crying.

The tension theory seems to me the most likely cause, although there is no real proof. The late evening is quite a busy time of day. You may be expecting your partner home from work, there will probably be an evening meal to prepare. There is the baby to feed, to bath, play with and put to bed. You are probably feeling worn out and your sympathy will be at a low ebb. Your baby is very quick to pick up tension and may well respond to your evening hypersensitivity with a crying bout.

What to do
There are no known remedies for colic. Although gripe water is a traditional remedy, its usefulness is unproven. As crying is so frequent an occurrence in a young baby I'm against using any kind of medication, even specially-formulated proprietary products. Take heart from Illingworth's studies – that babies with evening colic are otherwise perfectly healthy. Try to comfort your baby, using any of the methods previously described, but don't expect miracle cures. Above all, remember: these screaming fits *only* come at night and they'll only last 8 weeks out of a whole lifetime of pleasure that you'll have with your child.

General crying cures

If your baby still seems fretful try some, or all, of the following remedies as part of your crying cure. Most babies are soothed by both sound and movement, and many parents find themselves relaxed by them as well.

Movement
● Rock your baby – rocking chairs and swings are ideal for this.
● Walk or dance with your baby.
● Bounce the baby gently in your arms or on a bed or in the cot.
● Put your baby in a bouncing seat that will move gently.

● Take your baby for a ride in the car or in a pram or a sling, even at night.
● If you are on your own, put your baby in a sling and just let her cry and get on with whatever you want to do and try to ignore the crying.

Sound
● Talk, sing or croon to your baby.
● Put on the radio or television.
● Put on the vacuum cleaner, or let a tap run forcibly into the sink for a few minutes.
● Give your baby a noisy toy. Shake it and rattle it.
● Play tapes or records of calm music.

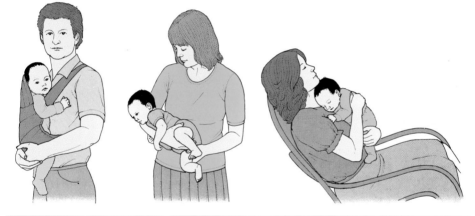

THE CAUSES OF CRYING   6m-1

Your baby will still cry if she's hungry, if she's in pain and if she's too hot or too cold and the cures for these will remain the same as for newborns (see p.182). However, as she gets older she will also be distressed by new things.

Boredom

Your baby will spend longer periods awake during the latter half of this year and she may cry out of sheer boredom if she's just left to lie in a cot, unattended, with nothing to look at or play with. Similarly, she'll be keen to stay with you and see what you're doing all the time because at the moment you're a constant source of amusement and affection. When you leave your baby, especially if she can hear you elsewhere, she's bound to cry.

What to do
● Always have mobiles or similar toys above your baby's cot so that she can swipe at them and watch how they move about (see p. 169). Leaves on trees, curtains blowing by an open window, lampshades moving – they all provide amusement for your baby.
● You'll have a more contented baby if you keep her near you whenever she's awake.

Anxiety

Your baby may well become increasingly wary and scared, especially of strangers and of your going away. During the second half of this year she will be extremely clingy and in parallel with this increasing dependence on you she will form attachments to comforters like her own thumb; a blanket or a dummy. The source of comfort varies with individual children but their need for it is common to all of them. The intensity and persistence of these attachments can last for two to three years. The objects are usually suckable or strokable, and children use them in moments of anxiety and tiredness to simulate the effects of continuous stroking and contact.

What to do
● Understand that this is just a period in your child's development that she has to go through.
● Never force her to go to a stranger if she really can't stand it.
● Let your baby have a comforter, even if it's a dummy. She'll grow out of using it in time.
● Give your baby lots of cuddles.

Frustration

Your baby's increasing physical capabilities may well lead to tears of frustration. Once she's started crawling she'll be able to move away from you more quickly and will want to explore her surroundings. What this in fact means is that she'll frequently have to be checked and stopped from doing what she wants to do, for her own safety, as well as to protect whatever it is that she's trying to explore.

What to do
● Make your home as "child proof" as possible by removing objects from low tables and shelves and by using the correct safety fittings throughout (see p.323).
● Remove the baby from the source of frustration. If, for example, she keeps going up to a dog and pulling its tail, either remove it or the baby from the room. Your baby's memory is very short at this time so she'll soon forget the object of her curiosity.
● Distract your baby with other games.

ALL ABOUT CRYING

In the one-to two-year-old most crying is due to emotional disturbance: to fear, anxiety, separation, deprivation of mother and mother love.

Insecurity

Between the ages of one and three, children spend less and less of their time physically close to, and touching, their mothers. But in contrast to this apparent independence there will be moments when your toddler becomes rather frightened and anxious. There is usually a period, around the age of one when this happens. You may notice that she's quieter and long

mischievous than usual; that she's become very shy of strangers and strange situations and clings desperately to your legs; she may even seem off food. These are all general signs of anxiousness to which you should respond immediately.

What to do
The best way of coping with these anxieties is to give your toddler extra affection and, while doing this, to encourage your toddler to be curious and adventurous, and to have a growing sense of self-confidence. Praise and reward each feat, each new achievement. Your toddler

experiences of being separated from you. If it was unpleasant the first time, your toddler is likely to find it more unpleasant a second time.

Children, undoubtedly, don't like being left. In a way, the better parent you are, the more your toddler is likely to cry when separated from you.

What to do
Never be scornful of fears and always try to be sympathetic and supportive. Reassure your child, more by actions than by words, that you are to be trusted and relied upon. If you say you will come back in half an hour, do so. If you say you are just going into the next room, go no further. If you say you will pop back in five minutes to check on a game, return as you promised. One of your baby's greatest sources of confidence is that she can trust you to keep your word.

In your attempts at sympathy and reliability do your best not to be over-protective. This will only curb whatever adventurous spirit your child has, and stop her from building up self-confidence.

requires your approbation and will do almost anything to get it, including showing off a new independence, so it really is quite easy to encourage her.

A child who is securely attached to the parent uses her as a base from which to explore, and goes on to explore confidently. Much research has demonstrated that the presence of the person with whom the child has a secure attachment enables her to cope with new, possibly fearful, experiences and with the accompanying anxiety.

Fear of separation

Simply because a toddler is so attached to the parent, separation becomes one of the greatest causes of distress, and fear of separation is one of the most potent causes of anxiety. When fear, insecurity, anxiety or separation cause great distress, then crying ensues. The degree of distress varies according to your toddler's age (you may find that it is much less by the time your toddler is fifteen months than when she was ten months), to the way you actually leave the toddler, and to the familiarity of the situation the toddler is in. Of course, it also depends upon your toddler's previous

Frustration

Towards the end of the second year, your toddler's adventurous spirit will almost certainly outstrip her co-ordination and degree of mobility. She will attempt tasks that are beyond her dexterity, sense of balance and physical strength, and this will cause great frustration. It's also inevitable that you will be the source of frustration because you have to stop your toddler doing certain things she wants to do for her own safety.

What to do
Try to be patient. The best form of support you can give is your help. Help with the painting; help with building a tower of blocks; help with climbing; help to make sand castles; help to prop up soldiers or farmyard animals. If the frustration at her inability causes crying, you can easily distract your child into another favourite game.

If she gets frustrated when she tries to copy older children's games, or tries to do something which an elder child can do easily, suggest that you play a game together that you know she can physically cope with. While it's important for your toddler to try new things, and to continue trying when she doesn't immediately succeed, too many defeats could have a retrogressive effect.

Don't be drawn into battles with your toddler – whether they're over using the potty or eating a certain food. She'll want to assert independence of mind and, where possible, you should respect this and not force the issue. Let your toddler decide whether she wants to use the potty, and don't worry if she wants only to eat green beans and ice cream. A calm acceptance of facts is better than arguing.

POSSIBLE PROBLEMS   1–2

Temper tantrums

A temper tantrum is an attention-seeking device. The tantrum will go on as long as you are giving your child your attention; it will be shortened abruptly if you withdraw it. The best thing to do is to leave the room; your child will come to no harm. A breath-holding attack is self-limiting, and your child will take a breath as soon as she becomes at all short of

oxygen. If she is kicking and screaming, simply move articles out of reach so that she cannot be hurt and leave her to kick and scream. Don't be tempted to cajole your child, to lose your temper, to smack or to threaten punishments. None will do the slightest good to bring the tantrum to an end, or to avert the next one. The only course of action is to leave your child alone.

Night-time crying

Quite a few babies cry as they are going to bed at night. You can do a lot to avoid this if you establish a bedtime routine. This doesn't mean that you are inflexible, rather that you give the evening a rhythm that you and your baby get used to. Bedtime and bathtime should ideally be happy. From the time your baby is six months old she should be enjoying her bath and if you treat it as playtime you are off to a good start (see p. 92). By the time bathing is over, your baby should be relaxed and getting a little sleepy. If supper is also casual, informal and happy, with a drink, a story, a game or a song, whichever your child prefers, followed by bed and a firm but loving goodnight, then just leaving your baby should work. As children get older they tend to express preferences for particular songs which they even like sung in a certain sequence, or favourite stories which they will follow with you in their story book. Some of them will drop off to sleep by listening to music or while you sit by them quietly reading or singing. Find the bedtime routine that suits your child best and follow it *every* night without fail (see p. 171). Familiarity brings security and that brings a happy child at bedtime, more likely to go to sleep without a fuss.

Prolonged separation

The effect of prolonged separation varies a great deal with age. Before the age of six or seven months, there are usually no signs of distress when, for example, babies are admitted to hospital or are separated from their parents for extended periods. From the age of six months to four or five years, however, children are acutely distressed, and it is possible that boys are more disturbed by separation than girls are. If young children have had an unhappy first experience of separation, they are more likely to be upset by a second separation or if they're admitted to hospital. The longer the separation, the more disturbance the child shows, especially if it is separation from mother, father and siblings.

The effects can be mitigated by receiving mothering from another individual, say a foster parent or a loving nurse, especially if the following are noted:
☐ Care is given to follow the baby's known daily routine and the pattern of child-rearing to which she is used.
☐ A brief period of familiarization is arranged so that the child can meet the person who is going to take care of her before the separation occurs.
☐ Memories of the past are kept fresh in the child's mind by the care-giver talking about them.

ALL ABOUT CRYING   2–3

As your baby gets older the reasons for crying become much more complicated. Her thinking becomes much more sophisticated and she has a much wider appreciation of the world and what is going on in it; she has insight into your motivations and understands your more subtle expressions of approbation and disapproval; she is becoming acutely aware of her own position in the family, amongst friends and in the world in general; she has new insecurities and anxieties. Fears are no longer confined to simple ones like the fear of separation and there are all sorts of new and unusual things happening every day that may cause fear. Because your child's appreciation of the world is growing, there is increasing potential for her to become upset by events. While she is gaining in self-confidence she is also becoming sensitive and more likely to feel shame, resentment, frustration, anger, jealousy and dislike, all of which may be upsetting and cause her to cry. Also, because she knows more of the world she is becoming aware of the threats that are around and how they may affect her. She has to face quite a lot of them alone. It is not easy for anyone, let alone a small child, and it is not surprising that she resorts to tears fairly often.

Fears real and imagined

Children suffer from classical fears between the ages of two and three. The fact that your child suffers from them is not a sign of abnormality. Two of them are described below.

Fear of the dark
This is very common and not at all abnormal. Help your child by leaving a night light on in the bedroom. You don't have to go to any expense; all you have to do is replace the standard bulb in your lamp by a coloured one with a low wattage. You can also help your child by showing that darkness is nothing to fear. So go for a walk at night and point out all sorts of interesting things that you don't normally see during the day, like the stars or the moon, or some nocturnal animals (the nocturnal house in a zoo, which you often have to walk around in darkness may also be a good idea). In the summer take your child out in the garden and lie on the grass, covered by a blanket.

Fear of thunder
Most children are fearful of thunder and lightning. The best you can do is to distract your child while it's overhead. You can tell a favourite story; turn the television set up loud, play music or get out that game you bought "especially for a rainy day".

Dealing with fears

Encourage your child to talk about fears as soon as she is able to. Listen intently and show your child that you are interested and sympathetic. Hear her out even if she finds it difficult to put the fears into words. Try to help by giving examples, and show that you identify with such fears. Never tease or shame your child about what she is feeling – that will only encourage her to hide it, and drive your child away from you. You should always be the sympathetic friend who will give help and comfort in a frightening situation. You are going to have to show your child how to face up to fears and these are some of the ways that you can actually do it.

☐ One of the best ways of reassuring your

child is to show her that you are exactly the same as she is. All children love hearing stories about when you were little, like them. Tell your child some of the fears that you had, and explain how you overcame them with *your* parents' help.

☐ If your child develops fear of a piece of household equipment, for instance the washing machine, help her to overcome it by explaining what it's for and how it works. Tell your child that machinery is nothing to be afraid of and to prove it, hold her in your arms while you fill it, and give a running commentary of exactly what you are doing. Go through the routine of putting in the powder and switching the machine on. Put your hand on it to feel the vibration and then slowly and gently put your child's hand on it with yours on top so that she knows that you are not frightened, and that with your support she needn't be frightened either.

☐ If your child is scared of getting lost or of being in an accident, talk her through it. For instance, you can say things like, "If you got lost what is the first thing you could do? Well, I think probably the best thing would be to go to the first house where you see a light, knock on the door and say, 'I am Jane Brown. My address is ... my telephone number is ... Please will you ring my mummy and daddy?'"

☐ Never ever brush off a fear as though it isn't serious. It is serious to your child and you should treat it as such. So, for example, if your child is worried by the lamp in her bedroom which casts an unpleasant shadow on the wall move the bed to a position where there are no shadows.

Dealing with irrational fears

One of the best ways to deal with irrational fears is to dispel them with some kind of physical activity. If your child is afraid of monsters or ghosts, say that you are a parent who can do magical things to them. Say that you are able to blow them away and give a big blow; promise that you will be able to get rid of them with the vacuum cleaner and switch it on;

guarantee that you can flush them down the toilet and do so. There are some people who say indicating to your child that you believe in monsters and ghosts in this way encourages your child to believe in them too, and that a better alternative is to say that there are no such things as ghosts. The one trouble with this ploy is that your child won't believe you. She can't; she can only believe you if her fears are rational, which they aren't.

Separation anxieties

Children well over the age of three still dislike being separated from their parents, even if you are only going to spend the evening out of the house. Up to the age of five or six it is quite usual for a child to shed a few tears until she is reassured about some of the details of the evening. These might include: what time you are leaving; how far away you will be going; who you will be with; what you will be doing and what time you will return. If at all possible, give your child these details with some references that she is familiar with: say that you are going to spend the evening with a relative, that it is about as far away as your child's play group and that you will just be having a meal and sitting around talking with friends and that at 11 o'clock Daddy will be bringing you home.

One of the most difficult separations for a child of this age is when the mother goes into hospital for the birth of a new baby. Apart from the jealousy that most children feel at this time (see p.274), there is the additional upheaval of the separation from the mother. It is important to prepare your toddler well in advance of the birth by talking about the new baby, about your going into hospital, and most importantly, about who will look after her while you are away. Ideally it should be someone with whom she is thoroughly familiar, who understands her routine and who can ensure that it continues while you are away. Try to let her visit you as often as possible while you are in hospital.

Making separation easier

☐ Always spend a few minutes with your child quietly doing something nice before you leave. Start getting dressed fifteen minutes early so that you have this amount of time to spare which you can devote entirely to your child before leaving the house. Never rush off without proper leave-taking.

☐ If you make a promise that you will be back by a certain time keep it and, as you are going, remind your child that you will always come back. If you are delayed, telephone to explain why and say that you will be home in a short while.

☐ It is quite a nice idea to have a goodbye ritual – to tell a story or play a game, to give a hug, to blow a kiss as you get into the car, to wave to your child as she stands on the step, or to honk your horn as you leave.

☐ Think up a few games – kiss a child's palm and fold her fingers around it, and say that if she needs a kiss while you are away there is one for her to have.

☐ Never keep the fact that you are going to go out a secret from your child. In fact, talk about it well ahead of your absence. Try to do it very casually the day before. Mention it the same morning and once or twice during the day. Suggest your child comes into your bathroom while you bath, and even helps you to get dressed. All children love playing with jewellery so give your child the free run of your jewellery box.

☐ When your child is very small, don't use time scales that she can't grasp; instead, compare time with some of her favourite activities. For example, if you are going to be away for an hour and a half say it is about the time it takes to make a cake; if it is half an hour say it is four cartoons worth.

☐ If you are going to have a babysitter ask her to come a good half hour before you leave so that she can get involved in some kind of activity with your child before you go. If you do this successfully your child may not even raise her head as you leave but simply say "Bye Mum".

Crying from overtiredness

This is one of the most common reasons for crying, especially in the evening. The child may have been allowed to stay up later than usual, perhaps because of a visit from friends or relatives, or on a special occasion such as Christmas Day, when children tend to be thrown out of their usual routines, with more excitement than they can cope with. The result is an exhausted child whose over-excitement will spill over into tears at the slightest problem. The more you try to jolly her out of it (and this is especially true when visitors are involved), the more hysterical and inconsolable her crying will become.

It is clearly better to prevent these situations developing in the first place, by trying not to let your child become over-excited and by ensuring that she has a rest in the middle of the day if you expect to let her stay up later than usual in the evening.

If you haven't been able to avoid it, and your child does become over-tired and tearful, try to deal with her as calmly as possible. Take her off quietly to her room and cuddle her until she has calmed down; if she has a favourite book or song, and she has quietened down enough to be receptive, read or sing to her. Or let her have a quiet, relaxing bath, get her ready for bed, and stay with her until you are sure that she has completely relaxed.

Dealing with injuries

You don't want your child to grow up being babyish about minor injuries, but you should never underestimate one, especially if you can see the damage. There is no point in saying that a small scratch doesn't hurt, because the sight of blood will scare your child and she will use pain as an excuse for your attention. Whenever your child comes to you with an injury give sympathy and support and use placebos whenever you can. The best possible placebo is a kiss and a cuddle and a gentle word. Next, try a favourite drink or snack, then suggest a small treat –

perhaps your child's favourite food for the next meal, or having tea as a picnic in the garden. Always keep your "magic" ointment by you. In our house it is 0.5% cetrimide cream which is just a simple antiseptic and can be used for all cuts and abrasions. It is very soothing and if your child believes that an ointment will work and take away the pain you are half way there.

Pre-school nerves

There are very few children who skip off happily to nursery school with a cheery goodbye and hardly a look backwards. Prepare your child well in advance for nursery school, no matter how self-confident she seems.

The first thing you have to do is to reconnoitre the various nursery schools in your district. This will mean quite a lot of time and effort because you should visit each one, talk to the teachers at some length, and sit in on at least a couple of classes so that you can get a good feel for the atmosphere and for how interested the teachers are in the children and how much individual attention they are prepared to give during different activities. One of the most important things you have to establish is that there is rapport between you and the teachers. If there isn't, there is no point in sending your child there, no matter how good the nursery appears to be.

Most good nursery school teachers will insist that you take your child along for a rather brief visit several weeks ahead of when she is going to start. Don't make a big thing of it. Fit it in between errands and don't stay for any longer than about fifteen minutes. Don't push her into it. Make the point of your visit a chat to one of the teachers and just let your child look,

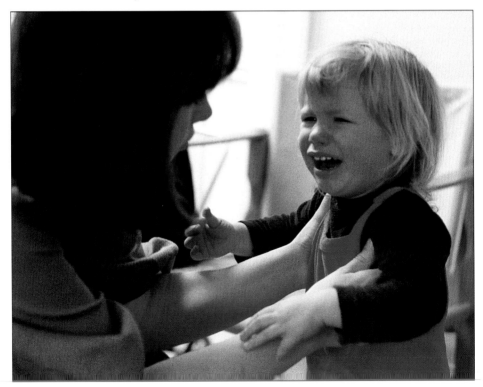

listen, observe and absorb. Let her wander around, touch, pick up and play with things, but don't force your child to do so. Some nursery schools might like you to do this more than once before your child actually starts.

On the first morning be prepared for a shaky start, and for the necessity of staying with your child for the whole morning. Many nurseries welcome this and they will suggest that you help your child by participating in the lessons and staying quite near her. This may not be necessary. As soon as your child feels that you are not going to leave, she will be quite happy if you sit at the back of the room. Take some work or a book along with you so that it is not a complete waste of time as far as you are concerned. If your child seems quite happy, say that you are just going to pop out to get something from the car and will be back in five minutes. Come back in exactly five minutes. If your child is distressed when you leave, don't go. If, on the other hand, she is quite happy, you might let another half hour pass and say that you are just going to do an errand and that you will be back in twenty minutes. Be sure that you are back in time. Over the next few days, using your child's reaction as a guide, see if you can leave her for longer. Some children adapt very quickly to a nursery and you won't need to stay after a few days. Others may still want you to stay for about half an hour at the end of two weeks. Just fit in with them. The most important thing is that your child should feel that school is a happy place and that it is not associated with the unhappiness of being separated from you and of feeling entirely alone. A good teacher, who feels confident about your child and confident about herself, will very firmly suggest that you leave when she thinks the time is right. Being over-protective about your child at a nursery school only makes it harder rather than easier for your child, especially if she's capable of coping without you. If you have good rapport with the teacher you should feel happy taking her advice in this.

All of my children liked a ritual when they first arrived at nursery school. We used to either play a game or draw on the blackboard, or try out a new toy or draw a picture with some new crayons. No matter what it was, we always did something which took about five to seven minutes before I said goodbye, and then they always came to the window and waved. This seemed to keep a child of not yet three quite happy when I departed and you may like to try some similar routine with your child yourself.

POSSIBLE PROBLEMS 2–3

Temper tantrums

A good method of handling temper tantrums when you are on your own with your child, in the privacy of your own home, is to ignore them (see p. 188). Alternatively you could distract your child by saying something unusual, amusing or silly, or try a tactic like switching the light on and off, or opening and banging a door several times.

However, as your child gets older, and there is a greater chance of her throwing a tantrum in a public place, there are a few different ways that you can handle them. The majority of temper tantrums are caused through anger and frustration – anger that she can't have her own way or that her body is not physically strong enough or well enough co-ordinated to do what she wants it to do, and every now and then your child needs, like everybody else, to give such anger full vent. You can help her by doing some of the following:
□ If your child is having a temper tantrum in a public place, don't get flustered; just take her outside the room into another as calmly as you can. Go outside of the shop and into the street; outside of the shop and into the car; out of the hotel foyer and into the rest room. You can deal with the tantrum more calmly where there are fewer people about.

195

☐ Don't ever forget to congratulate your child and praise her when the tantrum is over and she has got control again. After all, it's only a stage she's going through at the moment.

☐ A lot of anger and aggression can be got rid of by physically active games outdoors. That is why bicycles, skates and skate-boards are such good toys, because strenuous physical activity re-directs antisocial behaviour.

☐ If your child is expressing anger by shouting, join in for a few sentences and then gradually quieten your voice down, encouraging her to do the same, until you are both whispering. Then have a good giggle.

☐ Give your child some paper and crayons or fingerpaints and ask her to put on paper exactly what she is feeling.

☐ Let your child know that there is a set of "angry" toys like a drum to beat loudly, or a musical instrument to play like a xylophone or a particular marching song which can be shouted.

☐ It can help your child quite a lot to talk about anger and to let her know that you consider it to be a reasonable and valuable emotion to feel. It lets off steam but it also draws boundaries. Your anger tells her when she has overstepped the mark in all sorts of directions. Her own anger can be just as useful.

☐ Try to discuss with your child the causes of anger. Try to get to the root of the problem. It is one of the ways you can teach your child about sharing, tolerance, love, kindness, thoughtfulness for others, etc. If ever you think that such anger is justified, say so, and tell her why you think it is reasonable to be angry about something that has happened and then discuss the different ways that you might have reacted that wouldn't have been so hurtful and destructive.

☐ Show your child that anger is just as well expressed in words as in physical violence or destructiveness and let her know that angry words are much more acceptable to you than blows or breaking things.

196

BREATH HOLDING TIPS
As your child gets older she may try breath-holding attacks and her face might become quite blue during them. In this instance try the following:
● Blow gently on to your child's face.
● Sprinkle a few drops of cold water on to your child's face or apply a cold cloth.
● Gently pinch your child's nostrils together for a second or two.

Phobias

A phobia is different from ordinary fear. If your child is *afraid* of snakes, she is only afraid when she meets one at fairly close quarters. The rest of the time she doesn't give snakes a second thought. However, if your child has a *phobia* about snakes, she will become hysterical when she actually sees one, when she sees a picture of one, when she thinks of one, or when something reminds her of one. One of the things you have to understand is that, even as your child gets older, the explanation of a phobia really doesn't make any difference: she is not open to rational explanations. The only way you can help your child over a phobia is to convince her in some way that the object of the fear is harmless. There are a variety of ways in which you can do this:

☐ You can help your child to realize that such fears are unfounded by letting her know that you don't have the same fear but don't do it in a way which makes your child feel inferior

☐ Another way is to show that peers aren't afraid of the phobic objects. If, for example, the phobia is of dogs, it is quite a good idea to ask one of your friends who has a dog to bring it to the nursery school at pick-up time when your toddler can see that the others are quite unafraid of it.

☐ Never, ever ridicule your child's fears. No matter how unrealistic they seem to you, they are very real to her. Give rational explanations wherever you can and *always* behave in a sympathetic, helpful and rational way.

☐ If the phobia starts suddenly, look for something in your child's life which is causing stress. If it is associated with a parent going away, the death of a pet or starting nursery school, then there is a good chance that the phobia will be transient.

☐ But your child may be emotionally upset about something which is difficult to fathom out. You can try some real therapy by very gently introducing the object of her phobia while she is doing something very pleasant, like eating a favourite food such as ice cream.

Rows in front of the children

Of course your children have to grow up knowing the facts of life, one of which is that adults disagree occasionally, get angry and have rows, but for heaven's sake don't let them be frequent. If your partnership is going through a sticky patch, don't row in front of the children. Children, of course, want their parents to inhabit an ideal world where there is no rowing, no anger and no acrimony, and they get very insecure when the people they love most don't seem to love each other. The greatest deterrent to having a row with my husband came when my second youngest son, at four-and-a-half years old, snuggled up next to me a few minutes after we had had a row, looking very doleful. When I asked him what was wrong he said, "I don't know, but the world doesn't feel right."

Most children have the natural instinct to be peace-makers; mine certainly do. As soon as they hear a raised voice or an opinion vehemently expressed they start with diverting tactics like "Do you want a cup of coffee, mum" and then actually interject with, "Please don't get in a woos", which is their schoolboy term for getting in a state. It is like oil on troubled waters. It is very hard to lose your temper with anyone when your small child is pleading with you to stay calm. If you remember the deleterious effect it can have on your children to witness a row it can act as a great deterrent.

Baby battering

One of the things you should be aware of is that every parent at some time or other contemplates doing something physically violent to her/his children. Most mothers with newborn children who are fatigued and are walking the floor at nights trying to pacify a screaming baby will confess that they have thought of doing *anything* to stop the baby from crying. When my youngest son was about five days old and I was in such a situation I actually did think of throwing him against the wall. It is not abnormal to think such things. It's only abnormal to do them.

The highest incidence of baby battering amongst women is in the pre-menstrual period and it is a well-recognized part of pre-menstrual syndrome. Along with the depression, irritability, tearfulness, lethargy and feelings of unworthiness goes a lack of sympathy and patience with the children. Mothers who are ideal parents – very loving and caring, sympathetic and patient for the rest of the month – can become disturbed mothers for the few days prior to menstruation.

Most mothers are aware when they begin to lose hold on themselves and are able to control violent behaviour against their children. But if you feel yourself sliding down the slippery slope you should seek help, first from your partner or from a friend, but also from your doctor.

If you *ever* find yourself hitting your baby hard, sufficient to leave marks and bruises, don't feel that it is an admission of failure to seek help from your doctor. It is *essential* that you do, both for your child's sake and your own. Don't stand by and let your partner injure your child: try to make her/him see that what she or he is doing is wrong, and if she or he is impervious to your pleas, seek help on behalf of both of you. Contact your doctor, the police or your local health authority immediately. If you think that another adult is battering a child, never stand by without intervening. If you have seen evidence of battering, don't take no for an answer from the authority; be persistent.

12 Physical development

Watching your baby grow and develop is one of the most exciting aspects of being a parent, and during the first year you'll be astounded by how quickly your child changes. With each passing week he'll gain control over the various muscles in his body so co-ordination will improve, and with this improved co-ordination he'll be able to sit, crawl, stand and, eventually, walk and run. His manipulative abilities will improve and gradually, over the months, he'll develop fine control over his movements. Every child develops at his own rate, and the ages at which various skills or aspects of co-ordination are achieved, are only approximations. Don't force your child to go more quickly than he wants to—it will serve no purpose. Let him go at his own pace, while still providing all the encouragement and help that you can.

GENERAL DEVELOPMENT   0-1

The main changes that occur in your baby's general appearance, besides those of size and weight, are in proportion, posture and body control. Your baby's head gradually gets smaller in proportion to the rest of his body and his limbs lengthen and strengthen. During the first year your baby gains general control of his body so that it's no longer floppy and he can move it purposefully.

Your baby goes through the fastest growing phase of life in the womb. Growth and weight will continue to be rapid during the first six months, but the rate will slow down towards the end of the first year. In general, a baby of average weight will increase its length by a quarter during the first six months, and double its weight. The head will increase in circumference by about twice as much in the first twelve months as it will in the next eleven years (12.7 cm [5 in]).

Most size/weight charts plot the baby's weight in kilograms or pounds against the baby's age in weeks and its length in centimetres or inches (see p. 373). Except for the first few weeks of life when weight gain is watched rather closely, it's best not to watch your baby's weight obsessively. If your baby looks healthy and acts in a healthy way then it's highly unlikely that there's anything wrong. It is the long term trends that are important and, when considering your baby's weight, you should take account of different seasonal growth rates: growth is fastest in the spring and slowest in the autumn, so it's obvious that a year is about the minimum period over which you can study a child's growth realistically. And when you look at this growth you should pay attention to the regularity of weight gain rather than the amount. As long as your baby's weight is increasing over the weeks, even if it is a bit erratic, and he shows signs of being happy and thriving then you should not worry about weighing him too often. Furthermore, all size/weight charts are constructed for an "average" child. The average child is a theoretical statistic. Your baby is unique and his pattern of growth and weight gain will probably be quite different from any other babies that you know. That doesn't mean that he's abnormal.

199

Physical milestones

Milestones are "punctuations" in a baby's growth and development. These milestones occur with such regularity that it is possible to forecast with some accuracy when they will occur for most babies. This does not mean, however, that *all* babies will develop at the same speed. Just as there is a wide spread in the growth of size and weight so there is for the development of physical capabilities. While no two babies develop at the same rate or in the same way there are a few general principles which apply to physical development in all babies:

☐ All milestones are reached in the same order and your baby will not usually go on to another milestone before the previous one has been mastered.

☐ The rate of development is rarely constant. It goes through periods where it is very fast (growth spurts) and it may then slow right down. So, while development is continuous, many children can take huge steps forward in a developmental spurt and then slow down during a period of slow growth.

☐ A primitive reflex or movement has to be lost before a baby can acquire a par-

ticular skill. For example, your baby has to lose the primitive grasp reflex (see p.30) before he can acquire the skill to grasp an object purposefully.

☐ Development always proceeds from head to toe. The first milestone to be reached is control of the head; control of the body then progresses downwards to the arms, then to the trunk and then to the legs.

☐ When your baby is very young his movements are usually jerky. As he gets older the movements become smoother and more precise.

☐ A generalized activity very often makes way for a specific activity, so your baby at six months old may be making rather purposeless leg movements which resemble walking but they are quite different from the movements that your one-year-old child actually makes when he starts to walk.

☐ Development is measured not only in terms of *what* is done but *how* it is done. In other words, as your baby develops so do his skills.

☐ The brain and the nervous system control movement and co-ordination so your baby can only reach the milestones when the brain is ready. For instance, your baby will only learn to pick up a small object between his fingers and thumb when the nerve connections to the finger and thumb are fully developed.

☐ When a new skill is being mastered your baby may appear to lose a previously learned skill. This is simply because he is concentrating on the new one. As soon as it is mastered the old ones will reappear.

☐ Milestones can be affected by your child's personality. Independent, determined children nearly always try out and practise new movements more than others so it's not surprising that they master them earlier. A friendly, outgoing child often has a strong desire to communicate with others and may develop speech earlier than other children. You can encourage both of these characteristics in your child by the way you behave towards him (see p.249)

BODY MILESTONES

At one month
Your baby will have lost his very newborn appearance but his legs will still be bent. He may lift his head.

At two months
Your baby continues to stretch himself. He can lift his head to a 45° angle and hold it for a few moments.

At three months
Your baby's body will be completely uncurled and his legs will be extended. He'll hold up his head.

At four months
Your baby should be able to roll from side to side and on to his back. He'll support himself on his forearms.

At five months
When placed on his stomach your baby will push his head well clear of the mattress. He'll roll from back to side.

MANIPULATIVE MILESTONES

At one month
Your baby's hand will be held in a tight fist; he'll reflexively grasp anything put in his palm.

At two months
He'll hold his hand open more often and his grasp will become voluntary.

At three months
His hands will generally stay open although he may not be able to grasp anything for long.

At four months
Your baby will have discovered his own hands which he'll suck and play with.

At five months
He'll be able to grasp objects between both hands and will love sucking his own feet this way.

201

BODY MILESTONES

At six months
Your baby will be able to twist in all directions. He'll probably sit unsupported for a couple of seconds.

At seven months
Your baby's ability to sit will improve, although he may have to bend forward to balance himself.

At eight months
Your baby will be able to sit up completely unsupported and will be able to turn round.

At nine months
Your baby will make determined efforts to crawl and may be able to support himself on hands and knees.

At ten months
Your baby will be able to crawl with straight arms and legs. He'll pull himself to a standing position.

At eleven to twelve months
Your baby will probably be able to totter when supported but will "cruise" by himself (see p.211).

MANIPULATIVE MILESTONES

At six months
Your baby will be able to hold an object between finger and thumb and may be able to rotate his wrist.

At seven months
The finger and thumb become completely opposable. Your baby will hold an object in each hand.

At eight months
Your baby's dexterity will improve and he'll use a pincer movement to grasp small objects.

At nine months
Dexterity continues to improve. He begins to use his index finger to poke into holes.

At ten months
Your baby will be able to hold two objects in one hand. He'll be a bit clumsy in releasing them.

At eleven to twelve months
Your baby can hold crayons, feed himself, give and take objects. Co-ordination will improve daily.

Control of the head

Up to the age of six months, acquisition of head control goes something like this:

WHEN ON HIS BACK
● *From birth to six weeks*

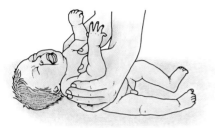

If you grasp your baby around the upper chest and lift his body from the mattress, his head will be so heavy and floppy that it will just hang back. This is why it is so important to support his neck and head carefully.
● *At six weeks*
If you lift your baby from the mattress by holding on to his hands he'll be able to hold his head in line with the rest of his body for a second or so.
● *At three months*

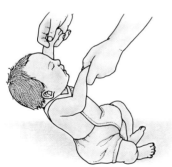

If you pull your baby up from a lying position by his hands he will keep his head up in line with the rest of his body without additional help from you.
● *At six months*
Your baby's head and neck will be so strong and well controlled that he'll be able to raise his head from the mattress and look at his toes.

WHEN ON HIS STOMACH
● *At one month*

Your baby will lie with his head to one side, with his bottom pushed up in the air and his knees slightly bent underneath his body.
● *At two months*
Your baby's body will be more fully stretched out and he'll be able to lift his head from the mattress for a moment or two.
● *At three months*
He will now lie quite flat and be able to raise his head and hold it in this position for quite a long time. He'll begin to take the weight of his shoulders and head on slightly outstretched forearms.
● *At four months*

Your baby will be able to raise both legs off the mattress. He'll be able to support his chest and head by propping himself up on his forearms. This way he'll be able to see what's going on around him.
● *At five to six months*
Your baby will probably be strong enough to take the weight of his head, shoulders and torso on his outstretched hands. He'll also be able to roll over from his back to his side.

203

Sitting

Before your baby can sit up he has to develop sufficient strength in his neck, shoulders and trunk so that he can control his head and keep his torso steadily upright. He also has to learn how to balance so that he doesn't topple over every time he tries to pick something up or twist around to see what's behind him; most babies don't achieve this before the age of eight or nine months.

● *At birth*

Your baby won't be able to sit up at all without support. If you hold him in a sitting position his back will be round and his head will loll forward. He'll be very wobbly, and will collapse immediately unless supported.

● *At one month*

Your baby's back will still be rounded and he'll only be a little steadier. However, he'll try and hold his head up for a second or two when held by you.

● *At four months*

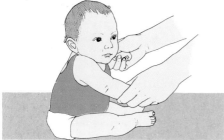

If you hold your baby in the sitting position he will be able to sit with his head held up; the lower part of his back will still be rounded but the upper part will be almost straight.

● *At six months*

Your baby will be able to sit up without support, but only for a few seconds. However, by this time he will enjoy sitting up in a chair surrounded by cushions for support.

● *At seven months*

He will be able to sit alone but will be very unsteady. His back will still be rounded and he will have to support himself with both arms, probably by placing them in front of his body as a kind of brace. However, in this position he won't be able to move his hands in any way because he'll be relying on them for balance. Any movement will result in his tumbling over.

● *At eight months*

Your baby should be able to sit up straight without using his hands for support. He will still be a bit unsteady so always make sure that he is surrounded by soft cushions in case he topples over.

● *At nine to ten months*

Your baby's balance will be so well developed that he'll be able to swing his torso to look around and will be able to reach forward without losing his balance.

Helping your baby to sit up

Now that you know how a baby learns to control his head and to sit up you can help your baby by playing similar sorts of physical games to those played in the first months of life to introduce your baby to the use of muscles for grasping, pulling and pushing:

☐ From the age of about two months you can help your baby to learn to sit up by supporting his tummy and shoulders and by talking to him so that he momentarily tries to raise his head to look at you.

☐ By the time your baby is three months old you will find that he is able to control head, neck and shoulders but that his back needs support because it's still rounded.

☐ At four months he'll be able to hold his head, neck and most of his back straight and all you'll have to do is hold on to his arms to keep his bottom steady and stop him from bending too much at the hips.

205

Propping your baby up

From as early as six weeks you should include your baby in what's going on by propping him in an upright position with pillows (see p.69). Although he'll not be strong enough to sit alone the pillows will provide all the support he needs. With all of my children I found the bouncing cradle the most suitable. It's soft and so it moulds to the baby's rounded shape; it can be safely padded with soft pillows and cushions. But the baby must be safely strapped into it to prevent him slipping and his head must be supported with a cushion or pillow. Because the cradle's so springy it responds to any arm movements and kicking and so your baby is encouraged to try to make things happen for himself. And because the chair is well angled the baby

is propped up and can see all around him. The bouncing cradle is very portable and it's easy to carry a small child and place him on the table or work surface next to you so that he can see you for both reassurance and education. The legs of the bouncing cradle are usually made of slippery metal so a useful tip to render them non-slip is to bind them with double-sided sticky tape; this way you can even put him on a shiny or slippery table or draining board. You can actually prop your baby anywhere as long as there is a straight, firm slope between his bottom and his head. Make sure that the baby is always well surrounded and supported by the cushions; if you do this carefully he can be propped in an armchair, between the back and the arm of a sofa, or in his pram.

Although most baby chairs are angled so that the baby can see around him, you may find that a very small baby slips down. If so, use a soft pillow behind him.

When you're cleaning up your baby's room you may want to prop him in one corner of his cot for safety. Always leave some toys with him, too, but never leave the room, even for a minute.

When you go out with a pram let your baby see what's going on by putting pillows under the pram base to raise his back and then prop either side to prevent him from falling over.

You'll naturally want to include your baby in family mealtimes. Until he can sit properly use a soft, washable cushion behind his back and bottom.

Crawling

Before your baby can crawl he has to be able to get into the right position. He has to be able to straighten his body so that his legs are outstretched; he has to learn adequate control of his head and neck, and he has to have the strength to push up on both of his arms so that his chest and head are clear of the floor.

It's difficult to specify at exactly what age a baby will start to crawl, so you should regard the times given below as stages more than ages. What's more, you shouldn't worry if your baby shows no interest in crawling. Some babies hate lying on their tummies and they are usually the ones who love seeing what's going on around them. They will probably leave crawling to a later stage; indeed, some babies never learn to crawl at all, but still go on to walk perfectly.

● *At birth*
Your baby will be born with a crawling reflex (see p.30), but will lose this as soon as his body uncurls from the fetal position.

● *At about four months*

Your baby will probably raise both chest and legs off the floor while making swimming movements with his arms.

● *By about six months*

Your baby will be able to support the top half of the body on outstretched arms and you may see the first signs of crawling when he bends his knees up below his body. Although he's moving into the crawling position he probably won't quite have got the hang of it, the result of which will be his rocking back and forth.

● *By about seven months*
Probably within a month of the previous stage your baby will have begun to take his body's weight on one outstretched arm when he wants to.

● *By about eight or nine months*

Your baby will have begun to pull himself forward on the floor with his head held erect, making kicking movements.

207

Helping your baby to crawl

While I am very much against *teaching* your baby to make orthodox crawling movements, you can encourage him to start moving forward from a lying or sitting position:

☐ The best possible way is for you to sit a few feet from your baby and to encourage him to come towards you, possibly using a favourite toy as an enticement.

☐ Help your baby whenever you think it's needed, particularly if he's getting tired and frustrated because his efforts are unsuccessful, and make sure that you always praise any efforts that he makes.

☐ As he becomes more adventurous you can help by placing a toy just out of reach so that he has to use all his own resources, including determination, to get hold of it.

☐ Babies learn by mimicry from a very early age so once he starts trying to crawl it's not a bad idea for you to get down on the floor yourself and crawl as well.

☐ Slippery floors, although usually dangerous, can be encouraging for crawling babies because even the slightest movement is rewarded with forward motion.

Shuffling

To move forward your baby has to co-ordinate hand movements and knee movements, but initially he may find this difficult and may devise a unique shuffling movement to propel himself forward. This can be anything from a sideways crab-like movement to a kind of shuffling on his bottom with one leg tucked underneath for leverage. It doesn't matter what kind of manoeuvre your baby works out – all are acceptable. The important thing is that he's mastered the art of moving forwards;

it is a great achievement and he should receive a lot of praise for doing so. You shouldn't discourage your baby from any odd movements he makes but rather let him discover how to control and move his body in his own particular way.

The crawling baby

Once a baby has learned the knack of crawling (or shuffling) he can pick up speed very quickly so a crawling baby is a baby to be watched. He's also a baby who needs a lot of room so that he can move about to the full extent of his capabilities. For this reason, and to encourage your child to be as curious and adventurous as possible, you should make sure there's enough clear floor space. Your crawling baby is also getting stronger every day so beware of anything that's rickety or fragile because he'll break it very quickly. Your baby will also get much dirtier now, and will put any object he finds on the floor straight into his mouth so make sure that he doesn't go near pets' feeding bowls or rubbish bins. Your baby's knees will take quite a bashing so put him into overalls or trousers and try to ensure that the floor is very smooth or covered with something soft to prevent grazing; your baby doesn't need shoes and should go shoeless until he's walking.

SAFETY TIPS
● Make your home child-proof.
● Never leave your baby alone.
● Remove all furniture with sharp edges and corners from the room.
● Remove anything breakable from a surface which is less than one metre from the floor.
● Make sure there are no electric wires trailing across the floor.
● Make sure all electric points are covered with safety plugs.

● Make sure that there are no switches less than one metre from the floor.
● Make sure that all doorways and stairways have adjustable safety gates.
● Try and keep the floor clear of small, sharp toys.
● Make sure all fires are guarded.
● Don't leave any cloths hanging from tables that a baby could reach up and pull.
● Make sure that all furniture and fixtures are sturdy and safely attached.

● Never leave anything hot on a table in the same room as your baby.
● Make sure that stair bannisters are too narrow for a small child to squeeze through.
● Make sure that all cupboard doors are closed firmly and that the handles are out of a crawling baby's reach; if they aren't, lock them or seal them up with masking tape.
● Make sure there are no containers of poisonous substances on the floor or within reach.

Standing

Because a baby's development progresses from head to toe, control over the muscles of the knees, lower legs and feet is rarely achieved before the age of ten or eleven months. It's only at this time that he's strong enough and has sufficient balance to take the whole weight on his feet and stand up.

ATTEMPTS AT STANDING
● *At three months*

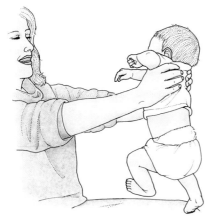

Once your baby can support his head, one of the most enjoyable early games is to hold him facing you with his feet touching your knees. When he's lifted up and down he'll feel his feet in contact with your legs and will learn the sensation of taking his own weight. Even very young babies love to be held in this way although you should take care to support the head.

● *At six months*
By now he'll probably make jumping movements by bending and straightening his knees and hips whenever he's held in a standing position.

● *At seven or eight months*
He may start a sort of dancing movement instead of jumping and he'll also start to hop from one foot to another. Babies quite often place one foot on top of the other then pull out the underneath foot and repeat the whole movement over and over again.

● *Around nine or ten months*

He can take his full weight on his feet, but can't balance yet. If you support your baby firmly underneath the arms he will be able to take his weight on his legs and will try to move one foot in front of the other. Supported on your lap, he will try to take a step or two forward. At this stage you must support your baby very securely to take most of the weight because his balance is still primitive.

● *At ten months or later*

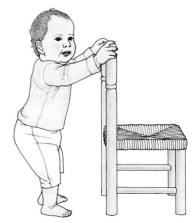

The muscle control of the knees and feet will have improved and he will start pulling himself up on any nearby furniture despite the fact that balance is still far from good.

Sitting down

Standing up is easy compared to sitting down, and it usually takes a baby three or four weeks to master getting back down to the floor again from a standing position. He usually does this by sitting down backwards with a thump, or by sliding his hands down the support until his bottom's on the floor. Until he's mastered this he'll probably just stand still and scream for your assistance. There may be a three week period of frustration for both of you before he learns to drop down into a sitting position. You can help by lowering your baby gently down so that he gains confidence in the movement and by not getting angry if you have to do it repeatedly.

"Cruising"

After your baby has gained sufficient confidence from pulling himself up into a standing position and getting back down on to the floor again it will probably be about four weeks before he starts "cruising". He does this by facing what he's holding on to and then gradually inching his hands along the support (a); the rest of the body is brought in line with the hands by taking small sideways steps, one foot after the other (b). As he gets confident using this method he'll hold on to the support at arm's length and will only use it for balance (c).

Once your baby has reached this stage it's then only a very few weeks before he will let go of the support and move forwards to the next piece of furniture. These first few steps are very unsteady. To increase the width of the base he keeps his feet quite wide apart and balances by holding his arms up and forward, slightly bent at the elbows. Not until your baby is quite proficient at walking will he bring his feet closer together and let his hands drop to his sides.

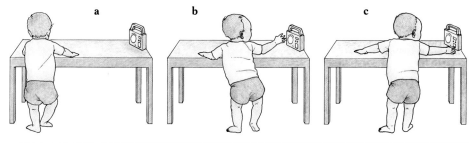

a   b   c

HELPING YOUR BABY TO STAND

● Don't put socks or shoes on your baby's feet. He has much better grip and balance when his feet are bare. If your house is cold, put bootees with suede soles on your baby's feet. Make sure that all your baby's clothing is loose so that movements aren't restricted.

● All the furniture in the room should be heavy, firm and stable so that there's no risk of it toppling on the baby as he holds on to it.

● Resist the temptation to hurry your baby with standing or walking. He'll do it in his own good time and nothing you do can hurry the process.

● Don't play tricks on your baby by suddenly removing your support. This will give your baby a bad fright and could damage his trust in you because until that moment you were the one thing that he could rely on.

● Don't start to use sleeping bags for the first time now – your baby will try to stand and will fall and may get hurt. However, if he's used to one it's all right to continue with it.

● Make sure that all wires and flexes are tucked away or firmly tacked down. He may start by cruising around furniture but a light flex may seem an ideal "hold" once he's on the move.

211

GENERAL DEVELOPMENT 1–2

During the second year your baby's body grows in length, loses its rather plump, podgy appearance, becomes firmer, stronger and more muscular, and starts to take on adult proportions. Balance and coordination improve and fine movements are mastered. By two years old, your baby son will have grown to half his adult height; your baby girl will have to wait another six or nine months to be that tall.

Size and weight vary very much from child to child just as they do from adult to adult. Weight gain is proportional to your child's size, so small children gain less weight, less quickly, than large children. Some size/weight charts are given on page 373 to show the variation between small and large children. At two years old you can see that there is a variation of almost 4 kilos (9 lbs).

BODY MILESTONES

At 13 to 15 months
Your baby should be able to stand unaided and take one or two steps to reach a support. However, he won't be able to get up from the sitting to the standing position without support.

At 15 to 18 months
Your baby will be able to raise himself to the standing position unaided. He will probably begin to walk without any support in the early position of feet wide apart and elbows high.

At 18 to 20 months
Walking will become steadier and the arms will drop down by his side. Your toddler will almost certainly want to walk upstairs.

MANIPULATIVE MILESTONES

At 12 months
Your baby will have mastered the adult grip, which is a fine movement achieved by bringing the finger and thumb together. If you ask your baby for something he will give it to you, and will be able to roll a ball across the floor.

At 13 to 15 months
Your baby will be able to hold two small objects in one hand; he will be able to put one block on top of another and may try to make marks with a pencil. When it is time to be undressed he may start taking off his shoes.

At 18 months
Your baby can build a tower of blocks, possibly three or four high. He will be quite skilled at manipulating food with a spoon and will be able to turn over the pages of a book. If you show him how, he will open a zip.

Walking

There is no right age for your baby to start to walk. Your baby's first unsupported steps will probably occur sometime between nine and fifteen months, but there's a wide variation either side of these figures. The reason for this is not known although very often there's a family history of early or late walking. Despite the very wide variation in the age at which babies learn to walk, they all have to pass through several well-defined stages of de- velopment before they can walk with con- fidence and good balance (see below). Babies can stay for a variable length of time in each phase and you should never make the mistake of trying to push your baby too hard to move from one to the other. You will give the greatest help if you are there with encouraging words so that your baby doesn't lose heart. Learning to walk is one of the most difficult things he'll ever have to do so make your baby proud of his achievements.

At 21 to 24 months
Your toddler will be able to maintain his balance while he bends over to pick something up and will not fall over.

At 2 years
Your baby will have learn- ed turning and screwing movements with the hands so he'll be able to open a door by turning the door knob and he may be able to unscrew a loose lid. He will probably enjoy washing his hands.

STAGES OF WALKING

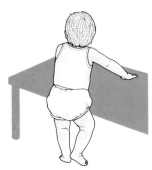  

1 *Your baby will probably have started cruising around the furniture before he was one. He'll slide both hands along the support and bring up his feet to align with the rest of his body. Balance will be a problem.*

2 *He'll still cruise but he'll stand further away from the furniture and take more of the body's weight on his feet. He'll start to move one hand over the other instead of sliding them together and, as he becomes more confident, will start to move both hands and feet together. This is a very important stage because, for a second, your baby has the confidence and the balance to take all his weight on one foot.*

3 *Your baby will really enjoy the independence of moving around rooms using any support he can, and the next stage will be the negotiation of gaps between two supports. He will only do this if he can hold on to both supports at once. At this stage he still has to feel securely supported, and will only let go of one support when he's holding firmly on to the other*

4 *Your baby will start to cross gaps which are wider than an arm's span. While still holding on to the support with one hand, he will move into the centre of the gap and, having got his balance, will release the support and take a step towards the next one, making a grab for it with both hands.*

5 *Your baby will now begin to "toddle". He will manage to stagger a couple of paces to reach the second support.*

6 *Your baby will now launch himself into an open space and take several unsupported steps with confidence. He may only take half a dozen steps before losing his balance and sitting down with a thud. However, you will find that he usually sets off to reach a goal and waddles rapidly from A generally a gorilla to it.*

HELPING YOUR CHILD TO WALK

● Arrange the furniture around the room so that he can progress down one side, across the end and up the other.

● Initially, the gaps between the furniture should be no bigger than the width of your baby's arms so that he can hang on to a piece of furniture with one hand and stretch out the other to reach the next support easily. If the gaps are too big your baby won't be able to reach the support that will enable him to cross the gap.

● While your baby is learning to walk make sure that the floors aren't slippery - one bad bang may give him such a fright that he's put off walking for several weeks.

● Make sure the room is baby-proofed, and that there are no flexes or objects which can be pulled over (see p.324).

● Shoes and socks are entirely unnecessary: bare feet are safer not only because there'll be no risk of malformed feet but because your baby will be able to grip well and get used to the sensation of weight. In the winter you can use slipper socks with suede or leather feet if it is very cold.

● A useful aid to complement cruising and your baby's first steps is a pushing trolley or cart. Make sure it has a stable wide base so it won't topple over and will only move at your baby's pace.

● Always stay close at hand when your baby is taking his first steps.

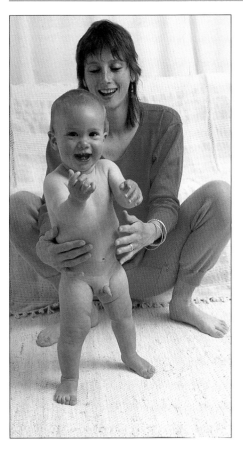

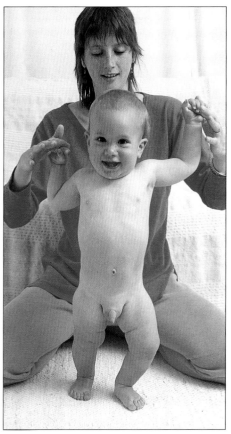

215

Your toddling child

When your baby first starts to toddle he will have little control over his movements: he will only be able to travel in one direction, he will be incapable of swerving, and he'll have great difficulty stopping once he's got up speed. However, by about nineteen months he'll be able to walk backwards as well as forwards and may even have mastered running. After he can run he'll be able to jump. By two years old he'll be able to veer and swerve while he's running and will be able to glance over his shoulder without losing balance. He will be able to stop quite suddenly without toppling over and will have sufficient balance to be able to bend down to pick something up without having to sit down first. If you encourage him he will be able to kick a ball, although it will be rather a dragging kind of kick because he can't maintain his balance on one leg for very long.

Your toddler will want, quite naturally, to race about as much as possible, but out of doors you'll have to be careful. He'll have no traffic sense as yet so you'll either have to hold his hand or use reins. I believe that reins are the most satisfactory solution for both of you: they hurt neither your arm nor your toddler's and they give your baby far greater freedom than he would have holding your hand. Although your toddler's strength will increase during this year don't expect him to walk much further than a couple of hundred yards at a time. If you're in a hurry, or can't bear the idea of constant stops and starts to look at things, then take a push chair of some sort and use that.

If your baby has a set-back in the development of walking, don't worry. He's learning so much at the moment that it's quite understandable that he may slow down in one aspect of his development to concentrate on another; he may also suffer lapses after an illness. Just relax and let your baby develop along his own lines.

SAFETY TIPS
● Remember, not only can your toddler walk, he can also climb, so fit bars to all the windows or, if you don't like the appearance, special fasteners which allow the window to be opened only a few inches.
● Keep possible hiding places like cupboards or chests securely locked so that your baby can't disappear and get locked in.
● Be sure that any locks on room doors are out of reach.
● Do not allow your unsupervised child into a garden with open access to a road. The road-training drill should be taught as soon as possible.
● Unless taught how to negotiate stairs properly, your toddler is bound to fall down them sooner or later. I taught all my children to go downstairs from the time that they could crawl, by sitting on the top stair, putting their legs down to the one below and then following with their hands.
● All clothing should be non-flammable.
● Keep all the handles of pans turned away from the front of the stove.
● Never leave anything hot lying around to cool off; keep it out of your toddler's reach until it is absolutely cold.
● A toddler can't cope with swing doors so don't have them.
● Glass doors should never be so clean that your toddler bumps into them, so make them obvious by fixing transfers or coloured paper on the glass.
● Keep all your medicines in an approved medicine chest, high up and always locked. Never carry medicines around in your handbag or leave them on your dressing table.
● Don't let your toddler run around wearing socks but not shoes. He can slip on any smooth surface.
● Don't put rugs on polished floors unless they've been backed with double-sided tape to make them grip.
● Don't let your child near anything which is small enough to be swallowed or pushed up his nose or into his ear.
● All sharp instruments, including kitchen equipment, should be kept out of your child's reach.
● Never leave sewing materials around.
● Never leave your child alone near water.

GENERAL DEVELOPMENT   2–3

By your child's third year the rate of growth and development will have slowed down. He will have almost complete control over his body, and many movements will have become automatic – he'll no longer have to concentrate or make an effort to do things requiring fine physical manoeuvring or co-ordination. He will have the co-ordination to build a tower of blocks, he will try to get dressed and undressed and may even manage to undo buttons.

PHYSICAL MILESTONES

At two years
Your child will be able to go up and down stairs alone but will put two feet on each step before moving on to the next. He'll kick a ball successfully without falling over.

At two and a half years
He'll be able to walk on tiptoe, jump in the air and on and off objects. However, he won't be able to stand on one foot yet.

At three years
He'll walk upstairs with a foot on each step but will have to put both feet on the same stair coming down; he'll jump off the bottom step. He'll be able to stand for a few seconds on one foot but can't skip.

MANIPULATIVE MILESTONES

At two years
He'll put on his own gloves, socks and shoes successfully. He'll manage to rotate his elbow accurately so that he can turn a door handle or unscrew a lid. He'll begin to draw pictures with pencils and crayons.

At two and a half years
He'll take off his trousers and underpants by himself. He'll be able to thread beads on to a string and will fasten large, easily placed buttons.

At three years
He'll dress and undress himself completely as long as all the fastenings are within reach; he'll manage the buckle on his sandals. He'll draw and colour quite accurately and will have mastered the complicated movement of using scissors.

217

CO-ORDINATION 0–1

During the first 6 weeks your baby's hands will be held in fists, although they'll probably open and close when he cries. By about 8 weeks your baby's hands will be open more often, and the grasp reflex (see p.30) will be replaced by a voluntary movement on your baby's part. Some parents get quite worried at this stage because their baby doesn't seem to hold on to objects as tightly as before. This is nothing to worry about – your baby is simply learning a new skill, which he will perfect within a couple of months.

Up to this age, he won't have tried to co-ordinate the movements of fingers and hands. Instead, he'll spend a great deal of time discovering how they look, feel and move; he'll hold them open most of the time and will move his fingers and watch them closely. It's as though he's assessing his powers before starting to use them.

Between four and five months old he'll have voluntary control over reaching – he'll probably move both arms towards an object and grasp it between his two hands.

At about six months old your baby will try to hold an object, either between two hands, or in one hand by squeezing it between the palm and fingers; there's no fine control. However, he'll be able to differentiate between large and small objects and will open his hand accordingly. He'll love the *feel* of things, so provide lots of different textures to clutch and handle, as well as different shapes. When he's lying down he'll probably reach out, grab a foot and put it in his mouth. He won't know exactly what to do with all objects, so if you offer a cube he may hold on to it, but if you offer a second one, he'll drop the first without thinking. At around this time he'll start to explore how he can use his hands in feeding. Hand/eye co-ordination will be sufficient for your baby to pick up finger foods and start feeding himself, although getting food to mouth is anything but accurate (see p. 140).

At about eight months old your baby will hold something out to you but will not yet have learnt how to let it go and give it to you. He will not reach this milestone until he's about a year old, when dropping things deliberately from his high chair or buggy becomes a very entertaining game.

From now on your baby's ability to grasp becomes more and more refined. By the time he is nine months old he'll have stopped holding an object in the palm of his hand and will hold it between his thumb and the side of his index finger, and by the time he is a year old he'll be able to pick up quite a small object between the tips of his finger and thumb, and will usually point at it with his index finger before picking it up. He'll be able to pass an object from one hand to another, and will be able to hold two objects at a time, one in each hand.

Between eight and ten months your baby really learns to manipulate. He squeezes things, slaps, slides, pokes, rubs, scrapes and bangs them. He explores every new substance with his hands, including food, and will mix, smear and splash anything that is liquid or runny. Most objects find their way straight to his mouth, whether they're feet, fingers, plastic lids or toys. As he gets more skilled at manipulation the fascination of putting things in his mouth begins to wane, and he begins to play games like pat-a-cake. He'll also have developed the social skill of being able to wave goodbye.

Hand/eye co-ordination

Age	Skill	How to give encouragement
Up to eight weeks old	Until he is about 8 weeks old your baby won't have learnt to use his hands. He'll be learning to focus; the maximum distance at which he'll be able to focus will be about 25 cm (10 inches).	Your baby will try to focus on anything which is moving, for instance a mobile which is highly coloured. However, your face will be the most interesting object in his whole life, so make sure that he sees that often and close. Hang interesting objects within his eyeline, no further away from him than 25 cm (10 inches).
Two to two-and-a-half months	Your baby will have opened his hands and will watch them with fascination. Focusing distance is not much more than 30.5 cm (12 inches) so he'll bring hands and fingers close up to his face so that he can watch them moving.	As soon as your baby's hands are open they are ready to have things put into them. The most interesting toys are the ones that make a noise, like a rattle. They are also useful because your baby starts to make a connection between what his hands are doing, what his eyes are seeing and what he can hear.
Two-and-a-half to three months	Your baby will watch his hands very carefully and with a lot of concentration. Once he does this you'll know that he has made the connection between seeing and doing. At about this age your baby may make a clumsy movement with either hand to get near to the object.	Your baby is learning to judge distances and to move his hands to where his eyes think something interesting is happening. One of the best ways you can help is to put a string above the cot or the pram with lots of interesting objects hanging from it. Let them swing freely so that your baby can reach up to touch them to make them move and, most important, to see them move as a result of his action.
Three to four months	Your baby will touch everything in sight, and will be learning how to measure distances using his hands and eyes. He'll look at an object and then confirm the distance by trying to reach it. He reaches the object but now, instead of using an open hand, he tries to make a fist before he connects with it.	Your baby will now be too old for swinging things. If something goes out of reach it will only frustrate him because he is longing to grasp it. Instead of having objects dangling from a string, secure them to the sides of the cot. Alternatively, hold out an object so that he can try to get hold of it. Always wait until he's touched it before handing it over.

219

Hand/eye co-ordination

Age	Skill	How to give encouragement
Four to six months	*Your baby's eyes will be mature enough to focus on objects at any distance and he will follow any moving object that catches his attention. As he approaches six months he'll no longer have to measure the distance between hand and object by looking backwards and forwards, from one to the other. A glance will tell your baby where the object is and where his hand is in relation to it. It will also tell him how big a movement he'll have to make in order to reach the object. At the same time he will be learning to grasp, so when he reaches out and touches the object he will open his fingers and curl them around whatever he wants to hold.*	*Your baby really needs lots of practice at reaching out and getting hold of things; he'll also have a great deal of fun doing it. You can encourage him to do this by holding out the most interesting objects you can find, for example anything that makes a noise or is an interesting shape. It could be a plastic bottle, a ball of wool, or car keys.*

Right- and left-handedness

If both you and your partner are left-handed one in three of your children will be left-handed; the chances of this happening with two right-handed parents is one in ten. There is no natural law which states that one hand is superior to the other so it should never bother you if your child is left-handed. Your child has no control over which of his hands is dominant; dominance is decided by the developing brain. Think of the brain as two linked halves, each of which controls different activities. One of these sides becomes dominant as your baby's brain develops. If it is the left side of the brain which dominates, the baby is right-handed. If it is the right side the baby is left-handed.

In the first few months your baby may seem to have no preferences but in fact the majority of newborns turn their heads more to the right than to the left. As your baby's co-ordination improves and he starts to acquire manual skills you may find that he starts to use one hand more than the other. Don't, however, be worried if he doesn't do this. Your baby will develop at his own speed. Never, ever, try to dissuade your baby from being left-handed. You may think that by "encouraging" your child to use his right hand instead of his left ' that you're doing him a favour for later life so that he'll never have to suffer the minor annoyances of right-handed potato peelers or scissors. You are not. And, what's more, you could well risk causing psychological side-effects like stuttering as well as reading and writing difficulties by altering what your baby's brain naturally wants to do.

CO-ORDINATION 1–3

By the time he's a year old he'll be able to pick up something quite small, such as a button, between thumb and forefinger. If you take a pencil or crayon and make marks on a piece of paper he will take the pencil when offered it, and will try to imitate the marks that you have made. By about thirteen months your baby will have learnt to hold more than one object in his hand. Co-ordination will also be improving so if you show him how to build a tower of blocks he'll follow your example, putting one block on top of another. He'll start to remove items of clothing (see p.64), and will love pulling around a toy on a string, hammering pegs through holes and fitting different shapes into the appropriate openings. He'll be able to feed himself without any help and without making too much mess by the time he's fifteen months old, he will attempt to brush his hair if shown and will be keen to help you around the house.

By about eighteen months your baby will be able to build a tower of blocks, four or five high, and turn over the pages of a book, probably two or three pages at a time. By the time your child is two years old his hands will be very well co-ordinated and he'll manage the complex movement of twisting something round in his hands so he can open a door by turning the door knob and unscrew a loose cap from a jar. Washing and drying the hands will be a favourite pastime and two-year-olds usually make their first attempts to dress and undress themselves. They can usually manage things like putting on their shoes but probably need help with their socks.

Always remember that your child will proceed at his own pace and that he cannot develop muscular co-ordination faster than the brain and nervous system are developing; no two children develop at the same rate. Don't make the mistake of expecting more from your child than he is capable of. He has a tremendous desire to please and if you constantly set your goals higher than he's naturally capable of

reaching he will then feel demoralized and unhappy because he has let you down. Even worse, he may become resentful and frustrated if he aspires to do things which are more complicated than his body will allow. Your primary role is therefore to help and encourage, not to set unachievable goals.

By the time your child is three years old he will probably be able to do the following things: he'll be able to build a tower of blocks, up to eight or nine high. He'll continue to dress and undress himself and will manage it with increasing skill. He'll undo buttons which are within easy reach although he may not be able to do them up. He will help with any household task or chore that you suggest and will love playing games that imitate the kind of jobs that you do whether it's mending something or doing the washing up. He'll be perfectly capable of carrying plates and dishes to and from the table, and will be a much more co-operative and able member of the family.

How to improve co-ordination

Between the ages of two and three your child is a great experimenter and you should feed this curiosity by opening up his world and planning new discoveries. This is the age when children find out about, and understand the force of, gravity – something always falls *down*. Anything which is round will roll; something which is square will not; liquids flow and have no shape; they take up the shape of their container. Large containers will hold more water than small containers. Solids on the other hand will often have a shape of their own and that shape can't be moulded. Clay and dough can be squeezed and made into different shapes.

These discoveries can only be made if your child's co-ordination, not just of the hand and the eye, but of the body and the limbs, develops and matures. Toys which demand good co-ordination will help your child to develop it. You can help him improve balance by simply encouraging him to walk along narrow strips. Always

stay close by otherwise your child could lose his confidence and fall. You can improve ball sense by throwing and catching, initially with something large and soft like a beach ball.

Children love jumping and somersaulting on to soft things, so put a mattress or a large piece of foam rubber down on the floor so that they can indulge in their acrobatics. In our playroom we always had three very large soft floor cushions for the children to tumble on. A simple tree swing made out of some stout rope and an old motor tyre is wonderful for developing strength, co-ordination and a sense of adventurousness. Climbing frames, as long as they are on a fairly soft surface like grass to cushion falls, have the advantage that they provide all sorts of physical activities that develop a wide range of movements that require good co-ordination. A really sturdy one will give your child good service for years and years and your child will use it in increasingly adventurous ways.

Encouraging adventurousness

Your child should become aware of, and enjoy, physical movement from very early on in life (see p.292). There is nothing more natural than for a young baby to be jogged about. After all he was constantly on the move inside the womb for nine months. Your child will get used to moving and being moved and having to use his body in a positive physical sense especially as he'll be carried around a lot when you go about your everyday life.

Once your child becomes mobile, it is better to encourage a spirit of adventure than to be over-protective. Of course your child will come a cropper once or twice, that is inevitable, but it's preferable to having a child who has no sense of physical freedom or confidence. You are also doing your child quite a disservice because for the next seven or eight years most of your child's pleasures will be derived from physical activities. If he can't move with the same pace and accuracy as other children he will be left behind and ex-

cluded from many enjoyable activities. Here is an example of what I mean by actively discouraging and actively encouraging adventurousness and independence. An over-protective parent is one who insists on holding the child's hand if he wants to climb along the edge of a low wall. Conversely a parent who encourages physical activity will be the one who introduces a child to balancing on a fairly narrow surface, practising at home on a plank supported at either end by a pile of magazines.

One of the best ways of encouraging activity in your child is to join in and do it yourself, so do so. You are your child's favourite playmate and you should be the person to introduce your child to new physical activities. You can also correct faults if they become apparent. Give your child tips and tricks on how to speed up and refine co-ordination. Just by imitating your own physical movements, your child will be learning new physical skills, without either of you knowing it.

VISION   0-1

It used to be thought that newborn babies could not see. It was thought that because they could not focus to any great extent their visual world need not be stimulating and could even be neglected. We now know that this is far from the truth. A newborn baby *can* see. The only difference between a newborn baby and an older one with mature eyesight is that the newborn baby cannot see as much, as easily, as well. In other words, your newborn baby sees in a limited way but sees nonetheless, and you have to fit the visual world into a range that he can perceive.

Your baby's visual powers will not be fully developed until he's between three and six months old. He won't be able to focus on anything further than 25 centimetres from his face. As his eye muscles become stronger and he develops binocular vision, his acuity will improve greatly.

Even although your newborn baby's eyesight is limited, his eyes are very sensi-

tive to two things: the human face, and anything that moves. If you bring your face to within 20 centimetres of your baby's you will notice that his eyes move and his expression changes. Even a baby only a few hours old will be able to bring both eyes together on to an object (convergence) and follow it if it moves. As he gets older his whole body may react with excited jerking movements when your face comes into focus.

Colour vision

When your baby is born the cells in the retina of the eye which see colours are not fully developed, so your newborn baby only sees the world in terms of muted shades. The first colours that your baby detects are red and blue, and then green and yellow. For the first few months of life your baby can only see the brightest kinds of colours so make sure that you have brightly-coloured objects around him.

Three-dimensional vision

Because your baby can only focus on objects which are closer than 30 centimetres from his face, the world appears rather flat and many details are not seen. However, even at two weeks a baby will automatically raise a hand to protect himself from something which is moving quickly towards him. It is necessary for your baby to have three-dimensional vision before he becomes mobile, and he probably won't crawl until he sees and understands the third dimension. A complete, three-dimensional picture of the world is not usually built up until your baby is about four months old and may not be perfect until six months old.

Checking eyesight

During the first few months of your baby's life you are the best person to check his sight although you shouldn't become obsessive about it. By the age of four months even an inattentive or lazy baby should focus on a brightly-coloured object held 20 to 25 centimetres from his face, especially if it makes a noise, like a rattle, and especially if it is moved. One of the most joyful sights in your child's life is your face, and your child should be reacting to your smile and bobbing head movements as you talk by the same age. If he isn't don't be too concerned but mention it to your midwife, health visitor or doctor when you next see them.

STIMULATING YOUR BABY'S EYESIGHT

● Put a fairly large photograph of your own face, your partner's face, one of your other children's faces, or indeed any face cut out of a magazine, at the side of your baby's cot so that he can practise focusing on one of his favourite objects – the human face. On the other side of the cot firmly attach a mirror so that he can look at his own face and also see it moving when he wriggles near it.

● Put very simple brightly-coloured pictures around the rest of the cot within the baby's range of vision (no more than 30 centimetres away for the first month).

● Put a mobile over the cot. This doesn't have to be an expensive item. It can be a couple of balloons or a few household objects hung on a coat hanger or on a wooden pole attached to the cot.

● String some interesting objects on elastic across the hinges of the pram hood so that your baby can watch them when he is lying in the pram.

● If your baby's cot is near the wall, you can use toys with rubber suction pads to stick out from the wall between the bars of the cot for your child to watch and focus on.

● As your child gets older it is important that toys move and make a noise so dangle soft, light objects on strings so that they swing when your baby swipes them. Anything that will jingle, such as a rattle or a toy with bells attached, will be entertaining.

● In the car stick toys on to the back of your seat. You can also hang them from the side windows or the roof, as long as it doesn't cut down visibility dangerously.

● Your baby's never too young to go to museums or art galleries with you. If he's in a back pack he'll be able to look over your shoulder at exactly the same things as you.

● When you leave your baby outside either suspend some toys or mobiles from a tree bough or from a washing line or piece of string hung between two poles. The washing itself will prove exciting to your baby if it's blowing about in the wind.

VISION   1–3

Around the age of one your child begins to see and rapidly follow moving objects, and his vision now is about as good as it ever will be in adult life.

The main changes that occur during your child's formative years are to do with the ability to *interpret* what he sees so that he can use it to express ideas in words, pictures and movements. In other words, it is the connections in the brain between the eyes, the tongue, the pen, the brush, the intellectual thought, the hand and the rest of the body that matures, not the ability to see *per se*. As with other aspects of your child's growing up you should try to encourage the development of your child's eye/brain and eye/body connections so that he can reach his full potential.

You should do this by providing stimulating ideas, stimulating books, stimulating toys and stimulating activities.

While I don't think regular eye check-ups are necessary in a child who is developing normally you should be on the look-out for any changes in the appearance of your child's eye, that is a lazy eye, a drooping eyelid or a squint. Be responsive to signs that your child can't see clearly, for example, bumping into furniture or not being able to follow the trajectory of a ball that's thrown to him. Seek medical advice at once; don't wait to see if the abnormality clears up. Like a disused limb, a disused eye deteriorates rapidly. Eyes need constant exercise and stimulation, that is how they keep healthy.

TEETH 0–1

There is no correct time for your baby to cut his first tooth. Some babies are born already having a tooth and yet it is still within the normal range to have none at twelve months old. It would therefore be misleading to give dates when you should expect your child to cut certain teeth, although it is possible to make a generalization about the order in which teeth erupt. As a general rule, teething starts around six months old, after which many teeth appear up to the end of your baby's first year; the order in which they come rarely differs between children.

HOW THE TEETH COME IN

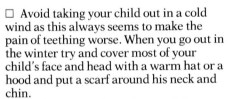

1 The first teeth to arrive are always the lower front teeth.
2 These are usually followed by the upper front teeth.

3 Upper side teeth come in next.
4 These are followed by the lower side teeth.

Teething

If you are on the look-out you will probably notice your baby's first tooth as it starts to push its way through the gum and form a small, pale bump. The only normal symptoms of teething are fretfulness and dribbling. You should never blame any other symptoms on cutting a tooth; it is a myth that teething can cause fever, diarrhoea, vomiting, convulsions, rashes or loss of appetite. Don't make the mistake of attributing any illness to cutting a tooth, so if you're at all worried consult your doctor immediately. No parent likes to see their child in discomfort so I would suggest you do the following:

☐ Offer your baby something firm to chew on like a raw carrot, a rusk or a cool teething ring. Your baby may find sucking rather painful, so give drinks from a cup instead.

☐ Try just gently rubbing your child's gums with your own little finger – this can help as much as anything. Certainly your attention and concern about his pain will bring comfort.

☐ Avoid taking your child out in a cold wind as this always seems to make the pain of teething worse. When you go out in the winter try and cover most of your child's face and head with a warm hat or a hood and put a scarf around his neck and chin.

☐ Don't give teething gels containing local anaesthetics. They only have a transient effect, and local anaesthetics can cause allergies.

☐ Don't use teething powders and teething medicines. Your baby has many teeth to cut, and if you use any kind regularly you will be exposing your baby to a large amount of medication, much of which may be unecessary and all of which may be accompanied by side-effects.

☐ Take care if you use the water-filled teething rings which can be frozen to form ice if placed in the freezer. Careless use of these teething rings has been known to cause frostbite in babies. These rings can be used quite safely to cool down the mouth if they are just kept in the fridge as opposed to the freezer.

☐ Avoid the frequent use of junior aspirin or paracetamol syrup. Both of these medicines are useful, but they should not be used with any regularity except under doctor's orders. Aspirin in any form certainly shouldn't be used frequently. Paracetamol syrup is the safest pain killer for a baby, but even so it should only be used on occasion, and if you need recourse to it to soothe your fretful baby for more than two doses then you should consult your doctor.

Looking after teeth

When your baby has several teeth, you can start good habits early by encouraging him with a game of tooth brushing. First of all let your child watch you so that he can see how brushing should be done. Then just make an offer of a soft toothbrush as something to play with. He will almost certainly want to do what he has just seen you doing and will try to make the same kind of movements by putting the brush into his mouth and moving it to and fro. This shouldn't be a serious business; it really should be playful. You are teaching your child to like and want to look after the teeth so you should avoid being censorious and make it a big laugh instead of a chore. To actually get the teeth clean, take a piece of gauze with some toothpaste on it and gently rub it across the gums and any teeth that your baby has. It's important to clean the gums even if there are no teeth because it keeps the mouth free of the bacteria which cause plaque and so provides a good environment for milk and

later permanent teeth to grow into. The easiest position will probably be with him on your lap, feet pointing away from you, mouth tilted up towards you.

Always use a fluoride toothpaste, and avoid varieties especially made for children as they often contain a sweetener. Your baby may want to eat the toothpaste but you should try to dissuade him if possible. Clean the teeth once if not twice a day and always after he's been given any medicine – children's medicines are often sweet and sticky to make them "more palatable".

Fighting decay

The three most important factors in the care of your baby's teeth are diet and the absence of sugar, good dental hygiene and regular check-ups. One of the best ways of taking care of your baby's teeth as soon as he has them is to see that his diet does not contain sugary foods such as sweets, chocolates, cakes, biscuits and very sweet drinks. Sugar, be it white or brown, is the arch villain in tooth decay. No child needs sugar. It is not necessary for health and you will be doing your child a favour if you don't encourage the development of a sweet tooth, not only for his teeth but also in relation to his weight (see p.149). Never leave a bottle containing milk or a sweetened drink lying around for your baby to suck on endlessly. His teeth will be constantly bathed in a sugary fluid which will encourage decay.

Your baby's diet should contain plenty of calcium and vitamin D as they are essential for the healthy formation of the permanent teeth which are already growing in your baby's jawbones. Foods which are rich in both of these nutrients are dairy products and fish; the fatty fishes like herring and sardine are particularly good.

Many people think that dental hygiene isn't important until your child has permanent teeth. This is not true, so *do* follow a sensible cleaning programme for your child's teeth and, as soon as he's about two, take him for regular check-ups (see p.229).

227

TEETH 1-3

At one time it was thought that milk teeth were not very important, but we now know that they are worth looking after. First of all they guide in the adult teeth so that they grow in the correct position and secondly, if the primary teeth are lost through decay, the bone behind the teeth can be affected, eroding the support the adult teeth need. Your baby will be teething for most of the second year and you should be prepared for the molars to be a bit upsetting. The first molars are usually cut between twelve and fifteen months when the upper molars appear first and are followed by the lower ones. The second molars appear between twenty and twenty-four months, in the lower jaw first and then in the upper jaw. In general the later teeth are cut the less trouble they cause.

Once your child has all his teeth, you should encourage the development of strong jaw muscles by giving plenty of chewy foods, and particularly fresh fruit and raw vegetables. As it happens this kind of food also has a cleansing effect as the fibres within them are shredded by the teeth. You should maintain the health of the teeth and gums by making sure that your child has regular check-ups.

HOW THE TEETH COME IN

 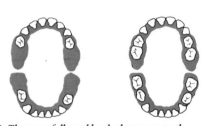

1 *The first upper molars erupt. Next come the first lower molars.*
2 *The upper eye teeth then come in, one each side.*

3 *These are followed by the lower eye teeth.*
4 *The second molars erupt first in the lower jaw. And lastly the second molars appear in the upper jaw.*

Dental hygiene and care

The Royal College of Physicians in England has stated in a report that children between the ages of two and twelve should take a fluoride tablet every day if the local water supply is not fluorinated. You should encourage your child to chew the tablet so that the fluoride coats the teeth as well as being absorbed into the bloodstream and being deposited in the permanent teeth which are developing inside the jawbone. There is no evidence to link taking fluoride with cancer.

Until your child has reached the age of about six or seven he won't be capable of cleaning his own teeth thoroughly so you should be responsible for the part of the tooth brushing routine which actually gets the teeth clean. He may object to this at first, and just clamp his jaws firmly shut. The best way around this is to make it into a game using a disclosing tablet. When chewed this exposes plaque as a dense area of colour.

Dentists generally agree that it doesn't matter how a toothbrush is used, as long as it removes plaque. At one time we were encouraged to brush the top teeth downwards and the bottom ones upwards so that the gum margins were protected. However, it has now been shown that there is nothing especially good about this method and the most efficient one, especially for children who don't have a great deal of co-ordination, is a gentle to-and-fro movement over all surfaces of the

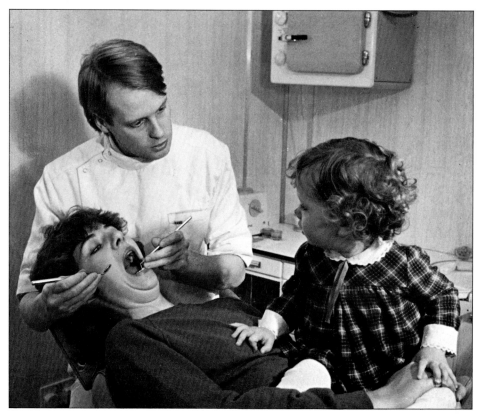

teeth. However, you must make sure that the bristles have rounded tips and that they aren't too hard. If the brush is too hard it may cause the gums to bleed, then recede and the teeth to eventually become loose.

Always encourage your child to have a regular tooth-brushing routine which should include never leaving the house for school without cleaning the teeth first, and never going to sleep without doing the same thing. Most children will put up a fight if they have to brush their teeth every time they have a sweet drink or a biscuit, but you can help them by providing them with a piece of cheese at the end of every meal. This makes the saliva alkaline and counteracts the sugary acid which erodes the protective enamel of the teeth and causes cavities.

Visiting the dentist

You should take your child for his first dental check-up sometime around the second birthday, and this visit should be as relaxed and pleasant as possible. Get your child used to the sight of the instruments and the smell of the surroundings by taking him with you when you go for your own check-up. If he can be trusted, and if your dentist has no objections, sit the child on your lap and let him watch while the dentist examines you. He'll no doubt watch with fascination and will be delighted to copy your example. Just before your child's visit play a game of going to the dentist and look into each other's mouths. Then, when you actually get to the surgery, prearrange for the dentist to look at your mouth just before he looks at your child's.

13 Intellectual development

In terms of teaching, your baby is the most responsive and most rewarding pupil that you could ever meet. He wants to do more things, explore more areas and widen his horizons more than anyone else you know. He also wants to please you, and the combination of these qualities gives him an appetite for learning that should thrill you. He wants to learn about everything from the first day of his life. Don't forget, he has five senses and he wants to learn through all of them. He is eager and keen to meet new sights, sounds, smells, tastes and touches. One of the most important things for you to remember is that he is never too young to learn although you'll have to tailor the way you introduce him to new experiences or the ways you try to teach him. You mustn't set him tasks which are beyond his capabilities as this will only lead to frustration, loss of self-confidence and possibly resentment towards you. Guide him in all things, but never try to force him.

LEARNING 0–1

Whatever you do don't waste the first crucial six weeks of your baby's life. Many people still think that because the baby isn't making sounds and moving very much he can't respond to what is happening around him and he can't learn. We know this to be entirely incorrect. Your baby's emotional and intellectual development during the first weeks of life is growing at exactly the same rate as every other form of development, from his size and weight to his ability to co-ordinate.

I believe that, initially, the most important person in a baby's life is the one who most consistently looks after him. In the majority of cases this is the mother. *You* are his most important teacher. As adults we learn the most important and the most memorable lessons of our lives from people whom we like and with whom we have a good rapport. If there is a special feeling of closeness, common ground, empathy and understanding with the teacher, then the lessons can be even more salutary and lasting. Exactly the same applies to your baby. All his learning will be made easier if he establishes strong bonds with you, his teacher, very early in life. A close runner-up to you is your partner. Your partner is your baby's next best friend; he should form a strong relationship with your baby as early as possible and be involved in as much of the "teaching" as you are.

The teaching you give your child is not teaching in a formal sense; there are no specific rules and no particular targets that your child has to reach. You should "teach" your baby by making the world interesting for him. Introduce him to new experiences, explain everything that you see and, above all, join in with every activity so that you and your baby learn together. You have to give encouragement at all times, give praise when even the smallest thing is achieved and provide constant support, especially if your child fails to do something that he really wants to do. Without your support your child won't gain the confidence he requires.

231

What your baby understands

● *The newborn baby*
Your baby will concentrate on your face if you bring it close to him, and he can distinguish your voice from anybody else's. When he hears your voice his eyes will move in the direction of it and he will try to follow your face if you move it close to his. He can recognize your face if you place it less than 30.5 cm (12 in) away from the time he's 36 hours old.

● *Four weeks*
If your face is close enough for him to focus on, he will watch you while you are talking and he will mimic your talking by opening and closing his mouth. He will also probably stop crying when you pick him up because he knows you to be a source of comfort. He imitates the movements of your face: he can use the right muscles to smile and grimace.

● *Six weeks*
He will smile back at you and his eyes will follow a moving toy.

● *Eight weeks*
If you hold something brightly coloured above his head, he will take a few seconds to focus on it and will then follow it as you move it from side to side.

● *Three months*
He will immediately see a toy held above him. He will smile when you speak and will make squeals and gurgles of pleasure. There will be obvious signs of curiosity and interest in what is going on around him.

● *Four months*
At feeding times he will show signs of excitement. He will laugh and chuckle when played with. He will love being propped up because he'll be able to see what is going on around him; he will turn his head in the direction of any sound.

● *Five months*
He ll be aware of strange situations and can express fear, disgust and anger.

● *Six months*
Your baby will become very interested in mirrors and in seeing himself in one. He will begin to show preferences for certain foods that you offer him.

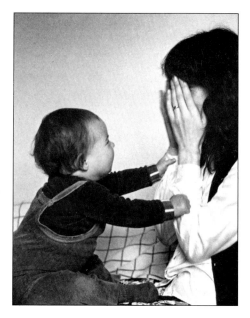

● *Eight months*
He will know his name and will understand the word "No". He will probably have developed little sound signals like a cough to attract your attention when he reaches out for something that he wants. He'll probably want to feed himself at around this time.

● *Nine months*
He'll show a will of his own and may stop you when you try to wash his face. He will concentrate very hard on toys and games and will even turn a toy over in his hand so that he can examine it carefully. When an object is hidden under a cloth he'll lift the cloth up to see the object.

● *Ten months*
He'll probably be able to clap his hands and wave bye-bye. He'll show that he · understands a small number of words, and very short, simple statements.

● *Eleven months*
He'll have learned, and will enjoy, simple games like "Peep-Bo". His other favourite game will be dropping things and having you pick them up. He'll become very noisy and will want to shake, rattle and bang anything that makes a noise.

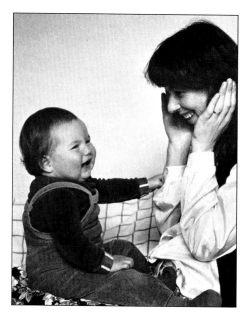

● *Twelve months*
He will do anything to make you laugh and will repeat it over and over again. He'll enjoy "reading" simple books with you and will help you to undress him by lifting up his arms when you take off his clothes. He may know a few simple words like bottle, bath, ball, drink.

Look at your baby

In the early days it is a prerequisite to face your baby; facial contact is terribly important. One of the few things that a baby responds to visually in the first days of life is a human face (see p.32). Your newborn baby has to see that face as close as 20 to 25 centimetres from his own, so bring your face up close to your baby's and make it "interesting". Move your head as you talk; raise your eyebrows and, most important of all, smile. Look deep into your baby's eyes all the time, and make constant eye contact. It has been shown that mothers who face their children while they are feeding or playing with them, and look into their eyes, are much less likely to use corporal punishment to discipline their children as they grow up. It's hardly sur-

prising that the children of such mothers are much better able to form relationships with people as they get older.

Have conversations

Your baby holds his first conversation with smiles. The conversation goes something like this: you are talking away to your baby about any subject you like with your face about 20 to 25 centimetres away. You are animated and you smile a lot. Your baby sees this as a friendly approach. Every baby has the natural human desire to respond in a friendly way, and so he smiles back. You are delighted with his recognition, his response and his friendly smile. You smile some more, you may laugh, you may cuddle him, you may kiss him. He *loves* that, so he smiles more to please you. You do more things to please him, and so the conversation goes on.

What is interesting about this kind of interaction between parent and baby is that your baby has learned two very important lessons. A smile from him gets a smile back. It may even get more substantial rewards like hugs and cuddles, as well as praise and approbation. The second lesson is that he has found a way of pleasing you and interacting with you. He will learn that he can initiate this interaction and will go on to use this method with other people. It is well known that the amount of smiling a baby does is related to his intelligence because it shows that he has learned that if he smiles the world will like him and life will be more pleasant. So you have given him a very good start in coming to terms with and managing the world around him.

Read to your baby

Children love books and will respond to them from a surprisingly early age if you look at them with your child and read to him from them. Reading from books together will teach your child about colours, the alphabet, numbers and names for simple objects. Your baby's never too young to be read to – your voice will be soothing to him, and you'll soon find that

233

books at bedtime are a useful and pacifying part of your evening routine. The bonus you may never expect is that once you have introduced your child to books he may want to read them alone. You'll have done him a great service because you'll not only have introduced him to the idea of entertaining himself, but also to a pleasure that will last him for the rest of his life – learning from books. This early start in life is invaluable.

I suggest you start off with board books which are brightly-coloured and robustly made. For variety, buy some pop-up books as well but resign yourself to your baby's rough treatment of them.

Learning spurts

Your baby doesn't grow, develop and learn at a constant rate. Learning spurts are well known and every child has them. During a learning spurt, your baby will gobble up new ideas, acquire new skills and put them into practice immediately. However, while he's going through these learning spurts some activities, and possibly certain skills that he's already learned, may appear to slip. Don't worry. They won't have gone for good. It is just that your baby is using all his concentration to learn something new, but once it is learned he'll regain all the other skills.

During a learning spurt you should try to make your child's life as interesting as possible. Of course if your child shows that certain things are enjoyable then you should do them as often as you can, but don't hesitate to introduce your baby to new things; he is ready to learn and absorb information at a very fast rate. And don't be too discriminating about the kind of entertainment you give either. Babies simply sieve out what they prefer and understand and let the rest go by. In the first year learning is an entirely piecemeal process, so you'll best help your baby if you provide as wide and interesting a range as possible.

Such spurts are invariably followed by periods when development appears to slow down. Treat them as recovery periods during which your baby can consolidate newly-learned skills and prepare himself for the next spurt. Don't get anxious about this – just let him practise the skills that he has already learned. You can help during these slower learning times by practising with him, saying something like "Let's sing that song again," or "Why don't we try to push the peg through that hole again."

Letting your child guide you

All the way through life, teachers who succeed do so by helping us to develop and reach our full potential. They maximize our strengths and minimize our weaknesses. As your baby's teacher you should try to make the best of his good points and play down his bad ones. You also have to give your child the kind of help he needs when he needs it. Giving help is worthless if the person who is being helped doesn't really require it or like it, so while you have to be an active helper, you mustn't be an interfering one. Your baby should not be learning what *you* want him to learn, he should be learning what *he* wants to learn, and this should be your first priority. You have to suppress any ideas of what you think a child of his age ought to be doing and respond to what he wants to do. This means that you have to be guided by your child. You have to respond to his needs. While it is your job as a good parent to introduce him to as wide a range of interesting things as possible, it is not your job to decide which of those things he should find interesting. In other words, having presented the menu, you must let him choose his own dishes.

LEARNING   1-2

During the first year of your baby's life the accent was on learning physical things: he learned to crawl, to stand up and possibly even to take a few steps. The ability to do these things brought with it a sense of physical achievement and a sense of independence. He was able to go and explore the world without having to wait for you to bring it to him. During this year he'll not only consolidate all the physical skills he acquired in his first year, but he'll also master one of the most difficult intellectual ones – speech (see p.248). Your child will be struggling to express his thoughts and desires through speech and with his increasingly able brain he'll now see himself as a separate entity to you; he'll be aware of "self". He'll probably be quite frustrated this year and you may notice that more tantrums occur during this period. He'll need a lot of affection, much encouragement and constant support.

Intellectual development

● *12 months*
Your baby likes looking at simple books with you and loves a joke – he will repeat anything that makes you laugh. He'll understand that he should hold up his arms when you dress him and knows the meaning of simple, frequently used words like shoe, bottle, bath. Your one-year-old may even say one or two intelligible words.

● *15 months*
He will show you that he wants to brush his own hair. He'll know what kissing means and will give you a kiss if asked. He'll be very thrilled by any new skill and will want to help you with any household chores like dusting. Even though he doesn't understand individual words he can understand quite complex sentences.

● *18 months*
When you are reading together he will point to things, like a dog, ball, cow. He will recognize a cow and say "Cow". He'll know the different parts of his body: if you ask him where his foot is he will point to it, and to his hand, his nose, his mouth or his eyes. He'll know the difference between his nose and Mummy's nose. If you ask him to fetch something he will.

● *21 months*
He will come to you, attract your attention, and take you to things that he is interested in or has a problem with. He'll love scribbling with a pencil. He'll begin to understand and obey simple requests and questions.

● *2 years*
He likes his own company and will play happily on his own. Instead of just scribbling with a pencil he will make up and down strokes in imitation of writing. He knows the names of many familiar objects and toys and will use the words with meaning. Once he learns the meaning of a word he may repeat it continuously.

Learning and speech

Learning to talk is one of the most important intellectual lessons that your child will ever master. Without it, many of the other learning skills will be handicapped and may even be prohibited. Learning to speak is almost an act of survival; a child quickly learns that he has to communicate to survive.

Early communication, as we have seen, is not with words; initially it's with cries. The first conversation is usually with smiles; later it may just be with a head movement. You may notice that your child just bobs his head to say thank you, and then a little later he may stand close to something that he wants and just shout for your attention. Once he has got it he will point to the object. These early lessons in communication tell him that life will be a lot easier if he can communicate with the world around him in the language which is commonly used, that is with words rather than gestures.

In learning to use words a child learns about the world around him and how people behave in it. Very often he will try to guess at the meaning of a word from the general sense of what is being said and the tone of voice which is used to say it. In discovering language, your child makes connections between sounds and what he understands about the nature of things which surround him. When he first uses words he'll use them generically, and they'll have a much wider meaning for him than they do for an adult. (Many children call every man they meet "Daddy", because Daddy is the name they use for the only man who is important to them, their father, but they don't realize the implication of their relationship.) "Nana" (banana) may be the generic name for fruit because that's the name he remembers first learning for a single fruit. However, with your help your child will learn the difference between a car and a lorry even though they both move on four wheels, and between a cat and a dog even though they are of similar size and shape and have tails.

Talk to your child

Your child is learning the art of communication so make sure that you communicate with him. If he wants something tell him that you understand what it is that he wants and give it to him, naming the object as you do so. Don't talk to him without looking at him. If he wants your attention stop whatever you are doing, turn to face him and listen. When your child first starts to learn language he learns it in broad strokes so while he may not understand individual words, he very often gets the gist of the sentence. Give him lots of clues to help with this. In the evening when it is time for bed, start tidying up the playroom, ask him to help you to put the toys away, stack everything neatly in its place, then go to the door and say "It's time for bed now" and put your hand out for him. Though he may not understand the words, he'll have got the sense of them.

During the early stages of learning to talk, you can give your child a great deal of help in learning to understand language. Children love the sound of speech and they love your attention. Combine the two and talk as often as you can to your child. Make sure that while you are talking you are looking directly at your child and make eye contact. Slightly exaggerate your facial expressions and your gestures. Exaggerate the emphasis you put on words, the inflection and the tone of your voice. If you can, try to match your words with actions. For instance, "I think it is time for your bath" – go into the bathroom and start running the taps. "Let's comb your hair" – pick up the comb and start combing his hair.

Learning and playing

To a child, play is learning; it's also very hard work. While he is playing, he is learning and growing up. Play helps learning in many ways:
☐ It can improve manual dexterity. Building a tower of blocks or, when he is older, doing a simple jigsaw, teaches a child that he can make his hands work for

him as tools and it prepares him for using his hands in delicate and refined ways.

☐ Playing with other children can help to teach a child how important it is to get on with others. Having playmates to the house teaches him to overcome shyness and introduces him to sharing; it presents him with problems to sort out without help from adults, and teaches him to control outbursts of antisocial behaviour. Through a special friend your child may learn to love people and understand feelings that he can't easily put into words. At the same time he will be learning to think about the feelings of others.

☐ Through play a child learns to communicate. Playing with other children demands a more complicated use of language. Talking while playing may be one of the sternest tests for your child because the more imaginative the play, the more complex the ideas, and these have to be expressed in words that his friends can understand.

☐ Play undoubtedly helps physical co-ordination. In fact it helps both physical and intellectual development. The freedom to swing, climb, skip, run and jump helps to perfect muscular co-ordination and physical skills. At the same time it also improves hearing and vision.

Provide the right games

As your child makes no distinction between learning and playing, you can help your baby to learn a great deal, simply by the material you provide for him to play with and the kind of toys you introduce him to. From a very early age, all four of my children loved playing with water, whether it was outside in a small paddling pool, or just standing on a chair at the kitchen sink with the taps running and an assortment of plastic dishes, cups, jugs, containers, and funnels nearby. Water games were always good for an hour's concentration and all the time my children were learning lessons: that water feels wet, that it will pour, that you can fill things with it, that you can empty them, that you can blow bubbles in it, that

things will float on it, things will sink through it; that vegetable dyes will dissolve in it and colour it and that other liquids won't; that when the tap drips it forms drops, and that cupped hands aren't watertight. And this wasn't the only game:

☐ Anything like play dough, plasticine, or pastry was interesting, too, because it could be moulded by their hands. They soon discovered that it would keep its shape if left to dry out, or, if they wanted to, they could roll it into a ball and start all over again.

☐ Sand, in the sandpit or sand tray, was also interesting because it was midway between a liquid and a solid. It felt like a solid but it poured like a liquid. If it was wet it would keep the shape of the bucket, and they could make sand pies; if it was dry the sand pies crumbled.

☐ One of the most important concepts that a child grasps during his second year is that of classification – of sameness and difference. Toys can help the formation of this idea. Farmyard toys, with a variety of horses, cows and chickens, allow your child to sort out the animals that look the same, especially if you help by showing him the differences and naming the animals repeatedly as you put them into little groups. The same procedure can be applied to many other objects – fruits, cars, shapes or tins.

☐ Children like being part of the domestic routine and learn a lot about what goes on in the house and what people have to do if they are allowed to participate. A small child can be given a little bowl with some flour to mix each time you bake; he can help with carrying and, when it comes to cleaning up, he can have a dustpan and brush. If your dustpan and brush is not too big, give him a real one rather than a toy one.

☐ For years, an essential part of our playroom was the dressing-up box into which were put all sorts of old clothes, uniforms, hats and shoes. Most children get immense pleasure from imitating other people. This is a very important learning step for a child because he begins

to recognize that he has to share the world with other people and get along with them. Dressing up to look like them is one of his ways of coming to terms with this.

☐ Children of both sexes like dolls. Boys should have their dolls too: they are their imaginary friends, their imaginary families and they help create an imaginary world into which he can escape. While your child is playing with dolls, be it a soft, cuddly doll or an action man, he is learning about, and possibly mimicking, human emotions. He will mother the doll, talk to it very firmly, tell it off, rant and rave at it, smack it, then dress it, put it to bed and kiss it goodnight. Through this kind of behaviour your child is working out the things that happen to him, and is learning to understand them fully and relate them to other people.

☐ Long before he'll be able to formally write or draw your child will love scribbling and using colours. A box of coloured chalks, a blackboard and an easel set at the same height as himself will be attractive because he'll be able to "draw" then rub out the scribbles and start again. Attach a sheet of paper to the easel and give your child a set of finger paints and let him make his own design of splodges, hand prints and finger smears on the paper. If you don't want to buy them you can make up your own (see p.299). Body paints are also great fun, especially when your child is playing with friends.

☐ Most children are musical and like to be sung to from the day they are born. Many children have mastered the tune of

239

their favourite song or nursery rhyme long before they can talk. As soon as your child is old enough you can buy him a simple musical instrument like a xylophone or a toy piano so that he can make his own music. Encourage him to do this by joining in with marching and clapping and singing. He'll enjoy it even more if you have your own instrument to accompany him with.

☐ The best way to help your child with learning is to join in with his learning activities, especially if you make suggestions about how to do something new with a toy and then demonstrate how to do it. However, you must do it tactfully and without interfering, and allow him to decide whether he wants to follow your advice or not. Many of your child's games won't be able to be played without a partner. You should offer to be "It" whenever you can, but only join in for as long as he wants you to; don't overdo it. Leave the initiative to him; he may want you to fill the bucket of sand and ask for your help, but the last thing he'll want is for you to turn the bucket upside down to make the sand pie.

☐ Your child's concentration span is increasing, but he may still have problems concentrating on something which is difficult. You can help him to concentrate by making the task easier or by giving him a helping hand. If you show how the task or the job can be completed, you can give your child a goal to work towards. He needs your support and encouragement and if you give it he will probably find the determination to go on longer than he would without you. It is very worthwhile doing this because your child will have a great feeling of achievement.

Let your child play alone

Some parents make the mistake of thinking that their child's every waking hour has to be filled with interesting diversions and stimulating activities. This is wrong and can even be harmful. One of the most important lessons that your child has to learn, and will learn quite willingly if left

to his own devices, is that he can be the source of his own entertainment. Very often a child wishes to be left to play by himself, to make his own decisions about what to play with and for how long. Let your child follow through little tasks that he has set himself, alone. If he can't do them he will ask for your help; if he doesn't, don't interfere. Interfering, interrupting, or introducing a new activity will do the opposite of making his life more entertaining. It will make it boring because he will never have the opportunity of seeing the activity through to completion. He will therefore miss out on the sense of satisfaction and achievement which every child needs.

Another common mistake is to believe that children need to play with toys. Many of the most popular play activities don't involve toys at all. They may involve physical activities like swimming or climbing, running, playing with a bat and ball, building a camp out of twigs and leaves, just carrying water to the sandpit and filling the moat, collecting pebbles or shells. Your child should be given the scope and the autonomy to do all of these things. If you don't encourage private activities, your child will have a very uncomfortable sense of withdrawal or even deprivation when he is forced to entertain himself if you are absent, and this may lead him into mischief, delinquent behaviour or, even worse, danger. So you should be pleased if your child shows signs of self-sufficiency and being able to do without you and to entertain himself while excluding you.

Leaving your child alone, however, will mean that you'll have to either ignore a mess or anticipate one. If he's playing water games, cover the kitchen floor with newspaper or old towels that will soak up the water. If he's painting, cover the carpet with a sheet of polythene. If he's playing with mud or clay, cover your child's clothes with a smock-style apron (see p.61) and ignore the mess half way up his arms, on his face and on his hair; it can all be washed off at the end anyway.

LEARNING   2–3

The way in which your child learns changes quite a lot in the third year, particularly in the second half of it. As a toddler, your child was learning about separate things, single events, one experience at a time. He may have satisfied his curiosity and explored that experience as far as he could, absorbing a great deal of new information in the process, but he rarely related it to anything else in his life. What happens in the third year, however, is that your child starts to think about his experiences and to learn from them. As your child develops the ability to think over new learning experiences his mind starts to work for the first time like a mini computer. Information is sieved and sifted, it is matched up to other experiences to see if they fit together or if they differ very greatly, and it is then put into similar or different pigeon holes. Your child starts to think and plan ahead, and becomes much more creative and imaginative. Gradually all the information that he has absorbed over the past years becomes available to apply to a given situation. Your child suddenly has an orchestra of thoughts which he can command at will.

This new ability to think, imagine and create changes your child's world considerably. Many familiar things close at hand in the house or garden no longer contain the same interest or excitement for him. He needs wider horizons; he needs to explore, to push the frontiers of his experience and knowledge further and further out.

Your child becomes very interested in how things work at this time and his conversation will constantly be punctuated with "Why". He is avid for information and constantly asks questions. It's as if his brain wants more and more information to put into the computer to start using immediately.

One of the most important steps in your child's intellectual development is when he understands that time is not just in the present but that there was a past and there will be a future; when he understands yesterday and tomorrow. Planning for the future is one of the most critical aspects of our intellect which makes us different from lower animals and it is in the third year that you will hear your child say for the first time, "I will eat that later," or "We can go tomorrow."

Intellectual development

● *2 years and 3 months*
He will try to build houses and castles with blocks and will repeat new words when you encourage him. He knows who he is and can say his name. He'll begin to pit his will against yours, and may become rather negative. He'll say the word "No" more and more often and won't always fit in with your wishes.

● *2 years and 6 months*
He loves helping you and will help with chores, putting things away, bringing things to the table. He'll know both his Christian name and surname. He can draw horizontal lines and vertical lines and can name several common objects. A boy will have noticed that his sex organs stick out

from his body whereas those of his mother, and of his little girlfriends, do not.

● *2 years and 9 months*
He'll begin to ask questions: he'll know the difference between boys and girls. He'll learn nursery rhymes and will be able to repeat them. He'll begin to understand numbers. He'll try to draw a circle but won't be able to complete it successfully without help.

● *3 years*
He'll become increasingly sociable and will like to play with other children. He'll know several more nursery rhymes and will almost be able to draw a circle. He'll know the difference between such words as on, under, and behind and will be able to form quite complicated sentences.

Learning and speech

As your child grows older speech plays an increasingly important role in communication between you and himself. Consequently, speech becomes more and more important in helping your child to learn. By now your child has got the hang of the basic rules of conversation. He knows, for instance, that people usually take turns at speaking; they know when it is their turn and they don't try to dominate the conversation. He also knows that instead of accompanying single words with gestures to explain what he means, he can vary the intonation of the words. He knows that an intonation which rises usually means a question and that a falling pitch indicates a statement. When your child was younger, speech was part of a simple pattern of communication telling you what he wanted or didn't want – it was used to greet you and to say goodbye and to give something a label. As your child's world widens he needs more sophisticated ways to express his thoughts.

One of the first expressions of this is his use of the possessive pronoun – "*my* doll, Mummy coat, Daddy nose". Another is the negative. Your younger child would just have said "No"; now he says "Can't" or "Won't". A little later he starts to express actions – "Dolly fall", "Dog bark", "Car bump". Another characteristic is the increasing use of questions combined with statements. "Daddy sleep, why Daddy sleep?" "Mummy must go shop, why Mummy go shop?" "Daddy gone out, where Daddy gone?" By the time your child is three he will be asking quite complicated questions in parallel with the way his thinking is developing. When you consider the following sentences, they contain quite sophisticated ideas: "I go get pencil and draw." "What that on table?" "See, this one better. But this not better."

Don't "talk down"

The kind of language you use with your child is very important. It's well known that adults change the way they speak to children as they get older. Sentences

become more complex, they contain longer words, they describe abstract ideas. Don't fall into the trap of talking down to your child and don't use baby language when it is redundant. Throw into your conversation the odd word that you know is unfamiliar to your child but which he can guess at from the gist of the sentence. This way he'll learn new words and will learn how to use them and how to express himself in an articulate way. Research has proven that the children of articulate parents who don't "tailor" their speech to their children, use words more easily and freely at an earlier age than the children of parents who persist in simplifying their language.

Learning and playing

In keeping with your child's expanding way of thinking, he starts to get more out of playing. Playing still involves learning but it's about learning different things.
□ Play now starts to put the world around him into perspective. Before, a game like a farmyard with animals was simply a matter of sorting the animals into different types and putting them in the right place. Now he sees it with different eyes. It introduces him to an aspect of life that he knows is different from the one he leads. After all, he is probably not surrounded by animals most of the time, so it helps to reduce the world to a scale he can handle.
□ Play increasingly becomes an outlet for emotions. Even an action man type of doll can bring out feelings of protectiveness and gentleness. He can also use the same toy to get rid of aggressive instincts which, if directed against other children, would be labelled naughty and antisocial.
□ Play creates an interest in other people. If the dressing-up box has a cowboy's outfit and a nurse's uniform your child can dress up and play a role. Even if he just puts a hat on at an angle and wears a pair of high-heeled shoes too big for him he can pretend to be his aunty and by acting out what he thinks she does, he is getting insight into her life and into other people's lives.

☐ Play develops a sense of territory and ownership. Safeguarding a new and cherished toy or his own private place to play, like a den, tent, or a play house, teaches a child to respect the belongings and privacy of others. Play stimulates curiosity, independence, an adventurous spirit and intellectual growth. Mechanical toys and puzzles stimulate analytical thought. Painting, drawing, making shapes with clay and fitting together patterns encourage creativity. As your child gets a little older, toys like a microscope, telescope, a chemistry set or a magician's outfit allow experimentation. These kinds of toys teach him to meet challenges and master difficulties.

☐ As your child gets older play helps to teach him how to cope with events beyond his control. He may break a treasured toy, he may fail to make a mechanical toy work or he may not have the competence to do what he wants to do. All these things help him to learn how to cope with problems which arise in his world. There may be several difficult choices to make but your child has to learn to make the decision. Play helps your child to get to know himself. As he gets older he has to interact with others, but before he can do that successfully he has to understand himself at least a little. Play allows him to find his physical and intellectual strengths and weaknesses.

☐ Play is an important aid in helping your child to mature. By the time your child is three he will be showing signs of having a sense of planning. He will keep his traffic jam of toy cars under the surveillance of a police car, with a pick-up truck standing alongside. This shows that he is thinking ahead. He'll start to exercise his capacity to delay when he plays with toys that need the glue to set or the clay to dry. If he is prepared to share one of his toys with a friend who reciprocates by lending your child one of his, then he is being taught the value of give and take.

Forming concepts

For your child to form concepts and put them to use in his world he has to have mastered two things. First of all he has to understand the basic concept of like and unlike. He learns to do this by recognizing similarities and differences in things and then fitting them together in his own mind. Once he can do this he has made an intellectual leap forward. From about eighteen months to two years old you will find that your child does this sorting automatically when faced with an array of objects which have certain things in common and certain differences. All things that roll and are round are sorted into one group. All things that have edges and are rectangular, like blocks, are sorted into another. Things which have four legs and meow are cats. Things which have two legs and fly are birds.

We give our concepts verbal labels (names) and in his third year your toddler develops his understanding of concepts by using language. It would be very difficult for your child to progress with concept formation if he couldn't talk. Your toddler might use the word cat for every cat he meets, including the family pet, the cat drawn in a book, the cat he sees in a neighbour's garden and a toy cat. In his mind he uses a single label for all these different things. But by the time he approaches three he'll have made several rather sophisticated distinctions. He'll know that they are all cats so he'll have a concept of what makes "cattiness" but he'll also know that they are subtly different: "My cat", "Your cat", "Toy cat", "Cat in book", "Go see Granny's cat".

Abstract ideas

When your child is two years old it is impossible for him to describe things which are not real; things which he cannot see, which he cannot pick up and touch. He doesn't know what pretty means, he hasn't quite got the hang of emptiness and fullness and, whilst he knows that when he blows bubbles they will float, he can't yet distinguish lightness or heaviness.

Your child may know the difference between one and several but he has no idea of the magnitude of numbers, so anything more than one may be "lots". He has very little concept of time, he can't visualize what tomorrow means or last week; he has difficulty coping with tonight. His understanding, however, improves throughout this year.

To have abstract ideas and to think in the abstract your child has to be able to picture things in his mind that are not actually there. If you ask him where a toy is, he has to remember when and where he was last playing with it. He has to see both things in his mind and then go and retrieve the toy. Once he is able to do this he can then make plans about things which are not actually there. So when you ask him where his boat is, he'll have a mental picture of the boat lying in the garden and will say: "Boat in garden, me get it in a minute". He'll carry on with his painting, finish it, wash his hands and then go out and get his boat without prompting. This means that he was able to carry the concept of fetching the boat in his head, have it interrupted by his painting, complete several unrelated tasks and then go back to the concept of bringing the boat in from the garden.

How to help your child develop

The most important way in which you can help your child develop is to listen to what he's saying. Because his world is expanding at a colossal rate, not only in terms of his physical capability, but also his new intellectual development, it is very important that you communicate openly and freely with him. You should listen carefully to everything he says, try to understand his thinking and answer his questions in terms that he understands. He is constantly asking you questions but you should be asking him questions, too, so that you are aware of what he is thinking and what interests him. Once you know these things you should present information and ideas in the most interesting ways you can think of.

Every time your child asks you a question or you have a conversation with him, you are presented with a golden opportunity of helping him to learn, even though the circumstances may be very casual and ordinary. If you are in the kitchen preparing lunch and your child asks you why you take the hairy bits off carrots you could start a discussion on how all plants have roots because they need food in order to make them grow, and next time you are out in the garden you could pull up a tuft of grass and show him that root system. Or if you are really ambitious you could try putting a bean down the side of a jam jar lined with wet blotting paper and watching the root actually appear and grow down. When you are out in the street keep up a running commentary on what is going on around you: traffic lights chang-ing, cars stopping at pedestrian crossings,

roadside drill, a policeman who is stopping and waving on traffic, tankers with oil in them, horse floats with horses in them, etc.

Around the age of three your child naturally becomes rather sensitive to what other people are feeling. He may show the first signs of sympathy by wanting to comfort you if you seem sad. Take advantage of this and start to teach him about the need to think of other people; that it is right to be kind and polite, helpful and thoughtful, co-operative and willing. Make sure he is introduced to people coming to your house like the window cleaner, the postman, the laundryman, the milkman. Tell him about each of their jobs and some of the problems they may have to cope with, and then suggest one of the ways he might help, for instance taking the letters from the postman at the door and bringing them to you.

Early reading

Some children have a natural bent towards reading early and writing before their peers. If yours is one of them, encourage and help but never push. Your child can only master these advanced skills when the brain and intellect are sufficiently developed. You are not to know whether your child's brain is capable of reading (and later writing) so you must wait to take your lead from him. Until this happens, simply continue reading to him and make the effort to point out and name objects in books and encourage him to repeat them.

I'm much against using "flash cards" when your child finds it onerous and a bore. In this instance you're only doing it for your own satisfaction and pride. This should never be the reason for making your child do anything. On the other hand, if your child is avid for new words and gets pleasure from remembering flash cards, do by all means encourage him as much as you can. You should not try to make him read. When he's ready he'll start pointing out words; only then should you start to help him.

Nursery school

As your child reaches three years old you should start thinking about whether he would benefit from attending nursery school. There he will meet lots of new friends, as well as interested and sympathetic adults who are good at knowing how to widen a child's horizons. He will have the opportunity to try a whole lot of new and interesting activities and he will have to learn to socialize and be a member of a group. Lastly, and most importantly, he will have to be able to manage without you.

The decision as to whether he is capable of doing without you for long periods of time will be one of the factors that you will have to weigh up when you are deciding the pros and cons of nursery school. If your child is very shy and clinging and doesn't talk easily to other adults and children, frets when you leave the room and follows you wherever you go then you are going to have problems with nursery school. In addition, most nursery schools won't accept children who are not toilet-trained. Add to all this the fact that attending nursery school for the first time is quite a traumatic experience for a small child and one for which you cannot really prepare him because there is nothing similar that you can introduce him to, and you may have a difficult decision. You can, however, fall back on the knowledge that most children manage it and indeed thrive on it so well that they miss school when they're on holiday. Bear in mind that with a little careful planning you can help your child get over the frightening first stages and he need not feel deserted.

Assessing nursery or playgroup

There are several different types of group for pre-school children. There are play groups, nursery schools and day nurseries. Ring up your local council and get a list of all pre-school groups in your area of which the authority has approved. Choose two or three from this list that you can visit and "assess".

Go about your assessment in a thorough way. First of all go and talk to the teacher in charge. Make an appointment to go and visit the group and sit in on some of the classes. If possible, spend a whole morning or a whole afternoon there so that you can get a feel of the routines, the amount of discipline, whether the teachers are strict, whether you approve of the way the children are treated, whether the environment is happy, informal and cosy and if the children seem happy. If you can, have a look at the facilities and talk to another mother whose child goes to that particular group.

Once you have decided where your child will go ask if you can take him along to sit in on a session so that he can get used to the place. This should be several weeks before he starts himself. If possible take him along for more than one visit.

When he gets there make sure that he knows who the teachers are and the sort of things that he will have to do. He might try sitting in one of the little chairs at the desk, or he may have a go in the sand pit or the water table or do a jig-saw puzzle, look at some of the books or play with some of the toys. Encourage him to play with other children but if he becomes very shy don't force him to be sociable. Many children get like this in strange situations and it's quite natural – let him take his time.

If your child is a bit worried or clingy most nursery schools welcome the idea that you sit with your child until he is happy to let you go. This may mean the whole session on the first day, a couple of hours on the second day, an hour on the third day, half an hour on the fourth day and ten minutes on the fifth. To try to see if he's ready to let you go just say that you want to pop out to the shops and that you will be back in a few minutes. Make sure that you are so that he can trust you to always return for him. For the first week or so, it is a good idea for you or your partner to take your child to the group and pick him up personally; don't let him cope with a strange mother doing a school run along with all of his other worries. And when you go to collect him, don't be late.

SPEECH 0–1

The moment when your child begins to speak is very exciting. For the first time you are given some precise information about what your child knows and thinks; it's as if language provides you with a window to look in on your child's mental ability. It's also the tool with which he can learn. He'll no longer have to rely on crying to communicate.

Despite a great deal of research we still don't know exactly how a child acquires language. What we do know, however, is the general sequence that all children follow. We also know that your baby learns a lot about language before he even starts to talk: long before he knows what the words mean he'll listen to any changes in sound, to the rhythm and the intonation of your speech. He'll also learn about verbal rituals before he begins to speak and will soon know that first one person and then another speaks.

For each month that your baby develops he will master new words and new grammatical rules. But learning to speak is infinitely more important than learning about vocabulary and grammar. What your child is mainly concerned with is communicating and interacting with the people around him, and his language shows how sensitive he is to the people he's talking to.

Children develop at their own speed and this fact applies to speech as it does to any other aspect of development. Don't get worried if your child doesn't seem to be as quick at picking up language as other children around you – give all the encouragement you can and let your child take the time he wants to.

How speech develops

Studies have shown that even a few days after birth babies will respond more to speech than to any other noise. They have also shown that even very young babies can discriminate between different speech sounds which is, after all, an essential part in the process of learning a language. For

example, in one study, one-month-old babies were observed to suck more rapidly from a bottle when they heard a new sound, especially if it was of the human voice. In these experiments the initial sound used was "Pa". As the sound was continuously played to the baby he got bored and eventually lost interest in sucking but, as soon as a new sound, "Ba", was introduced his sucking rate increased once more. What's so interesting is that the baby was able to distinguish between two such similar sounds as "Pa" and "Ba", before he could actually say them.

● *Up to six weeks*
As soon as your baby's born he'll start to make sounds. Initially they will be cries – cries for food, for affection, or because he's uncomfortable. Along with these he'll start to make little burbling noises as a mark of pleasure and contentment.

● *Around six weeks*
He'll begin to respond to your smiling face and your voice with a more exaggerated gurgling. Although he's not literally talking to you he *is* communicating, and what's more he's learning to communicate in the way that adults do. For example, on hearing your voice your baby will burble something at you, then wait for your reply before responding again.

● *Three to four months*
Your baby will make soft, cooing noises. At this stage the sound will be of single syllables with an open vowel sound. The first consonants he'll use will be p, b and m so it's hardly surprising that he'll say "Maa" or "Paa", although he won't understand the significance of what he's saying at this time.

● *Seven months*
He'll be increasingly responsive to sounds, whether of the human voice or music. He'll expand his cooing into two-syllabled words by repeating the initial syllable: "Maama", "Beebe", "Daada". This stage will be followed by explosive sounds of exclamation. "Al", "Iml".

248

● *Eight months*
Your baby will continue to babble, but he'll also learn how to shout to deliberately attract your attention. If he's near you when you're having a conversation with someone he'll pay close attention to whatever you're saying and will then turn to watch any reply that's made to you. His babbling may become quite musical and he could try to imitate you when you sing a nursery rhyme to him or put on his musical box.

● *Nine months*
Your baby's speech will become noticeably more elaborate as he starts to join up the syllables he knows and pronounce them with sentence-like phrasing. So, with the rising and falling intonation of adult speech he'll say: "Ca-mama-dah-ba". Once he starts to make up sounds like this, technically called *jargoning*, you'll know that he's just about to start talking.

● *Ten to eleven months*
Your baby will probably say his first "real" words some time during this month. The emergence of these first words is as much controlled by your baby's physical ability to articulate and make speech sounds as it is by his intellectual ability to make connections between objects and labels. The words he chooses will almost certainly be the names of things which are important to him: people (like mama, dada); animals (dog, cat); objects (cup, ball).

Simplifying words

The change from babbling to saying precise words means that your child has to change from making a stream of ill-controlled sounds to planned, thoughtful, controlled speech. Furthermore, the sounds have to be in a certain sequence so that the words are understandable to another person. All this is rather much for a young child so the pronunciation of early words is very often simplified.

Nearly all children reduce the number of consonants that they say at the beginning (or the end) of words so that spoon becomes "poon" and smack becomes

"mack"; he might say "du" for duck, "be" for bed, "ca" for cat. This aspect of speech is one of the last to be mastered in English and children quite often have difficulty with consonants until they are four or five years old. This is quite normal.

Another way that children simplify the pronunciation of words is to put the consonants in the same place in the mouth where the basic sound of the word is made. This accounts for doggy being pronounced "doddy" or "goggy".

The other preference that children show is to substitute a more explosive sound with a less explosive one so that instead of pie your child may say "bie" and "doe" for toe and "bop" for pop.

Helping your baby to talk

□ One of the first kinds of words that your baby learns are label words identifying the names of things. So in conversations with your baby stress the names of objects and repeat them frequently. When you are feeding your baby talk repeatedly about the spoon and putting the food on the spoon and licking the food off the spoon. Make an effort not to use pronouns. Say "I'll get your coat" instead of saying "I'll get it." Say "Here is the ball" instead of "Here it is." Your child is busy learning the difference between himself and other people so use his name constantly rather than "you". "William is a good boy", "Where are William's shoes", "William and Mummy will go into the car."

□ Don't expect too much of your baby's pronunciation – if he can't say a word properly but you understand what he means don't insist he keeps on trying until he says it perfectly. He'll only get frustrated.

□ Go to some effort to understand his own private, invented words or ones which are mis-pronounced. If he is trying to explain something to you, go through a long sequence of alternatives until you find the word that he actually wants. His pleasure in having communicated with you when you find it will be enormous and will encourage him to try again.

249

☐ Help your baby to learn about how to apply words by describing and talking about things which are actually in front of him. Your baby can then make the connection between an object and what you're talking about if you repeat the word, especially if he can see, hold, touch and play with it. So, while you are playing with a ball, you should repeat the word ball as often as you can, and also discuss the innate properties of a ball – that it is round, it will roll, and it will bounce.

☐ In teaching your baby to talk you really have to be something of an actor. You must bring drama and interest to what you are saying. This means exaggerating your pronunciation and your intonation. Make it clear that you're asking a question. Show when you're pleased and when you're serious. Carry this through in your actions as well as in speech and in facial expressions.

☐ Your baby learns language from you more easily than from any other person but don't expect him to pick it up from the general babble of adult conversation in which he's not included. He won't be able to distinguish the single sounds and sentences. Always look directly at your baby while you are talking to him. Stop what you are doing and look intently at your baby when he "talks" to you. Pay him the compliment of listening to his efforts when he tries to talk back.

☐ Ask your baby questions like "Where's your teddy?" and "Was that nice?" He may not be able to answer you initially but he'll understand what you're saying and may well point or nod.

☐ Don't oversimplify what you say to your baby – he needs the stimulation of adult speech, not a kind of pulpy baby talk.

☐ Take advantage of your baby's interests by talking about things on which he is already concentrating. He may not be

interested in a story about a fictional character, but he will be riveted by a story in which he is the central character. He may not be interested in animals but he will be interested in all animals if they are discussed in terms of mother animals and their babies because he can relate to that.
□ Encourage him to use the few words that he has learned by using them in your conversations. He will be delighted to hear his own primitive conversation coming back at him, and this will encourage him to be adventurous with speech and to try out new words.
□ Never, ever scold or correct early errors of pronunciation or understanding. With my own children I found some of them so charming that I left them uncorrected until quite a late age. In our house we all said "aterator" for radiator, "gamilla" for vanilla, "binoclickers" for binoculars.

Bi-lingualism

Children seem to thrive on having two languages to learn. When small babies are learning to talk they have the ability to make all linguistic sounds. They find a new language much easier than we do. It also seems to be quite easy for them not just to pick them up, but also to think and speak in two languages. Recently I watched a small godchild looking from her French mother who was speaking French to her English father who was speaking English. She's just two and a half years old; but she replied to her mother in French and her father in English. I would encourage small children to be exposed to more than one language rather than restrict them to one alone.

Spotting when something is wrong

Don't worry if your baby doesn't speak this year. As in everything else, children develop speech at different rates. However, if your child is still not speaking by the time he's two and a half you *must* seek expert help. If deficient hearing is responsible then it's crucial to have the faults sorted out before he starts nursery or primary school. If it's a real speech defect you should go to the best paediatric department, with a special group of therapists for children with speech disorders. Many problems can be sorted out if seen early enough and given expert help.

SPEECH   1–2

This year your child will make great strides forward both in terms of physical and intellectual development. He'll increase his vocabulary, and his grasp of grammatical construction will greatly improve. In order to speak properly he'll have to unlearn some of the habits he got into when his speech consisted of babbling. For example, in babbling, consonants are frequently dropped, and duplicated words are common. Once your child gains control of his speech he'll constrain the errors and substitutions that he used to make.

The beginnings of classification

As your child learns to recognize and identify objects he'll begin to classify and group them. However, at the beginning this process won't be completely accurate. He'll look at several objects and use the same word to identify all of them if they have one or more features in common. This is referred to as overextension. The reason he uses words generically like this is because he hasn't the ability to articulate all words, but his desire to communicate with you is so strong that he has to use the nearest word that he can. Your child will link words together on the following bases:
Shape
Balls, apples or stones may all be called "ball".
Size
A handbag, a polythene bag and a shopping basket may all be "bag".
Sound
A whistle, a siren and a car horn may all be "beep".

Movement
A bicycle, a car, a bus and a train may all be "choo-choo".
Although your child overextends in this way he does know the difference between two things he calls by the same name. For example, he may use the word "guck" for truck and duck, and yet when faced with pictures of them both and told to point out a truck and a duck he'll quite easily make the distinction.

In the same way, children can underextend words. For most children the word animal usually just applies to mammals and the animals that they meet in their everyday life; they very often have difficulty in understanding that fish, insects and birds can be categorized as animals too. Whatever early words your child learns he'll soon begin to use them to mean a variety of things. A single word can be a label for a greeting, a demand or a question. At the beginning your child may often add gestures to single words to give them meaning. Later on he'll learn to change his intonation as a signal for different meanings.

Expanding vocabulary

Your baby's vocabulary will continue to expand and the words he'll learn most readily will be those whose use affects his daily life – people and animals, foods and most things from his daily routine. Early words nearly always include the names of animals like duck, dog, cat, horse, cow, plus the kind of noises that they make. Your child will also know the names of his favourite toys and, very importantly, the words which he can use to change or regulate the world around him by his interaction with you. So there may be words like no, up, more, out and open.

Some children learn a whole load of words as soon as they begin to speak but it's more usual for them to acquire between 1 and 3 a month. By the time he's two he should be able to say about 200.

Helping your child to understand

Understanding always goes before usage

and your eighteen-month-old child will understand a lot more of the speech that he hears than his own language suggests. To help him you should make available far more information than your words alone provide.
□ Talk to your child as often as you can and always look at him when you do so. In this way your child will be given the maximum number of opportunities for learning and understanding language.
□ Help your baby's comprehension by acting out what you are saying with facial expressions and gestures, and make your words accompany actions that involve him. "Mummy will put on Jennifer's coat", "Mummy will take off Mummy's shoes."
□ For your child to learn that communication is always two-way, you shouldn't babble on with long sentences and stories without giving him the opportunity to participate and contribute. Punctuate your conversations with questions that demand a response of some kind.
□ Your child finds it very difficult to understand language if there is a great deal of background noise that obscures speech sound. So if the television is on keep the sound low and don't play your radio loudly.
□ Give him the confidence to try conversation with strangers by acting as his interpreter. In this way he won't feel embarrassed and will have a go.
□ Give him as many cues and clues to your meaning as you can, even though you know that he cannot understand exactly what you are saying. For example, at bathtime take him into the bathroom, run the tap, feel the temperature of the water and undress him, giving him information about what you are doing all the time and then say, "Now you are ready for your bath". Having had all the visual action and speech clues presented to him, he will certainly understand the meaning of your last comment.

The first sentences

Sometime before your child's second

252

birthday he'll start to string words together. This is an important milestone because it shows that he's now aware of the relationship between objects. Your baby's first sentences will be limited in their meanings. They'll probably explain something that has just happened or describe what someone is doing. His sentences will be concerned with the following:

What's happening:	Me run
	Cow go moo
	Truck bump
Who possesses what:	My dolly
	Mummy dress
	Granny bag
Where things are:	Doll in box
	Daddy in garden
	Ball in bath
Repetition:	Me more milk
	Play again
Where something's gone:	Drink all gone
	No more toy

His sentences won't follow adult grammatical rules, that will develop later, but they will have a logical construction of their own. He'll learn fairly early that certain words are used in combination. He'll repeatedly hear "Pick up", "Put on","Go out", and will continue to use them as one word even when joining them on to others. So he'll have "Car pick up", "Door go out".

His first attempts at tenses will be slightly awry. He'll make the past tense by adding "d" to anything – "I wented", "You goed", "I gaved". To make words plural he'll add an "s" to the end – "Look, fishes", "Mouses", "Gameses".

Looking at books together

As with other aspects of her development, you are your child's first introduction to books. If she regularly sees you sitting reading a book or magazine, she soon will start copying your behaviour. You will find her sitting, studiously "reading" her book – which may well be upside down – and turning over the pages at intervals! Gradually her attention will turn to the content of the pages as she starts to recognize objects. Popular books with this age group are those with clear, recognizable pictures of familiar, everyday objects which you can look at with your child, pointing and referring to the object by name. As your child's vocabulary expands during this year, she will be able to point to objects herself when asked. She will soon start to appreciate simple, illustrated stories, especially those with a repeated "chorus" which she will start to anticipate and join in with – e.g. *The Gingerbread Man* or *The Three Billy-Goats Gruff*. As well as having a regular refrain, the most popular stories for this age group have simple, recurring themes – often involving the downfall of the big, fierce "baddie" (the wolf, the troll, the wicked witch) or the victory of the small or weak hero over his bigger and stronger opponent (the little pig in Three Little Pigs). Toddlers often want the same story read over and over again; for some reason, they find something in the story that they

need. If that is what your child wants, let her have it – even though you are bored with reading it.

The value of nursery rhymes

Children love nursery rhymes – from the first game of "This little piggy" to all the old favourites – and will join in enthusiastically with whatever actions are involved. As with story books, the attraction of nursery rhymes lies in their simplicity, drama and recurring motifs and, above all, in the rhythm which babies and toddlers respond to from a very early age. Don't worry if you think you don't have a great singing voice: your child won't mind. In fact, you'll never have had such an appreciative and adoring audience!

Nursery rhymes play an important part in the development of your child's language skills, as well as providing an enjoyable and entertaining form of communication between you. Many can be sung as the accompaniment to activities – e.g. "See-saw Marjorie Daw" or "One, Two, Buckle my Shoe" – thus

teaching and reinforcing the concepts in an enjoyable and memorable form. All will expand your child's vocabulary, extend her powers of imagination, and encourage a love of music and rhythm.

SPEECH   2–3

During the third year, the structure of sentences will become more complicated and your child will start to fit whole phrases together. He'll begin to understand and use negatives, not just a simple "no" and "not". He will also start to phrase words so that they make a question and not just put "why" in front and, for the first time, he will begin to fully appreciate the relationship between one object and another. He'll start to use adjectives – big, small, fat, thin – and then comparative adjectives – bigger, smaller, fatter, thinner. He'll understand and use words that imply spatial relationships – this, here, that, there, and will learn the relationship between "I" and "my", "you" and "yours". He'll also learn how to use phrases with conjunctions like "and", "then", and "but".

Having conversations

In his third year your child becomes a natural chatterer so take advantage of this tendency to show him how conversations are carried on; the to and fro pattern of verbal exchanges, how to make subjects interesting with questions and how to move on through various points of interest in any subject.

One of the best ways of involving your child in a conversation is to ask him what he likes or what he is doing or how things work. Having asked him the question you have to show real and sincere interest in his response for him to learn that conversation is worthwhile. Similarly, when he approaches you with a question or an appeal for help or just a request that you come and see something that is exciting, you have to show a genuine interest in what he is doing and saying. In this way you can contribute to what he is thinking, understanding and learning. If you respond to his running commentary of things that he is doing with a series of absent-minded "mms" he'll not only get little in return that he can learn from, but he will quickly learn that you are not interested so he'll stop referring to you.

You can help him in everything that you do by giving descriptions that are slightly more detailed than you would normally use. For instance, if he is having difficulty getting his sweater over his head, you can say something like "Oh dear, the opening in your jumper is too small for your head." In this rather elaborate way of saying "I'll help you" there are at least three new ideas and three new words that you have introduced him to. If he can't lift something and you can, you can point out that you are able to because you are stronger than he is and the object is heavy. Talk about colours, shapes and textures whenever possible. "You are going to have the *red* sweet. I'll have the *yellow* one." "Look at the pretty blue flower with the long stem. Let's smell the flower." "Daddy's car has four wheels. This truck has lots of wheels, let's count. One, two, three, four, five, six, seven, eight."

You can also help him out with conversation. If you ask him what he has been doing in the garden and he can't quite get the words together, you could point him in the right direction by saying: "What did you make in the sandpit? ... How did you get down from the top of the climbing frame? ... Where did you go on your tricycle?" You can prompt his responses by "What happened next?"

One of the favourite things that all my children enjoyed in a conversation was for me to leave a blank that they could fill in with the word that they knew. So in reference to getting down from the top of the climbing frame I could prompt them with "Oh you mean you slid down the _____", and my children would gleefully contribute "slide". Or in discussing what they had done in the sandpit I would say "Oh you made sandpies with your _____" and my children would shout "bucket".

Helping with grammar

As your child begins to understand the more complicated aspects of grammar you can help, as before, by simply repeating what he has said in the correct form. So, as he starts to apply the constructions more and more widely, help him to use them in the correct way with new words and expressions.

Negatives
With your help your child can learn to put the negative where it belongs. By listening to what you say they learn to use won't, can't, wouldn't, hadn't, wasn't.
Your child says "I not eat biccit."
You say "You haven't eaten your biscuit."
Your child says "no sweeties left."
You say "Oh dear – there aren't any more sweeties."

Questions
In the same way you can teach him how to ask questions correctly and use the appropriate words that precede questions.
Your child says "go out?"
You say "Where shall we go?"
Your child says "more?"
You say "Would you like some more ice cream?"
Your child says "coat on?"
You say "How do you put your coat on?"
In this way your child learns to use the "wh" words, such as what, who, which, where, and why.

Adjectives
One of the best ways to teach your child about adjectives and the relationship of one object to another is to do it by opposites. So if your child says big ball, you can look around for a smaller ball, and introduce him to the concept of opposites like

big and small. You will be able to show him that compared to each other one is bigger than the other or that one is smaller than the other. Similarly you can get over the concepts of wide and narrow, thick and thin, deep and shallow, heavy and light, hard and soft – always demonstrating with the appropriate object and if possible making it into a kind of game.

Possessive pronouns
Your child says "I bring book here", you can say "Oh you were over there and you brought your book to me here."
Your child says "I hate *this* biccit."
You say "Oh then I'll have your biscuit and you can have my biscuit."
Your child says "This Jennifer coat that Mummy coat."
You say, "Yes, that is *your* coat, this is *my* coat."
This way your child learns how to use the words "my" and "yours".

Asking and answering questions

When your child approaches his third birthday he will ask you questions continually. While you may get tired of answering the constant whys you should be happy your child is showing so much curiosity in what is going on around him and making so many attempts to try to understand the world and to express his ideas in words.

Your child's questions should always be treated seriously and you should try to give the most accurate, truthful answer you can. Don't fob your child off with an answer like "Because that is the way it is" or "Things are just made that way" because that can't advance his understanding at all. You have got to give him information that adds to his knowledge in a form that he can cope with. So when your child says "Why is it raining?" don't respond with "Because it is." Try, instead, a simple explanation like clouds are full of water and the water is falling back to the earth in rain drops.

Your child's questions are usually very simple because he hasn't learned to use words to express his questions fully enough. So you should always examine the question to see what the point of it is. If your child says "What's that?" and you say "A ruler", he may want more than a name. So you could say "It's a ruler and you use it to measure things; look, this book is 23 centimetres long. It's also used to draw straight lines; let's draw one together." He may often ask questions which seem unanswerable at first like "Why birds fly?" But what he may really means is "Why do birds fly, how do birds fly, why do birds flap their wings?", and you should try to supply all this information. Test out bits of information and then say to your child "Is that what you mean?"

If you don't know the answer to a question, be truthful, say that you don't know but also add "Let's go and look at it in the book." Or "Let's go and ask Daddy", or "Perhaps your brother will know."

Sometimes parents shy away from giving truthful and accurate answers to children because they think a child won't be able to cope with the truth. This is often the case with questions about death, and about sex. You must *always* answer these questions truthfully and should never avoid a difficult answer. However, don't make the mistake of thinking that when you tell the truth you have to tell the whole truth. You don't. It would be a mistake to try to do that because your child doesn't understand enough to cope with the complexities of a full and accurate reply. What you can do in awkward circumstances, however, is to supply that part of the truth which they can cope with and can understand (see p.280).

POSSIBLE PROBLEMS   2-3

Dyslexia

Very few people understand what the term dyslexia really means, and I'm against its loose usage because it may quite incorrectly label a child, thus preventing him from receiving the simple help that may be all his difficulties require.

There's no question that some obviously intelligent children do encounter difficulties learning to read, but even the experts are still arguing about who may appropriately be labelled as dyslexic, and what causes the condition.

Dyslexic children are likely to be impaired to varying extents in many language skills. However, for most children classed as dyslexic, it is the problem with reading which is regarded as the most severe.

The main view held by psychologists is that the deficit is in the brain and muscle processes which, firstly, make sound and, secondly, maintain and manipulate the sounds from memory. It is also believed that dyslexia has a genetic component: a tendency inherited from parents, involving unusual brain function. It is not related to intelligence, though the problem will be more obvious in intelligent children, whose difficulties in learning to read may thus be put down to laziness.

It is important that a correct diagnosis of dyslexia is made, so that the child can be helped by specially trained teachers.

Lisping

Lisping is another common speech defect in children who are just learning to talk. It occurs, to start with, because the child simply has not mastered all the sounds needed and so he substitutes a similar sound that he can make. This can become a habit, however, or the child may be copying another child with a lisp. Neither of these is anything to worry about and usually stops without treatment.

Lisping may, however, indicate a more serious underlying problem: it may be due to a degree of deafness, to a cleft palate, or to a faulty action of the tongue. Although these possibilities should have been excluded at your child's regular developmental check-ups, if you are at all worried about persistent lisping, consult your doctor so that speech therapy can be started if necessary.

14 Social behaviour

The foundations of your child's social behaviour are laid in babyhood. The way you treat your child and the way in which he responds to you, and to the outside world, will be part of his character's make-up. Social development in early childhood goes through fairly well-defined stages. From being a very non-gregarious newborn your baby will join in the surrounding social group by imitating others. He will first imitate facial expressions, gestures and movements, then speech sounds and, finally, patterns of behaviour. One of the most important guides in this early period is the mother, or mother substitute. Babies who establish warm, loving, outgoing relationships with their mothers are motivated to make friendly relationships with other people by the pleasure they feel in this early relationship. There will be a slightly troubled time, probably in the second year, when your child will be struggling so hard to assert independence that he slips into a negative stage of doing nothing that you want, and everything that you don't want him to do. You have to go with your child on this, realizing that he's not turning into a monster, and that he still needs your help to steer him along the path to independence. Your job will be made a lot easier if you use your wits to make it seem as if your child's getting it all his own way. In the end you'll have a lovable young child who has learned to respect the feelings of others, and one who has an overwhelming desire to share his happiness with those whom he loves.

Your baby is different from all others. He is unique, and no matter how many books you read, none can tell you about him. You are going to have to discover your baby for yourself and little by little, with careful observation, paying close attention to all the signals, you will come to know and prize his individuality. It is one of the most precious possessions a child has, and one of the most important jobs you do is to nourish that individuality. Help it to grow and flower and maintain it intact.

Getting to know your baby as a person is like reading an exciting story very slowly. You will gradually find out if he likes very gentle treatment or slightly rougher handling; you will find out if he has a ready sense of humour, enjoys a joke and is eager to join in with things, or whether he prefers to be quiet. It may take you several weeks to know how he behaves when he is really well and happy, and until you do you may well worry about whether he's ill or not. It may even take you a couple of months to know his crying patterns – an early signal of whether he's going to be a fretful baby or a placid one (see p.179). But don't worry. You will gradually come to know all of your baby's idiosyncracies: whether he feeds quickly or slowly; whether he needs a lot of sleep or is wakeful; if he likes to be cuddled or not.

While you are learning about your baby you will have to make many reassessments and adjustments as you fit your daily routine to his needs.

259

Social milestones

By the time that your baby is six months old he will have learned a lot about being a sociable human being. In ways that we do not quite understand, he will have become an expert at the flow of social exchange. He'll know how to start a conversation with you and how to get you to play. He will have learned how to hold your attention by smiling, by babbling and by being interested and curious; and how to end a conversation by looking away or appearing bored. The stages at which he acquires this ability are outlined below:

● *By three months*
He won't like to be deprived of social contact and will quite often cry when he is left alone. He will stop crying when an adult reappears and when he is talked to or is diverted by a toy or a rattle. He will turn his head when he hears human voices and will smile when an adult smiles at him or makes a kind of clucking sound. He will express pleasure when others are present by smiling, kicking and waving his arms. He will recognize his mother and other familiar people by acting sociably, and will show fear of strangers by turning away and possibly even crying.

● *By the fourth month*
He may lift his arms in anticipation of being picked up. He will focus on faces and will nearly always follow the direction of the person who leaves him. He will smile at a person who speaks to him and when anyone shows particular attention to him he will show delight. He will laugh when he is being played with.

● *Between the fifth and sixth month*
He will show quite a different reaction to smiling and to a scolding tone of voice. Familiar people are greeted with a smile, and strange people with recognizable expressions of fear.

● *At six months*
Social behaviour becomes much more active so he may pull the hair of the person who is holding him or rub their nose or start to pat the person's face.

● *At seven to nine months*
He will socialize by imitating speech sounds and gestures.

● *By twelve months*
He will refrain from doing things if told "No", and will show fear and dislike of strangers by rushing to his mother, and possibly even crying when the stranger approaches. He may become slightly clingy at this age.

Responding to your baby's behaviour

The generally-accepted definition of a good baby is one who cries very little, settles down easily and sleeps for long periods; the definition of a bad baby is the opposite. On the basis of these definitions all of my friends had good babies and I had bad babies. However, I would not describe any of my babies as bad. They were demanding and occasionally difficult but this arose only because they wanted my attention and, to me, this seems perfectly normal.

In the first few weeks you and your baby have to get used to each other. Don't be put off by how your baby behaves initially. He has no control over how he responds to the outside world and may exhibit tendencies which will not remain beyond the first couple of months.

He may be miserable, jumpy, excessively wakeful or excessively sleepy. What you must do is deal with your baby's needs as competently and calmly as possible, giving all the love that you have.

"Difficult" babies

A baby who is really difficult, who for instance cries and cannot be comforted by any of the usual methods (see p.182), is extremely hard to deal with calmly. The sound of a baby crying constantly is irritating and upsetting at the same time and, if your baby also rejects your efforts to comfort him, you may then feel spurned and inadequate. You may even become angry because you believe that the baby is crying on purpose. This is absolutely impossible: your baby cries because he is biologically programmed to do so until his needs are understood and fulfilled. When you fail to do this a vicious circle ensues. You become tense because the baby won't stop crying. When you're tense you cannot cope calmly with your baby who therefore cries even more. Ill-temper increases on both sides.

What to do
Try very hard not to lose your temper or to get too worked up.
● Share the responsibility with your partner and take it in turns, wherever possible, to deal with your baby.
● Follow the advice on crying (see p.182), and don't forget, yours is not the only baby in the world who is going through this "difficult" spell. Whatever you think, this spell will be brief.
● Don't treat your baby's behaviour as a deliberate rejection of you – at the moment he can't help behaving like this as he is desperately trying to adapt to the new world. You have to accept the baby as he is and deal with him accordingly; as he grows he *is* going to change.
● Accept any offer of help from friends and relations. You'll need your rest, and if friends can look after your baby, even for a couple of hours between feeds, you can recharge your batteries.

Sleepy babies

These babies are often called placid babies. Your baby may sleep twenty-one hours out of twenty-four; he'll make few demands on you, will rarely cry, won't be very alert and won't take much notice of his surroundings. He may fall asleep mid-feed, he won't respond when talked to and he won't show much emotion.

What to do
A baby like this is marvellous initially because he leaves you to regain your strength after delivery. However, he is missing an awful lot in life and should be coaxed into realizing that being awake is much more fun.
● Don't try to keep your baby awake forcibly. He knows how much sleep he needs and you should respect this. However, you should make sure that he's not going for too long without food. If, for example, he can sleep through the night you must wake him up before you go to bed because it is otherwise too long for a new baby to go without liquid.
● Whenever he is awake provide as much stimulation and affection as possible. Surround the cot or crib with mobiles and photographs so that even if you're not there he has something to focus on and be occupied by.
● Try carrying the baby in a sling so that at least he has your warmth and smell, even although he's asleep.

Wakeful babies

Instead of sleeping the usual sixteen out of twenty-four hours for the first few weeks of life your baby may sleep as little as twelve, and he'll take these in short bursts. He'll be full of life, interested in everything that's going on and will be very keen to learn. Wakeful babies are usually very sociable and affectionate. Though he may exhaust you, he'll be very rewarding.

What to do
Until your baby's old enough to entertain himself, you and your partner will be the sole form of entertainment, and he may

261

demand your attention all hours of the day and night. If you don't work out some sort of shift system with your partner you may become so fatigued that you cannot carry on. Don't be resentful of your baby's wakefulness; try to accept it and take practical steps to make sure that you get enough sleep.
● Carry the baby around in a sling.
● When you're at home take the crib or basket wherever you go and place it *safely* on a table or work surface so that your baby can hear your voice.
● Have plenty of pictures and mobiles over the cot or crib so that he'll be occupied even when you're not there.
● Prop the baby up on a bed or in the pram from about six weeks (see p.69).
● Keep the baby's room warm because this sometimes encourages sleepiness.
● Take the baby into bed with you (see p.173).

Discontented babies

You may have a discontented baby, one who is irritable when he's hungry yet doesn't enjoy feeding. He takes the feed slowly and with difficulty. After it he isn't very sociable and doesn't like to be held. When you talk to him he doesn't seem to take much notice; he seems tired but fretful and not very relaxed. When laid down to sleep he starts to cry.

What to do
Don't feel that you'll never succeed in making your baby comfortable and happy or you'll begin to feel inadequate and eventually resentful. Try to keep all negative emotions out of your head. Your baby's behaviour is aimed at the outside world to which he's not yet acclimatized, and not at you. Don't interpret your baby's unhappiness as a personal criticism. Try very hard, no matter how much your baby rejects you, to get him to smile at you. Try to engage him in play; sit with him on your lap and try some physical exercises (see p.292). Get your baby to respond. Once he does this then you know that you've turned the corner and you're really just

to know each other.
● When he cries, try all the crying remedies.
● Keep his room warm and cosy; try wrapping him snugly (see p.166) before he's put down to sleep so that he feels secure.
● Give as many feeds as he want and *never* keep him waiting and crying.
● Put lots of mobiles above the cot to occupy his attention.
● Carry him around with you if that provides comfort.

Jumpy babies

All newborn babies are sensitive to loud noises and sudden, jerky movements, but jumpy babies over-react to quite normal stimuli. When he gets hungry he doesn't show hunger with the usual persistent cry but within a few seconds is screaming hysterically. When he's picked up his body stiffens and if he's put down again the body may jerk. He seems alarmed by any kind of noise or rapid movement.

What to do
● Understand, once again, that your baby's behaviour is not a rejection of you as a parent. It's just an inability to deal with the new world that he's in.
● Keep the baby wrapped (see p.166), most of the time. This means that when he's moved there's no risk of his arms or legs flopping which gives a sense of insecurity.
● Pick him up gently and slowly. When you bend down speak softly and gently; you could even try singing a song.
● If he seems to feel more secure when he's near you put him in a sling and carry him with you all of the time.
● Don't give your baby baths, just top and tail him every day (see p.88). Never take all of his clothes off at once; always leave the vest or the nappy on and try to keep the body covered, even by a towel, for as long as possible.
● Don't leave him in a noisy room. For example, avoid rooms which face noisy roads or schools, and rooms which have whirring clocks or telephones.

Your baby as part of the family

During the first few weeks of your baby's life the household will revolve around him, but from then on he'll have to learn to fit in with the household and the rest of the family. It is important that your new baby learns to live with a group of people for whom there are routines, accepted customs and modes of behaviour, quite a number of guidelines and a few rules. Your baby can't be expected to fit into family routines if he isn't introduced to them, so include your baby in family activities like mealtimes, games, outings, shopping,

household chores, looking after pets and visiting friends as soon as possible. All of these encounters are important to your child because through the working of the family group he will learn about the working of people in general. In this way he'll relate how he behaves with the family to how he should behave with strangers. Through the family your baby will learn the social customs and attitudes of your society. One of the ways your baby learns is by imitation – so by watching and copying how you behave, your child develops his own behaviour patterns.

263

DISCIPLINE 0–1

Very few children under the age of a year need true disciplining. Up to this age a child is not open to reasonable argument and your main form of discipline will simply be to say "No" and, if your baby doesn't obey, to resort to the physical removal of either the baby or the object. I don't believe that young babies should ever be smacked or punished.

As they grow up all young children need to be shown by their parents the boundaries of socially acceptable behaviour. Many of these limits are implicitly set by the way members of the family behave to one another. Setting a good example by your own behaviour is the best way to teach your child what good behaviour is. It is part of your responsibility as the parent to give your child guidelines on behaviour and you should start to do this during your child's first year. If you fail to do this your child will soon find that other children and adults won't tolerate someone ill-mannered and selfish. You are going to have to keep to some guidelines in your home, as in any other organized group of people, for the sake of efficiency, justice and safety.

Understanding bad behaviour

No baby behaves badly deliberately, although many a tired and exhausted parent feels convinced that they do. Your baby may cry constantly and be very irritable and grumpy but this is usually due to being over-tired, hungry, ill, anxious or scared of your leaving or of meeting strangers. This is not your baby's fault and should never be blamed for what really is beyond his control. Nor should you blame yourself if you've done everything within your power to prevent or correct what is causing your baby's unhappiness.

Towards the end of this year one of the major causes of "bad behaviour" will be frustration. Your baby may be a fairly strong-willed character to begin with and as he gets older and becomes more independent he's going to want to express this. A battle of wills will ⟨...⟩ ⟨...⟩ and he'll

no longer accept that you have total control over his life. He will challenge your preferences and will begin to assert himself strongly. Objections to your choice of food will be common, so let your baby choose what he wants to eat, and the order in which he eats it (see p.144). Similarly, if he expresses a desire to wear certain items of clothing let him go ahead and wear them. If you don't allow your baby some freedom at this time he will become very frustrated and angry.

Doing things alone may bring their own frustrations because your child's ambitions will often exceed his capabilities. He won't be able to make his body do what he wants it to, and he'll find that he cannot manage the world in the way that he wants to. This will inevitably result in tears and possibly temper tantrums (see p. 188). Try not to get annoyed at this – every child goes through similar behaviour – but do give him your assistance. If you don't offer to help at this point he may waste a lot of energy trying to do something that is beyond him and repeated failure will be very demoralizing. When your baby is in this kind of mood, bullying and pressurizing will simply cause more stubbornness. You have to be tactful, humorous even, and a little devious. If you let your baby feel that he is taking control you will find that he very often fits in with what you want. So, instead of saying "Don't" to your baby who is throwing plastic mugs everywhere, make the clearing up into a game. Sit down and suggest that he tries to pick them all up before you have time to count to ten.

When to say "No"

During your baby's first year there are very few reasons for saying "No." I prefer to keep the rules for my children to a minimum, and I had only one unbreakable rule in their first year. That was when they were doing something which was unsafe for themselves and others. In these in-stances I would say "No" firmly and at the

same time remove the object from my child, or stop my child from performing the dangerous activity. I did not wait for my child to stop. As I was trying to teach my child what was unsafe, I always offered an explanation of why I was stopping him from behaving in a certain way. I simply stated what was dangerous about it and repeated it every time the same thing occurred in the hope that my child would remember, learn and not do it again. I did not chastise and I tried not to become angry. Only as they got older and learned the rule did I give them the opportunity to resist without my intervention.

I believe other aspects of discipline are better taught by praise and reward for good behaviour, or by example with an explanation from other members of the family. However, this will only be successful when your child has the intellectual ability to recognize what's wrong and can decide what the correct way of behaving actually is.

POSSIBLE PROBLEMS   0–1

Disliking your baby

Many women believe that mother love will be turned on like a tap as soon as their baby is born. It therefore comes as rather a shock when after even two or three days they don't feel anything for their baby that resembles love. They may feel tenderness and protectiveness towards this tiny new being that is dependent on them, but they don't feel a strong, binding love. This is very common and is not at all abnormal. Love usually does develop after one or maybe two weeks, but until it does concentrate on enjoying your baby physically: the fit and the feel of your baby against your skin; the smell of your baby as you put your nose into the crease of his neck; the grip of your baby as you put your finger into his tiny palm and feel it grasped tightly.

Sometimes, however, mother love never comes and, for whatever reason, a mother finds herself disliking, resenting and spurning her new baby. Sometimes a mother and baby are just what child psychologists would call "a bad fit". Neither is suited to the other. Society has been used to blaming the mother for this situation because she isn't capable of adjusting to her child's needs and personality but we now know that this is

265

not true. A woman can have great mothering instincts and a strong desire to look after and tend to her baby and a great urge to love him. She can do everything but the last thing, and it is now recognized that this is as much the baby's fault as the mother's; they are a "bad pair". A mother who finds that she cannot relate to her baby with loving feelings should consult her doctor because she needs help, and so does her baby.

Antisocial babies

Just as there are adults who keep themselves to themselves, are rather taciturn and don't enter willingly into social exchanges, so there are babies who can be described as antisocial. These babies don't smile very much, they don't respond to being talked to, they don't enjoy playing games, and they don't like being cuddled. On the other hand, they can become grizzly if placed in a pram or cot and left alone. They are rather irritable and get upset easily. They tend to cry a lot and are slow, difficult feeders. When such a baby is tired he is fretful but doesn't go to sleep. Nothing you do seems to make this kind of baby happy, and you may feel that you are lavishing love to no effect; it hardly seems worthwhile.

The sad thing about this kind of baby is that he never learns the rewarding lesson that he will get back what he gives. A baby who smiles a lot and exudes joy gets friendship, love, companionship and help in return. The baby who is miserable or who just stays in neutral gets nothing in return. Life is that much less pleasant for him and so he may grow up to be a rather unpleasant individual. As a parent you *have* to make sure, as best you can, that your child doesn't grow up with this negative feeling. Even although you may find it difficult, you have to try really hard to get your baby to look at you, to listen to you, to smile at you. If you can only get to this stage, where your baby is responding to your overtures, most of his unhappiness and yours will be a thing of the past.

Backward babies

Babies develop at all speeds from very fast to very slow and it can be difficult to distinguish normal slowness from backwardness. If you feel that your baby is not really keeping up with the general social milestones (see p.260), consult your doctor. However, minor defects may not show up for several months, so follow your instincts if you suspect that your baby is not developing quite normally and seek early help. The earlier you get help the greater the chance you have of dealing with the abnormality, and of preventing the baby, the family, you and your partner from suffering unnecessarily.

If, in addition to being socially backward, your baby's physical development is abnormal, then the burden of looking after the child can be a great strain. In reality the parents have to continue to look after such a child like a newborn baby, seeing to its every need. This can result in a deteriorating atmosphere within the home, and in such cases you must seek help. It's often comforting, as well as actively helpful, to talk to people in similar situations so check your local directories for groups as well as contacting any relevant national agencies.

Head banging

Towards the end of the first year some babies take to banging their head against the side of the cot. This is rarely a sign of abnormality, and there's little risk of brain damage; what is more, the baby will grow out of it quite quickly. However, you should minimize the risk by padding the sides of the cot with a quilted fabric, and by buffering the cot and the wall if this causes an irritating banging noise. Try giving your baby a relaxing bath before he's put to bed and give him an extra long cuddle (it's thought by some psychologists that such children may need more physical attention and stimulation). Music from a mobile or from a radio may also be soothing. If your baby continues to bang his head for several months talk to your doctor about it.

PERSONAL DEVELOPMENT 1–2

During the second year much of your toddler's behaviour is attention-getting. He will try to do this by speaking, by crying, by hitting or by doing other things which he knows are forbidden. When he's successful at getting attention he'll show how satisfied he is by smiling or laughing.

Two-year-olds often seem to be very negative and their favourite word appears to be "No." This is a transitional stage between babyhood and childhood, and during it your toddler will be trying to assert his independence. He'll want to do everything immediately, and will frequently want a specific routine adhered to. Your toddler's mood may change frequently and his emotions may veer between extremes of lovingness and temper tantrums. One of the things that you must do is follow your child's mood when he shows this kind of negative assertiveness. Unless your child is given the opportunity of being independent at this stage such early resistance can lead to strongly negative behaviour.

On a much more positive level, two-year-old toddlers become much more co-operative in play. Early play with an adult teaches toddlers how to be socially co-operative, as long as the adults are patient in showing children how to share. Your toddler will learn to share by being shared with. Gradually he will begin to co-operate with other children in play although in the beginning other children may be unwilling to share. Encourage your child to persevere and don't give up showing your child by your example.

Likes and dislikes

A child begins to show all kinds of assertiveness during this year and it is quite natural that he should demonstrate preferences dramatically. He is very keen to grow up and to show that he is growing up. He no longer sees himself as a mirror image of you; he now sees the two of you as separate people, and therefore finds no reason for doing exactly what you want. He is determined to exercise his independence and will refuse offers of help and shrug off your assistance, even when he really needs it.

Your child is developing likes and dislikes, and has a very strong urge to fulfil his own desires, even though they may not be the same as yours, and yet the conflict which this may bring may make him feel very unhappy. Your child is torn between the very strong drive to exert independence and the drive to be loved by you. Even when he is trying to win a battle with you he needs your help and emotional support because he is too immature to manage without them. Your job is to take the middle road and to try to balance the need for independence with the need for love and protection. It isn't always easy. Your toddler's thinking is immature; memory is short, and judgement is unreliable. He cannot think ahead and is therefore impatient when things don't get done immediately. At the same time he is eager to control and dominate the world around him. His strength of will is ahead of his intellectual capacity so you'll have to decide when it is time to baby your toddler and when it is time to encourage and push him on, allowing independence and adventurousness, while still guarding against any dangers. Do be flexible in allowing your toddler to exercise these likes and dislikes, and don't enforce your will simply to win or to show your authority. You can always win by pulling rank, but you shouldn't be unreasonable for the sake of it. Judge the situation carefully. There are very few situations where it is important for you to get your own way (one would be if your toddler's safety was

threatened), so where it doesn't matter, let your child do what he wants to.

Personality

Your child is born with his own personality which shows itself within the first few weeks of life. However, there are certain social situations which will develop a child's personality during early childhood. They can bring out both the good and bad aspects of your child's personality and you should try to make sure that the good traits are accentuated and the bad ones played down.

□ If your child has a strong desire for approval, he will be motivated to fulfil the expectations of those around him. The desire for your approval and the approval of other adults usually comes before the desire for the approval of friends. Whenever you can, get your child to do the "right" things for your approval.

□ Young children express their sympathy by trying to help or comfort a person who is sad or in distress, but they are unable to sympathize until they have been in a situation similar to that of a person who is distressed.

□ When children understand the facial expressions and speech of others they develop the ability to empathize and to experience what the other person is feeling.

□ Children who tend to be rather dependent, who like to be helped and given attention and affection, are motivated to behave in a socially approved way. Independent children are motivated less by the desire for approbation.

□ Children who are friendly express their friendliness by wanting to do things for and with others, and express their affection in all kinds of words and gestures.

□ Children who are not allowed to be constantly in the limelight of family attention, and who are given opportunities and encouragement to share what they have, want to think of others and do things for them rather than simply concentrating on their own possessions, their own interests and getting their own way.

The timid child

Some children are naturally shy, keep themselves to themselves and speak very little. Don't immediately think that your child is retarded and become over-anxious and over-protective. A child who is quite talkative on home ground may be completely silent and withdrawn in a strange place or when confronted with strangers. This happens in many children around the age of one. In a new situation don't increase your child's difficulties by insisting that he join in immediately. Allow him to sit quietly on your knee or to stand by your side while he takes in what everyone is doing and becomes familiar with it. After half an hour or so, when you can sense that he is feeling more comfortable, gradually encourage him to join in your conversation. Even a shy child, if encouraged in this gentle, slow way, will join in with new friends and new games after an hour or so. But do remember to introduce new experiences slowly and allow your child to get used to them before moving on to other ones.

If your child's very timid and shy he may become very upset if you try to leave him with a sitter. You must try to understand your child in this and still give him your love no matter how irritating the situation is. He'll grow out of this clinginess with your help, but he'll need to gain a sense of security first.

269

Playing and sharing

Your toddler should mix with others as soon as possible. In the first year your child becomes used to interacting, not only with members of the immediate family, but also with the extended family such as grandparents, aunts, uncles, nieces, nephews, cousins and friends who come to the house. Your toddler will be a great deal more comfortable with strangers and adults if he starts off feeling that every friend of yours is a friend of his and that there are other members of the family who will help and care for him and whom he can rely on and trust.

If you help your child to accept others readily then he won't have too much difficulty mixing with other children when expanding experience and the desire to strike out make him want the company of others of the same age. At about the age of eighteen months children will usually tolerate other children although they won't necessarily play together; they may play side-by-side doing the same thing, but rarely interact. A little later, when they start to play with toys, grabbing and hitting between children is not abnormal. However, if your child repeatedly does this then you must explain that it's not a good way to behave, and point out that he wouldn't like the same doing to him.

While your child has to learn to share, it is hardly realistic to expect him to automatically give a toy to another toddler if he wants it. This is not because your child is selfish or a bully; it is because he hasn't appreciated the concept of sharing. If your child makes a grab for a toy that another child is playing with, you can teach him about sharing by saying that if he has the friend's toy, he must give one of his to the friend. A child of two is usually able to understand the justice of this reciprocity. You have to deal with sharing in very simple terms because intellectually he is not grown up enough to have more adult behaviour forced upon him. It is not until he is about two and a half to three that you can use reason and expect your child to be more altruistic.

Encouraging generosity

You can encourage your child to be generous from a very early age. As you are the most important person in his life it is easiest to be generous with you. You can take advantage of his desire to please you by teaching little generous acts (like giving Daddy a sweetie) and to then go on to encourage more and more unselfishness in his behaviour towards you and other members of the family. It is only natural for your child to want to please and be friendly with people who obviously care for and love him and for whom he feels affection. Having accepted generous behaviour as the norm towards people whom he loves, it is a fairly logical extension to show unselfish, generous behaviour to people who are just friends. So, ask your young baby to give you a sweetie or to give Daddy a sweetie, or to give you one each. If he finds a particular activity exciting and pleasurable you can ask if you can join in and share the pleasure and excitement and then encourage your toddler to do the same with other members of the family and friends who come to the house. By the time your child is eighteen months he should be able to share activities and treats with anyone who enters the home and is seen as a friend. If he can do this he

is well on the way to being generous and unselfish with his peers.

Only children

Although only children undoubtedly benefit from the constant love that they receive, and grow up feeling very close to both parents and friends, there are few who don't confess to having wanted brothers and sisters at some stage in their lives. This is rarely a serious problem but one of the things you can do to mitigate any possible problems is to introduce your baby to other babies of the same age. As your baby reaches the sociable age, around eighteen months to two years, you should make a real effort to find friends for him and to have them visit you at home.

It's easy for parents to over-indulge an only child and to make them feel too important. You're going to have to curb your desire to give him all that he wants and, just as important, all your attention. It's important that he learns to accept that he can't have everything that he wants and be the permanent centre of your world, just as a child in a larger family has to (see p.263).

It may be a temptation to be possessive and over-protective. This can only be bad for you and your child. Not only will you feel bereft when your child becomes independent and needs you less, but your child will lose out on a sense of curiosity, a sense of adventure and independence and may become clingy. You mustn't shy away from disciplining your child, either. Like any other child he has to be shown the right way to behave if he's to grow up able to mix well with others.

271

DISCIPLINE

It has always been known that children need discipline, but mainly for the comfort of adults. In the old days it was believed that discipline was necessary to ensure that children conformed to standards that were socially acceptable; more recently it has been found that children need discipline simply to be happy and well-adjusted. Children like to know what the boundaries of behaviour are. Discipline is essential to a child's development because it fulfils certain needs.

□ Through discipline, children learn how to behave in ways that mean they are praised. They interpret this praise as an indication of acceptance and love. Both of these things are essential if your child is to adjust successfully to growing up and being happy.

□ When discipline appropriate for the age of your child is applied it serves as motivation. This encourages your child to strive to accomplish what is required and this brings a great deal of comfort and satisfaction.

□ Discipline, above all else, helps a child to develop a sense of self-control and of conscience. This inner voice will later guide him in making his own decisions and controlling his own behaviour. Without it he'll be indecisive and may act in an antisocial way.

□ Undisciplined children are often scolded. This gives them a feeling of guilt and shame. These feelings will inevitably lead to unhappiness and poor adjustment.

□ Discipline enables children to win social approval which makes them feel contented, happy and secure.

When to use discipline

Discipline, overdone or underdone, can be equally bad for children because both of them lead to insecurity. There is no place for ruling your child by fear, force, corporal punishment or humiliation. While

Disciplinary guidelines

Remember that learning the rules of social behaviour and learning about self-control takes time; it doesn't take months, it takes years. Don't expect too much from your child and don't expect him to remember what you said last time. He isn't necessarily defying your previous instruction, he may have simply forgotten it – a child of two has a very short memory, so be forgiving and repeat your instructions. Words never mean as much as actions and you really do have to show your child how to behave. Here are some of the things that you can do:

● Have as few "rules" – those instructions which can be broken under no circumstances – as possible. "Don't" is a very negative word and, if you are not careful, by the time your child is two you could be prefacing everything you say by "Don't". "Do" is a very positive word so reinforce with positive "dos"

and cut down on the "don'ts".

● Don't give vague instructions; try to be very clear. Instead of saying "Don't be naughty" tell him *exactly* what you don't want him to do.

● If you give your child an instruction, always give a reason why. If you tell your child that his tricycle has to be put under cover when he's finished using it at night, explain that it may otherwise get rusty in the rain and not work. Try to refrain from saying "Because I say so" when he asks you why.

● Always reward good behaviour with praise and affection, possibly even with a treat if your child has accomplished something difficult. You can distinguish between good and bad behaviour just by withholding praise and rewards from acts that you don't approve of.

● There is no better way of getting your child to do something than to show that you do it too. If you want your child to take off his dirty shoes at the door, or to

you can tell your child the reasons for your wanting certain things in a certain way, you cannot use reason until he is about two and a half or three, so disciplining has to be very simple and easy for your child to understand and it has to be in direct relationship to what he is being punished for. There must, therefore, be no delay between what your child does and the discipline he is given, and the disciplinary action has to fit whatever it is your child has done. If you become extremely angry over minor misdemeanours and if you do this with any frequency your child will simply be left bewildered and may even lose love and affection for you. Reserve disciplining for really serious misdemeanours like destructiveness, being physically violent or telling lies. In this way your child gets very clear messages of what is intolerable and of what, on the other hand, you disapprove. Your child's memory is short and if you brood over what he's done he will simply not understand. He will think that you are purposely withdrawing love from him and be very perplexed, so make all discipline clear, swift and then forget it.

Avoiding problems

Children are very receptive to fairness and justice, and if you adhere to these two principles you will probably avoid most difficulties in disciplining.

Corporal punishment will only lead to problems. I think it should be avoided at all costs. In any case research has shown that children don't know what they are being smacked for. They cannot remember, so they don't associate the punishment with the crime, and smacking doesn't act as a deterrent.

I think it is quite wrong to give a child the message that physical violence is ever acceptable and certainly not as retribution for something he has done wrong. I feel it is not only inefficient but very unkind.

Never punish a child as a calculated act. Your child knows the difference. The child is much less damaged by a sharp word or a

put on wellingtons before he goes out in the wet, show that you are prepared to conform to this procedure, too, by doing the same with your shoes.
● Be consistent. Don't let your standards slide and give one instruction on one occasion and the opposite on another (although you can show that under certain circumstances you are prepared to be flexible). There is no reason at all why your child shouldn't have several ice creams on his birthday, because he knows that that day is special, but he should learn not to expect the same on the following day.
● Always admit your mistakes no matter how young your child is and always be generous when you do something wrong. It makes your child feel that the world is fair and just, so don't be afraid to say, "Naughty Mummy," or "Mummy shouldn't have done that" or "You are quite right, I won't do it again."

slap in the heat of the moment which is quickly forgotten when the air is clear, than by a protracted argument with a threatened punishment as soon as you have got your child home or, even worse, when your partner gets home.

You will not go far wrong if you are very clear about your motives for disciplining. Make sure that they are for the happiness and safety of the child, and not simply as a means of impressing on your child your authority and superiority.

POSSIBLE PROBLEMS   1–2

The aggressive child

Aggression is a basic act of hostility and the ways in which we use it usually mean that it is unprovoked by anyone else. Most children have feelings of aggressiveness to some extent and usually express them in verbal or physical attacks on another child, very often choosing a child who is smaller than they are.

Aggressiveness, bullying and destructiveness are modes of behaviour that usually represent cries for help. They frequently result from parental neglect, absence, over-discipline, under-discipline or too much smacking. A child who behaves in this way is really not at fault, although he may be very hard to help. It is worth remembering that a nasty little boy or a nasty little girl is usually nasty because someone has been nasty to them. You shouldn't be too ready to blame them but should look beyond, to their home and their environment. Weaning a child off his normal pattern of behaviour, and the distrust of adults, may take years because he has to re-learn the attitudes which he has been learning from the day he was born.

If your child starts to show signs of being very aggressive, try to nip it in the bud. Don't punish and don't smack your child; this will only make the aggressive behaviour worse. Instead, show very firmly that you are not prepared to put up with it and that he will gain nothing but your disapproval if he continues. Show that if he can change he will be highly rewarded, and will gain lots of praise for all good efforts. If your child seems to be highly disturbed, or if you're at all worried by his behaviour, you must seek medical help immediately.

Jealousy

Rivalry is a perfectly normal emotion for a child to feel. Sometimes it can have a positive effect and can act as a spur to make the child do his best. In this instance it adds to his friendliness and his desire to socialize. However, if it leads to quarrelling and boasting, your child will have a hard time of it.

A child feels one of the strongest forms of jealousy when a new baby arrives. This is because your child feels that he's been "dethroned" and that he has lost the special place he had in your life. He may try all sorts of attention-seeking devices and may even revert to such babyish behaviour as losing bowel control, refusing to feed himself or refusing to dress alone. Or he may direct his jealousy directly at the baby and

try to hurt it. Alternatively he may feel unable to cope with these jealous emotions and may internalize them so that he becomes quiet and stays away from you; he may even reject you altogether.

It is very easy to understand all of these emotions. You must try to help your child by preparing him for the arrival of a new baby and by showing that his place in your affections is quite secure. Put aside a special time when he has all of your attention; involve him in looking after the baby by asking for assistance in certain easy tasks, and praise and reward all helpful behaviour on his part, and whenever he shows love and affection for the new arrival.

Over-indulgence

It is very easy for any parent to over-indulge or spoil their child. After all, you probably love him more than any other human being in the world. You have a natural desire to please your child and to make his life happy. It is therefore very easy to err on the side of giving a child too much, of making life too easy for him and of allowing him to become the centre of your universe. You will have to control these desires in yourself for the sake of your child.

One of the ways in which you can help your child not to be egocentric is to make sure from early on that he is not always the centre of your attention. He must learn that the world does not revolve around him; that the household and the family do not see him as the pivot for their constant attention. If you let your child know quite clearly that there are times when he's expected to do without you and to do things alone, you will be doing him a favour. None of these should involve cruelty or force. You should show your child as much love as you can, but he should be made to see that everyone has certain boundaries within which they live. As he gets older you should also teach him that you have a need for privacy just as he does, although you're always there if needed.

Don't make the mistake of thinking that over-indulgence has anything to do with the number of possessions your child has or how much affection he gets. It is to do with allowing your child to grow up so that he impresses his will on you and on others by using power games such as wheedling or bullying. It is a parent's duty to prevent this occuring.

Stuttering

Nearly all children of this age have jerky speech which, on occasion, may turn into a real stutter. This may be because your child has so many ideas in his head that he thinks more quickly than he can speak. It may also be that he is very excited and simply can't articulate properly. Stutters can also appear for a short time and then disappear again. Initially the most important thing that you can do is to remain calm and not draw your child's attention to the stuttering. Don't jump in with the word that you think your child is looking for but simply accept your child's speech. Making your child feel nervous and self-conscious about the way he talks will only increase his tendency to stammer.

Temper tantrums

Between one and two years old temper tantrums are normal, attention-seeking devices (see p.188). Children of this age have not yet acquired the judgement to match their strength of will, and clashes with parents are therefore frequent. If anger or frustration are excessive they may culminate in a tantrum. Children usually throw themselves on the floor kicking and screaming because they do not have the control to do anything else. It is their way of showing their helplessness to overcome their problem in a controlled way.

Far and away the best thing that you can do is to stay calm. If you don't your child will catch your mood and it will make his behaviour worse. Ignore your child and, if possible, leave him alone. A tantrum loses much of its point for a child if there is no audience.

As your child gets older he will become better able to tolerate delays and accept compromises. At the same time you will become more expert at anticipating problems and forestalling head-on clashes and will become more skilled at finding distractions.

A "naughty" child

There are some children who are habitually naughty. There are some who are habitually disobedient. I think you ought to make the distinction between being naughty and being disobedient because these two things have to be handled differently.

To me, a naughty child is one who is immature and not able to exert sufficient self-control to do what he knows is right. A disobedient child, however, is quite mature and knowingly flouts your wishes and rules.

A naughty child is often forgetful and simply forgets your remonstrances. You can tell him off for doing something wrong and find him doing it again an hour later. He'll be genuinely surprised to find himself in the wrong again so quickly. Such naughty children frequently get so wrapped up in an activity that rules go by the board. This kind of child needs more repeated tellings than the average, and careful, sympathetic correction. Usually a naughty child is apologetic and contrite. I feel apologies and contrition should receive warm acceptance and understanding. However, there does come a point when a naughty child needs punishing, but physical punishment should never be used. I favour withdrawal of treats and pleasures which can be reinstated when a given goal has been achieved.

Your child may go on being naughty for a long time. Be prepared for this and don't become too angry; sheer naughtiness is more of an irritation than a serious annoyance. You may feel you can sympathize to a certain extent with naughtiness: if you don't feel like this try not to be too hard.

Disobedience is another matter. Most of us feel little sympathy. A constantly disobedient child rarely apologizes or expresses any kind of repentance. If you have a disobedient child your life may become awfully miserable with a constant stream of negatives, rows and recriminations. Guard against this if you can. A child has a limited repertoire with which to respond to your anger. Brutality in your behaviour leads to brutality in his. Physical punishment from you encourages violence, truculence and aggression in him. It's hard, but try a programme of positive actions and words. Try to explain to him why he shouldn't be so disobedient; explain when his actions are dangerous or anti-social and suggest how he should behave. Outlaw punishments, reward all good acts. It often works. Whatever you do don't alienate your child. You are all he has. Always show your love, always let him know he can come to you.

PERSONAL DEVELOPMENT   2–3

Your young baby's dependence on you stemmed from the fact that you were the centre of his universe, you were the caretaker and the affection-giver. He couldn't get through life without your help and support and he sought your approbation and affection.

However, as he gets older and sees himself as an independent person, not just a reflection of you, he begins to see you as a separate personality and as a whole person. He is experiencing many different feelings and new emotions with which he has to become familiar. He begins to know real love for many of the things around him: his favourite toy, a pet, a favourite grandparent. All of these feelings bring your child closer to the adult idea of love. If he sees that you are tired he is genuinely concerned, and if you are unhappy he is sincerely sympathetic. When he is enjoying something he wishes to share the experience with you and offers to share it. If you need help, he will offer it spon-

taneously because he really wants to give it. If you are upset or frightened, he feels profoundly sorry for you, and tells you so with words and expressions. He has a strong desire to make you feel better and happier, and does so in the only way that he knows, by telling you that he loves you and by hugging you.

This is quite a step forward in your child's personal development, because all these feelings and actions are truly un-selfish. He is putting someone else before himself; he is genuinely caring and loving; he wants to understand someone else and do what is best for them; he wants to bring them pleasure and comfort, and these are grown-up things to want to do. Always encourage and praise him when he ex-hibits these tendencies.

Imitation and identification

Your child has always learned by imi-tation and as he gets older he begins to learn by "identification", too. He begins to put himself in your position and into the position of others and starts to behave as he would have others behave towards him. This means that he is starting to control himself and take command of himself. You may even overhear your child scolding himself when he has done something that he thinks you will disapprove of. The difference is that he now disapproves of it in himself.

You will find your child observing and identifying with most of the adults who are close to him and any interesting ones who are not. He may give in to his imagi-nation by dressing up and acting out rôles, and by being all kinds of different people. But most of all he'll practise being you. He will play Mummy or Daddy with dolls and toys and you may even hear the imitation of exact phrases that you use with exactly the same intonation you have in your voice. These are all ways of exploring and experimenting with the way he thinks the world works.

277

Making friends

Your child's galloping desire to learn brings with it the desire for the company of children of a similar age. He will probably be showing signs of gregariousness and of wanting to join in games with others during this year and he'll need the stimulation of other children's ideas and their company.

You cannot make friends for your child but you can help him to find friends. Your child has to learn how to make friends slowly, just as he has learned all the other lessons in his life, so introduce your child to making friends with only one at a time.

Start off on home ground first and invite a child who lives nearby so that your child is in familiar surroundings and has a sense of confidence about what he is doing and where he's doing it. Make sure that you are near at hand to give him help and support should he need it, and encourage him to settle down to playing by playing along yourself. Once he has got over the first hurdle of making friends, try inviting two or three children to the house at the same time – one of the best ways to introduce this idea is to have a tea party or to have a picnic around the paddling pool.

Once your child becomes a member of a group of friends make it clear to him that they are welcome at your home and that he can bring them into the house once he has asked your permission. As your child makes his first steps into the outside world, it is important that he has a comfortable feeling about it and has confidence about his own place within it, so helping gather around a small group of friends whom he knows and with whom he gets on, is an important way of laying down the right patterns for later life.

Encouraging security

All children have fears. Anxiety and fear are perfectly normal emotions, but they make a child feel very unhappy and uneasy, and it will be some time before your toddler has the ability to cope with fears or avoid the things which make him afraid (see p 122)

One of the most common early fears is of your absence or of being abandoned. The easiest way to cure this is to show your child that you will always come back as you promised and when you said you would. Fear will not be cured by staying with your child; that will only make him more fearful because he never learns to cope without you.

Your small child also begins to feel anxiety if he finds that his own feelings are getting out of control, like frustration, anger and jealousy. The way to help here is to listen and observe your toddler as closely as possible, so that you can pick up all the clues as to what is causing the anxiety and then reassure him. Just talking about some of the fears and explaining what is happening will give the reassurance that he needs.

Remember that whether you think your child's fear is reasonable or unreasonable, as far as your child himself is concerned the fear is still the same. All fears have to be handled sympathetically and gently. Never suddenly present your child with whatever makes him most frightened. You wouldn't dream of asking your child to stay outside in a thunderstorm if he was afraid of thunder, so why should you expect him to pat the dog he's scared of? Whenever your child shows fear, accept that fear as real and don't brush it aside as nothing. Always tell your child when there is nothing to fear, but don't just tell him not to be afraid, because he won't understand that. Explain why there is no reason to be frightened, always tell him that you understand why he is, and always sympathize with his fear. Never ridicule the fear; that will simply make your child secretive, and it is much harder for him to cope with a fear alone, than to cope with your help.

Handling genitals

Babies usually become aware of their genital organs toward the end of the first year but handle them without any obvious pleasure. Handling eventually does bring a pleasurable sensation, and then fondling becomes more like real masturbation. Most children of both sexes masturbate, and it's simply unreasonable to expect them not to. There are many misconceptions about masturbation but, despite the myths, it will not lead to blindness, homosexuality, insanity or any other such fictions.

It is perfectly normal for a boy to handle his penis. After all, he handles every other part of his body that sticks out, so why not that. In young children, masturbation is rarely done for any length of time or for any purpose. The pleasure it brings is more of a general pleasure than a specific sexual one. It is not until children are much older that they feel sexual excitement from masturbation.

There is no reason to discourage it, nor should you stop your child from masturbating. That will only cause furtiveness, and worse, it may stop your child discussing anything about genital organs in later life. Unless masturbation is an obsessional means of escaping from reality, the best way to treat it is by paying no attention to it at all. If by accident it happens in public, distraction is the best course of action, but never, ever, scold your child for it.

Nudity and sexuality

A child's sex education begins with the first cuddle. All children take pleasure in physical contact and joy in their parents' reciprocity. They grow up realizing that people touch one another as an act of friendship as well as an act of love.

As your child gets older he will become pleasantly aware of his body, without being at all self-conscious about it. You can encourage this by having an open attitude to nudity within the family. Like everything else, a child learns patterns of behaviour and attitudes from you. The child who sees his parents unclothed and unembarrassed will take nudity as a matter of course and is unlikely to grow up concerned about nakedness. On the other hand, if you are worried about it he will almost certainly worry too; if you're furtive he will also be encouraged to be furtive.

It is perfectly natural that a child should be curious about the differences between male and female bodies. Your child will probably have been aware of the difference in genders since the age of fifteen months or so, and once he sees his parents naked he'll be aware of sexual differences. Curiosity about his mother's breasts and his father's penis is best satisfied by a frank chat and a good look. Neither of these things is likely to stimulate sexual feelings and your child will be embarrassed only if you are.

Answering questions

Children who are encouraged to ask questions, and who are given explanations, take for granted that their parents will listen to them. These children grow up to be happier and less authoritarian than children whose questions are ignored and who are rarely supplied with explanations. Parents who take note of what their child says are showing that they consider him an individual with something useful to say. If your family believes and operates in this free and easy manner, it's going to be a much happier unit.

In the early years your child regards you as omniscient and will naturally turn to you for advice on most subjects. If you remain approachable and welcome questions your child will grow up feeling that

he can talk to you about anything. Discouraging your child when he is young and uninhibited will only make any inhibitions worse as he grows older. If you want to be the confidant of your children you should try to keep the channels of communication open at any cost.

You should not avoid answering questions, even if they embarrass you. If you are concerned about when you tell your child about sex, the answer is that you explain the first time that he asks you. A child's curiosity should always be met by your willingness to answer truthfully. It is much better if he learns about sex in an accurate, matter-of-fact way from you than in a secretive melodramatic way from friends who may well have some of the information wrong.

From about three years onwards, a child can handle at least part of the truth on sexual questions, although it is not until he is about six or seven that he can understand the mechanics of sex. I told my own children about fertilization, conception and the growth of a child in the womb, and childbirth whenever they asked about it. I left discussions about sexual intercourse until the age of six or so depending on the child. All discussions on sex should include aspects of caring, loving and the responsibilities involved in intimate relationships.

DISCIPLINE   2–3

As your child becomes old enough to reason with you, you can explain what discipline is and he should grow up feeling that discipline is based on mutual responsibility and participation in decisions. Don't expect blind obedience from your child. It is far better to reason and persuade. Never coerce a two-year-old; it will only lead to a battle of wills and resentment.

If, however, you take the trouble to discuss why it is wrong to behave in a certain way and right to behave in another, you will find that your child is interested in motives and in very much

more likely to do what you want because he understands why you want it.

On the other hand, don't make the mistake of talking over every decision, and never just telling your child what to do. Don't, for example, over-burden your child with responsibility for his own conduct or safety. He is simply not old enough for that. When you think the situation warrants it, give a simple order unless you feel that your child is going to be recalcitrant, in which case a softer approach may be more successful.

Good disciplining should give your child the opportunity to make a choice. Part of growing up is about exercising choices and options and he has to learn this skill like any other. You should choose very carefully when you are going to give a choice: let it be one he will find fairly simple, one you don't really think is important which way the decision goes. Don't, however, try to fool your child by giving a choice when your decision is already made; you won't fool him.

When to use discipline

To my mind the times when you have to insist on discipline fall into a small number of categories:
□ When your child's safety or the safety of another person is threatened. This will include dangerous games, dangerous toys, or dangerous activities around the house involving fire, electricity and sharp instruments. There have to be rules, for instance, whenever fireworks are used or whenever

you make a camp fire or have a barbecue outside.
□ Children have to grow up learning that the wishes and comforts of other people must be honoured. I have been very strict on matters where thoughtfulness, helpfulness, unselfishness and courtesy with anyone are concerned.
□ I feel that there can be few concessions about honesty. With my own children I have always been severe with lying and stealing. I have not done this through punishment but rather by proving to the child that it is better and easier on them to tell the truth, no matter how bad it is, and no matter how dreadful the crime seems, than to tell a lie. The punishment for a lie is always worse than the punishment for telling the truth and admitting that something wrong has been done because I want my children to know that I appreciate the courage it takes to own up to something.

Bed-wetting

It is perfectly normal for a child under the age of four to wet the bed occasionally (see p.161). One in ten boys still wets the bed at the age of five. You should remember that bladder control, like any other skill, develops at different rates in different children. As a child grows older one of the characteristics of bladder control is the ability to hold urine for longer and longer, but it may take some children a very long time to last the ten or so hours through the night (see p.160). You can help in quite a few ways.
□ You can discourage drinks after six p.m.
□ You can make certain that your child empties his bladder before going to bed.
□ You can lift your child without waking him and see that he passes urine before you go to bed.
□ You can put a potty by the bed so that if he should wake he can pass urine without any problem.
□ You can make sure that his pyjamas don't have difficult fastenings and can be

taken down quickly.
□ You can leave on a dim light in the room so that your child can see what to do if he should wake up in the night.
Worry and anxiety are nearly always the root cause of your child's problem and so it seems to me unkind to say or do anything to aggravate your child's sense of inadequacy. You should never draw attention to wet beds or make a fuss about them; you should certainly never scold your child. You can, however, take one or two steps to make sure that a wet bed causes a minimum of inconvenience to everyone by laying a rubber sheet on top of the ordinary bed sheet, and then putting a small sheet over the rubber sheet. This one can be whipped off and washed very easily and quickly while the rest of the bed linen remains dry.
You should only take your child for medical advice about bed-wetting if he's willing. By the time that you can establish that bed-wetting is a real problem and not just a variation of normal, your child may be old enough to participate in the deci-

sion to seek help. If you talk it over frankly with your child and he really does not want to go along and have medical tests and examinations (other than those which exclude a remediable abnormality) then don't subject him to them. All children outgrow bed-wetting and yours will too. You should make the process of reaching that grown-up stage as comfortable and unembarrassing as possible. If he agrees to have tests done make sure they are thorough and exclude all abnormalities. Don't accept treatment without a full investigation.

Stuttering

Transient stuttering is a common accompaniment to learning to talk. Stuttering or stammering that goes on in the long term usually has the same causes as bed-wetting: tension, anxiety or fear. It may start out of the blue after a severe shock or accident. Stuttering sometimes continues into adult life but, as we all know, stuttering is no bar to leading a perfectly normal,

happy and fruitful life. I believe that stuttering should be treated in exactly the same way as bed-wetting. You should accept it in your child when he is young, pay no attention to it and never ridicule or draw attention to it. And you should be perfectly frank and unembarrassed to talk to your child about it, when he is old enough, say around five or six. If your child is very concerned and can't handle embarrassment at school and with strangers, and you would like advice and help from a speech therapist, then seek it. If, however, your child is perfectly happy to carry on stuttering, then don't cause unhappiness by dragging him from clinic to clinic. One of my stepsons stutters and is perfectly happy to do so even to the point of reading the lesson at school. We've asked him if he wishes to see a speech therapist and he doesn't, so we haven't pushed him. Stutterers don't stutter while singing or saying poetry. If your child concentrates on giving his speech rhythm it may help.

An aggressive anti-social child

We've all experienced feelings of aggressiveness towards other people, especially when we feel that our security – as represented by our territory or our possessions – is being threatened. It is only by great self-control that we conquer such feelings, and that is something that takes many years of learning and maturity to achieve. It is not surprising, therefore, that many young children give full rein to their aggressive instincts.

When aggressive behaviour in a child becomes a regular feature, however, it is usually a response to two things: a lack of effective restraint and discipline from the time he was born, and a feeling of insecurity in the child, who may be experiencing a lack of parental attention, love and affection. In both ways the parents are almost entirely responsible for the child's difficult behaviour.

If you have an aggressive child you should examine in close detail the way that you and your partner behave, and if you're honest with yourselves you'll almost certainly find that you are falling short in your position as teachers and role models for your child. It is fairly easy to prevent a child ever becoming aggressive but it is very difficult to retrain an aggressive child to be less so. One of the first and most important ways that you can teach gentleness and flexibility in your child is to be flexible, tolerant and gentle in all your dealings with the child. Don't forget your child will imitate everything you do, including being aggressive.

If your child suddenly becomes aggressive or starts bullying, this is a sure sign of some tension or unhappiness in the child's life, and you should look carefully for the cause of it. It will nearly always be found in the child's relationship with you, your partner or the rest of the family, or to tension in the home. Don't think that you can pull the wool over a young child's eyes by sweeping things under the carpet; a child will pick up on the atmosphere, and this, can cause great insecurity.

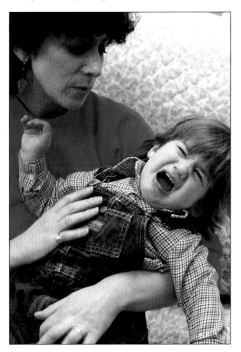

Stealing

Most little children are used to taking things that belong to others – their mother's make-up, a sibling's toy, or their father's keys – just because they want to play with them, and when this occurs at home it normally isn't a problem. However, small children are incapable of understanding the "property rights" of others, and you may discover that your child has taken something — either while you were out shopping or visiting a friend's home. If this is the case, explain to the child that this is stealing, and that stealing is not allowed. Eventually, your child will get the idea.

It isn't necessary to have the child accompany you when you return the object, unless the habit has become persistent and you feel that extra enforcement is necessary. Most children feel penitent enough on being found out.

Shyness

Some children are shy by nature, and studies show that up to ten percent of infants are born with a nervous system that predisposes them to shy behaviour. Such children show their shyness by giving evidence of disliking new experiences; even when taken to a family gathering or party, they will spend most of the time clinging to their mothers' skirts or hiding their faces. They also show reluctance in conversing with strange children or adults, and typically prefer to play alone rather than in a group. When such a child grows older and attends school, he or she may be diffident about making new friends.

If your child is shy, my advice is not to criticize him or to try to change his nature – not only is this unrealistic but it also may add to the problem. Instead, when you know that a new experience is in the offing, try to prepare him ahead of time so any strangeness is diminished. And, when he will be meeting new people, allow him plenty of time in which to get used to them before you expect him to feel comfortable in their presence.

"Habits"

Nail biting, thumb sucking and carrying a comforter are not abnormal in a young child. You should not try to stop them, and certainly never by force, ridicule or deprivation. They are nearly always caused by tension of some kind and they happen in about half of otherwise quite normal school children. For the most part they are unconscious, nervous habits and are best cured by encouraging a pride in appearance. The majority of children stop nail biting when they become concerned about their appearance and become interested in the opposite sex. At this age social considerations begin to outweigh their personal habits. Thumb-sucking and carrying a comforter can go right on to the 'teens. I don't believe in discouraging either habit. As they get older children sense what is acceptable, impose self-control and only indulge in their habit in private. No one can persuade me there's much that needs correcting about this mature behaviour.

A cheeky child

It is not always easy to draw the line between cheek and impertinence. Occasional cheekiness is, to my mind, perfectly acceptable; I like it in a child. It suggests spirit, mischievousness and a healthy attitude towards authority.

There is the mistaken belief that questioning decisions is being cheeky. This is because some parents feel that it undermines their authority, but if you encourage your child to talk things over with you, you will encourage the sense of responsibility for disciplining himself rather than blindly obeying your decisions. In this way he will grow up aware of the value of persuasive argument. On the other hand, if you encourage your child not to say what he thinks because you interpret arguing as being naughty he will rarely get the chance to understand the reasoning behind your decisions.

The other good aspect of being cheeky is that it provides a verbal mechanism for getting rid of anger and frustration. Anger is a perfectly acceptable emotion in a child, but isn't acceptable if your child is venting his anger in a physical way and is being aggressive and bullying. It is much better for your child to shout about anger than to hit someone. So when your child is cheeky weigh up why you think he is being so and if the reasons are healthy ones, just keep it in check. Insolence goes beyond cheekiness because it flouts good manners. It ignores thinking about how the other person feels and it may be hurtful. If your child goes over the boundary into insolence you are going to have to teach him that this is not acceptable.

Selfishness

All children are selfish, but as your child comes out of toddlerhood the most important lesson that you can teach is "Do as you would be done by." He can't always have the sweets he wants because they have to be shared with others; he may not have the biggest, rosiest red apple because there is only one and another child may want it; he has got to learn to lose because only one child will win and he won't always be the one. The most important way of convincing your child that he should not be selfish is to try to get him to feel how other children will respond to selfishness. If he can understand that gen-

erally speaking all other children are feeling the same way as he is then it is obvious that people have to take turns at getting what they want, whether it is being the top dog, getting the prize, having more rides on the tricycle than anyone else, or hogging the swing. It's up to you, by your actions, to show your child the benefits of unselfishness.

An over-indulged child

An over-indulged child is a self-centred child. Here are some of the things that you may have been doing that will make your child egotistical:

☐ If you are over-protective you can make your child feel that he is extra-special. Children who are waited on hand and foot by others and protected from experiences grow up to expect that others will continue to do things for them instead of making the effort to do them themselves. This stifles independence and co-operativeness.

☐ If you show favouritism towards a child you encourage a sense of self-importance. Children who are not favoured have feelings of inferiority or martyrdom. Either way it encourages the child to become self-centred rather than outgoing and thoughtful about other people.

☐ Some parents set too high a goal for their children, and encourage them to become egocentric when they strive for these goals.

One of the best cures and possibly the only cure if you won't change your ways for an over-indulged child is to let him go to school early. He really does need the levelling process of a play group or a nursery school, and getting used to mixing with a group and being considered as no different from anybody else. Later in life he may respond well to boarding school. If neither of these things is possible, an over-indulged child can still be pulled down a peg or two by choosing bright, out-going, intelligent friends for him. Contact with another sensible adult can help your child through the painful process of losing this sense of self-importance.

285

15 Playing

Until the beginning of this century it was thought that play was fun but a waste of time. When children reached school age they were expected to work, and play was kept for the time when work was completed or for holidays. It was thought that as young children were incapable of doing anything useful, they might as well spend their time playing. We now know that play can have a much more important rôle in your child's development. In the last fifty or sixty years research has shown that play provides a platform for learning, especially about becoming sociable. To learn to become sociable a child has to have contact with children of the same age, and these contacts will mainly be made through play. Many parents concur with this research and believe that for their children to be healthy and happy and to grow up well-adjusted, they should be given liberty to play for as long as possible. To this end they provide their children with all sorts of play equipment and toys, with an emphasis on their educational value.

PLAY   0–1

During the first year your baby will go through what is called the exploratory stage. Until he is about three months old play will mainly consist of observing people and objects and of making rather random attempts to grab hold of anything that is held in front of him. After three months your baby will gain enough control over his hands and arms to enable him to grasp hold of, and examine, small objects. As soon as he can creep, crawl or walk his world will explode. He'll be able to forage for himself and will examine everything within his reach.

Suitable toys and games

Never in a baby's development is play more synonymous with learning than in the first few years of life. Your baby is learning to see properly, he is discovering how to use his hands and how to master hand/eye co-ordination (see p.219). He may learn quite a lot about these things by simply watching and moving his own hands and fingers, but he will practise and perfect his newly-learned skills with any toys that you give him.

SUITABLE TOYS
- Mobiles
- Rattles
- Mirror
- Music box
- Large/small balls
- Soft toys
- Squeaky toys
- Bendy toys
- Activity centre
- Books
- Cooking utensils

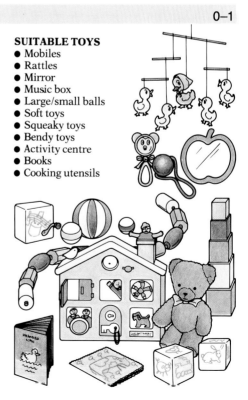

What toys to give
● *From about five weeks*

His visual field will be increasing and he'll enjoy watching anything which moves, so hang mobiles above his cot and changing mat. They're easy to make from household items if you don't want to buy them (see p. 290).

● *Three months*

He'll love objects which make a noise so provide him with a rattle or any form of toy which he can shake or strike out at. Choose a lightweight, unbreakable, washable rattle that has a slight enough handle for your baby to grasp easily (at this stage he won't have the muscle strength or co-ordination to grip on to anything for more than a few seconds).

● *Four months*
Plastic beakers filled with beans, or water-filled canisters will also make interesting noises and he'll be able to hold them between both hands.

● *Six to ten months*

Any object that is fairly small and has crevices, holes or handles that your baby can poke his fingers into or wrap them around will be ideal. They should be brightly-coloured and, if possible, make a noise, like rings with bells on them.

Put a fairly large specially-designed baby mirror in his cot – he'll love staring at his own face. Never be tempted to put one of your own mirrors in the cot – it could easily break.

Musical boxes seem to provide endless fascination for small babies and can play a part in your bedtime routine (see p.167). The best ones have a string which the baby can pull.

Activity centres which have a series of knobs and buttons which your baby can push or turn to make noises can be attached to a cot or the bath. As your baby's manipulative abilities improve he'll love playing with this.

● *Ten to twelve months*
Once your baby can pick up something small he'll be able to hold chalks, pencils, crayons and, eventually, paint brushes. He'll be more mobile now and will enjoy being able to pull or push toys like trains, cars or walking dogs. Provide him with some toys on strings so that as he sits on the floor he can draw them in towards him.

Games to play together

Play peek-a-boo with your baby, either when he's in his cot or if he's sitting on your lap. You can vary the game by hiding your face behind a headscarf or towel instead of your hands.

Buy a large inflatable beach ball and gently roll it towards your baby. Once he can sit unsupported he'll be able to bat a ball back to you with his hand. You could even throw a small ball gently into your baby's lap for him to "throw" back to you. Show your baby how to fill up a container with toy animals, plastic spoons, anything really which isn't breakable. Encourage your baby to have a go and you'll soon find that he'll sit for hours filling up and emptying his container.

Babies seem to have endless patience with stacking beakers or rings, both of which help your baby with co-ordination. They come in a variety of styles although the basic principle is the same. The ones with large pieces are better for younger babies because they're easier for unco-ordinated hands to grab hold of.

Making use of household objects

A baby under one year old really doesn't
need formal toys, although he'll inevitably
be given some. Everything he comes
across is interesting. Anything that smells
interesting, looks interesting or sounds
interesting will appeal to your baby and
many household items, which we take for
granted, will hold a world of excitement
for him. Here are a few things that you
might try as entertainment for your child:

☐ Wooden spoons and spatulas, small
saucepans and lids, colanders and sieves,
funnels, a set of plastic measuring spoons,
plastic cups with lids, plastic bottles of
different sizes with their caps on, small
plastic boxes that you might use in the
fridge, plastic ice cube trays, a whisk, an
old egg carton, old loaf and bun tins. Just
hand them to your baby and he'll discover
what *he* wants to do with them.

☐ Anything which rolls: the cardboard
tube inside kitchen rolls and toilet rolls,
cotton reels.

☐ Round objects like balls: balls of every
type, balls of wool, balls of string, grape-
fruit, oranges, apples.

☐ Things which are very light: balloons, a
sponge, foam rubber, polystyrene.

☐ Things which are flat and hard: a
wooden plate, a table mat, a ruler.

☐ Things which are stretchy: elastic
bands, elastic itself, a piece of cloth cut on
the bias.

☐ Anything which has a hole that a child
can poke his fingers through: a roll of
sticky tape, a roll of sticking plaster, a
napkin ring, a set of shaped plastic biscuit
cutters.

☐ Things which are quite large and heavy
but perfectly safe, like a cushion, a football, a soft-backed book, rice or dried fruit
in a tough polythene bag, a loaf of bread.

☐ Anything which rattles: transparent
plastic jars with pulses, coloured beads or
paper clips inside. But do make sure that
the lid is firmly on.

☐ Objects with different textures:
pieces of felt, strips of fine sandpaper,
thick strands of wool, a fabric-filled
bean bag.

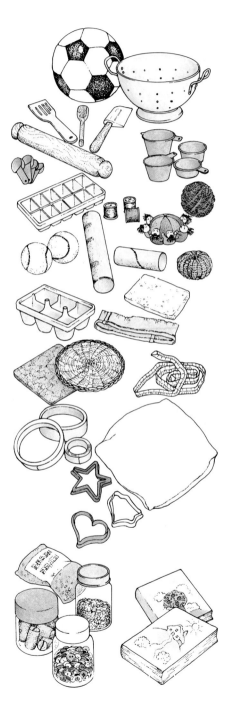

SAFETY TIPS

● Never give your child anything to play with which is so small that he might swallow it by accident or gag on it, push it up his nose or into his ear.

● If you buy a toy that is painted make sure that the paint is lead-free. Young children put everything into their mouths and children have been known to get lead poisoning from toys or furniture covered with paint containing lead.

● Never give your child a toy that is made from a hard substance which has sharp edges.

● Never leave your baby alone while he is playing, not even in a play pen.

● Always provide non-toxic crayons and pencils. For your own sake, make sure that crayons, pencils and felt tips will wash off surfaces and fabrics.

● Don't buy toys made from thin rigid plastic. They break easily and leave dangerously sharp edges.

● When you buy soft toys check for a safety label. If there's no label make sure that there are no sharp pieces of wire used to hold any additional pieces on, and check that eyes and noses are firmly secured to the fabric.

PLAY EXERCISES

You can help your baby's physical development from a very early age by playing simple games as part of your daily routine. What you're aiming for should be strengthening but, above all, entertaining. Think of these exercises as an excuse to sit down with your baby and play together. You'll probably find one of the best times is after you've given your baby a bath and he's feeling calm and contented. There are, however, certain points that you should bear in mind:

☐ Never force your baby's limbs into unnatural positions.
☐ Always check that your baby's smiling and contented. As soon as he cries, stop.
☐ Exercise him on a soft carpet or towel, never on a slippery surface.
☐ Dress him in something comfortable. As long as the room's warm enough and he's not in a draught, his nappy will be sufficient clothing.
☐ Never exercise your baby when he's tired or hungry.

Crossovers
1 (*top left*) Sit cross-legged on the floor with your baby on your lap, as shown.

2 (*bottom left*) Stretch your baby's arms out to the sides, no further than shoulder height.

3 (*bottom right*) Bring his arms back across his chest and then start the exercise again.

Flier
1 Lie on your back and put your baby on your shins with his chest on your knees.

2 Stretch his arms out to the side – as you do so he should raise his head. Then bring his hands back to the original position.

Arm stretch
1 Put your baby on his back and let him grasp your thumbs. Move one arm above his head.

2 Lower the extended arm and at the same time raise the other arm above his head.

Push-ups
1 Put your baby on his tummy, with his arms out in front of him. Hold his lower half securely around the hips.

2 Slowly raise your baby's legs, so that his back forms a right-angle with his arms. Lower his legs and repeat after a short rest.

293

BABY MASSAGE

Massage is a wonderful way to express your love for your baby; in the early days it helps the bonding process between you and your child; it helps to calm an unsettled baby and can help an anxious mother to come to terms with handling her fragile new baby. Older babies and toddlers also benefit from massage; it is an effective way of soothing a fretful baby and can help an over-excited toddler to relax.

Work from the head down, with light strokes, ensuring that both sides of the body are massaged symmetrically. Make sure the room is warm and disconnect the phone. Lay the baby on a warm towel or sheepskin, or on your lap.

Lightly massage the crown of the head with a circular motion, then stroke down the sides of the face. Next, massage the forehead, working from the centre out, then the eyebrows, eye sockets, over the cheeks and around the ears.

Gently stroke the neck from ears to shoulders and from chin to chest. Then stroke the shoulders from the neck outwards. Stroke down the arms to the fingertips. Then with fingers and thumb gently squeeze the arm from top to bottom. Massage the wrist and hand, stroking each finger with fingertips and thumbs.

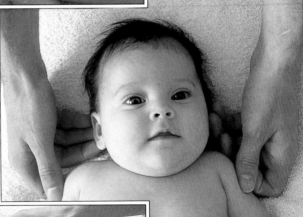

Continue down the chest, following the curves of the ribs. Massage the abdomen in a circular motion working outwards from around the navel, using fingertips or fingers and palm of hand.

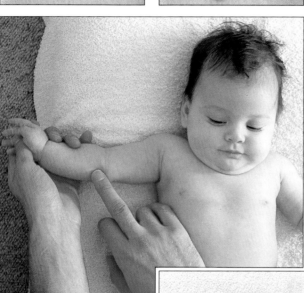

Massage the legs, working down from thighs to knees, shins, calves and ankles. Gently squeeze all the way down, as with the arms. Massage ankles and feet and from heel to toe. Then stroke each toe individually. Finish by some long, light strokes the whole length of the body from neck to toes.

Once you have massaged the baby from head to toe on the front, turn her over and do the back, again working from the head down.

You can increase the pressure of your strokes if you feel your baby likes it. Use sweeping strokes and do each part two or three times. On small areas, use just the fingertips. On some areas you will need two hands and on others one.

295

PLAY

Like almost everything else your child is doing and experiencing, play develops. Your child is now entering the proper "toy" stage. This usually begins towards the end of the first year and goes on to reach its peak between five and six years old. When children first play with toys they just examine them and explore them. As they get older they use their imagination to breathe life into the toys. They endow toys with human qualities, they set up houses, homes and camps and imagine that their toys are capable of talking and feeling just like themselves.

Suitable toys and games

Your toddler's co-ordination will improve greatly this year, as will his manipulative skills. Toys which make use of both of these will provide the most enjoyment, but be prepared for your child to be a bit ham-fisted at first and give him quite large, straightforward items. Household objects will continue to be popular, but other toys may stretch both co-ordination and mental processes further.

SUITABLE TOYS
- Posting box
- Stacking blocks
- Building blocks
- Hammering table
- Push/pull toys
- Dolls
- Cars
- Crayons and felt tips
- Paints and brushes
- Blackboard
- Books
- Plasticine
- Sand pit
- Paddling pool
- Slide
- Swing
- Frame
- Trolley

Manipulative toys

"Fitting" toys, where your toddler has to fit a shaped block into the correct hole, are ideal. A variation of this is sometimes called a "post box" and consists of a plastic box or cylinder with shaped holes cut into the surface. Your toddler can "post" his appropriately shaped blocks through the correct holes with the extra pleasure of them disappearing with a clunk. Stacking blocks provide hours of fun because they can be used in the bath, in the garden and on the beach, as well as on the floor. If you haven't already got them, building blocks are perennial favourites with children because they can be used as part of imaginary play to make so many shapes or objects – towers, forts, corrals, houses. Buy the ones sold with a trolley and you'll combine manipulation and walking.

Playing with paint

All children love to paint and draw, but during this year you may find it difficult to interpret exactly what's been drawn. Make sure that you prepare both the painting area and the child by covering the table and floor with a waterproof covering or newspaper and your child with an overall.

Two paint techniques that your child might enjoy trying out are block painting and butterfly painting. In block painting you have to provide the equivalent of a rubber stamp. This can be a small sponge, a ball of cotton wool, a cork, half an apple or a potato – anything, really, which your child can hold easily and use in a stamping movement. Make up the stamp pad by sprinkling two tablespoons of powder paint on some moistened squares of kitchen paper which you've put in a flat dish.

Gently use the back of a spoon to mix the paint into the paper.

In the second technique blobs of coloured paint are dropped on to a piece of thick paper. This is then folded so that the two sides mirror each other. If your child has learnt how to blow through a straw he can blow the paint into shapes before they're blotted.

Only keep paintings that you and your child both agree are worth keeping. Display them with magnets on refrigerator doors or, if you find a place where your child's fingerprints always seem to mark the walls, such as down the side of the staircase, cover these with your child's drawings. Your toddler's pictures make ideal cards to send to relatives or to say "thank you" for presents; they're also easy to make into calendars.

BLOCK PAINTING

1 *Prepare the painting area by covering it with newspaper. Give your child a sponge to dip into the paints.*

2 *Having dipped the sponge into the paint he should then blob (or smear) it on to the paper.*

3 *When he's done this a couple of times give him another object to use with differently coloured paints.*

BUTTERFLY PAINTING

1 *Prepare the painting area. Make up some watery paint that your child can put on with a spatula.*

2 *If your child is old enough give him a straw to blow the paint about on the paper.*

3 *Fold the paper in half but let your child open it out to see the mirror-image butterfly.*

What paper to use

Inexpensive makes of paper, wallpaper, shelf paper, old envelopes or brown paper bags, even old newspaper, can be painted on. Alternatively, buy a roll of lining paper and just cut off what your child needs. Make a reusable colouring board by covering a piece of cardboard with clear, stick-on paper. In this way paintings can be washed off with a damp cloth or paper towel (you'll probably have to experiment with paints to see which one sticks on the surface best).

What brushes to use

When your child begins to paint use thick brushes so that he sees immediate, bold results. Provide pastry brushes, cotton wool balls, orange sticks and pipe cleaners for variety. Let him use his fingers or his feet from time to time because he's bound to love getting messy with the paint. An alternative brush can be made from an old roll-on deodorant bottle: with a teaspoon, lever out the ball from the neck of the bottle, fill with paint and replace the ball.

PAINT TIPS

● Buy powder paints and mix the quantity that you need; only buy blue, red, yellow and white.

● Keep paint in small plastic jars, preferably in the non-spill variety which have a hole in the top for the paint brush.

● Plastic egg cartons make a difficult-to-spill artist's palette for your child.

● Another useful kind of paint holder is a large piece of foam rubber in which you've cut holes for the paint pots.

● To thicken up powder paint without using extra powder add some liquid starch.

● Children love making their own paint so make up a little liquid starch in a small container and pro-

vide some bottles of food colouring. They can add this until they have the colour that they require.

● If you add a little bit of detergent to finger paints it makes cleaning easier.

● You can make a paint that will stick to a shiny surface such as glass or aluminium foil by mixing food colouring, egg yolk and dry detergent.

● If you buy your child felt-tips or crayons make sure they're the fat, chunky ones because they're easier to hold.

Preserving drawings

You can preserve a crayon drawing by ironing it on to a piece of cloth. Lay it face upwards on the ironing board, cover it with a piece of light coloured cloth and then iron it firmly at a low-to-medium temperature. The drawing will transfer to the cloth. Make sure you let it cool before you move it from the ironing board. Another tip is to spray drawings with fixative, or even hair spray if you use it. This will keep the colours from being rubbed off. Alternatively, there is a "magic" solution which is estimated to keep a drawing for 200 years! Dissolve a tablet of milk of magnesia in a quart of soda water and let it sit overnight. The following day soak a paper drawing in the solution for an hour; remove from solution and leave until it is completely dry.

PAINT STORAGE TIPS
● Take a fairly large block of synthetic foam rubber or polythene foam and make holes in it. Stand up all your child's bottles, brushes and jars in it.

● A cutlery tray makes a very good store for bottles, jars and paint brushes.

● Put drawing paper on a kitchen towel dispenser and attach it to the wall in your creative corner.

Creative materials

Fingerpaint
Mix 60 ml of liquid starch with either four drops of food colouring or one tablespoon of powder paint.

Glue
Mix 250 g of flour with one teaspoon of salt in a pan. Add 600 ml of water slowly until it's absorbed into a paste. Simmer for five minutes then cool and refrigerate in an airtight container until required.

Modelling dough
Mix three parts of flour to one part of salt then stir in one part of water. Colour with food colouring and store in an airtight container.

Mock-clay dough
Mix together equal parts of salt and flour. Add a little oil and then add enough water to mix to a stiff dough. Knead until soft and stretchy.

Playing with water

Most children love playing with water and by the time that they're in their second year will have forgotten about any fears they may have had. You can help your child have fun by trying some of the following:

☐ Let your child play in the bath. All my children loved empty plastic bottles in the bath which they used as water pistols. As before, provide beakers and colanders so that your child can create a variety of effects (see p.92).

☐ Paddling pools are ideal summer playthings and they needn't be expensive. The smaller, round variety which you blow up serves just the same purpose as a more elaborate permanent one.

☐ In the summer lay a tarpaulin sheet on the ground and play a hose or plant spray over it. When it's completely wet it'll make a perfect slide for your child.

☐ Make a small hole in the bottom of a plastic container and fill it with coloured water. Attach it to the back of your child's tricycle (and later, bicycle). He'll be able to see the coloured trail the water has left as he cycles along.

☐ All children love messy games so if you have a tap in the back garden put a container of soil near it so that he can mix water with the soil and make up his own mud. Be prepared for the mess – but your child will adore it.

☐ Make an "iceberg" that can be played with in the bath or in a paddling pool. Put some food colouring into a balloon then fill it with water. Put it into a pan just in case it bursts and then place it in the freezer. When it's solid prick the balloon and peel it off – you'll be left with a perfect, round "iceberg".

Playing with sand

Sand-pits are marvellous play areas for children. Whether you buy a ready-made one or make your own by filling an old plastic paddling pool, an old rubber tyre or a cement-lined hole, you should always use washed river sand. Although more expensive than builders' sand it doesn't stain like the latter. Always cover the sand-pit over when not in use or every cat in your area could use it as a litter tray.

Slides, frames and swings

As your toddler becomes more co-ordinated throughout the year you may want to invest in a large piece of play equipment. If you decide to buy a swing, buy the kind which your toddler has to be bodily lifted into and out of. If you buy a slide make sure it has safety sides and *no* parts which will splinter.

SAFETY TIPS

● Never let your toddler go near or handle fireworks.

● Keep him well away from any kind of pool containing water. No matter how small or shallow it is, even if he can swim, he should never be left unattended.

● Take special care if you go to children's playgrounds with fast-moving roundabouts and concrete bases, and avoid the times when older, more boisterous children are using the equipment.

● Any game that involves metal implements is potentially dangerous, e.g. metal buckets and spades or toy pistols. So is any game with sharp or pointed instruments, e.g. bows and arrows or toy knives.

Rough and gentle games

Not all children like the same sort of game, nor does the same child like the same kind of game all the time. Some children have an obvious preference for more athletic, boisterous games, while others prefer quiet, contemplative activities.

Having had four sons, I found that two of them were of the former type, and two of them the latter. From an early age I indulged the two who preferred rough and tumble games by providing large, soft cushions in the playroom and foam-filled soft furniture for them to jump and leap about on and do their acrobatics. Outdoors there was a rope to climb, a tree with a favourite way up and down, a climbing frame with rope ladders and netting for them to cling on to, a tyre swing, and I think they had their first tricycle around the age of about thirteen or fourteen months. Ball games like football or bat and ball were always favourites and had the advantage that they tired the children out.

With the latter two children, we had to provide lots of books and countless sets of paints, easels and drawing boards. At a very early age the children made toy ships or toy steam engines from household junk like empty egg boxes and toilet roll tubes, yogurt cartons and plastic margarine containers, and as they got older they went on to making paper aeroplanes. One of our sons became quite an expert on origami at the age of three. Both of these children loved musical instruments and had recorders, toy flutes, toy xylophones and toy guitars before graduating on to proper instruments at a later age.

Are the toys creative enough?

There is hardly any toy or game that isn't creative for your child. Whatever he plays with or sees when he's awake will help him create imaginary worlds. He'll create patterns with colours and shapes and will create miniature models of his own home all the time that he's playing.

By far the most enjoyable and beneficial are games that don't need too much super-

vision from you. They allow your child to follow any interesting development if the fancy takes him, and in this way he can concentrate on doing something of his own choosing. He can use his own judgement so that his interest is completely fulfilled. If you constantly interrupt him and tell him to be clean and tidy, or careful, or if you try to help him too much, his interest in the game will wane. He will lose sight of the point of his game and will become disheartened. This sort of adult interference can result in a child being unable to concentrate when he gets to school.

Is my child stimulated enough?

If you provide the right environment and the right equipment, you needn't worry about whether your child is being stimulated enough. At this stage your child is developing his thinking about playing, and what he needs is freedom to allow his thought processes to expand so that he can follow new ideas as they occur to him, and see play through to its conclusions. It is your job to provide the floor space, the tools and uninterrupted time so that he can look after his thinking himself.

Your child is attacking play very much like an explorer. He must be given privacy and time to himself with no interruptions (unless he asks for them). It is your job to be an assistant, to provide the equipment and make sure that he has all the facilities that he needs. Once you have provided all these facilities, it is up to your child to decide what to do, not you, and you shouldn't interfere.

How you can help

You can't teach your child to use his imagination, but you can encourage his natural gift for fantasy by doing the following:
□ Play make-believe games with your toddler.
□ When you tell a story act out the characters' parts and make up all the various character's voices. If your child has a favourite, suggest that he takes that part.

☐ Play "What's this" games. Get your child to shut his eyes then gently stroke some object across his skin. He's got to guess what it is.
☐ Help your child in his imaginary world by giving him some glove puppets – either bought ones or brown paper bags with faces drawn on them.
☐ Start to stock a dressing-up box. Put in some of your old shoes, shirts, skirts, dresses, hats and scarves. Have some special cheap jewellery as well. If you can find some authentic uniforms from second-hand shops so much the better. Make a cloak from a length of fabric and attach a clasp at one end.

☐ Provide good fantasy toys like dolls; children of both sexes love dolls because they're so easy to incorporate into their imaginary worlds. Stuffed animals, house-cleaning, gardening or carpentry sets are also ideal.
☐ Play at being an animal. Get down on all fours and move about the floor making all the animal noises that you know. This will show your toddler how to do it.
☐ Play telephone conversations. If you've bought your child a toy telephone pick up the real phone and pretend to have a telephone conversation with him.

STORAGE TIPS

● Always keep any plastic containers with lids for storing blocks, marbles or small toys. Those made for ice cream or even margarine are ideal.
● Use brightly coloured labels for easy identification of what's inside your containers.
● Large glass jars are good for storage because you can immediately see what's inside them.
● Never throw out any shoe boxes – they make good beds for dolls as well as houses or barns.
● Loop a plastic mesh basket over the taps in the bath to store all bath toys.
● Use a flat-topped chest for storing larger toys. This can double up as a table.
● Your child's toys are bound to get strewn around your home. Try to keep a basket in each room to make for quick and easy tidying up.
● Keep a special bag or box of toys in the car at all times.

CLEANING AND PREPARING TOYS
● Always buy machine-washable stuffed toys.
● Alternatively use a carpet shampoo and brush to clean stuffed toys.
● Try to buy plastic toys which can be put into the dishwasher.
● If plastic toys have got out of shape, soak them in hot water and then re-mould them with your fingers.
● Clean and deodorize smelly toys by sponging them with a cloth that has been wrung out in a solution of baking soda.
● You can dry-clean your toys by shaking them in a bag containing a generous amount of baking powder.

PLAY 2–3

Your child will probably still play with some of his existing toys although the ways in which he plays with them may differ. He may continue to play with building blocks but instead of just piling them on top of each other will use them as part of a larger concept: he may use them to form the wall surrounding an imaginary garage forecourt.

During this third year your child will want to imitate the way you behave and the way you look. Manipulative skills will be greatly improved so larger jigsaws and more fiddly puzzles will be popular.

SUITABLE TOYS
- Large-piece jigsaw
- Plasticine
- Lego building bricks
- Scissors (blunt-ended)
- Glue
- Prams and push-chairs
- Tea sets
- Toy washing machines, cooking utensils
- Play house
- Tricycle
- Cars and trucks
- Climbing frame

Imitative games

As part of his imitation of the adults around him, your child will create a little world of his own. You don't need to buy a proper play house for him to do this. A couple of chairs, or a small table draped with a large blanket will make an instant tent or playhouse, as will an old playpen covered with a sheet. Children love playing in the dark, so draw the curtains if that's what they want. All of my children loved playing with cardboard boxes of any size, as long as they were big enough to climb into. Small ones became boats and cars, piles of them were made into castles, forts and houses. Boxes laid on their sides became tunnels and when laid end to end became trains. More elaborate "houses" can be made by taking a large box or a series of tea chests with all the nails and strips of metal taken off and cutting out doors and windows. Your child can draw in curtains and put pictures on the wall inside, and outside he can draw shutters, a door and a knocker. If you put several stools or small chairs in a line across the room your child will make them into a train, a boat or an aeroplane.

Manipulative games

Your child will use his hands to explore objects and discover what they do – it'll be an important part of the learning process for him. All of the games and ideas listed below require good co-ordination.

□ During this year your child will have enough co-ordination to help with tasks around the house, and he'll still see this as a form of play because he's so keen to copy what you do. He'll be able to handle an electric mixer, as long as you keep an eye on him; he'll be able to snap the tops off beans and tear the tops off spinach.

□ Many children love taking anything mechanical to pieces so don't throw away old clocks, old motors, cameras or record players; let your child have fun taking them to pieces. And if there is anything around the house that needs to be dismantled, such as an old wall or fence, or if there's stone to be broken up for crazy paving, let your child join in.

□ Your child might enjoy trying out spatter painting. To do this he places leaves, grasses, coins, whatever shape he wants, flat on to a piece of white paper. He then takes a toothbrush, well soaked with paint, and gently draws a knife across it so that the paint is spattered randomly across the paper. To make it look even more exciting he can continue doing this with different colours. When the paint is dry he can remove the objects.

□ Give your child a small plot in the garden which is entirely his. Provide him

with his own trowel and watering can and help him plant some bulbs or vegetables which grow quickly like marigolds, radishes and beans.

☐ Your child will probably be able to deal with jigsaws of up to six pieces. Wherever possible you should try to buy ones with easily identifiable bits when the puzzle's apart. Your toddler will find it much easier if he can see what's a leg or an arm or a tree rather than just a shape. Buy wooden jigsaws where possible: they're easier to handle and don't bend like the cardboard variety. If you find your child still can't hold them make it easier by gluing on small plastic hooks from the hardware store. Start off with the inset puzzles where the pieces fit into pre-cut areas on a tray. Your toddler will soon pick up how it's meant to work.

☐ With some jigsaws you may have to show your child exactly how to assemble the pieces. When you do this explain to him why certain pieces go together and interlock. "Look, this bit has two bumps which look like eyebrows . . . this piece is for the head which always goes on top of the body." Once you've done this and helped your child through it himself a couple of times he'll happily sit and do it over and over again.

☐ Make a puzzle out of your child's favourite picture by pasting it on to heavy card and covering it with clear contact film. With a craft knife, cut the puzzle into about six pieces made up of triangles, diamonds and squares.

☐ Stop the puzzles from getting mixed up by marking the back of each piece with a specific colour.

Learning through play

There is no time in your young child's life when play does not contribute to his development. Quite often your child's needs and desires can be fulfilled in play when they cannot satisfactorily be met in any other way. For instance, a child who is unable to be a leader in real life may gain great satisfaction from being a leader of his toy soldiers or band of Indians or

cowboys. For most children, play involves experimentation. Through trial and error, your children can discover that creating something new, something that they haven't met or done before, can be very satisfying. Once they have fulfilled their creative interests in play, they can then transfer them to the real world.

At home and in school children learn what the generally accepted roles of the different sexes are. Knowing what they are, accepting them and taking up the relevant role are different things. Very soon after joining a playgroup your child learns that he must play that role if he wants to become an accepted member of the group. It may be within this group that your child meets the most rigid enforcement of moral standards that he'll ever experience. There is nothing like a group of children at play for encouraging the development of desirable personality traits. By contact with friends, your child will be given lessons every day in how to be generous, truthful and co-operative, how to be a good sport and pleasant to be with. These lessons are especially forceful, because your child is constantly seeking the approval of his friends and peers, and the playgroup in general.

Learning about colours

Always mention the colour of something that you are using or looking for. For instance, "I'm looking for the green packet." "Where's that red tin gone?" "Oh, I've found the jar with the blue label," "I'm going to use this yellow pencil." Always describe the colour of your child's clothes. "That's a pretty pink dress," "What a nice red jumper." Always point out the colour of flowers, in your garden, your window box or in the park, and show your child the different colours that animals, and birds especially, can have. Show your child how colours are made, "Look, if we mix a little bit of red with this white we will get pink; yellow mixed with blue will make green." Teach your child the colours of the rainbow; rainbows are magical to children.

Learning about letters

Teach your child the alphabet song so that remembering it is all the easier. Serve alphabet soup or alphabet spaghetti and help your child to spell out his name with the letters. Alternatively, buy your child magnetic letters that he can play with on the refrigerator door. My children liked us to spell out words by drawing the letters in the palms of their hands while their eyes were closed, and they tried to recognize the letters and build up the word. Play word games when you read a story. As you read a sentence, leave out a word and get your child to say what it is. "The cat was sitting warming himself by the ......" As you point to the fire in the picture your child can shout out "fire."

Learning about numbers

Always take the opportunity to count while you are doing routine things. For instance, count one, two and three as you do up the buttons on your child's dungarees or jacket, or when you're washing his hands or feet. Help with number learning by counting things as you shop.

Count bottles and jars and arrange them into groups such as two bottles, three cans and four packets. Draw numbers on small sheets of paper and help your child to number little groups of his toys, for instance, three balls, five blocks, seven farmyard animals. When you go for walks count the number of houses or gates, trees in a garden or ducks in a pond.

TELEVISION

Some babies are introduced to television while they are still in their cots. Their parents see television as a built-in baby-sitter because it keeps children amused when there is no-one else who wants to look after them. For quite a lot of children television is more popular and consumes more of their playtime than all other play activities added together. Here are some of the reported facts about television:

● Television is at its least useful when a child is left to watch it alone. Even if he's watching a highly educational programme he'll get less out of it if he watches it in an entirely passive way. If he watches it with other children who comment on it, or with an adult who asks questions and makes observations, the programme acts as a springboard for ideas and discussion rather than one-way, non-participatory communication.

● Some parents let television interfere with the usual eating and sleeping routines, leading to upset digestion and tired children.

● Watching television can curtail other play activities, especially outdoor play and playing with other children; it may leave little time for creative play.

● Television often presents information in a more exciting and dramatic way than school books and school teachers. Children therefore often find books and school work boring.

● Television cuts down on conversation and other social interactions in the family.

● Characters on television are often pre-sented as exaggerated stereotypes and children come to think that people in a given group have the same qualities as the people portrayed on the screen and this influences their attitude towards them.

● If a child watches too many programmes portraying crime, torture and cruelty, this may blunt a child's sensitivity to violence so that he accepts violent behaviour as normal.

● Two groups of children were studied for the effects of violence on television. One saw violent programmes, the other did not. The studies showed that the young children who were allowed to watch the violent programmes were noticeably more aggressive, both with other children and with their toys, than those children who had not been exposed to the same programmes.

● Children are great imitators and as the law breakers often seem more glamorous than the heroes, children tend to identify with the villains.

● Light entertainment that children watch doesn't necessarily provide a good lesson in pronunciation and grammar and children can pick up habits which are often sloppy.

● Television can present models for the behaviour of the different sexes and for life roles and careers. This in turn gives rise to similar expectations in children which are not always the best.

● If children are really interested in programmes they have seen on television it may act as a motivation to follow up what they have watched by reading or asking grown-ups about the subject.

16 Outings and travel

Your new baby can go everywhere with you so long as you are composed and well-prepared. If you are well organized and self-assured, outings with your baby can be a great joy, and the sooner that you start after bringing the baby home the better.

For the first few months, at least, most babies are looked after by their mothers, especially if they're being breast-fed. I have, therefore, addressed this part of the book mainly to mothers. Looking after a baby doesn't preclude a mother from resuming the active life that she had before. One word of warning, though. New mothers shouldn't be too ambitious, or undertake strenuous shopping expeditions that involve walking long distances, or carrying heavy bags. I made the mistake of doing this seven days after I had my baby and I was so tired that I had to sit down on the pavement or I would have fainted.

LOCAL OUTINGS   0–1

Planning your outings

It's always worth spending fifteen to twenty minutes planning how you're going to get to your destination, what you're going to need for the journey, where you're going to feed your baby and how you're going to change him. Until you feel confident, take your partner or a friend along with you. An extra pair of hands to share the load, and an ally to share the novelty and possibly any problems, will make any trip more enjoyable.

You'll have to make sure that there's somewhere that you can feed your baby in peace, especially in the first months when your baby won't have settled into a predictable feeding routine. You'll have to change your baby as well, so try to find out if there's a nearby department store or public convenience with a mother and baby room you can use. There should be a work top at waist height for easy changing which will save you having to change your baby on the floor, or even worse, on your lap. In the summer, it would be pleasant to sit in a nearby park to feed your baby.

What to take for a young baby
- A changing surface (which can be a fold-up mat or a fabric nappy
- Disposable nappies
- Baby wipes
- Breast pads if breast-feeding
- Bottle and feed if bottle-feeding
- Hat
- Sweater
- Toys for distraction
- Plastic bag for dirty nappies

What to take for an older baby
- A changing surface
- Disposable nappies
- Baby wipes
- Baby food and spoon
- Non-messy snacks
- Feeding beaker with fruit juice
- Bib
- Hat
- Sweater
- Toys for distraction
- Plastic bag for dirty nappies

311

Using a sling

Slings are one of the most convenient methods of carrying a baby as well as one of the oldest. They hold your baby securely against your chest so that you and your baby have the security of being close to each other; they also leave your hands free. Buy a washable sling because your baby is bound to posset over it, and do try it on before you make your final choice. It's got to be easy to put on and to wear. The shoulder straps must be wide enough to support your growing baby's weight comfortably and both you and your partner must feel relaxed wearing it. It has been said that a baby shouldn't be carried in a sling until he can support his own head. This is not true. You can carry your baby in a sling as soon as you and he are happy about it – your baby will find close contact with you so soothing and reassuring that he'll probably curl up with his head quite well supported and doze.

PUTTING ON A POUCH SLING

1 *Clip the sling on round your waist then swivel it to the back.*

2 *Pick up your baby and manoeuvre his legs into the leg holes.*

3 *Pull one side of the sling up over the baby and on to your shoulder. Swap hands and repeat with the other side.*

PUTTING ON AN ENCLOSED SLING

1 *Put on the sling. Slip your baby comfortably on to the inner seat. Zip up the seat section.*

2 *With one hand still supporting the baby pull the outer cover around him and do up the inner zip.*

LEANING FORWARDS

Always cradle your baby's head if you have to lean forwards or stretch to one side

Using a push-chair

If you don't carry your baby in a sling, a push-chair becomes absolutely essential. Small babies fit quite snugly into the curved shape of the push-chair, but do make sure that the baby is well supported with pillows on either side and that he's safely strapped in. Even a tiny baby, if awake, can be propped up to take in the interesting sights around him.

There will be plenty of occasions when you'll have to collapse the push-chair – getting on a bus or going to certain shops for instance – so it's a good idea to practise before you make your first expedition. Make sure that you can kick it shut, open it up one handed and, above all, operate the brakes.

SAFETY TIPS
● Never leave your baby unattended.
● Always make sure that the push-chair is fully extended and in the locked position.
● Never let go of the push-chair for a moment without putting the brakes on.
● Always put the safety harness on your baby.
● Never, ever, put shopping on the handles of the push-chair.
● From an early age teach your child to keep his fingers away from the wheels.

PUSH-CHAIR TIPS
● One disadvantage of push-chairs over prams is that in cold weather your child is more exposed. If you don't use leg muffs (see p.45), lay a blanket over the push-chair before you put the baby in. Once you've put him down, wrap the blanket over and around him.
● If your baby falls asleep before you get home either put the push-chair into the lie-back position or tuck him up comfortably with pillows.

COLLAPSING THE PUSH-CHAIR

1 *Put shopping on the ground and take your baby out of the push-chair. If you have a reclining push-chair, slot the back into the upright position.*

2 *Grip one of the handles and put your foot under the collaps-ible strut. Pull your foot upwards.*

3 *Lean forwards, pushing the handles down until they lock into position; this allows you to carry the push-chair easily.*

313

Using a back pack

A back pack is a useful means of carrying an older baby who can sit up well and who has become rather heavy to carry in a sling. Once again, it leaves your hands free, but it also allows your baby to see much more of what's going on around him. This becomes increasingly important the older your baby gets and the more his understanding grows. Before you buy a back pack you should do the following:

☐ Try on the back pack, with your baby in it, before you buy.

☐ Check that the baby's seat comes half-way down your back. This is very important because it places the strain on your back and not on your shoulders; it also keeps the baby stable.

☐ Make sure that the pack has a safety strap to keep the baby in place and a waist belt for you to keep it secure. Check that the shoulder straps are well padded.

☐ Check that your baby can sit comfortably and that the leg openings don't restrict him in any way.

☐ Try to buy a pack with a built-in loading stand so that you can put it on without any help; such back packs often convert to free-standing seats.

Put the baby into the back pack and lift it up and against your partner's back. He can then slide his arms into the straps.

If you're alone put the baby in the pack first then rest it on a chair or table. Squat down and slide your arms into the straps.

Going shopping

Try to shop early in the morning when the shops are least busy. When you go to a supermarket and your child can sit un-supported, put him into your shopping trolley and wheel it down the *centre* of the aisles. Your baby will want to grasp or pull everything in sight which can easily cause chaos with a supermarket's carefully stacked packets or tins. If you're still feeding your baby plan to shop between feeds; if you're going to be out for a while aim to have most of your shopping done before you have to find a quiet spot to give the next feed.

Having a car is one of the greatest freedoms a new parent can have. There's no worry about how to cope with public transport, there's no difficulty in managing any shopping and it provides an ideal feeding and changing area.

SHOPPING TIPS

● When you're carrying your child in your back pack remember your child's grasping fingers can reach jars and tins in a shop.

● When you take your child into the supermarket keep him supported and under control by using your own reins to tie him into the trolley.

● For emergencies keep a few disposable nappies, wipes and plastic bags in the glove compartment of the car for quick changes.

● If you take toys on expeditions attach them to the pram or trolley so you don't have to keep picking them up.

● Shopping seems to make children hungry and therefore fretful. Avoid this by bringing a snack.

● You can always use the opened boot of the car, with a blanket laid over it, as a surface on which to change your child.

● Keep a spare changing bag in the car

314

Eating out

In the first months your baby will doze off almost anywhere, so eating out will be quite easy. However, by the time he's nine months old he'll be capable of keeping himself awake; he'll be keen for any new experience and a restaurant, with strange people doing even stranger things, will fascinate him. Choose your restaurant carefully. If possible go for ones which seem friendly towards both children and their parents and which provide high chairs. In case they don't, always take along a portable high chair (see p.41) and ask to be put at a table out of the main areas of activity. Always take your own snacks with you, and as soon as you've settled your baby in his seat, give him these to occupy him. Have plenty of toys for distraction as well (rearranging paper napkins is a good quietener). You may find it works better if you feed your child before you and your partner start.

Using public transport

My advice is wherever possible, don't. Neither buses nor trains were designed for parents with young children. If you're shopping on your own, with a push-chair, a changing bag and a grumpy baby, getting on public transport can seem like the last straw. However, there are some tips to get over the worst problems.

☐ Always travel outside of the rush hour, even if that means waiting in a coffee shop, or walking round a gallery for an extra hour; it's worth it.

☐ Where possible, carry your baby in a sling or back-pack. This leaves your hands free. It also makes getting on and off a lot easier.

☐ Carry plenty of distracting toys.

☐ You may be asked to leave your push-chair in the special luggage section. If this is the case make sure you get up in plenty of time before your stop to retrieve it.

☐ Never be embarrassed to ask for help.

LOCAL OUTINGS   1–3

By the time your child is walking you may find that your greatest problem is keeping him safely restrained and happily occupied when you go out. You'll also have to be prepared for very slow journeys with endless stops to look at the many objects which take your child's fancy. Most parents continue to use their push-chair, although reins, back packs and bicycle seats are useful alternatives.

Using the push-chair

As your child gets older he won't be happy just sitting in the push-chair, but will want to walk along with you. This may be inconvenient, especially if you are shopping, and you will have to do your utmost to persuade your toddler to stay in it. In my experience the best way of doing this is to take along one of your child's favourite toys as well as a snack. If your child is so restless that he makes shopping impossible then the only alternative I can suggest is to take along a pair of reins and put your child in them (see p.47). You can

What to take	● Sweater/Coat
● Toys	● Sun hat
● Books	● Change of nappy
● Drink	until toilet trained
● Snacks	● Potty,
● Comforter	if necessary

either stack your shopping in the push-chair, leaving your hands relatively free, or you can collapse the push-chair and carry it over your arm while you carry the shopping in the other.

Using a bicycle seat

If you have a bicycle you may find it fun to take your toddler on the back. There are two kinds of bicycle seat – front-mounted and rear-mounted. These lightweight plastic structures fit neatly and securely on to the bicycle frame and can accommodate a child of up to 80 kilos (40 lbs). Make sure that your child's feet are well away from the wheels and that there's a strong safety belt. If you decide you do want to use this method of transport, you may want to buy a protective helmet for your child as well.

Shopping with an older child

As soon as your child can toddle you'll be faced with a new problem: how to keep an eye on, and occupy, a lively young child and concentrate on what you have to do. The only efficient way of getting about, especially when shopping, is to take your partner or a friend along with you. In this way, one adult can get on with the shopping while the other occupies the child. (There is also the added bonus of another pair of hands to help carry shopping home.)

The most important tip is to keep your toddler on reins so that you can concentrate on what you're doing without having to worry about what he's doing. It also helps to sit your child in the supermarket trolley so that he can't run away. As you go around the shop ask your child questions like "Can you see the baked beans?" "Which is the largest tin?" "Which apples do you want – the red or the green ones?" Most children love being involved in this way and you can even let them choose their favourite foods and put them in the trolley. My supermarket solution to this method of keeping them quiet was to let my children put anything into the trolley as we were going around and then take it

all out at the end, unbeknown to them: time-consuming, but peaceful.

If you aren't going food shopping but, say, clothes shopping instead, still keep your toddler on reins but take along his favourite books. When you go into the changing rooms sit your child on the floor beside you and encourage him to look at the pictures, maybe telling you what's in them or what the story is about.

SHOPPING TIPS

● Encourage your child to become familiar with shopping. Give him the wrappers or boxes of things on your shopping list and suggest he finds them for you by matching them up with products on the shelves.

● Toddlers can get lost in shops. Dress yours in an easily spotted coat or hat in a bright colour.

● As soon as possible, teach your child his name, address and telephone

number. In the meantime, insert a label with this information inside his coat in case he does get lost.

● I used to use a referee's whistle on a string round my neck to summon my children. We had a code: one whistle – come briskly; two whistles – run; three whistles – emergency.

● Any outing can be a lesson in disguise. In the supermarket you can teach your child about healthy eating (that beans are

better than spaghetti) or best buys (that large tins work out cheaper than small ones).

● You can make sure your child can find his way home if he strays by giving the same running commentary as you approach your house. "And here's that big fir tree on the corner, now we turn right, straight on past the church, and here's our own road, and our house is over there, the fourth house on the left."

MANAGING TWO CHILDREN

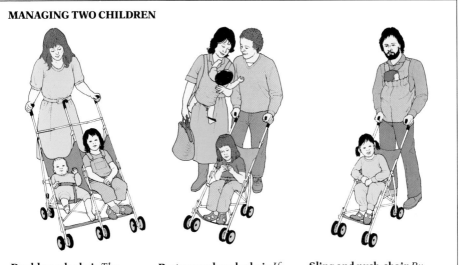

Double push-chair *The independently adjustable sections make it ideal for children of different ages.*

Partner and push-chair *If two of you go out together any trip is going to be easier whichever method is used.*

Sling and push-chair *By carrying your youngest in a sling your hands are free to push the push-chair.*

Special excursions

Going out to the shops or to the park will probably be part of your toddler's daily routine but there will be occasions when you want to plan a special excursion like the zoo or a boat trip. In your plans, take your child's personality into account. What's his attention span? Is he very active? If he is, don't plan to go anywhere where he's going to be confined to his push-chair for long or you'll ruin everybody's day. If, when the day arrives, your toddler's in a bad mood, postpone the outing; similarly, if you no longer feel like it. Take enough snacks for the whole day and include quite a variety of them.

CAR JOURNEYS   0–1

Travelling is a normal part of everyday life, and the sooner your baby learns about it the better.

Car safety

The most important aspect of travelling by car is the safety of your baby. Never sit in the front with your baby on your lap. You should always use a child restraint (car seat) suitable for your baby's age, weight, and size. Make sure that the restraint complies with current standard and safety regulations and is compatible with your car. Before choosing a restraint, seek independent consumer and safety advice.

The movement of a car is very soothing to most babies and they quite often sleep soundly through long journeys and arrive more refreshed than you do. By the time your baby's old enough to sit in a car seat he's going to need entertaining and this will be the most taxing part of any car journey you take.

Feeding your baby

Obviously feeding is much easier if you're breast-feeding because there's no preparation or sterilization involved. If you're bottle-feeding, however, you're going to have to find some way of making up your

317

baby's feed in sterile conditions. You must *never* try to keep a made-up feed warm because any germs will quickly multiply. If you can't get hold of disposable bottles and feeds, either mix the formula, when you need it, in a sterilized bottle with some boiled water that you've kept in a thermos or, alternatively, make up the feed in your usual way, cool it in the refrigerator and carry it in an ice-pack.

Once your baby's weaned you'll have to take along baby food, a plastic spoon, sugar-free rusks, a bib and a drinking cup with a spout. You can feed your baby directly from the jar but if he doesn't finish it all off you *must* throw it away.

Changing your baby

Disposables are by far the easiest to use when you're travelling. If you have a hatch-back you can change your baby on a mat laid out in the back; otherwise lay your baby on a mat along the back seat. There's no need to do more than top and tail your baby when you're travelling so all you need are some specially designed baby wipes and a plastic bag to put dirty nappies in.

CAR TIPS
● Never leave your child alone in the car, especially in the heat when the temperature can be much higher than outside. Avoid heat stroke by only taking your baby on essential short journeys early in the morning and at night. Secure a suction sun blind or nappy on the window to protect him from the sun.

● Remove all loose objects from the back window ledge in case of accidents.
● Tie a variety of your baby's favourite toys on short pieces of string to the car seat.
● Always keep a bag with spare nappies and cleaning equipment in the car.
● Have a rug or cot quilt to put over the baby when he falls asleep.
● Have your baby's favour-

ite tapes to play in the car.
● Keep some special toys for car journeys and introduce them one at a time.
● Have a large container of diluted fruit juice in the front with you, and give your baby quite frequent but very small drinks.
● Once your child is weaned he'll like to have a few snacks during the journey. Make these non-messy.

CAR JOURNEYS   1–3

It's between the ages of one and two and a half that car journeys become most difficult. Your child will hate being made to sit still in one place, at just the time when he's discovered all the exciting things his body's capable of, like walking and running. Secondly, he'll want to assert *himself*. A new sense of independence emerges at this time and he'll be keen to express what he wants to do, especially when you don't want him to do it. It's your job to amuse him and keep him occupied – for all your sakes. Some of the tips that I found most valuable with my children were as follows:
☐ Make an early start or travel at night.
☐ Pack soft clothing in such a way that it will do double duty eg. anoraks in a pillow case make good pillows for a child to nap on.

☐ Be prepared to change seats so that all the passengers get varied views during the journey.
☐ You can buy or make special covers for the front seats of the car with pockets which can carry games, snacks, drinks, books.
☐ Curb restlessness by stopping for five minutes every hour or so, so that the children can run about, investigate and stretch their legs and imaginations.
☐ To make these stops worthwhile warn your children in plenty of time to put on shoes, hats and coats.
☐ Stop your temper getting frayed if there's a spill or accident by putting some spare clothes for each child in the car with a plastic bag for soiled clothes.
☐ Always tape knives, forks and spoons to the inside of the food containers.

☐ To minimize mess in the car have a store of carrier bags to put rubbish in and a supply of paper tissues and baby wipes to clean sticky hands and faces.

☐ Have a few *nutritious* snacks in plastic bags so that you never have to say no if your child wants to nibble eg. raisins, cornflakes, pieces of cheese.

☐ Always take more drinks than you think you'll need, such as small sealed containers of milk or juice.

☐ Most children love grapes (the seedless kind) and they quench thirst as well as satisfying hunger.

☐ If you take toys in the car tie them to coathooks or handles so that they don't get trampled on the floor or roll under seats.

☐ To give your child some surprises wrap favourite toys in several layers of paper. Unwrapping will keep him occupied.

☐ Get your child to take some responsibility for his own entertainment by letting him select a few of his toys and put them in his own case or bag.

☐ Magnetized games prevent bits getting lost.

☐ Sew or stick velcro on to toys or games so that they will stay steady or in one place.

☐ A child's favourite music playing in the car or a story telling cassette will give you half an hour of peace – take a selection of tapes.

☐ Keep a few treats hidden away for the moment when your child gets grumpy.

☐ Play "I Spy" games. Ask your child to look out for a certain object: a black cow, a red truck or a fire engine.

☐ Don't stand for any misbehaviour like screaming or shouting or kicking. This can be very dangerous. If your child does this pull in to the side of the road and say that you're not going any further until he behaves.

Preventing car sickness

Some children are more prone to car sickness than others: the balance mechanism of their inner ear is more sensitive to the swaying movement. Most children who suffer from car sickness grow out of it as they get older, but there are a number of things that you can do to minimize the risks:

☐ If you've noticed that your child gets car sick, ask your doctor to suggest a suitable drug. These are usually given half an hour before you leave.

☐ Don't give your child rich or greasy food within a few hours of leaving.

☐ If your child wants a snack during the journey give him dry biscuits or a glucose sweet that he can suck.

☐ Don't become over anxious. Children quickly pick up on their parents' moods and this can make them apprehensive and therefore more prone to car sickness. Excitement and apprehension do play a part in sickness and it's been shown that children tend to suffer more on outward journeys than on return ones.

☐ Keep your child occupied.

☐ If your child goes very pale or very quiet, stop the car. Provide a plastic bag or bowl to be sick in, if necessary.

☐ Always keep baby wipes to clean your child up in case he is sick and something tasty like mints for your child to suck to take away the taste.

AIR TRAVEL   0–3

Travelling by air is by far the easiest means of public transport to use, but you should still plan out your journey meticulously, especially if you're travelling alone. You can't always get things right, so, like me, you may have to grin and bear it once or twice. I shall never forget making the journey from New York to London with my eighteen-month-old son crying for the whole seven and a half hours, despite all the efforts of my husband and myself.

When you make your reservations say that you're going to be travelling with an infant. Ask to be put on a flight that's not crowded and ask for a bulkhead seat, because there's more leg room there. Ask if they provide cots; if they do, order one so that your baby will be comfortable during the flight. Bulkhead seats are advisable if you have a toddler, too, because you can lay a towel on the floor in front of you for him to play on. Carry a small baby in a sling so that your hands are free. Alternatively use a push-chair. Ask the air staff if the airport provides push-chairs – you'll quite likely have to walk a long way to reach the boarding area and if you're trying to manage hand-baggage and a baby you could find it exhausting. If they don't provide push chairs take your own – it can be carried as hand baggage.

Arrive at the airport with plenty of time to spare. This means that you'll be able to check-in before the queues start and get yourself organized without getting into a flap. Carry everything that you need in a lightweight shoulder bag – toys as well as nappies and changes of clothing – so that your hands are free.

What to take with you
● Child's passport and inoculation documents, if necessary.
● Lightweight bag for baby's equipment.
● Travel cot if cot unavailable at destination.
● Push-chair, carry cot or sling.
● Plastic sheet for nappy changing.
● Bouncing chair if used.
● Pack of disposables; buy supplies at destination.
● Nappy changing equipment (see p.78).
● Potty if needed.
● Plastic bags for dirty nappies.
● Vacuum flask for days on beach.
● Bottle-feeding equipment if required.
● Non-spill mug and plastic dish if weaned.
● Toys and games.
● Comforters if used.
● Quick-drying, non-crease clothes.
● Sun-hat, if necessary.
● Long-sleeved and long-legged clothes.

MAKNG THE BEST OF PLANE JOURNEYS

● Request bulkhead seats and cot, if required, when making reservations.

● Change your baby's nappy just before boarding.

● Keep some food or drink at the ready to give your baby at take off or landing to help equalise the pressure in his ears and avoid discomfort.

● Shortly after boarding ask the most pleasant looking flight attendant you see for help and find out when it will be convenient for him or her to warm your baby's food and drink.

● Make sure your inflight baby bag, with bottles, equipment and changes of nappies and clothing, is clearly labelled in case it gets mislaid during the flight.

● Don't try to eat or drink hot food while you're holding the baby for fear of spillage and scalding the baby.

● Take along a few of your child's favourite toys but only bring them out one at a time and at intervals spaced through the journey.

● Let your baby play with all the inflight equipment – spoons and forks from the food tray, plastic safety instructions from the seat flap, earphones for the films or for music.

● Amuse your child with the same kinds of games as you'd play in the car (see p.318).

Towards carefree foreign holidays

Your baby's never too young to travel. According to my mother, she took me on a camping holiday when I was six weeks old and I took one of my sons to Italy when he was barely three months. Children usually rise to these occasions. My baby son lay gurgling in Rome airport for two hours while we found our lost luggage and for the first three days of the holiday he calmly accepted trial and error until we found an Italian milk formula that suited him.

The type of holiday you choose is up to you and your individual tastes – it may be camping, staying in a luxury hotel or swapping house with another family. If you are going to go to a hotel make sure that they have adequate facilities for young children. Without them you're not going to enjoy the holiday yourselves. Check that they provide high chairs, play pools, laundry (if you're using fabric nappies) and early meals for children. If you're going to a beach it's advisable to choose one which is sandy and shelves very gently.

Ask your doctor's advice well ahead of your trip about health precautions, vaccinations (see p.368), medication or special creams that you should take with you. With a baby, consult your health visitor about food, facilities and hygiene in the country or area that you're going to.

If you're adventurous with the family diet at home let your children eat what they want to abroad. If you or they are more conservative and you're not self-catering, make early arrangements with the hotel for them to have simple, plain meals. Don't introduce your child to exotic food for the first time in a foreign country.

SUNBATHING TIPS

Try to avoid exposing your baby's skin to direct sunlight at any time. Babies have little skin pigment so they have much less protection from the sun than adults, and exposure to the sun's ultraviolet rays can lead to skin damage and skin cancer in later life.

● Use sunscreen of at least factor 15 on all exposed skin, and apply it 20 minutes before going out. Repeat every three hours, or more frequently if she gets wet.

● In very hot weather, avoid taking your baby out in the sun between 11am and 1pm when the sun is at its highest.

● Dress your baby in a wide-brimmed hat and loose light clothing that covers her shoulders and neck, such as a shirt or dress with sleeves and a collar.

● Be aware that your baby is still at risk on cloudy days.

● Make sure the pram or buggy has an adjustable hood or umbrella to shade your baby.

● Be particularly careful near snow and water where reflected light is strong.

17 Home safety

Accidents in the home cause 37% of deaths in children between the ages of one and four. Most of them are avoidable so you should take the time and care to make sure that the chances of accidents in *your* home are minimized. Most accidents are caused by a chain of events rather than a single occurrence. The chances of an accident happening are increased by the following:
□ If your child is tired, ill or hungry.
□ If the mother is pre-menstrual, tired or pregnant.

□ If your child is considered hyperactive.
□ When there's great excitement in the home, like going on holiday or expecting the arrival of a new baby.
□ If you and your partner aren't getting on, or if you're actually rowing.
□ If your child hasn't got anywhere safe to play.
□ If the correct safety precautions haven't been followed.
□ If the equipment you use for your baby doesn't comply with safety standards.

SAFETY EQUIPMENT
As soon as your child becomes mobile you must protect him from potentially dangerous objects or situations in the house.

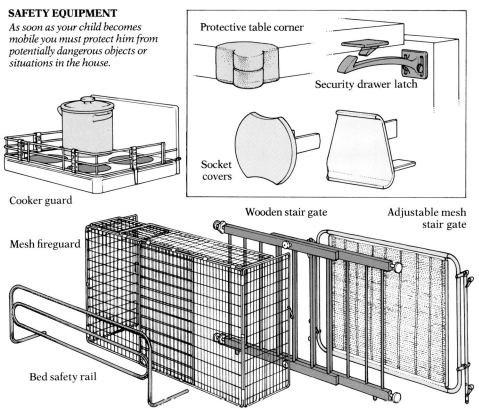

Protective table corner

Security drawer latch

Socket covers

Cooker guard

Mesh fireguard

Wooden stair gate

Adjustable mesh stair gate

Bed safety rail

ROOM-BY-ROOM SAFETY

GENERAL TIPS

● Buy all medicines in childproof bottles, and always keep them out of the reach of your child in a locked medicine chest.

● Always keep medicines and chemicals in the clearly labelled containers that they originally came in. Never put a poison into a bottle which previously held anything harmless like lemonade or squash.

● Store all drugs and chemicals as far away from food as possible.

● Don't leave aerosol cans lying around – the nozzle could easily be depressed by your child and could cause eye damage.

● Always keep a fireguard in front of a fire.

● Make sure that the flex of electrical appliances is kept out of the reach of your child.

● All electrical flex should be in good condition and not frayed or otherwise damaged.

● Fit safety socket covers to all power points.

● Cover hot radiators and pipes with towels or seal them off with pieces of furniture. Teach your child from an early age that radiators are hot and shouldn't be touched.

● Screen and bar all upper storey windows and never leave anything that your child could climb up on near them.

● If you own a gun always store it, with its ammunition, in a locked cupboard.

● Keep pins, needles, matches, lighters, sharp knives and scissors out of the reach of your child, in a locked or childproof drawer.

● Buy flame-resistant clothing for your child.

● Any furniture you have should be too solid and heavy for your child to pull over.

The bathroom

☐ Make sure that it is possible to open your bathroom and lavatory door from the outside.

☐ Medicines, scissors and razor blades should be kept out of your child's reach.

☐ Don't leave perfumes and cosmetics lying around.

☐ Keep the lavatory lid closed.

☐ When you run your child's bath always run the cold in first so there's no risk of his being scalded; test the water before putting your child in.

☐ Fit handles to the sides of the bath.

☐ Use a non-slip bath mat.

☐ Have a non-slip floor surface.

☐ Teach your child how to swim as soon as possible.

☐ Any windows should be barred and fitted with safety catches.

☐ The bathroom cabinet, which must have a childproof lock, should be out of the reach of your child.

☐ Don't fit a bathroom cabinet above the lavatory – your child could climb up on the seat to open it.

☐ Never leave your child alone in the bath.

☐ Electrical bathroom heaters should be fixed high on the wall.

☐ Hot towel rails should be covered with towels and your child should be taught from an early age that they're hot and shouldn't be touched.

☐ Don't mix lavatory cleaners with bleach as they can give off dangerous fumes.

☐ Keep all cleaning agents, bleaches and disinfectants in a locked cupboard.

All heaters should be
wall-mounted

Put heated towel rails
out of your child's
reach

Have a childproof
lock on the medicine
cabinet

Have safety handles
on the bath

Have non-slip bath
mats

Keep the lavatory lid
closed

Lock away all
cleaning substances

325

The kitchen
☐ The floors should be non-slip.
☐ All work surfaces should be well lit.
☐ The floor should be uncluttered.
☐ Windows and glazed doors should be fitted with toughened safety glass.
☐ Try to use sliding doors on cabinets. If this isn't possible keep the doors closed and preferably locked.
☐ Keep drawers closed and locked if possible.
☐ Always wipe up spilled liquid at once.
☐ Keep work surfaces as clear as possible so that sharp implements such as knives can be spotted immediately.
☐ Fit a cooker guard.
☐ Never leave a boiling pan or chip pan unattended on the stove.
☐ Always turn the handles of pans towards the back of the stove.
☐ Never reach across a heated burner or ring; you could knock a pan off the stove.
☐ Whenever using electrical equipment always follow the manufacturer's instructions exactly.
☐ Don't use tablecloths. Even a crawling baby can reach up and pull whatever's on the table on top of himself.
☐ Keep matches in a safe, cool place.
☐ Don't cook with your toddler around you. Arrange a play area in a special part of the kitchen so that you can still talk to each other.
☐ Keep the flex on any electrical equipment short.
☐ Don't store things that you use frequently on a high shelf. When you have to reach into a high place stand on a well-made kitchen ladder, and make sure that your balance is good before you reach up.
☐ Always keep cloths away from the stove in case of fire.
☐ Buy a dishwasher or washing machine with a safety lock on it.
☐ Keep a fire blanket next to the stove in case anything catches fire.
☐ Keep plastic bags well out of reach of your child.
☐ Your child's fingers could easily catch in a swing door. Either get rid of it or secure it in an open position.

☐ Never leave a room with the iron on; it's all too easy for your child to topple both board and iron on top of himself.
☐ Any glasses that your child uses should be unbreakable.

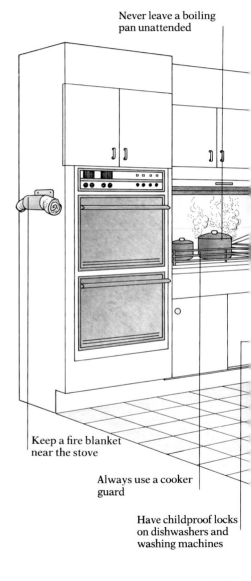

Never leave a boiling pan unattended

Keep a fire blanket near the stove

Always use a cooker guard

Have childproof locks on dishwashers and washing machines

Have a special play area for your child

☐ Keep your baby and his toys away from the immediate cooking area so that there's no risk of your tripping and spilling hot liquid over him. Either put him in a play pen, baby bouncer or chair.

☐ If you put your child in a play pen in the kitchen make sure that it is at least two feet away from your work tops.

☐ Store all cleaning materials – bleach or soap powders – out of reach of your child.

Keep knives well away from your child

Store all cleaning substances out of reach

Put pets' bowls out of your child's reach

Make any clear glass more obvious by putting transfers on it

Don't have long flexes on electrical appliances

327

The living room

☐ Run flexes around the walls.
☐ Disconnect appliances when not in use.
☐ Keep flex on electrical appliances short.
☐ Don't place hot or heavy objects on low tables.
☐ All shelving should be securely fixed to the wall and should be well out of the reach of your child.
☐ Anything breakable should be out of the reach of your child.

☐ Use a fixed fire guard with a fine wire mesh.
☐ Fit safety glass to windows, especially French windows, so that it won't shatter even if your child falls on to it.
☐ Never leave hot or alcoholic drinks lying around within reach of your child.
☐ Don't leave lighters or matches lying about.
☐ Keep the television out of reach.
☐ Make sure your houseplants aren't poisonous (see p.330–331).

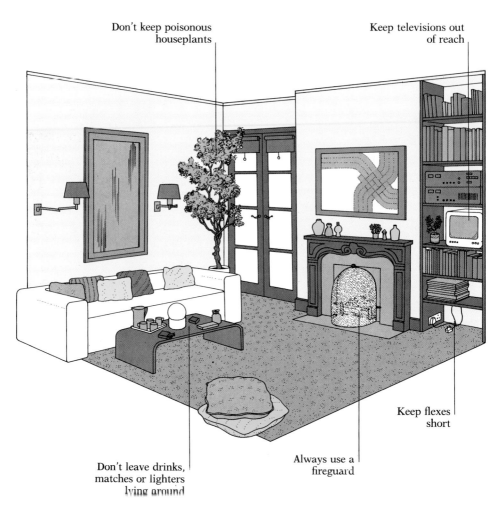

Don't keep poisonous houseplants

Keep televisions out of reach

Keep flexes short

Don't leave drinks, matches or lighters lying around

Always use a fireguard

The bedroom

☐ Put bars and safety locks on all windows and don't leave furniture near them.
☐ All furniture should have rounded corners; if it doesn't, put on special plastic safety corners.
☐ Store toys and games at a low level so that your child doesn't have to stretch or be tempted to climb up to get at them.
☐ Don't leave toys lying around on the floor.
☐ Don't put an electric fire anywhere near your child's bed at night because he could throw off his blanket or quilt and cause a fire.
☐ If the bedroom's upstairs leave a safety gate at the top of the stairs.
☐ Buy non-flammable nightclothes.
☐ Wall-mounted lights are safer because they have no flexes trailing on the floor.
☐ Never leave your baby with the cot side down.
☐ Never leave your baby alone on the changing table, even for a second.

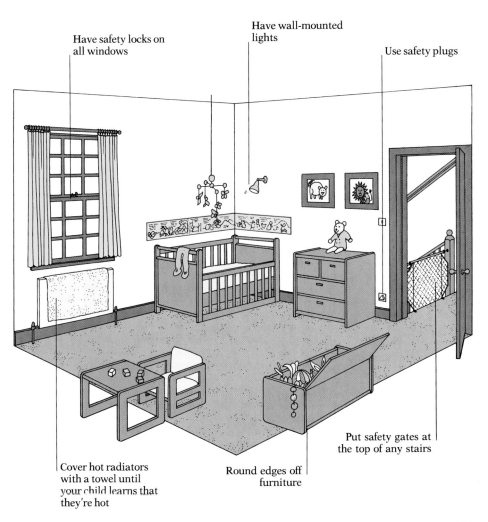

Have safety locks on all windows

Have wall-mounted lights

Use safety plugs

Cover hot radiators with a towel until your child learns that they're hot

Round edges off furniture

Put safety gates at the top of any stairs

Halls, stairs and passageways

☐ Fit a safety gate to the top and bottom of the stairs.
☐ Never leave anything lying on or near the stairs. Make sure that doors, hallways and stairs are well lit.
☐ Electric switches should be in convenient places.
☐ Bannisters should be secure and only have narrow gaps.
☐ Don't have open-plan staircases – your child could easily fall between the stairs or off to one side.
☐ Stair carpets should be fitted well so that they don't slip. Any tears or holes should be patched immediately with heavy-duty tape.

The garden

☐ Have childproof locks on all gates.
☐ Fence off a swimming pool or pond.
☐ Never leave a paddling pool with water in it; empty it and either deflate it or store it upside down.
☐ Fit any rainwater butts or similar water-collecting devices with a lid. Your child can drown in as little as 5 cm (two inches) of water.
☐ Remove all poisonous plants from the garden.
☐ Pull up any mushrooms or toadstools as soon as they appear.
☐ Bury any animal excreta before your child has the chance to poke it, play with it or even eat it.

POISONOUS PLANTS

▲ *Causes skin irritation*
▨ *Causes mouth- and throat-lining irritation*
◉ *Causes stomach and intestinal irritation*
◆ *Causes poisoning of the system*

Poison oak

Houseplants

Caladium	▨ ◉
Castor Bean	◉ ◆
Dieffenbachia	▲ ▨
Elephant's ear	▲ ▨
Mistletoe	◉ ◆
Philodendron	▲ ▨
Poinsettia	▲

Ivy	◉
Laurel	◆
Oleander	◆
Rhododendron	◆
Wisteria	◉
Yew	◉

Jack-in-the-Pulpit	▨ ◉
Mayapple	◉
Moonseed	◆
Poison Ivy	▲
Poison Oak	▲
Rosary Pea	◆
Snakeroot	◉ ◆
Yellow Jessamine	◆

Flower Garden

Autumn Crocus	◆
Belladonna Lily	◉ ◆
Christmas Rose	▲ ◉
Daffodil	◉
Foxglove	▲
Hyacinth	◉
Hydrangea	◉ ◆
Iris	◉
Larkspur	◆
Lily of the Valley	◆

Rhododendron

Forest Growth

Baneberry	◉ ◆
Bittersweet	◉ ◆
Bloodroot	◉ ◆
Deadly Amanita	◆
Fly Agaric Mushroom	◆

Poinsettia

Ornamental

Bleeding Heart	▲ ◆
Daphne	▲ ▨ ◉

☐ Store all gardening tools in a locked shed.
☐ When mowing the lawn keep your toddler well away.
☐ Never work on your car when your child is playing outside.
☐ Your clothes line should be at a higher level than your child can reach.
☐ Lock away all pesticides, plant sprays and car cleaners.
☐ Never leave lengths of rope lying about.
☐ Fence off your rubbish bins so that your child can't get in and rummage about inside them.
☐ Make regular checks on the safety of any swings, slides or climbing frames in your garden.

ROAD SAFETY
It's never too early to teach your child the safety code for crossing the road. Whenever you want to cross the street always go to a pedestrian crossing. Stop by the kerb, hold your child's reins or his hand, look in both directions for traffic and listen. If traffic is coming, let it pass. Look in both directions again and when nothing is coming walk across; don't run. Continue to look and listen as you cross. Keep up a running commentary of what you're doing and why, what you're looking for and what you're listening for.

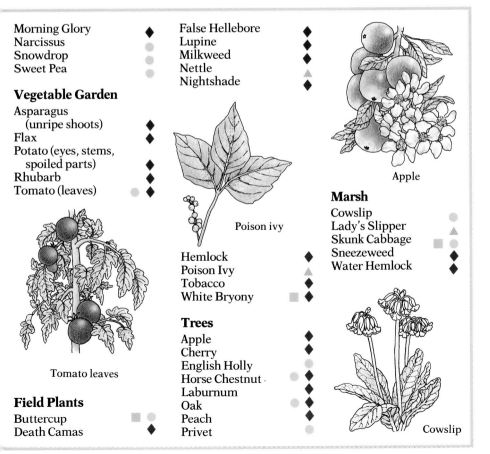

Morning Glory ◆
Narcissus
Snowdrop
Sweet Pea

False Hellebore ◆
Lupine ◆
Milkweed ◆
Nettle ▲
Nightshade ◆

Vegetable Garden

Asparagus
  (unripe shoots) ◆
Flax ◆
Potato (eyes, stems,
  spoiled parts) ◆
Rhubarb ◆
Tomato (leaves) ◆

Poison ivy

Hemlock ◆
Poison Ivy ▲
Tobacco ◆
White Bryony ◆

Trees

Apple ◆
Cherry ◆
English Holly
Horse Chestnut ◆
Laburnum ◆
Oak ◆
Peach ◆
Privet

Apple

Marsh

Cowslip
Lady's Slipper
Skunk Cabbage
Sneezeweed ◆
Water Hemlock ◆

Tomato leaves

Field Plants

Buttercup
Death Camas ◆

Cowslip

331

EMERGENCY FIRST AID

A basic knowledge of first aid is always useful; the knowledge could help save your child's life in an extreme situation.

Choking

Hold a small baby face down and pat his back between the shoulder blades to dislodge the foreign body from his windpipe. The best way is to support him along your forearm, but you can also hold him upside down. With an older child hold him firmly around the waist and tip him forward over your arm until his head is at about the level of your knee. Then go through the same procedure as described for a baby, sharply hitting his back between the shoulder blades until he coughs up the object. Your child may only cough the object into his mouth. To prevent reinhalation hold his head and chin steady with your left hand and hook the object out with your right forefinger. Be very careful not to push whatever's in his mouth back down his throat. If you're at all concerned about your child, seek medical aid immediately.

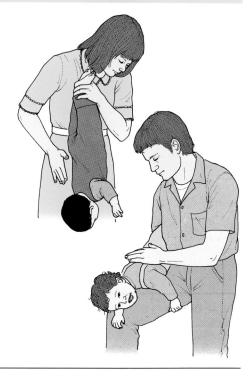

Heavy bleeding

1 Take any piece of clean cloth and press the edges of the wound together until the blood clots and bleeding stops.

2 If there's a bone protruding, or if there's something in the wound like glass, press round rather than on it.
3 Lay your child on the ground and raise the affected limb above the level of his body – this both cuts down on the amount of blood that gets to the limb and allows blood to flow to the vital organs (brain, heart, kidneys) more quickly which counters the risk of shock. Contact your doctor as soon as possible because the wound will probably need stitching.

4 If your child is bleeding from a place that is difficult to compress, like the groin, lay him down and flatten the blood vessel that is bleeding by pressing your fist or the heel of your hand against the underlying bone.

Unconsciousness

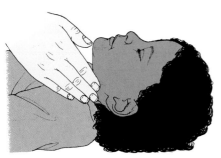

1 First check that your child is still breathing and that you can feel his pulse. The easiest place to feel it is a short way under the jaw in line with the tip of the ear lobe; this is the carotid artery.

2 Having done this, put your child into the recovery position. Turn your child on to his stomach and bend one of his arms up to support the upper body. Bend his knee up to support the lower body and turn his head to one side. Dial for an ambulance immediately. If your child isn't breathing you must give him mouth-to-mouth resuscitation.

Mouth-to-mouth resuscitation

1 Tilt your child's head back so that the airway is open, and check that nothing's blocking his throat.

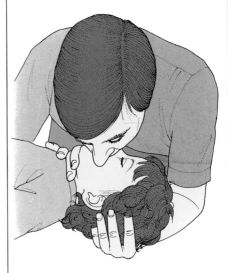

2 For a baby up to 12 months, seal your lips around his nose and mouth and breathe into his lungs at a rate of ten breaths per minute. For a child one year or over, seal his mouth only and pinch his nose. Check his breathing after four inflations. (If the casualty is a baby, puff very gently into the lungs.) Continue doing this until breathing starts again then place him in the recovery position. Seek medical assistance as soon as possible.

333

External chest compression

If mouth-to-mouth resuscitation by itself is unsuccessful and your child's heart stops, you must perform external chest compression in conjunction with mouth-to-mouth ventilation.

Resuscitation must be continued until the circulation returns and the pulse is felt. If it is difficult to feel the carotid pulse in an infant, check the brachial pulse. This can be located on the inside of the upper arm, halfway between shoulder and elbow. Place your thumb on the outside of the arm and your index and middle fingers on the inside. Press your fingertips lightly towards the bone to find the pulse.

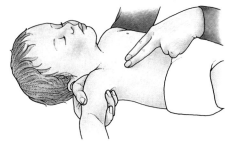 

For babies under two

Place your index finger centrally between your baby's nipples. Then place the next two fingers just below the centre of the breastbone and press down sharply to a depth of 2.5cm (1in) five times in three seconds.

For children

Lay your child on his back on a firm surface. Place the heel of one hand just below the centre of the breastbone. Using light pressure, press at a rate of 100 compressions per minute, to a depth of 2.5-3.5 cm (1-1½ in), with 5 compressions to one ventilation.

Shock

Often after a traumatic injury, one that is accompanied by excessive bleeding, severe burns, recurrent vomiting, severe diarrhoea, or extreme pain or fear, a child will fall into a shocked state. Symptoms include pale, cold, clammy skin; shallow and rapid breathing with yawning and sighing; sickness and vomiting, and, most seriously, unconsciousness. If you suspect shock in your child, you should act immediately. Send someone for medical help while you attend to her.

1 Lay her down, preferably on a blanket and keep her head low and to one side so that any fluid in her mouth can drain. Raise her legs, unless you suspect a broken bone, to keep the circulating blood in the centre of the body.

2 Loosen any tight clothing and, if it is cold, cover your child with a blanket. Do not use a hot water bottle or electric blanket.

3 If your child becomes unconscious, follow the techniques on page 333. If breathing or heartbeat stops, begin mouth-to-mouth resuscitation and external chest compression. Do not give your child anything to eat or drink. If she's thirsty, simply moisten her lips with water.

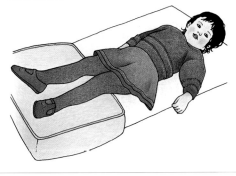

Electric shock

Switch off the power source immediately. If you cannot locate the power source *don't* touch your child; you could get a shock yourself. Find something which does not conduct electricity, such as a piece of wood or plastic tubing, and use it to push your child away from the wire or socket. Make sure that whatever you use, and your hands, are dry before you do this. If his breathing has stopped send for medical help, then give mouth-to-mouth resuscitation.

Sometimes an electric shock can cause medical shock, with low blood pressure, thready pulse, pale face, clammy skin, sweating, dizziness and rapid breathing. If this is the case take your child immediately to the nearest hospital casualty department. If it is only a frightening shock reassure your child and then lie with him until he has settled down.

Clothing on Fire

1 Fire rises; it is also made worse if your child runs around in a panic. If your child is on fire put him on the ground as quickly as possible with the flames uppermost.

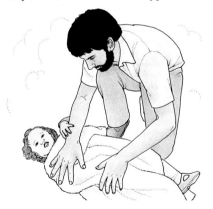

2 Wrap the child firmly in a blanket, bath towel or coat, made from cotton or wool (not synthetic fabrics which melt in contact with the heat). Roll your child over and over on the floor to smother the flames.

3 If there's nothing available lie on the child yourself to smother the flames, but make sure that you lie flat or a tunnel will be created and could cause the flames to fan up and set you on fire too. Have your child examined by a doctor as soon as possible.

335

Burns

Burns need urgent treatment because of the risk of infection and, with deep burns, shock. Superficial burns, those involving damage only to the skin, can be treated safely at home. Deep burns, which affect the entire thickness of the skin, must be treated by a doctor.

1 Remove your child from the source of danger and comfort him, as burns can be very painful.

2 Cool the affected area immediately, under cold running water or in a cool bath for at least 10 to 20 minutes; this stops the heat damaging your child's skin further.

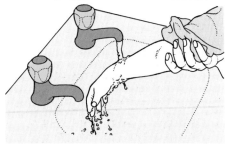

Make certain a young child isn't made too cold.

3 Carefully cut away and remove any clothes soaked in boiling fluid or chemicals, making sure you do not burn your fingers. Do not remove clothes if you think you will cause further damage to the skin.

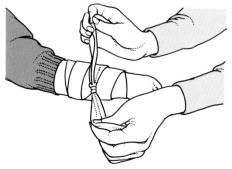

4 Cover the injury with a sterile dressing or similar non-fluffy material, larger than the burn. Do not put any fats, ointments or lotions on a burn.

Broken bones

Rough play not infrequently results in broken bones. Children are most prone to greenstick fractures, where the bone bends rather than breaks, and where there is minimal damage to the skin. Suspect a fracture if your child cannot move the affected area normally or without pain; if there is bruising and/or swelling around the site of the injury; if the area appears deformed.

1 Don't try to straighten any bent or curved limb. If there is a serious wound or if bone is sticking through the skin, cover the area with a sterile dressing. Don't touch the wound.

2 If there is no bone sticking through the skin, immobilize the joints above and below the affected area to prevent worsening of the injury; put an affected arm in a sling; immobilize a leg by tying knees and ankles together. If possible, keep the affected part raised.

3 Do not give your child anything to eat or drink in case he needs to be given a general anaesthetic.

4 Call an ambulance if the bone is sticking through, otherwise take your child to the nearest casualty department.

Hypothermia

Hypothermia develops when the body temperature falls below a certain level – usually by exposure to extreme cold outdoors or inadequate heating indoors.

A baby who has become dangerously chilled will appear quiet, drowsy and limp and will refuse food. His hands, feet and face may be bright pink. If you suspect hypothermia in your baby, you should request urgent medical help. In the meantime get into bed or a sleeping bag with him so that he is warmed up gently by the heat of your body.

Poisoning

If you even suspect that your child has swallowed a poison contact your doctor or local hospital immediately. You child may have severe stomach pains and will probably vomit. Hold him in such a way that there's no risk of his inhaling and choking on any vomit. *Never* attempt to induce vomiting in your child – you could cause more harm if what he's swallowed is corrosive. Corrosive substances include caustic soda, weed killers, paraffin, disinfectant, bleach and other ammonia-based household cleaners. Look for signs of burning around his mouth. If there are any he's probably swallowed one of these substances. Give him water or milk to drink to cool the burning.

If your child's unconscious place him in the recovery position; if he's stopped breathing give him mouth-to-mouth re-suscitation, taking care not to burn your own mouth.

FIRST AID KIT
1 A packet of absorbent cotton wool
2 Sterile gauze squares in various sizes
3 A box of adhesive dressings in various sizes
4 A roll of 5 cm (2 in) gauze bandage
5 2 or 3 crêpe bandages
6 A roll of 2.5 cm (1 in) adhesive tape
7 A sterilized eye pad with bandages
8 Triangular bandage made of a stiff material
9 Safety pins
10 Blunt-ended tweezers
11 Blunt-ended scissors
12 A simple antiseptic cream.
13 Milk of magnesia for indigestion
14 Sun screen with the highest protection factor
15 Junior paracetamol
16 Calamine lotion
17 A bottle of antiseptic for cleaning wounds
18 Insect-repellant spray

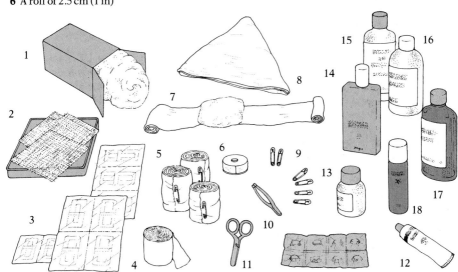

Home medicine

Any parent is going to be distressed when his or her child becomes ill. The difficulty can lie in not being able to identify what's wrong with the child and in not being able to tell how serious the ailment really is. All children get ill at some stage but modern medicine is so efficient that few illnesses now pose the threat that they once did. Doctors are on hand to identify and prescribe for the ailment, it's the parent's job to provide the essential nursing and comfort.

WHEN TO CALL YOUR DOCTOR 0–3

You must start off believing that most doctors won't mind if you consult them for reassurance. Along with many other doctors I very quickly learned that one person whose opinion can't be dismissed is the mother's. A mother usually knows instinctively if her child is well or not. And if any sensible mother feels strongly enough that her child is unwell then a doctor ignores this at his or her peril. So when in doubt consult your doctor, especially if any of the following signs is noted:

Temperature
● If the temperature rises above 38°C (100°) and your baby is obviously ill.
● If the temperature rises above 39.4°C (103°F) even if there are no apparent signs of illness.
● When a fever, having been high, drops and then rises again.
● When the temperature is accompanied by infantile convulsions (see p.352).
● When your child has a stiff neck, a headache and sensitivity to light, as well as a fever.
● When your child has had a temperature of more than 38°C (100°F) for three days.
● When your baby's skin feels cold and he is drowsy, unusually quiet and limp though his face, hands and feet are pink (possibly hypothermia).

● If the fever is accompanied by a rash, especially of red or purple blood spots that don't disappear when pressed. Check this by using the base of a glass and looking through it.

Wounds
● When your child has had any kind of serious accident or burn.
● When your child has lost consciousness no matter how briefly.
● When the wound is deep or has caused serious loss of blood.
● When your child has been bitten by an animal, a human or a snake.
● When acid gets into your child's eye.
● When the eye has actually been pierced by an object.

Pain and discomfort
● When your child feels sick and dizzy and complains of headaches.
● When your child complains of blurred vision, especially after being hit on the head.
● When your child has severe griping pains at regular intervals.
● When your child has a pain in the right side of his stomach and feels sick.

Breathing
● If your child's breathing becomes laboured and you notice that his ribs are being drawn sharply inwards with each breath.

Loss of appetite
- If your child's normally a good eater.
- If your baby's under six months.

Vomiting
- If the vomiting is violent, prolonged or excessive.
- If your baby is very young – it may cause rapid dehydration.

Diarrhoea
- If your baby's very young – it could cause dehydration.
- If it is accompanied by abdominal pain, temperature or any obvious illness.

What to tell your doctor
Once you've decided to call your doctor he or she will probably ask you the following questions. It's important to give accurate answers.

☐ "What is the baby's temperature and were there any fluctuations in it – if so, what were the readings?"

☐ "Was the onset of the fever quick or slow?"

☐ "Is the child's throat red? Does it have any white spots?"

☐ "Are the neck glands swollen?"

☐ "Are there any additional symptoms like vomiting or diarrhoea?"

USING A THERMOMETER   0–3

Your child's temperature will probably fluctuate between 36°C and 37.5°C (97.5°F and 99.5°F). It will be at its lowest at night when your child is asleep and highest in the afternoon; it'll also be high if your child has been running around.

Although you'll probably be able to tell your child is feverish just by looking at him there may be occasions when you have to take his temperature. Don't, however, rely on the temperature reading as an accurate reflection of your baby's health. Children can be very ill with no fever, or well with a high temperature.

Types of thermometer available
Clinical thermometers come in a variety of styles. It does not matter which you use, but you should not try to take the temperature by mouth until your child is six or seven years old and can be relied on not to bite the thermometer. It is possible to buy special baby thermometers that give readings down to 25°C (77°) – this is useful as babies lose heat more rapidly than adults and can have a lower temperature than normal when ill. Another feature to look out for is the time the thermometer takes to register – some take only 30 seconds, although using the armpit method (see opposite page) always takes longer than taking a reading by mouth.

The latest digital thermometers are particularly good, with an easy-to-read digital display, and a high degree of accuracy. You can also use simple temperature indicator (liquid crystal) strips which are reusable. They are made from heat-sensitive plastic that you place against your baby's forehead. Although less accurate than conventional thermometers, they do give a quick indication of whether your child has a fever.

Reading a conventional thermometer
Holding the thermometer up to the light, rotate it between your first finger and thumb until you can see the mercury column quite clearly. You will see a thin line when the column is viewed from the side and a thick line when it's viewed straight on. It is the thick line that you should observe. Before taking your baby's temperature always check to make sure that the column of mercury is well down below the beginning of the scale.

On the front of the thermometer there is a scale with a small arrow at 36.9°C (98.6°F) which is the average, normal body temperature. Having taken your child's temperature for the required amount of time, remove the thermometer, wipe it and read it. Wash with soap and cold water before storing.

TAKING A TEMPERATURE READING
By conventional thermometer
Rotate the thermometer until you see a thick strip of mercury. Read the temperature off the mercury column.

Normal temperature

By digital thermometer
Read off the temperature from the digital display. Some models have a facility to recall previous reading.

Normal temperature

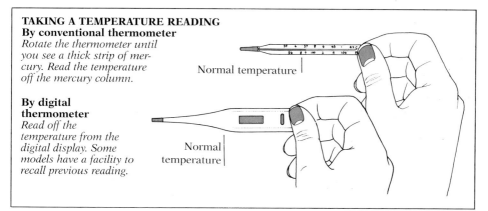

Taking your child's temperature

The best method of taking an accurate measurement of your baby's temperature is to hold the thermometer under one arm. In the past some people used the rectal method, but this is no longer recommended because of the danger of puncturing delicate tissues. It's not sensible to try taking the temperature by mouth until your child is at least seven years old, and can understand that she should not bite the thermometer, although the digital thermometer is safer than the conventional thermometer from this point of view.

ARMPIT METHOD

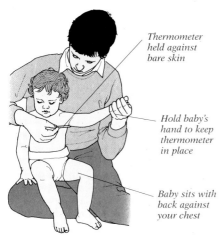

Thermometer held against bare skin

Hold baby's hand to keep thermometer in place

Baby sits with back against your chest

Remove your baby's clothes and sit her on your knee with her back against your chest. Using a digital or mercury thermometer, place the bulb in the centre of your baby's bare armpit. Hold her arm to her side and keep the thermometer in place for three minutes. The temperature in the armpit is about 0.6° (1°F) less than the actual internal body temperature.

STRIP METHOD

Hold the temperature indicator strip at both ends with your finger and thumb and press it flush to the centre of your baby's forehead. Hold it gently in place with your thumbs, allowing your other fingers to encircle your baby's head so that the baby doesn't shake the strip free before it has had a chance to register the temperature. Keep your fingers clear of the numbered panels. Leave the strip in place for about 15 seconds. Numbers and colour panels will show up in sequence, before coming to rest at the reading for your baby's temperature. Most strips indicate a level for normal (often indicated by the letter N) and levels for fever.

341

GIVING MEDICINE 0-1

Most baby medicines are made up as paediatric syrup which has to be taken with a spoon or a dropper. With a newborn baby make sure that any implements used have been sterilized in a sterilizing solution. Your baby may start to cry when he takes the medicine. Don't worry about this; it's far more important that your baby swallows it and keeps it down. When a child is ill I think the importance of taking the medicine outweighs every other consideration; this is one situation in which blackmail is justifiable. Do this by using the most powerful reward that you can think of as a means of getting your baby to accept the medicine.

USING A DROPPER

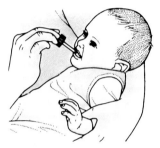

Cradle your baby in the crook of your arm so that his head is slightly upright – never have him lying flat because this makes swallowing difficult. Take up the amount of medicine specified into the dropper's glass tube. Place the dropper in the corner of your baby's mouth and gently compress the teat.

USING A SPOON

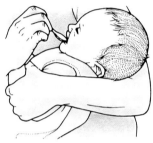

Sterilize the spoon. Sit with your baby on your lap and gently open your baby's mouth by pulling down his chin. Place the tip of the spoon on to his lower lip, raise the angle of the spoon and gently let the medicine run into his mouth at the right speed for comfortable swallowing.

USING YOUR FINGER

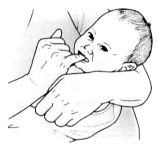

If both the dropper and the spoon prove ineffective try dipping a carefully-washed little finger into your baby's medicine and letting him suck it off. It's more important that your baby takes the medicine than that he takes it in an orthodox way.

ADMINISTERING DROPS

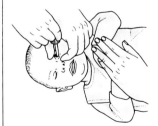

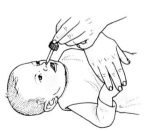

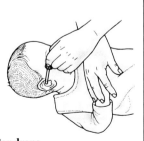

Eye drops
Pull down his lower lid and let the drops fall between his eye and the eyelid. Get someone to hold the baby still.

Nose drops
Lay your baby on a flat surface and angle his head backwards. Gently drop the liquid into each nostril.

Ear drops
Lay your child with his head to one side before administering the drops in the usual way.

GIVING MEDICINE   1–3

Medicines for older children usually come in a liquid form, which is simply taken off a spoon, or in tablet form. Ear or nose drops would be given in the same way as for a younger baby. If your child is making a great deal of noise about having drops you *must* keep calm. Get your partner to help you by holding the child firmly while you administer them.

As your child gets older try not to make a fuss, or be very insistent that he takes the medicine as this will make your child respond negatively. It usually helps if you show your child that you are willing to take some yourself. If your child really doesn't like the taste then try diluting it with your child's favourite drink.

Giving tablets
If the doctor prescribes tablets for your child make them more palatable by crushing them between two spoons and then mixing them with a spoonful of honey, jam or ice cream. Whatever the medicine is

make sure that you follow your doctor's instructions precisely, giving the medicine at the intervals stated. This is important because some medicines have to have constantly high blood levels in order to be effective and the level of medicine in the blood will drop if the interval between doses is longer than stated.

Put the tablets between two spoons, as shown, and press down on them. Mix the tablets with honey, jam or thick yogurt and give this to your child.

NURSING YOUR CHILD   0–3

Few mothers will escape being called upon to act as a nurse – all children fall ill at some time. Mothers, however, make excellent nurses because they put the health and comfort of their children before almost anything else. Many children become "mummyish" when they are ill and want to be with their mothers all the time. Very often it's not just the mother's company they require but the mother's physical contact. Ill babies need a lot more nursing, cuddling and affection than usual. If you're still breast-feeding you'll probably find that your baby wants more "comfort sucks". You should make sure that these are given.

Should he go to bed?
Unless your doctor advises otherwise, you should trust your own common sense and your child's natural inclinations. If he wants to stay up he should be allowed to

do so. Even if he has a temperature he should be allowed to stay up if he wants to. But do make sure that he gets plenty to drink so that he doesn't become dehydrated, that he rests when he feels tired and that the room temperature is kept even and warm.

There is nothing sacrosanct about bedrooms either. One of the most potent medicines is the sight and sound of you and the reassurance they bring, so your sick child will be very much better off being near you. If possible rig up a couch, sofa or comfortable chair so that he can be in the same room as you. This way your child will have the opportunity of seeing, talking to and being entertained by anyone who comes into the house rather than being cut off from the rest of the family in his bedroom. When your child is tired, however, it is time to put him to bed. But don't just leave him alone. Make sure that you visit him at regular intervals (every half an hour), and find the time to stay and play a game, read a book, or do a puzzle. If you have other children, encourage them to do the same thing.

When he's on the road to recovery make sure that enough happens in his day to make the distinction between night and day. If he hasn't been watching television, let him watch it before he goes to sleep. Then read him a story to calm and quieten him, as you would usually do.

Feeding your sick child

There are no longer any hard and fast rules about the sort of food that you should give your child when he's sick and unless directed by your doctor you can feed your child whatever he wants. It's time for you to relax most of the rules, dietary and otherwise. Let him eat and drink what he wants, and as much as he wants. You'll probably find that he prefers little but often. If your child is off his food never force him to eat. For two or three days food really isn't important, but liquids are. If your child has a temperature, and especially if he's vomiting, you should make sure that he drinks plenty of liquids (at least one litre a day). The most nutritious liquids are probably milk and fresh fruit juices. If your child isn't keen on milk you can disguise it as milk shakes and flavoured drinks, custards and ice cream; yogurt can also take the place of milk. Fresh fruit juices with all their vitamins and minerals are excellent, so indulge your child in his favourites. There is nothing especially nutritious about the fizzy glucose drinks that are recommended.

Even although your child will seem to eat very sparsely while he's ill he will quickly make up the deficit as his appetite increases. The return of his appetite is invariably the sign that your child is on the mend. When he is on the road to recovery, spoil him with his favourite foods and perhaps those that have been previously restricted to treats. He'll be keen to make up for all the lost meals, and any weight-loss will be made up quickly.

Treating your child's temperature

The first thing that you have to do is make sure that your baby is not wearing too many clothes. Remove a few layers if he is; make sure that he is not covered by more than a couple of blankets and that there is a good supply of fresh air in the room (by leaving a window open slightly).

A good method of reducing your child's temperature if it's above 39.4°C (103°F) is by tepid sponging. This means exactly what it says: wiping your child's skin down with tepid water. You should check on your child's temperature every ten minutes when you are doing this and stop when the temperature falls below 38.5°C (102°F). There's no risk of chilling him if you stop as soon as this temperature is reached.

Cover a waterproof sheet with a towel and lay your child on it. Fill a basin with tepid water. Dip a sponge or a soft flannel into the tepid water then gently rub it all over your child's skin – first the face and then the trunk and the limbs. Tepid water allows the blood vessels to stay dilated and when the water evaporates from the surface of the skin it absorbs heat from the blood and has a cooling effect. Don't think that you will bring down the temperature faster by using cold water. You may not bring the temperature down at all because cold water causes the blood vessels of the skin to contract which means that the blood cannot lose heat efficiently. The faster the evaporation takes place, the greater the cooling effect, so if you have a fan it will help to bring your child's temperature down if you use it on him.

After tepid sponging make sure that your child's skin is dry. Do not dress him in pyjamas but cover him lightly with a cotton sheet. If his temperature rises again you can repeat the tepid sponging.

Keeping your child isolated?

We now know that there is no point in practising the old-fashioned rule of isolating a child with an infectious disease from the rest of the family. This practice, which involved sterilizing all utensils and having a separate laundry for the sick child's clothes and bed linen, is now out of date. It has been shown that there is little point in taking any of these precautions because most infections are caught and passed on within 48 hours and during this time the symptoms are very often unclear. The chance is that by the time your child develops a fever the other members of the family have been exposed to the bacterium or virus anyway, and will be carrying it themselves.

Keeping your sick child amused

When your child is ill relax all rules. Let him play whatever games he wants to, even if you've previously disallowed them in bed. If he wants to paint put a polythene sheet across the bed and let him get on with it. Be flexible about tidiness – the bedroom is bound to get untidy but don't make a fuss about it.

Your child could easily get bored lying in bed, especially if he's not really well enough to play by himself. If you can, move a television into his room – it will provide him with ready stimulation and will make him feel special which will do a lot to keep his spirits up. Make sure you'll be able to hear any demands for channel changes, or give your child the remote control device. Whatever else you do, give him your company. Sit on the side of his bed, cut pictures out of magazines for him, help him with his colouring book, play games, sing songs, chat, read a story – just be there. You're the best cure there is. As your child's nurse you're in a unique position to please your patient. You can turn his unhappiness into happiness and you should devote yourself completely to this task.

345

COMFORT AND RECUPERATION TIPS

● Give your child treats. For a sore throat give ice cream, for queasiness give mashed potato.

● Cool cotton sheets are soothing to a feverish child. Change the bed regularly.

● When your child is being sick always be there, and always cover his forehead with the palm of your hand. Give him something like a mint or a chocolate to suck afterwards to take away the bad taste.

● Put a table next to the bed for his toys, books, fruit juices or water.

● Make an invalid's work table by cutting a semi-circle out of an inverted cardboard box. This can be placed over your child's lap. Alternatively you can put a sanded wooden plank over two chairs, either side of the bed.

● Buy some new toys for your child. Don't give them to him all at once, but give them one at a time.

● If your child isn't feeling too ill you could try wrapping the toys up so that you can play a game together. Ask him to guess what's in the packages by feeling them, then let him have the fun of tearing all the paper off to see his present.

If your child has to go to hospital

It's almost inevitable that your child will have to go into hospital at some stage, although the majority of hospitals try to avoid admitting children under the age of four where at all possible because of the upset it causes, both to the child and to the parents. If, however, your child has to go in the following advice may help to make the situation less traumatic.

□ Don't lie to your child about what will happen. Explain why he's got to go in but say that you will see him most of the time that he's there.

□ Go with your child to the hospital. Well-run wards or departments allow the parent to undress the child and even provide beds so that the parent can be with the child for the length of his stay. Try to get your child admitted to such a hospital.

□ Make sure that you pack your child's comforter if he has one, as well as some of his favourite toys and games. This is very important. The worst aspect of going into hospital is the change in routine, removal from all that's familiar, and the people he loves and trusts most.

□ Expect your child to behave slightly oddly when he comes out of hospital. The stay in hospital may affect his sleeping rhythm as well as his bowel and bladder control. Take account of this; your child will gradually get back to normal.

□ If you know that your child is going to have to go into hospital you could introduce the idea of it during play. Buy a toy stethoscope and practise being a doctor on your child's teddy or dolls. Get your child to join in by handling your "instruments", maybe pretending to be the doctor.

□ Explain what hospitals are all about – how they are places to go to make people better (you could even explain that animals have hospitals, too). Make them seem as natural as fire stations or supermarkets are to your child.

□ Include books on hospitals or doctors in your child's "library". The more he reads and sees about hospitals the less frightening the experience will be.

☐ Don't do anything in the ward off your own bat. Ask nurses how you can most help and then do as the nurses say. Most nurses are extremely grateful for any help at all and you may find yourself helping with feeding, teaching, bathtimes etc.

☐ Be prepared to help children other than your own. Many children are in hospital without any visitors at all and a caring, loving word, a short game or a story read can be a great comfort to them.

☐ Be prepared to muck in. Don't make your visiting time simply a half an hour three times a day. Stay for several consecutive hours and do anything that's necessary. Your child will love to see you and will feel a great deal happier when you're not there if you spend several hours with him and keep your promises about visiting.

☐ If your child is extremely sick, even unconscious, still visit regularly and spend time with him. If you can, talk to him, read a story to him, play his favourite music, don't remain silent, make as many sounds as you can. Children respond to many different sounds even smells. It might be worth recording, for instance, the bark of your child's dog, or the voice of a baby brother or sister and playing it to them repeatedly by the bedside.

MEDICAL INDEX

Asthma

In a person suffering from asthma the allergic reaction shows itself in the lining of the air passages. This lining is very sensitive. It not only responds to the allergen with wheezing but it also responds more than usual to infection and emotional disturbances. The lining of the airways goes into spasm and secretes large amounts of mucus. Your child will have difficulty breathing out, his face will become pale and his lips may even turn blue. The allergen that causes your child's asthma will be something that he's inhaled. It can be dust, pollen, feathers or fungal spores. As mentioned on page 349, many small babies wheeze if they have an attack of bronchitis or bronchiolitis (inflammation of the smaller tubes). This baby can legitimately be labelled a wheezy baby but it is wrong to condemn all babies who wheeze with the label asthmatic. They are not. Once they grow a little bigger and the bronchial tubes become wider the wheezing will stop. This condition is not allergic in origin.

What to do

If attacks of asthma persist in your child ask your doctor to refer you to a paediatric chest physician who can sort out any problems for you. As your child gets older the consultant will probably test him to various allergens to see if he is hypersensitive to a specific substance. If this substance is isolated you can then do something about avoiding it. For instance, if your child is sensitive to feathers and house dust (both of these being very common causes of allergy), you will have to get rid of any bedding which contains feathers, down or hair, and you will have to make sure that the furnishings plus the carpets and curtains in your child's room do not hold a lot of dust. The clue to a house dust allergy is a small mite (the house dust mite) which lives in house dust and causes the allergic condition. There are nearly always more mites in damp houses than in dry ones, so there is a scientific rationale for a child's asthma being worse in a damp house than in a dry house.

Besides the allergic component of asthma there is nearly always an emotional one. While asthmatic children tend to be very bright and intelligent, they are also very sensitive children. They need a lot of care and attention and they reward you with their happiness and friendliness. If your paediatrician suggests that emotional factors are playing an important part in your child's asthma then it is up to you and your family to see what you can do about improving the atmosphere in the home and minimizing stress in your child's life.

It is very important that you and the rest of the family don't get asthma out of perspective. Many parents of asthmatic children are over-anxious and over-protective, and over-stress the condition so that eventually the whole household revolves around the asthmatic child. This is an unwise way of behaving because your child may soon learn how to manipulate you and the rest of the household around his asthma attacks.

The treatment of asthma is rather complicated so make sure that you get very clear instructions from the paediatrician as to what you should do under certain circumstances, and certainly what you should do if an asthma attack comes on suddenly out of the blue.

Balanitis

This is the inflammation of the tip of the penis in uncircumcised boys. It may be caused by nappy rash, which is often a reaction to detergent or it can be due to an infection. It is not serious but for the child's comfort, you should treat it promptly. The penis will be red and swollen, there may be a pussy discharge from the tip and the foreskin cannot be drawn back.

What to do
If you notice any redness around the tip of the penis, draw back the foreskin very gently. If the foreskin won't draw back, leave it and consult your doctor. If the foreskin will retract, wash and dry the penis thoroughly and apply a simple antiseptic ointment such as Savlon. If your child is really in pain consult your doctor. He may prescribe an antibiotic cream to relieve the inflammation and infection. If the foreskin is tight your doctor will wish to see your child again to check it and, if it fails to be stretched by the time your boy is six, he may need circumcision.

Bites
The chances of your child being bitten by an animal like a dog, or another child are relatively high; the chances of your child being bitten by a snake depend on where you live.

What to do
The treatment given for a cat, dog or other mammal bite depends on the depth of the wound and whether your child's tetanus inoculation is up to date. If the bite is superficial, clean the wound and then bandage it if necessary. If, however, the wound is serious, or on your child's face, then you *must* see your doctor. He or she will need to know the date of your child's last tetanus inoculation and, if it's out of date, will give him a booster. Bites from other children should be cleaned and bandaged, but if you're at all worried by them you should contact your doctor.
If your child is bitten by a snake get him to hospital immediately. Do not let him walk, but lay him flat on the seat of your car. If possible, identify the snake. If you are in an area where poisonous snakes are prevalent, seek advice as to whether you should keep emergency serum on hand.

Blisters
Blisters are formed as a protection to the body where it has been chaffed, burned or rubbed.

What to do
A blister should be left intact. Never prick it; leave it intact as long as you can. If a blister is on an exposed area simply cover it with a small pad of gauze kept in place with tape. The blister will subside of its own accord and the skin will become dry and fairly hard. It will change its colour to a rather dark pink and it will gradually fall off. Don't do *anything* to disturb this natural process.

Bronchitis and pneumonia
Bronchitis is a frequent complication of the infectious childhood diseases (see p.366). Infectious diseases like measles and whooping cough are often accompanied by chest infections. What happens in this situation is that the infecting organism of measles or whooping cough enters the lungs and weakens their defences. The bronchial tubes become inflamed and produce a lot of mucus, the functioning of the lungs begins to deteriorate and the mucus can't be expelled. It then forms into little pools and these become infected. The initial signs of bronchitis or pneumonia are an increased breathing rate; difficulty with breathing and possibly a rather bluish colour around the mouth. When pooling of mucus occurs in a small air passage, the deeper part of the lung beyond this blockage becomes sealed off and the fluid may collect to the extent that it renders a little section of the lung completely solid; this is a small area of pneumonia. If a larger air passage becomes blocked off, the area of pneumonia can be quite extensive.

What to do
If you notice any of the above symptoms contact your doctor immediately. While you are waiting for your doctor do the following things: try to keep the air moist by boiling a kettle in the room – never leave your child alone in a room in which a kettle is boiling. Stay with your child; make him feel comfortable and secure. Try

to support your baby's back by leaning him on two or three pillows because breathing is easier in the upright position. Don't, whatever you do, panic. Stay calm.

Your doctor, after examining your child, will probably prescribe antibiotics, which you should administer according to instruction.

Burns
It is almost inevitable that your child will burn himself on a radiator or hot tap at some stage, despite your efforts.

What to do
Leave a minor burn alone and never burst a blister. Don't apply anything to it. The best treatment is to cover the burn with a piece of clean gauze (a freshly laundered cotton handkerchief will do). Ask your doctor's advice if you are worried.

If your child has been severely burned he must be taken to the nearest hospital casualty department for proper treatment.

Catarrh and runny nose
Neither persistent yellow catarrh (catarrh which continues for longer than five or six days), nor a runny nose is normal. Both of these signs indicate that your child may be suffering from chronic sinusitis or a chronic infection of the nose and throat. Both of these need consultation with the doctor and fairly rigorous treatment with antibiotics. If this doesn't work you should ask your doctor to refer your child to an ear, nose and throat specialist.

What to do
As the ear, nose and throat and the lungs are connected by a very small set of tubes, anatomically speaking, an infection in any one place can very quickly creep along the tubes to infect another. For example, chronic tonsillitis will go on to chronic infections of the middle ear unless it is treated. These chronic infections can cause irreparable damage to your child's health so have them seen to if any symptom in the ear, nose or throat goes on for longer than a week.

Chickenpox
This is a relatively mild infection which children invariably catch as it's one of the most contagious of all childhood diseases (see p.366). Your child will be contagious from twenty-four hours before the rash starts to the time that they scab over. The chickenpox virus is a close relative of the one that causes shingles (herpes zoster), so adults, particularly older ones, can catch shingles from a child with chickenpox.

Chickenpox often starts with a temperature of 38°–39°C (100°–102°F). In very small children, however, there is hardly any rise in temperature; the rash may be the first sign. This will appear in waves over three or four days and will be extremely itchy. At first the spots are like dark red pimples, but within a couple of hours they will have developed a small blister on top which resembles a drop of water. This will eventually scab over and drop off. The rash usually starts on the trunk and then spreads to the face, the scalp, the arms and the legs. In the worst cases it can also appear inside the mouth, nose, ears, vagina and anus.

What to do
The most important thing to do is to stop your child from scratching the spots. If you don't do this the scab may come off and the resulting wound may become infected and leave a scar. The best treatment for this is calamine lotion, applied at regular intervals. Keep your child's nails short to minimize the risk of infection should he pull the scabs off. Your child may find that the itchiness is so intense that he can't get to sleep. In cases like this ask your doctor for a sedative. If your child is still wearing nappies leave them off as much as possible to prevent infection.

Colds
A cold is caused by a virus which we cannot treat specifically. There is no antibiotic to which the virus is sensitive so it cannot be killed. This means that it has to be overcome by the body's own defence mechanism and this usually takes ten to

fourteen days, whatever we do.

The common cold virus infects and inflames the membranes of the nasal passages and throat. This produces the well known symptoms of sore throat and runny nose. Quite often the viral infection weakens the body and allows a secondary bacterial infection; at this point a clear nasal discharge would become yellow and pussy. At the same time the tonsils and adenoids may become swollen and so may the glands in the neck. Tonsillitis complicating a cold usually requires antibiotic treatment so consult your doctor (see p.362). Colds are common in young children, and five or six colds a year is quite common. Babies under six months are less likely to catch colds because of the antibodies they receive from their mothers, especially if they're breast-fed.

What to do
In a young baby a cold can cause quite a lot of distress because it may block the nose and prevent breathing during feeding. Don't let your child suffer in this way; consult your doctor as soon as possible. You will probably be given nose drops to use before each feed and these will keep the nasal passages clear long enough for the baby to feed. Never use nose drops for more than a few days at a time unless they are prescribed by your doctor.

Because all the upper air passages, the nose and the sinuses in an infant are connected by very short tubes, an infection of one part can quickly spread to another. For this reason a cold in a child may rapidly become sinusitis, bronchitis, tonsillitis, and sometimes otitis media (infection of the middle ear). If your child complains of a sore throat or earache (see p.354), consult your doctor immediately because specific antibiotic therapy will almost certainly be needed.

Older children seem to feel the tiresome symptoms of a cold less then adults. They rarely feel under the weather and seem to suffer it quite cheerfully so there is no reason to use proprietary cold cures for a child in the way one might for an adult.

Cold sore/Herpes simplex

Cold sores have nothing to do with a cold other than the fact that it is the high temperature accompanying the cold which activates the virus in the skin. The herpes simplex virus lives permanently in the nerve roots buried in the skin. The virus is dormant for most of the time, but if the body is heated up for any reason, by a cold or any other viral infection, by sunlight, by ovulation in the middle of the menstrual month, the viruses are tickled back into action and give the well-known symptoms of first an itching in the skin, then a tenderness and soreness in the skin and then the emergence of a swelling which later turns into blisters. All this happens in about 24–36 hours but the blisters alternately weep and scab and take 10–14 days to clear up.

What to do
If you notice the herpes blisters coming up take your child to your doctor immediately. Idoxuridine solutions are available which, if painted on to the affected area early enough, can contain or minimize the attack of herpes.

The herpes virus is passed on by direct contact. Most children who get cold sores, usually around the lips, nose and possibly on the cheeks and chin, get them through adults who kiss them. It is quite common if one parent in the family has cold sores for others to catch the virus from that one parent; it is equally possible for your child to infect others as well.

Conjunctivitis

Conjunctivitis is an inflammation of the conjuntiva, the outer covering of the eye. It makes the eye look red, and it can feel itchy or sore.

What to do
If your child develops "a red eye", examine it first to see if there is a foreign body trapped underneath the lid, and if so remove it. If the eye looks clear but is sore whenever your child blinks or looks at a bright light, and if the eye waters a great

deal, then keep the eye closed by putting a small pad of cotton wool with two pieces of tape placed crosswise to keep it in place. In case the conjunctivitis needs specific antibiotic treatment take your child to your doctor.

Convulsions

In some children we never discover the cause for convulsions but in the majority of children between the ages of one and three convulsions or fits are caused by a rise in body temperature. Young children's brains are more easily affected by this than adults; the irritation stimulates the nerves controlling the muscles which in turn react by contracting violently. When having a fit your child will become unconscious and will twitch uncontrollably. His eyes will roll up and he may froth at the mouth slightly. His breathing will be heavy and his teeth will be firmly clamped; he may become incontinent during the fit. When the convulsion is over your child will fall asleep – he may drift straight into sleep or he may briefly come to and then sleep.

What to do
Never leave your child alone. Although you desperately want to call for help you must stay by your child until the fit is over to make sure he doesn't hurt himself. Loosen his clothing and remove any nearby furniture in case he kicks or rolls against it, but don't try to restrain him. Don't try to place anything in his mouth. Contrary to popular belief, people rarely bite or swallow their tongues during a convulsion and you could do more damage by trying to prize open his jaws. Once the fit is over, place him in the recovery position and call the doctor at once.

If your child has a fit of this sort you should try to prevent high fevers from occurring in the future. Use tepid sponging (see p. 344) and remove extra clothing and blankets when he gets hot. Ask your doctor if anti-convulsant drugs would be of benefit to your child.

Coughing

Coughing is the body's natural reflex to irritation of the throat, the very back of the nose and the membranous lining of the air passages. It usually accompanies an infection of the upper airways, the throat or the sinuses. The purpose of the cough is to remove excess mucus or phlegm which has come up into the back of the throat from the lungs or the nose and sinuses. By coughing the phlegm is loosened, brought up into the mouth and then swallowed. Any germs existing in it are then killed by the acid in the stomach. (A common cause of coughing at night is mucus dripping from the nose and sinuses into the back of the throat.)

What to do
A cough which is merely a response to irritation and not to the presence of excess mucus is called an unproductive cough because it doesn't cough out any phlegm. A cough which does get rid of the mucus is called a productive cough.

An unproductive cough serves no useful purpose and can be extremely irritating to a small child; it can even prevent sleep. It is important to differentiate between a dry, unproductive cough and a wet, productive one which produces phlegm, because the treatments are entirely different.

Cough suppressant medicines are used to suppress unproductive coughs and expectorant medicines are used to help a productive cough get rid of phlegm. You should keep a bottle of cough suppressant medicine, prescribed by your doctor, in the house in case your child develops an unproductive cough.

You can ease the irritation of a night time cough by turning your child on to his side or his front, or by propping him on pillows (if he's over a year old). Never let the coughing get so severe that a prolonged bout of it causes your child to vomit; always consult your doctor before this happens.

A productive cough, however, should never be suppressed because it is serving a useful purpose. It is helping to overcome infection by clearing mucus from the air passages. A productive cough that lasts for more than 48 hours should be treated by a doctor.

Croup

Croup quite often accompanies a cold and usually only occurs in children between the ages of one and five. The name is given to the sound of air being inhaled through a constricted windpipe, past inflamed vocal cords. Your child may go to bed feeling quite well but then wake with a very tight chest and have great difficulty breathing in; exhaling will be easier.

What to do
If you notice this kind of breathing you should call your doctor immediately. On occasion the breathing can be so laboured that there's a risk of suffocation. If this is the case take your child straight to a hospital. Otherwise, stay with your child until the doctor arrives. Difficulty with breathing can be very frightening and your presence will reassure him. To make breathing easier, prop up your child in an upright position with pillows, and make sure that he is comfortable. If he's very alarmed take him on your lap, hold him firmly and try to get him to breathe with you. Listening to you breathing in and out will take his mind off his own fear – if he's relaxed his breathing will be easier. Make sure that the air of your child's bedroom isn't too warm as this can dry and irritate the already inflamed air passages. Open the window and let some cool air blow in. Moistened air is soothing to the passages so try taking him to the bathroom, running the hot tap of the shower with the door and the windows shut. This will make the atmosphere steamy and if you sit in there with your child on your lap (maybe telling him a story at the same time), it might help. If you can do nothing else, boil a kettle in your child's bedroom. Once you have placed a boiling kettle in your child's room *never* ever leave. When the doctor arrives ask him for advice about treating croup so that you can deal with it easily in the future.

Cuts and grazes

Examine any wound to see how deep it is and whether it is bleeding profusely. If it is both deep and bloody see your doctor.

What to do
Clean the area with a diluted antiseptic solution. If you don't have this by you, dissolve one teaspoon of salt in a glass of water and use this as a cleansing solution.

Drowsiness

Drowsiness in a normally alert child can be a symptom of a fever, hypothermia (when the body temperature falls below normal), or dehydration. It can also occur before or after a convulsion, following a blow to the head, or as a result of medication, such as antihistamines. If a child is drowsy but contented, it is feeding well and has a normal temperature, there is no cause for alarm; your child is probably just feeling a little sleepy. If, however, a child becomes drowsy whilst recovering from an infectious disease such as measles or chickenpox, and he complains of headache and neck pain, this could indicate encephalitis, meningitis or Reye's syndrome, all of which are serious conditions and require immediate medical attention.

What to do
Check your child's temperature. If it's over 38°C (100.4°F), he has a fever and if it is under 35°C (95°F), he will be suffering from hypothermia. In either case, consult your doctor immediately.

If drowsiness is accompanied by diarrhoea and vomiting, keep up your child's fluid intake to prevent the risk of dehydration. If his condition does not improve, consult your doctor.

Check to see if your child has received a blow to the head; check if your child has a headache or neckache; smell your child's breath and check the drinks cabinet – he

353

may have drunk alcohol. Check the medicine cabinet for sleep-inducing drugs. In any of these cases, contact your doctor immediately.

If your child has had a convulsion, leave him to rest after the fit has passed and seek medical advice.

Earache

Earache is a common ailment in babies and young children. The main reason for this is the anatomy of the ear. Think of the ear as two sections separated by a membrane, the ear drum. The first section is a passage leading from the opening of the ear to the ear drum. This is the auditory canal. The second section, behind the ear drum, is the middle ear. Inflammation of the outer ear is called otitis externa; inflammation of the middle ear is called otitis media. The Eustacian tubes, which are rather short and wide in small children, link the middle ear to the back of the throat. Their purpose is to equalize pressure in the ears, but they are often the source of ear problems in small children.

Otitis media is the most common ear ailment both because of the construction of the Eustachian tubes and because babies spend most of their time lying down. The combination of these two factors makes it much easier for bacteria to travel from the nose and throat straight to the middle ear. Inflammation of the mucus membrane of the Eustachian tubes causes them to become blocked. This traps the bacteria in the middle ear, where they multiply.

Obviously, no small child can tell you that his ear hurts, but if he has inexplicable fever, vomiting, diarrhoea and loss of appetite, and certainly if he pulls at his ear, you'd be right to suspect that his ears are troubling him.

What to do
Call your doctor immediately if you suspect your child has earache. He will examine your child to confirm the diagnosis and, if the cause is otitis media, will prescribe antibiotics and possibly nose

drops. The antibiotics will combat the bacteria and the nose drops will keep the Eustachian tubes from getting blocked up, risking further infection. Never, ever put anything into your baby's ears, and don't apply hot compresses to the outside of the ear. Leave the treatment to your doctor. Similarly, if the cause of the earache is a boil, or something else in the outer ear, don't treat it yourself. Call your doctor.

Eczema

Infantile eczema often goes hand in hand with asthma and the two are quite commonly seen together. Eczema produces a fairly generalized rash on the face, behind the knees and on the inner side of the arms and wrists. The rash is usually itchy, dry, red and scaly; in its worst state it can weep quite profusely. You will notice that the eczema waxes and wanes. It may be brought on by a cold or if the baby has had a sleepless night or a tummy upset.

Like asthma, infantile eczema is nearly always associated with an allergy and it is usually hereditary. Often asthma or other allergic conditions may run throughout the family, so you may find that a relative has penicillin sensitivity, another has asthma, another has eczema, another has hay fever.

What to do
The best treatments for infantile eczema come from paediatric dermatologists. You should ask your doctor to refer your baby to a specialist so that you can get the most modern treatment. An experienced dermatologist will also know when to introduce a new treatment when other medications seem to have stopped working.

The story on infantile eczema is rather good: many children improve around the age of two, and many more do so by the age of seven. Usually it will have disappeared by the teens although the person always retains the possibility of coming out in eczema in later life if they ever have a severe trauma, mental or physical.

For the everyday care of a baby with eczema of the skin I would suggest the following: avoid over-bathing – soap and water are dehydrating. Use baby lotion on cotton wool which will do the same job just as well. Pay fairly good attention to cleanliness, particularly round the nappy area and face. Avoid wool next to the skin as it can be irritating and make the eczema worse. Rub in the soft, bland creams and ointments that your doctor provides you with exactly as prescribed.

Epilepsy

After febrile convulsions the next most common cause of fits in children is epilepsy. Epilepsy can take two forms: petit mal and grand mal.

With petit mal your child suddenly "blanks out" for a couple of minutes and looks very pale and vacant. He won't fall down or become incontinent but he'll be completely unaware of his surroundings. When he snaps out of the fit he'll carry on as normal, as if nothing had happened. Contact your doctor if you notice anything like this.

A child suffering from grand mal exhibits exactly the same symptoms as one suffering from febrile convulsions.

What to do
You should deal with them in exactly the same way, then seek immediate medical advice. Your doctor will probably order a electroencephalogram (EEG), to confirm epilepsy. It has been shown that it's psychologically inadvisable to treat children suffering from epilepsy as "epileptic". Treat your child as normal, but take certain precautions – leave the bathroom door open in case an attack occurs in the bath and keep a close eye on him when he's swimming or sailing.

Fever

The range of normal body temperature is 36–37°C (96.8°–98.6°F). Anything over 37°C (100°F) is a fever, although the height a temperature reaches is not necessarily an accurate reflection of the seriousness of the sickness. A fever is not in itself an illness but rather a symptom of one. Apart from any illness, your child's temperature will reflect the time of day and activity level: after a very strenuous game of football, for example, the temperature could temporarily be over 38°C (100.4°F). A temperature of over 37°C is always serious in a baby under six months old. If the temperature remains high, there is also a slight risk of a convulsion occurring.

What to do
If you suspect that your child has a fever, take his temperature, then check it again in 20 minutes to see if it has varied. Note down each reading.

Put your child to bed and remove most of his clothing, even if the room is cool. A child with a fever need only be covered by a light sheet. Lower a temperature of over 40°C (104°F) by sponging your child all over with tepid water. Take the temperature every 5 minutes and stop sponging when the temperature drops to 38°C (100.4°F). Never use cold water for this as it causes the blood vessels to constrict, preventing heat loss and therefore driving the temperature up.

Give paracetemol elixir only if other methods of reducing the fever have failed. Never give aspirin to a child with the symptoms of chickenpox or influenza as this has been linked to the development of Reye's syndrome.

Encourage your child to drink as much liquid as possible by offering small amounts of fluid at regular intervals. Consult your doctor immediately: if your child is under six months old; if your child has a convulsion; if he has had a convulsion in the past or if febrile convulsions run in the family; if the fever lasts more than 24 hours, or if you are worried about any of the accompanying symptoms.

Fingers caught in door

Until your baby learns how doors work there's always the risk that his fingers may get trapped.

What to do
If the skin is badly broken and there is any serious bleeding take your child to the nearest casualty department immediately. If the finger is bleeding profusely place your thumb and forefinger on either side of the crushed finger just beyond the palm of the hand where the finger actually starts. This will stop the blood from getting to the end of the finger and prevent haemorrhage. Other than this don't use any other form of first aid. Don't try to put your child's hand in any particular position, let him take up the position of maximum comfort. Don't give your child any painkillers.

If your child's pain and the swelling fingers do not subside within 24 hours put the arm in a sling to keep the hand upright, but make sure that your child moves his elbow several times an hour so that it doesn't stiffen. Above all consult your doctor.

German measles (rubella)

This is a viral disease, like measles, but it isn't as serious or as contagious (see p.366). The initial symptoms resemble a mild cold with a runny nose, a sore throat, and a temperature of 38°C (100°F). The rash usually appears a couple of days after your child starts to feel unwell. The spots, which start behind the ears and on the forehead before moving down on to the body, are pale and flat and are not as close together as those in measles. They only last for a couple of days. The glands on the back of your child's neck will almost definitely be swollen and they may stay like this after the rash has gone.

What to do
You should call in your doctor to get an accurate diagnosis. This is important. It's important for any pregnant woman with whom your child has been in contact; it's also important in relation to possible inoculation at puberty. The infection is so mild that there is nothing specific that you should do, other than keep your child comfortable and amused. You should,

however, keep him indoors until the rash has been done for a few days. A combined vaccination against measles, mumps and rubella (MMR) is now available and can be given at around 15 months.

Gluten sensitivity

Gluten sensitivity is an allergic response to the protein which is contained in most cereals and grains. Unwittingly, therefore, you feed your baby with an allergen because gluten is contained in baby cereal, in most other cereals and in anything made with flour (be it brown or white).

A child with gluten sensitivity initially shows a "failure to thrive". This means that the child will perhaps not have as much energy as you'd expect, may be a little sleepy and won't gain weight quite as quickly. You will also notice that the stools alternate between a fatty consistency so when you to try to flush them away they won't go – they stay and float – and quite loose stools. This is because the allergic reaction in the lining of the bowel prevents the correct digestion and absorption of fatty substances. Your child may have frequent bouts of diarrhoea and be irritable a lot of the time. If the condition goes undiagnosed in girls it can lead to a delay in the onset of menstruation. In its very advanced stage gluten sensitivity, or coeliac disease, produces quite abnormal body configuration. The abdomen becomes distended with hardly any fat on the limbs or body, the muscles of the legs and arms become wasted, the tongue becomes smooth and there may be swelling of the ankles. Oddly enough these children also tend to have long eye lashes. However, gluten sensitivity is not very common and the fact that it is caused by a common food-stuff should not make you unnecessarily wary or over-anxious about your child's diet.

What to do
Once a diagnosis has been made your child has to be given a gluten-free diet, which means that wheat, rye, barley and oats will have to be excluded. This diet will be

provided by your consultant and dietician. Your child will have to remain on a gluten-free diet for life. The first thing that you will notice is an improvement in the mood of your child. This usually appears within a few days, and is followed by a greatly improved appetite and consequent weight gain. You will then notice a change in the appearance of the stools and the frequency of bowel movements, although this may take weeks. After being on a gluten-free diet for six months to a year your child should be within the normal range for weight, although his height will take about two years to recover.

Hayfever

Hayfever is similar to asthma except that the allergic reaction occurs in the mucous membranes of the nose and eyelids, not the chest. The condition is also known as allergic rhinitis and causes sneezing, a runny nose with clear discharge and itchy, watery, red-rimmed eyes. It occurs in spring and summer and is usually due to a reaction to pollen from flowers, grasses and trees. Hayfever is periodically troublesome, but it has no serious consequence.

What to do
If your child is sneezing a lot, check his temperature to make sure that he isn't ill with an infection such as influenza or a common cold. Discourage your child from rubbing his eyes; this will make them worse. Bathe his eyes with cool water to ease the irritation.

Consult your doctor as soon as possible if you think your child may be suffering from a more serious infection, or if the hayfever is making your child miserable.

If your child's condition is severe, your doctor may arrange for your child to have a series of tests to track down the allergen that is causing the symptoms of hayfever. Once one or more allergens have been determined, a special vaccine can be made for your child and a course of desensitizing injections given over a period of weeks to protect him. These don't always work,

however, and have to be give during the winter.

There are various measures you can take to try to minimize the severity of attacks. Watch the pollen count each day and, if it is high, discourage your child from playing near freshly mown grassland, for example. Use synthetic fillings for your child's pillows and duvet, rather than feathers. Keep your house as dust-free as possible. Even if our child isn't allergic to dust, a dusty atmosphere makes hayfever worse. Prepare an emergency pack for outings. It should contain paper handkerchiefs, eye drops to reduce the eye irritation, a moist towel to soothe your child's eyes, and whatever medication has been prescribed.

Hives (see Urticaria)

Infectious fevers (see p.366)

Measles

This is a highly infectious disease; it can also have quite serious complications, namely pneumonia and meningitis (see p.366). Your child is most likely to catch the disease between the ages of one and six; it takes its most serious form under the age of three.

It generally takes 1–12 days for the symptoms to appear after your child has been infected. The first symptoms are similar to a normal cold – runny nose, a hoarse cough and a fever. For the first two days the temperature will be 38°–39°C (100°–102°F). It may fall briefly before becoming as high as 40°C (104°F). It's at this stage that the rash usually appears. It starts off as small, scarlet-coloured, slightly raised spots. These go on to merge into irregular areas of a reddy-brown colour. The rash generally starts on the throat and behind the ears. It spreads to the face and then to the rest of the body. Your baby's eyes may become red and sore.

What to do
Call your doctor who will probably confirm measles, especially if he or she finds small red spots, each with a white

centre, inside your child's mouth; these are known as Koplik's spots. While your child has the fever follow the general instructions for coping with high temperatures (see p.344). Bathe his sore eyes with lukewarm water and cotton wool and dim the lights if that makes him more comfortable. He probably won't be very hungry when he's feverish, but make sure that he takes adequate amounts of liquid by providing small but frequent drinks. If your child still has a high temperature four days after the rash has appeared call your doctor again. Similarly, if your child has earache or laboured breathing, if he has a phlegmy cough or if he becomes semi-conscious, call your doctor immediately.

Between the ages of one and two your child can be inoculated against measles, mumps and rubella (MMR) (see p.365). If your child is exposed to measles before he's been inoculated your doctor may give him gamma globulin which will either prevent the disease or reduce its severity.

Meningitis

Meningitis is an inflammation of the meninges, the membrane that surrounds the brain and spinal cord. It is caused by viral or, much more seriously, bacterial infection. Your child may be unwell and irritable, with a high temperature, and may vomit. An older child may complain of a severe headache and a stiff neck, and a baby may have a bulging soft spot (fontanelle). The child may develop convulsions. Bacterial meningitis also causes a rash of small, flat purplish spots which don't disappear when pressed. Check this by pressing a glass against the rash and looking at it through the base.

What to do
Viral meningitis is serious, but bacterial meningitis is life-threatening and the disease can develop very quickly, so it needs urgent action. If you suspect meningitis, take your child to the Accident and Emergency department of the nearest hospital.

Meningitis is confirmed by taking a sample of cerebro-spinal fluid through a lumbar puncture. If it is bacterial meningitis, your child will be treated in hospital and all close contacts will be immunized to prevent further spread of the disease.

Mumps

This disease is uncommon in children under five (see p.366). When the infection does occur, however, you may first notice that your child seems under the weather. The positive symptom will be if the glands swell up in front of and under the ear on one side of your child's face. This swelling will be accompanied by fever, during which your child may become delirious. The other side of your child's face will swell up some days later, after your child's temperature has fallen and then risen sharply again. His neck will be stiff and his throat will be sore and he's likely to complain of a very dry mouth. The MMR vaccination prevents mumps occurring.

What to do
Call your doctor. Although there's no specific treatment, you can do a lot to make your child comfortable. Reduce his temperature, with your doctor's approval, by tepid sponging and baby paracetamol. Give liquid foods if your child finds it difficult to chew; give your child plenty to drink.

Nettle rash (see Urticaria)

Nose bleeds

Haemorrhaging from the nose is most often caused by damage to a patch of small blood vessels lying very near the surface of the skin, just inside the nose. This is usually because the nose is injured during rough games, or because your child persistently picks his nose.

What to do
This small patch of blood vessels can bleed rather a lot but try not to panic. Calmly hold your child's head down.

Never hold it upright or tip it back because blood which is swallowed can irritate the stomach and cause vomiting. This will only increase the blood pressure in the head and create a tendency for the nose to bleed again.

Apply gentle pressure with your thumb and first finger on either side of the nose until bleeding has stopped. This will usually happen in two or three minutes. If nose bleeds occur quite frequently take your child to the doctor who may refer him to a specialist for cauterization of the delicate areas inside the nose.

Rashes

Most rashes have an internal cause and in young children they are a classic symptom of some of the more common infectious fevers (see p.366). They may also indicate an allergy.

What to do
Rashes usually involve damage to the small blood vessels in the skin and there is very little that one can do to correct this by applying anything on the skin surface. However, try to relieve the symptoms of itching and burning by applying a cooling lotion, like calamine, since prolonged scratching may break the skin and introduce infection. It is better not to use anti-sting or anti-burn sprays on a rash because they very often contain local anaesthetics which may produce allergies in the skin.

If the rash becomes infected you should consult your doctor; if you notice that there are tiny blisters in the rash then you should seek medical advice immediately.

Roseola infantum

This disease is often confused with German measles (see p.366). Your child will suddenly get a very high fever of 39°C (102°-104°F), without any other symptoms. As soon as his temperature returns to normal he'll develop a rash of pale red spots.

What to do
Contact your doctor so that you get an accurate diagnosis. No specific treatment is needed, other than keeping the fever down (see p.344).

Scarlet fever

Also known as scarlatina, this severe throat infection is caused by a strain of streptococcus bacillus (see p.366). It starts with a sore throat and a fever, the tonsils become swollen and inflamed and your child may have headaches and vomit. About three days after this a rash of tiny spots may appear around the neck and in the armpits; this will then spread over the whole body. The tongue's surface may become red and swollen, and if the infection goes untreated the skin may start to peel from the fingertips, the palms and the soles of the feet.

What to do
Call in your doctor for an accurate diagnosis. He'll probably give your child antibiotics or sulphonamides to mini-mize the severity of the illness. Other than this there is nothing specific that you can do, although you should watch out for any signs of earache developing. If it does, contact your doctor again.

Sleep-walking

Sleep-walking, when a child wanders about the house while asleep, is a sort of "mobile dreaming". A sleep-walking child does not walk about with his eyes closed and his arms held straight out in front. His eyes will be open but he will be asleep; he won't see you and won't understand anything you say to him. Many children go through a short phase of sleep-walking, but this soon passes.

What to do
If you find your child sleep-walking, don't try to waken him. Lead him slowly and gently back to bed. There is no need to consult your doctor unless the sleep-walking is very frequent and you need

359

reassurance that nothing is seriously wrong. Protect your child – for instance, by putting a barrier at the top of the stairway at night, and by making sure that no windows are left open. Try to reassure your child if you think you know the underlying cause of the sleepwalking.

Splinters

All splinters, except large ones or others which are deep and cause your child discomfort, should be left alone. If your child isn't bothered, you shouldn't bother. Many small splinters are expelled by growing skin anyway and simply emerge on the surface and get rubbed off.

What to do
If a splinter becomes infected just break the skin of the pussy area with a sterile needle. The pus will drain away and the splinter should become free of its own accord. If you attempt to remove a splinter or open up an infected one you should do the following: calm your child as much as you can. Never say that it will be painless; it won't and your child won't trust you again. Sterilize the needle by boiling in hot water for five minutes or, better still, waft the tip of the needle through a flame five or six times. Get the help of another adult who can hold the part with the splinter in it steady, despite the tears and protests from your child; when the needle is cold gradually break the skin at the most superficial part of the splinter. Use a pair of eyebrow tweezers to pull the end out once it is freed, then bath the area with a solution made up of a glassful of water and a teaspoonful of salt. Finally, put a little antiseptic cream on the area, and leave open to the air.

Sprains

Because they're so active and especially when co-ordination isn't very good, children can sprain their hands and ankles quite easily. In a sprain a ligament is quite often torn, and this causes swelling. Your child won't want to put pressure on the joint, and will find it painful to move.

What to do
The best treatment for a sprain is rest; any kind of strain on the sprained part should be avoided. However, if you feel you must do something, you can help it by applying poultices. Dissolve magnesium sulphate, bicarbonate of soda or even salt in a glass of water until some of the powder remains in the bottom of the glass. Make a poultice with this super-saturated solution by wringing out a pad of gauze or linen in the solution and bandaging it fairly firmly to the bruised area. You can repeat this poultice every one or two hours if you want to. Your child may find it more comfortable if you bind the affected joint with a crepe bandage.

Sticky eye

A sticky eye is fairly common in the first day or so after your baby is born and it is nearly always due to blood or amniotic fluid getting into the baby's eye during birth.

What to do
There is always the possibility that the sticky eye is due to a bacterial infection so consult your doctor in case antibiotics are needed. However, usually all that is needed is careful cleansing with a cotton wool swab soaked in sterile water. When you wash the eye you should draw the swab from the inside corner, near the nose to the outer corner and then throw it away. You should use a separate swab for each eye. When you lay your baby down to sleep make sure that he isn't laid on the side of the sticky eye because the unaffected eye might become contaminated with pus when your baby turns over.

Stings

It's almost inevitable that your child will be stung by a bee or wasp at some stage, and that he'll be very upset when it happens.

What to do
If your child has been stung do not try to squeeze it out. This may spread the irritat

ing chemical which is on the end of the sting into deeper parts of the skin. Instead, remove it with a pair of tweezers. Don't use proprietary sting preparations that contain anti-histamines; they may cause an allergy of the skin and are better avoided. One of the best household remedies to relieve the pain is to take a piece of cotton wool or gauze which has been soaked in a solution of bicarbonate of soda, and to hold it in place over the sting with a piece of tape.

Occasionally your child may be stung inside the mouth in which case you should call your doctor immediately. While you are waiting get your child to rinse his mouth out with a bicarbonate of soda solution. If you cannot contact your doctor, and you see that the inside of his mouth is swelling, give your child a piece of ice, an icy lolly or ice cream to suck, find an adult to accompany you and take the child to hospital. If necessary you should lie the child down in the back seat of the car and take him to the hospital alone.

Styes
A stye is an infection in the hair follicles of the lower eyelashes. It looks like a small boil on the eyelid – a red swelling with a central area of pus.

What to do
Eyes are very precious. Never take chances, and consult your doctor if you are at all worried. Don't use any of the patent treatments available from chemists as they may make specific antibiotics less effective should they be prescribed by your doctor. You may notice that the eyelash is loose and if your child is co-operative you can release the pent-up pus inside the stye by just pulling the hair out. It won't be painful because the infection will already have dislodged it from its hair follicle. Another thing that you can do is to bathe the stye with a cotton wool bud dipped in a salt solution made by adding one tea-spoon of salt to a glassful of lukewarm water.

Squints
Your newborn baby may squint until the age of eight or ten weeks, by which time he'll have learned to use his two eyes together (stereoscopically).

What to do
There is nothing wrong with this kind of early squinting but if it persists after three months go to your doctor and ask to be referred to an eye specialist. Early treatment is important otherwise the imbalance of the muscles of the eye, which usually causes a squint, may remain uncorrected.

Sunburn
Most children's skin is very sensitive to sunlight – more sensitive than adults' and with the potential for long term damage. You should be careful about exposing their skin to the sun at any time.

What to do
Preventing sunburn is a lot better than treating it. Protect the exposed parts of the skin with a sun-screen cream of at least factor 15 about 20 minutes before going out. Repeat every two or three hours and every time your child has been in the water.

Always cover your baby's head with a wide-brimmed hat and dress him in loose light clothing that covers the shoulders and neck – such as a shirt with sleeves and a collar. Make sure the pram or buggy has an adjustable hood or sun-shade with which to shade your baby.

If the sun is extremely strong it is better to keep your child indoors, especially between 11am and 1pm when the sun is at its highest.

Remember that your baby is still at risk of ultraviolet rays even on cloudy days in summer.

If by chance your baby does get sun-burned, calamine lotion is a good cooling application, and paracetamol elixir will do a lot to relieve the soreness in the skin and bring his temperature down. If your baby is restless and ill take his temperature; if it is raised this may herald heat stroke and you should call a doctor.

Teething

Teething is the term used to describe the eruption of a baby's first teeth. Teething usually begins at about the age of six or seven months, with most of the teeth breaking through before your baby is 18 months old. Your baby will produce more saliva than usual and will dribble; he will try to cram his fingers into his mouth and chew on his fingers or any object that he can get hold of. He may be clingy and irritable, have difficulty sleeping and he may cry and fret more than usual. Most of these symptoms occur just before the teeth erupt. It is important to realize that the symptoms of teething do not include bronchitis, nappy rash, vomiting, diarrhoea or loss of appetite. These are symptoms of an illness, not teething, and should be treated as such.

What to do

If you can't work out why your child is so irritable, and he has no other symptoms of illness, feel his gums. If a tooth is coming through you will feel a hard or sharp lump and the gum area will be swollen and red. You should not need to consult your doctors unless your baby has other symptoms which cannot be attributed to teething, or you are unduly worried. Nurse your baby often. A teething baby needs your comfort and closeness. Don't think that the arrival of teeth means a necessary speeding up of the weaning process. Babies with teeth can still be breastfed with no discomfort to the mother.

Distract your child with a chilled teething ring (never freeze the ring or your baby may get frostbite) or a piece of carrot or apple – something with a firm texture. Stay with your baby in case he chokes on the food.

Try not to resort to analgesics such as paracetamol elixir. Over the course of the teething process, doses of such painkillers could become too large. Only use analgesics on your doctor's advice.

Rub the swollen gum with your finger. Try to avoid teething jellies that contain local anaesthetics, as these have only a temporary effect and they can cause an allergy. If your child refuses food, encourage him to eat by giving him cold, smooth foods such as yogurt, ice cream or jelly.

Thread worms

This is the most common type of infecting worm. These thin, 6 mm ($^1/_4$ in) long white worms live in the rectum and the females crawl through the anus to lay their eggs on the surrounding skin. This produces the classic symptoms of itching, especially at night. When your child scratches his bottom he may pick up some of the eggs under his fingernails. If he then puts his hand in his mouth the eggs will be ingested again.

What to do

If you notice your child scratching his bottom, especially at night, save your child's stools and examine them for the thread-like worms. If you find them, consult your doctor immediately. He will prescribe a single-dose treatment which will eradicate not just the worms, but the eggs as well. Because worm infection spreads easily to other members of the family everyone should be given the antiworm treatment, and all of you should take a second dose two weeks after the first. Keep your child's nails short, and make sure he washes his hands after going to the lavatory.

Tonsillitis

The job of the tonsils is to trap infections as they enter the body through the mouth, and localize them in the throat. For this reason tonsillitis is usually part of a throat infection. The tonsils also send warning signals to the rest of the body when an infection is beginning so the body can alert all its defences. The adenoids serve exactly the same function but are at the back of the nose instead of in the throat. It is fairly logical, therefore, for the tonsils and adenoids to be thought of together. Tonsils are most important to a child up to the age of ten years and this coincides with the time they are most likely to meet infection and their defences have to be very strong. If your child has tonsillitis he will complain of a very sore throat and his tonsils will look red and swollen; they'll probably have white patches on them.

What to do
You should call in a doctor to check your child over; he'll probably prescribe antibiotics to combat the infection. To make your child's throat feel better give him as much ice-cream and cold liquid as he wants.

Despite their useful function it used to be fashionable to remove tonsils and adenoids. Nowadays, ear, nose and throat surgeons feel that certain criteria must be fulfilled before tonsillectomy can be considered. The criteria would probably include recurrent, severe attacks of tonsillitis, possibly associated with ear infections and deafness. Despite these criteria tonsils are rarely removed in a child under the age of four. The most serious side effect of tonsillitis is infection of the middle ear leading to chronic deafness. You should always be on the look-out for signs of deafness if your child has recurrent attacks of tonsillitis, and if they should occur, have your child referred immediately to an E.N.T. specialist.

Toxocara

This roundworm is found in cats and dogs. Its eggs are passed on in their faeces so your child is at risk when he plays on ground where animals have defaecated. He can ingest the eggs if he puts his dirty hands into his mouth. The eggs burrow through the intestinal wall and are carried in the bloodstream to the lungs. They are then coughed up, swallowed and continue to develop in the intestines. There are generally no symptoms, although if your child has more than one worm he may have abdominal pain and suffer from a loss of appetite.

What to do
Prevention is better than cure. Don't allow pets into your child's play area at home and take care when you go to public parks. If your child is diagnosed as having toxocara he will be prescribed a medicine to get rid of it. Follow your doctor's instructions carefully.

Urticaria

Urticaria is the general term used for an allergic skin reaction and it is also known as nettle rash or hives. Most children have a tendency to develop hives but this is gradually lost as they grow older. It is very easy to diagnose because it is the only skin rash which will disappear completely within a few minutes.

The rash, which is very itchy, often looks like a fairly bad nettle sting; it can also form large red patches with uneven edges. It may result in swelling of the eyes, the lips and possibly the tongue. If the latter occurs you must get in touch with your doctor immediately. One of the commonest offending agents is aspirin which gives rise to the rash, swelling of the face, eyelids and mouth.

What to do
You can do quite a lot to relieve the itchiness by cooling it with applications of calamine lotion. There is no need for any specific treatment unless the attacks are persistent. In this case you should ask your doctor to be referred to a paediatric dermatologist who will investigate your child's rash and try to find a cause.

There is a particular form of urticaria called papular urticaria which is caused by flea bites, usually from the fleas on the family cat. I well remember a case of a child who used to appear in our clinic once a month and it turned out that it was the day after she had been to visit her granny and it was granny's cat who had the fleas. The cure for this is to get rid of the fleas on the cat, not to get rid of the cat.

Vomiting

Vomiting is the violent expulsion of the

contents of the stomach through the mouth. A baby may posset up small quantities of curdled milk after a feed but this should not be confused with vomiting. Vomiting has many causes but in the majority of cases there is little warning and after a single bout your child should be comfortable and back to normal.

Vomiting can be a symptom of a specific disorder of the stomach such as pyloric stenosis, or a symptom of an infection such as an ear infection. It frequently accompanies a fever, and even the common cold can cause vomiting if your child swallows enough nasal discharge to irritate his stomach. If your child has a bad cough this can also cause him to vomit up food that he has recently eaten. Other causes of vomiting include appendicitis, meningitis, migraine headaches, food poisoning and travel sickness. Some children vomit because of excitement and anticipation, but this is usually limited to toddlers.

Vomiting should always be taken seriously because it can rapidly cause dehydration, particularly in a baby or young child.

What to do
Put your child to bed and place a bowl for him to vomit into within easy reach. Give your child frequent, small amounts of liquid, preferably cold water with a pinch of salt and 5ml (one teaspoonful) of glucose added, every 10–15 minutes. Check your child's temperature to see if he has a fever too. Keep your child cool by wiping his face with a cool, damp cloth. Get him to brush his teeth to take away the taste.

Consult your doctor immediately if your child continues to vomit over a six-hour period; if vomiting is accompanied by diarrhoea or a fever over 38°C (100°F); or if the vomiting is accompanied by any other worrying symptoms such as earache. Your doctor will diagnose the cause of the vomiting and treat your child accordingly. He will also make sure that there is no danger of dehydration. Feed your child bland foods when the nausea and vomiting

have passed. Reintroduce solid foods slowly.

Warts

Warts are small benign lumps caused by the wart virus. They are made up of an excess of dead cells that protrude above the surface of the skin. They can appear singly or in alarming numbers over all parts of the body, including the face and genitals. If they occur on the soles of the feet, they are known as verrucae. It takes about two years for the body to build up resistance to the wart virus, and after that time the warts usually disappear spontaneously. Warts are spread by direct contact with an infected person.

What to do
If your child wants the warts removed, or they appear on a part of the body where they would easily infect other people, try the patent wart cures from your chemist. These work by the application of a weak acid solution to the wart and the daily removal of the resulting burnt skin. You should follow the manufacturer's instructions carefully and avoid applying the solution to healthy skin. Don't use patent wart cures on warts that appear on the face or genitals: you may cause scarring.

Consult your doctor as soon as possible if you are unsure whether the lumps are really warts. Any growth or lump on your child's skin which you are uncertain about should be checked by a doctor. Consult your doctor as soon as possible if the warts continue to multiply or appear on the face or genitals and you want them removed.

Whooping cough (Pertussis)

This is one of the most dangerous diseases, especially if your child is under a year old (see p.366). As with most of the childhood diseases, whooping cough starts off with a runny nose, a cough and a slight temperature. This period can last for up to two weeks. This will be followed by severe, paroxysmal coughing when your child will have difficulty drawing breath. This is when the characteristic "whoop" occurs.

A vaccination against whooping cough can be given at the same time as the diphtheria and tetanus vaccination (see Immunization Chart, below).

What to do
Call in your doctor immediately. He will prescribe antibiotics which, if administered early enough, prove effective in stopping chest infections. He'll also show you how to tap your child's chest to loosen the phlegm that is pooling there. When your child starts on a coughing bout, hold him firmly and try to calm him down. If he's tense he'll find it even more difficult to catch his breath. Prop him in a half-sitting position to make breathing easier between bouts. Eating may provoke vomiting. Try giving small amounts of easily-eaten food (mashed if necessary), and try giving them immediately after a coughing fit.

IMMUNIZATION 0–3

Immunization is one of the most successful forms of preventive medicine and has helped to eradicate many formerly lethal diseases throughout the world. However its continued success depends on strict maintenance of an immunization programme in the community, and it is the responsibility of all parents to ensure that their children are fully protected. Some parents are anxious about the possible side effects that may occur as a result of a vaccination. If you have concerns, it's important to talk them through with your doctor and health visitor. The risk of complications is very small whereas the risk of harmful effects from the diseases themselves is much more serious. However, if your baby develops side effects at any stage of the programme your doctor may delay or stop immunizations.

IMMUNIZATION CHART

Age	Vaccination	How given	Reaction
2 months	*Polio* *HIB (haemophilus influenzae type B)*	*By mouth* *Injection*	*None* *Possible lump at injection site; slight risk of fever*
	Diphtheria, tetanus and whooping cough (DTP)	*Combined injection*	*As above*
3 months	*As 2 months*	*As 2 months*	*As 2 months*
4 months	*As 2 months*	*As 2 months*	*As 2 months*
12-15 months	*Mumps, measles and rubella (MMR)*	*Combined injection*	*Fever; rash; slight risk of high fever or convulsions*
4½-5 years	*Polio* *Diphtheria and tetanus* *MMR*	*As 2 months* *Combined injection* *As above*	*As 2 months* *Possible lump at injection site* *As above*

365

COMMON CHILDHOOD INFECTIOUS DISEASES

Disease	Incubation Period	Symptoms
Measles (see p.357)	*10–12 days*	*Runny nose, cough, inflamed eyes, fever, vomiting, diarrhoea, Koplik's spots on the inside of the cheeks, rash behind the ears, then on the face, then on the body*
German measles (see p.356)	*17-18 days*	*Slight temperature, enlarged glands at the back of the neck, rash behind the ears then on the forehead, then the rest of the body*
Roseola (see p.359)	*7-14 days*	*A high temperature with slight cold symptoms; a pink rash when temperature goes down*
Chicken pox (see p.350)	*14-16 days*	*Dark red, irritating groups of spots which emerge every three or four days*
Whooping cough (see p.364)	*5-14 days*	*Slight temperature, runny nose, slight cough then a convulsive cough followed by whooping breath*
Mumps (see p.358)	*17-21 days*	*Swelling and soreness of the glands at the sides of the face, in front of the ears, painful swallowing and dry mouth*
Scarlet fever or Scarlatina (see p.359)	*2-5 days*	*Lack of appetite, fever, vomiting, swollen glands, tiny red spots*

eatment	Complications	Immunity	Prevention
o specific treatment other an junior paracetamol to duce the fever. If secondary fection of the ears or lungs ccurs antibiotics will be ecessary	Earache, pneumonia, encephalitis	Lifelong	Inoculation combined with mumps and rubella vaccine at 15 months
o specific treatment	None to your child but fetal damage could occur in a pregnant woman	Lifelong	Inoculation combined with measles and mumps vaccine at 15 months
o specific treatment	Possibly infantile convulsions	Usually lifelong	None
elive itching with alamine lotion. Treat fected spots with escribed cream	Rare	Lifelong	None
ntibiotics must be given arly to be effective; fresh r. Possibly raise your iild's head in bed to ake breathing easier	Very rare nowadays although there's possibility of bronchitis or pneumonia	Lifelong	Inoculation between 3-6 months
lenty to drink, soft food chewing is painful	Meningitis, inflammaion of the testicles	Lifelong	Inoculation combined with measles and rubella vaccine at 15 months
enicillin with rest in bed s long as fever lasts	Rare	Lifelong	None

367

IMMUNIZATION AND TRAVELLING ABROAD 0-3

If you are planning to take your baby or toddler abroad, it is vital that you find out beforehand about the health risks in the country you are going to be visiting and the precautions, including vaccinations, you may need to take. You can get this information from your travel agent, the embassy (in London) of the country you are going to visit, or from the Department of Health, who issue a useful leaflet (SA 40) *Before You Go: The Traveller's Guide to* *Health* which gives comprehensive advice on the subject. They also publish a companion leaflet, (SA 41) *While You're Away*, which is worth taking with you.

If vaccinations are required, you should see your doctor at least two months before departure as some take time to be effective and some cannot be given at the same time as other vaccinations. Some vaccinations are available free on the NHS; others have to be paid for.

Holiday health precautions

First-aid kit
Take a first-aid kit with you containing: a packet of adhesive dressings, sterile needles, insect repellant, antiseptic cream, water sterilization tablets and any medicines that have been prescribed by your doctor.

Water
Babies' feeds should, of course, be mixed with boiled water as usual. Otherwise, unless you know that the local water is safe, use bottled water or sterilize it by boiling or using sterilization tablets. This applies not just to drinking water but also to the water you use for cleaning teeth or rinsing the mouth out.

Food
Beware of raw vegetables, salads, unpeeled fruit, cream, ice-cream, ice cubes, under-done meat or fish and uncooked or reheated food. Freshly cooked foods are safer.

Travelling in Europe

If you are travelling in Europe, free or reduced cost emergency medical treatment is available in the European Community countries. To get medical care you need an E111 form (available from your local Social Security office) which should be applied for at least one month before your trip starts. You can apply for Form E111 if you live in the UK and are a national of the UK. Children have to be included as dependents on Form E111

Travelling outside Europe

The UK has made arrangements with some countries outside the European Community for urgently needed medical care to be provided free or at reduced cost to UK nationals or residents. You may have to produce evidence of UK nationality and residence in order to qualify for such treatment. Check before you go what is available in the countries you intend to visit.

Taking medicines abroad

If you need to take any prescribed medicines for your baby or toddler with you, your doctor may be able to supply a limited quantity under the NHS. You should check if there are any restrictions on taking drugs, prescribed or pharmacy-bought, into the country you are visiting. It is advisable to have a letter from your doctor with details of any medicines prescribed, to avoid any problems in going through Customs.

Travel insurance

Whatever countries you intend to visit, it is very important that you take out adequate private medical insurance. The arrangements provided for emergency medical treatment in EEC countries, or in countries covered by reciprocal arrangements, do not cover every eventuality; the cover is not always as comprehensive as in the UK and it never covers the cost of bringing a person back to the UK in the event of illness.

DISEASE AND PRECAUTIONS

Disease	Risk Area	Vaccination
Cholera	Africa, Asia, Middle East, especially in conditions of poor hygiene and sanitation	2 injections. NB Cholera is contracted from eating or drinking contamined food or water
Malaria	Africa, Asia, Central and South America; possibly southern Europe and United States (Check before travelling)	None, but anti-malarial tablets are available which should be taken before, during and for a month after your trip
Polio	Everywhere except Europe, North America, Australia and New Zealand	Given as a routine to babies in the UK
Rabies	Many parts of the world, including Europe	Not routinely available, but consult your doctor for advice
Tetanus	Places where medical facilities are not readily available	Given as a routine to babies in the UK
TB	Africa, Asia, Central and South America, some poorer inner city areas elsewhere	Skin test and injection, preferably 3 months before travel. Not necessary for short visits and when staying in modern hotels, but advisable for longer visits if you will be living or working closely with the local population
Typhoid	Everywhere except Europe, North America, Australia and New Zealand, in conditions of poor hygiene and sanitation	2 injections, 4-6 weeks apart. Typhoid is contracted from drinking contaminated water
Yellow fever	Africa and South America	1 injection at least 10 days before travelling. Infants under 9 months should not be vaccinated, and should not therefore be exposed to the disease

369

19 Personal records

During your baby's first year the date of every milestone achieved, every inoculation given, each tooth cut, will seem permanently etched on your mind. However, as the years pass, and second or third children join your first, you'll find that you forget not only the unimportant facts, like when your baby rolled over on to his or her back, but also important points like inoculation dates. For this reason we've included a set of charts which will help you keep track of the events affecting you all.

Baby's name_____

Born_____ **19**__
At_____

BIRTH RECORD
Baby's name_____
Time of birth_____
Date of birth_____
Duration of pregnancy_____
Mother's health during pregnancy:
 Illness_____
 Medication_____
 Problems_____

Delivery:
 Type_____
 Monitoring_____
 Drugs_____
 Problems_____
 Consultant_____
 Hospital_____
 Length of stay_____

Height_____ Weight_____
Blood type_____
Type of feeding:
Breast_____ Bottle_____

Baby's name_____

Born_____ **19**__
At_____

BIRTH RECORD
Baby's name_____
Time of birth_____
Date of birth_____
Duration of pregnancy_____
Mother's health during pregnancy:
 Illness_____
 Medication_____
 Problems_____

Delivery:
 Type_____
 Monitoring_____
 Drugs_____
 Problems_____
 Consultant_____
 Hospital_____
 Length of stay_____

Height_____ Weight_____
Blood type_____
Type of feeding:
Breast_____ Bottle_____

DEVELOPMENT RECORD

Holds head up for a
 few seconds _____
Smiles _____
Laughs _____
Sleeps through night _____
Rolls over _____
Sits unsupported _____
Crawls/Shuffles _____
Cruises _____
Walks _____
First tooth _____
Starts solids _____
Is weaned _____
Feeds self _____
Looks for hidden toy _____
First words _____
Points to parts of the
 the body _____
Makes simple
 statements _____
Pedals tricycle _____
Stays dry throughout
 nap _____
Can do up buttons _____
Draws a circle _____
Gains bladder
 control _____
Gains bowel control _____
Starts playgroup/
 nursery school _____
First visit to the
 dentist _____

DEVELOPMENT RECORD

Holds head up for a
 few seconds _____
Smiles _____
Laughs _____
Sleeps through night _____
Rolls over _____
Sits unsupported _____
Crawls/Shuffles _____
Cruises _____
Walks _____
First tooth _____
Starts solids _____
Is weaned _____
Feeds self _____
Looks for hidden toy _____
First words _____
Points to parts of the
 the body _____
Makes simple
 statements _____
Pedals tricycle _____
Stays dry throughout
 nap _____
Can do up buttons _____
Draws a circle _____
Gains bladder
 control _____
Gains bowel control _____
Starts playgroup/
 nursery school _____
First visit to the
 dentist _____

ILLNESS, INJURY and ALLERGY RECORD

Illness	Duration	Date
____	____	____
____	____	____
____	____	____
____	____	____
____	____	____
____	____	____
____	____	____

Injuries		Date
____		____
____		____

Allergies_____

ILLNESS, INJURY and ALLERGY RECORD

Illness	Duration	Date
____	____	____
____	____	____
____	____	____
____	____	____
____	____	____

Injuries		Date
____		____
____		____

Allergies_____

IMMUNIZATION RECORD

Immunization	Date/Age
Diphtheria, pertussis, tetanus	
Diphtheria, tetanus booster	
Polio	
Polio booster	
Measles, mumps, rubella Adverse reactions	

IMMUNIZATION RECORD

Immunization	Date/Age
Diphtheria, pertussis, tetanus	
Diphtheria, tetanus booster	
Polio	
Polio booster	
Measles, mumps, rubella Adverse reactions	

FAMILY MEDICAL HISTORY

	Birth date	Illnesses
Father		
Mother		

Family allergies and chronic conditions

TELEPHONE NUMBERS

Doctor

Health centre

Health visitor

Local hospital

Dentist

Playgroup/ nursery school

HEIGHT AND WEIGHT CHARTS   0–1

As in every other aspect of development, your child will grow and put on weight at his or her own rate. While it is interesting to both plot your child's development and compare it to the average, you should never became obsessive or anxious about it.

The graphs in the left-hand columns of the following pages plot the typical growth patterns of children of high, low and medium birth weight. The graphs on the right-hand columns are for your use.

To record your baby's weight first weigh your baby. Then go along the bottom axis until you find his or her age. Cast your eyes up the vertical axis until you reach your baby's weight. Mark the point at which the two axes meet. For height use length and age as the axes.

Key
•••••••••••••• Large baby
—————————— Medium baby
– – – – – – – – – Small baby

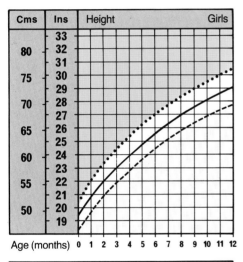

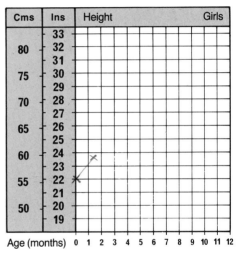

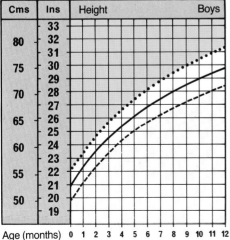

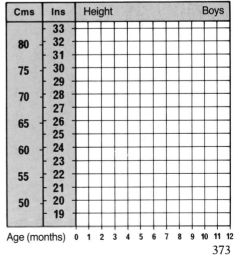

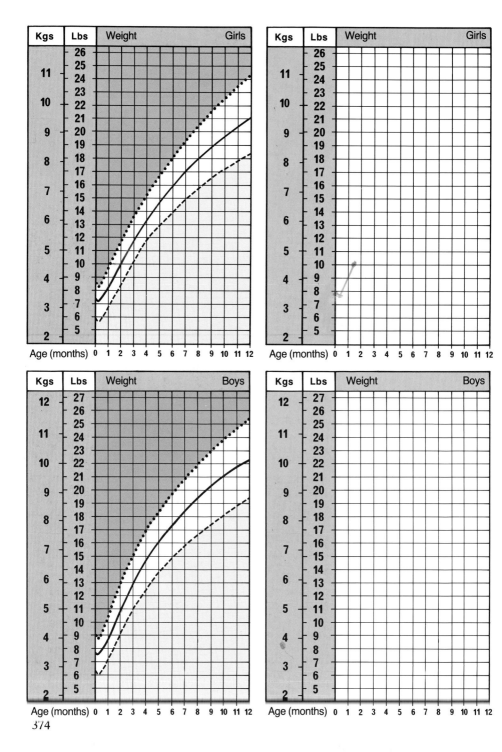

HEIGHT AND WEIGHT CHARTS   1–3

Key
············· Large baby
────────── Medium baby
– – – – – – Small baby

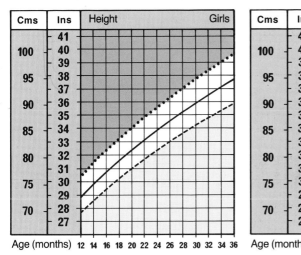

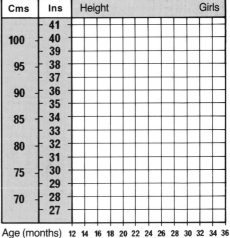

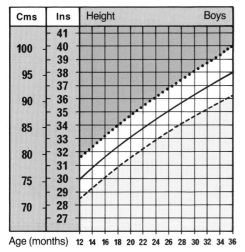

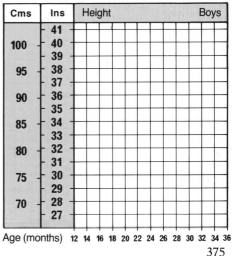

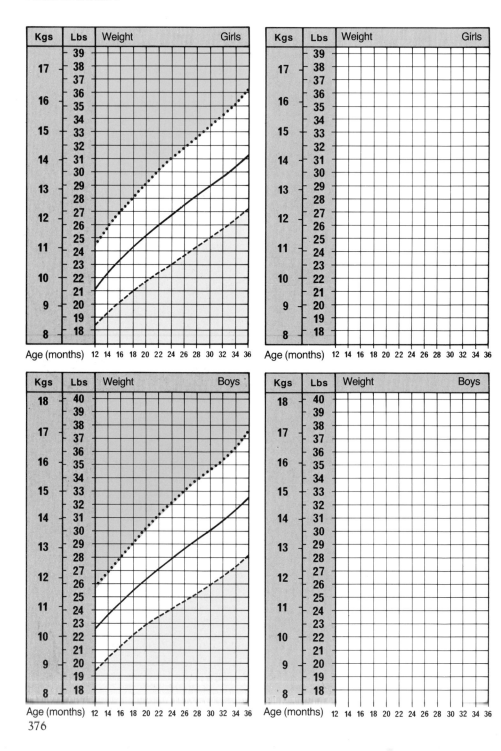

USEFUL ADDRESSES

Association of Breastfeeding Mothers
PO Box 207
Bridgwater TA6 7YT   020 7813 1481
http://home.clare.net/abm/

Association for Improvements in
   Maternity Services (AIMS)
5 Portholl Road
Brighton BN1 5PD   01753 652 781
http://www.aims.org.uk/

Council for Disabled Children
8 Wakley Street
London EC1V 7QE   020 7843 6000
http://www.ncb.org.uk/

Cry-sis Helpline
BM Cry-sis
London WC1N 3XX   020 7404 5011

Gingerbread
16-17 Clerkenwell Close
London EC1R 0AA   020 7336 8183
http://www.gingerbread.org.uk/

La Leche League (Great Britain)
PO Box BM 3424
London WC1N 3XX   020 7242 1278

The Maternity Alliance
45 Beech Street
London EC2P 2LX   020 7588 8582

Pre-School Learning Alliance
69 King's Cross Road
London WC1X 9LL   020 7833 0991
http://www.pre-school.org.uk/

Royal Society for Mentally
   Handicapped Children and Adults
   (MENCAP)
123 Golden Lane
London EC1Y 0RT   020 7454 0454
http://www.mencap.org.uk/

National Childbirth Trust (NCT)
Alexandra House
Oldham Terrace
London W3 6NH   020 8992 8637
http://www.nct-online.org/

National Childminding Association
8 Mason Hill
Bromley BR29EY   020 8464 6164
http://www.ncma.org.uk/

Meet-a-Mum Association (MAMA)
Waterside Centre
26 Avenue Road
London SE25 4DX   020 8771 5595

Twins and Multiple Births Association
   (TAMBA)
Harnett House
309 Chester Road
Little Sutton
Ellesmere Port CH66 1QQ   01732 868 000
http://www.tamba.org.uk/

Acknowledgements

Dorling Kindersley would like to thank the following for their help in the preparation of this book: Debbie Lee and Sandra Schneider for design help; Vision International, Gary Marsh, Kuo Kang Chen, Coral Mula, Les Greenyer, Nick Oxtoby, O'Connor Dowse and Peter Searle for their art and photographic services; Wendy Hawley and Jacob, Linda Cole and Ben, Mike Staniford and Polly, Janet Abbott and Stephen for being models for reference shots; Babyboots, Mothercare, YHA Services, DBNMA and La Cicogna for kindly lending us equipment and, finally, all the parents who gave us their personal tips on baby care.

FIRST EDITION

Photography
Anthea Sieveking

Photographic Services
Adrian Ensor
Negs

Illustration
Edwina Keene

Additional Illustrators
Jim Robins
Lindsay Blow
Richard Lewis

SECOND EDITION

Editorial
Irene Lyford

Design
Sally Powell

Models
Zoë Carroll Pettit
Katerina Armenakis

Typesetting
Tradespools Limited, Frome

Reproduction
Bright Arts, Hong Kong
I GS, Bath

Illustration
Gillie Newman
Karen Cochrane
Nicholas Hall